MOBILIZING

PUBLIC

OPINION

STUDIES IN COMMUNICATION, MEDIA, AND PUBLIC OPINION

A series edited by Susan Herbst and Benjamin I. Page

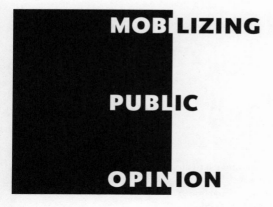

MOBILIZING

PUBLIC

OPINION

Black Insurgency and Racial Attitudes
in the Civil Rights Era

TAEKU LEE

The University of Chicago Press
Chicago and London

TAEKU LEE is assistant professor of public policy at Harvard University.

The University of Chicago Press, Chicago 60637
The University of Chicago Press, Ltd., London
© 2002 by The University of Chicago
All rights reserved. Published 2002
Printed in the United States of America
11 10 09 08 07 06 05 04 03 02   1 2 3 4 5

ISBN: 0-226-47024-5 (cloth)
ISBN: 0-226-47025-3 (paper)

Library of Congress Cataloging-in-Publication Data

Lee, Taeku.
    Mobilizing public opinion : Black insurgency and racial attitudes in the
civil rights era / Taeku Lee.
        p.   cm.—(Studies in communication, media, and public opinion)
    Includes bibliographical references and index.
    ISBN 0-226-47024-5 (cloth : alk. paper)—ISBN 0-226-47025-3 (pbk. : alk.
paper)
        1. African Americans—Civil rights—History—20th century. 2. African
    Americans—Politics and government—20th century. 3. Civil rights move-
    ments—United States—History—20th century. 4. United States—Race
    relations. 5. Racism—United States—Public opinion. 6. African Ameri-
    cans—Attitudes. 7. Whites—United States—Attitudes. 8. Public opin-
    ion—United States. I. Title. II. Series.

E185.61 .L477 2002
323.1′196073—dc21

                                                                    2001053858

CONTENTS

TABLES AND FIGURES

INTRODUCTION

I'm sure that my mother never thought that her black, barefoot child would become in a position of power; I'm not the kind of material this society whips up to make a mayor. I come out of a struggle . . . I was not groomed to be a mayor . . . I'm grassroots.

—Unita Blackwell

The individual man does not have opinions on all public affairs. He does not know how to direct public affairs. He does not know what is happening, why it is happening, what ought to happen. I cannot imagine how he could know, and there is not the slightest reason for thinking, as mystical democrats have thought, that the compounding of individual ignorances in masses of people can produce a continuous directing force in public affairs.

—Walter Lippmann

The political status of African Americans in Selma, Alabama, at the time of the civil rights movement was an extreme example of the marginalization and exclusion facing black citizens throughout the Deep South. African Americans comprised more than half of the eligible voters in Selma's county of residence, Dallas County. But with the combined force of grandfather clauses, literacy and character tests, all-white primaries, poll taxes, and direct (sometimes violent) intimidation working with frightening potency to chill political participation, only about 2 percent of the voting-age black population were in fact registered.[1] This kind of formalized second-class citizenship became increasingly intolerable to civil rights activists in the South. In 1963, two Student Nonviolent Coordinating Committee (SNCC) workers, Bernard and Colia Lafayette, arrived in Selma to start a voter education effort to change matters. White segregationists in Selma were quick to respond. A local chapter of the Citizens' Council was organized and local elites such as Sheriff James Clark Jr., State Circuit Judge James Hare, and State Circuit Solicitor Blanchard McLeod began concerted efforts to defeat voter registration efforts.

In a pattern of activism akin to other civil rights campaigns throughout the South, tensions began to mount and the public's attention increasingly turned to Selma. By early 1965, the Southern Christian Leadership Conference (SCLC) and Dr. Martin Luther King Jr. propelled the conflict in Dallas County to the center stage of the civil rights movement. The movement strategy of provoking police brutality with nonviolent direct action fit well in Selma. Sheriff Jim Clark's bigotry and short temper were notorious. Indeed, during several successively intensified clashes, Amelia Boynton, Anna Lee Cooper, C. T. Vivian, and others succeeded in inciting Sheriff Clark and Alabama Public Safety Director Colonel Al Lingo to vicious and violent responses that shocked much of the nation. By the time the SCLC's leaders, Martin Luther King Jr. and Ralph Abernathy, engaged in civil disobedience and joined the hundreds of activists already in jail, the national media had converged on Selma. Racial frictions rose to a fevered pitch in Selma and beyond. On February 18, a demonstration in nearby Marion, Alabama, led to the clubbing of NBC's Richard Valeriani and the shooting death of a protester, Jimmie Lee Jackson, by state and local law enforcement officers. Just days later, far away from Selma, Malcolm X, the "shining black prince" of the movement, was assassinated while speaking to followers at Harlem's Audubon Ballroom.

In the aftermath of these deaths, the SCLC decided to organize a massive protest march from Selma. Early on the afternoon of Sunday, March 7, 1965, six hundred civil rights activists set out from Brown's Chapel African Methodist Episcopal Church, the nerve center for movement activism in the Selma campaign. Despite entreaty from the Kennedy administration and fiat from Governor Wallace, these six hundred souls resolved to march on foot fifty miles along Highway 80, fully aware that they were putting themselves directly in harm's way. Their destination was Montgomery: the state's capital, the "cradle of the Confederacy," and the site of a celebrated bus boycott almost a decade earlier. They would barely make it beyond the city's limits.

The denouement of the march on "Bloody Sunday" needs little reminder to anyone familiar with the civil rights movement. The activists marched uneventfully through downtown Selma but barely crossed the murky Alabama River on the Edmund Pettus Bridge before they were met by a detachment of law enforcement officers. About fifty Alabama state troopers and several dozen of Sheriff Clark's posse waited on horseback, fitted with gas masks, billy clubs, and blue hard hats. Major John Cloud declared the gathering illegal and gave the marchers a two-minute warning to disperse. The major rejected Hosea Williams's efforts to engage in dialogue and then peremptorily gave the order for the law enforcement officers to set upon the marchers with reckless fury and punishing force.

Newsmen on hand captured the surreal chain of events with film and camera. By sundown, scenes from Selma were broadcast in living rooms throughout the nation. One television station, ABC, interrupted their evening movie, *Judgment at Nuremberg*, to air a film report on the assault. The raw footage ignited a firestorm of public outrage. George Leonard, a magazine editor, described the reaction as he and his wife watched the evening news from the comfort of their living room in San Francisco:

> A shrill cry of terror, unlike any sound that had passed through a TV set, rose up as the troopers lumbered forward, stumbling sometimes on the fallen bodies. . . . *Unhuman*. No other word can describe the motions. . . . The bleeding, broken and unconscious passed across the screen, some of them limping along, others supported on either side, still others carried in arms or on stretchers. It was at this point that my wife, sobbing, turned and walked away, saying, "I can't look any more." . . . I was not aware that at the same moment people all up and down the West Coast were feeling what my wife and I felt . . . [that] hundreds of these people would drop whatever they were doing; that some of them would leave home without changing clothes, borrow money, overdraw their checking accounts; board planes, buses, trains, cars; travel thousands of miles with no luggage; get speeding tickets, hitchhike, hire horse-drawn wagons; that these people, mostly unknown to one another, would move for a single purpose: to place themselves alongside the Negroes they had watched on television. (Leonard 1965, xx, emphasis in original)

Congress and the president also reacted with a sense of urgency and outrage. On the floor of the House of Representatives and the Senate, fifty members of Congress publicly condemned the events of Bloody Sunday. Michigan's John Conyers, for one, declared that the entire Michigan congressional delegation (which included Republican conservatives Gerald Ford and Ed Hutchinson) stood behind the Leadership Conference on Civil Rights demand that President Johnson immediately propose voting rights legislation and use of federal authority to prevent further violence in Alabama.

At the same time, representatives throughout the nation began to receive a flood of mail from their constituents, and many of these elected officials explicitly cited these correspondences in their public statements. Senator John Pastore from Rhode Island, for example, expressed anguish that "[t]elegrams from horrified citizens—neighbors of mine—pour in to me. . . . They reveal the deepfelt dismay—the heartfelt resentment that helpless Americans anywhere in America could be subjected to such savagery" (Garrow 1978, 177). Wisconsin senator William Proxmire opened his statement on the floor of Congress with a telegram from John Lavine, a newspaper publisher in Chippewa Falls, Wisconsin. Proxmire introduced Lavine's correspondence by noting that Chippewa Falls is "a town in which people are careful and stable in their attitudes [and] certainly not characterized by emotional reaction." As with many other correspondents, Lavine urged direct federal intervention, observing,

> Never in our experience have [we] received such reaction from normally political, nonemotional leaders of our community and "workingman" alike as we have as a result of the brutality in Alabama. Isn't it possible that this bloody disregard of Americans' constitutional rights can be protected by the intervention of Federal marshals and/or law enforcement officers? Please understand, we and the many citizens who have contacted us, are generally not advocates of this type of intervention, but we see no other recourse in this situation. It is not a time for words; it is a time for action. (Garrow 1978, 178)

By 9 P.M. on March 15, President Johnson delivered a special address to Congress, a message that was viewed on television by 70 million Americans. In the first special address to Congress on domestic policy in nineteen years, Johnson proposed sweeping voting rights legislation. Perhaps equal in symbolic significance, Johnson struck a deep chord with movement activists and movement sympathizers throughout the nation by explicitly co-opting Dr. King's rallying cry from the 1963 March on Washington, "we shall overcome." Johnson, who was interrupted forty times by applause during his forty-five-minute speech, declared that "at times history and fate meet at a single time in a single place to shape a turning point in man's unending search for freedom. . . . So it was last week in Selma, Alabama." [2] With public outrage and the renewed resolve of racially liberal elites behind the proposed legislation, the Voting Rights Act of 1965 passed by a vote of 328 to 74 in the House on August 3 and by a vote of 79 to 18 in the Senate the next day. By August 6, 1965, Johnson signed what he called "one of the most monumental laws in the entire history of American freedom" (Garrow 1978, 132). It was, by his own reckoning, a crowning achievement of Johnson's presidency.

ELITE OPINION THEORY AND THE CIVIL RIGHTS MOVEMENT

This is a book about how our views on an issue such as race become activated and articulated during the course of sustained mass unrest and social
protest. What happens with mass audiences as they witness the unfolding
conflict in Selma? When do such events arouse our political opinions and
stir us to action? Are our views and actions responsive to the influence of elite actors or to that of movement-based individuals and organizations?

For many Americans, the mid-1960s—the 1964 Civil Rights Act, the
election of Lyndon Johnson, Selma, and the 1965 Voting Rights Act—signify a defining moment in U.S. political history. For some political commentators, this is so because it honors the potential for democratic government to achieve just outcomes. Faced with an especially egregious instance
of racial repression in the South, the nation's leaders chose not to abide by
tyranny against a minority and instead affirmed equal political status for all
its citizens. Philip Klinkner and Rogers Smith, for example, claim that "[i]n
many ways, this advance toward racial equality stands as the most important and proudest achievement of the twentieth century in America" (1999,
287). For other political commentators, the mid-1960s are a defining moment because of its enduring influence on American politics for the rest of
the twentieth century. Thomas Byrne Edsall and Mary Edsall argue that the
highly charged 1964 presidential election "set in motion a larger political
process" that not only led to Lyndon Johnson's election and the subsequent
passage of the 1965 Voting Rights Act but also fundamentally transformed
our ideological views and our partisan attachments (1991, 8). More recently,
Stephan Thernstrom and Abigail Thernstrom (1997) suggest that it is the
juxtaposition between the celebrated legislative successes of the mid-1960s
and the ensuing eruption of urban uprisings that has cast a long, troubled
shadow on race relations and racial politics since the civil rights era.

For many public opinion scholars, the mid-1960s also signify elite-
driven, top-down influences on mass opinion at work. This consensus
among academics—that the political beliefs and sentiments of ordinary
individuals are shaped primarily (if not exclusively, by some accounts) by
elite actors—is at the heart of this book. The list of works that take an elite
approach is too numerous and diverse to list here.[3] In the coming chapters,
I focus chiefly on elite theory's two most prominent exemplars, especially
vis-à-vis racial attitudes in the civil rights era: Edward Carmines and James
Stimson's "issue evolution" model (1989) and John Zaller's "receive-accept-
sample" model of mass opinion (1992).

To preview some of the coming arguments: Carmines and Stimson support their version of elite theory with substantive claims that parallel the Edsalls' on the influence of the mid-1960s on partisanship and ideology. To wit, they boldly assert that "[t]he 1964 presidential election marked the decisive turning point in the political evolution of racial issues" (1989, 47). As we shall see in detail, one implication of Carmines and Stimson's account is that history is made by political elites at distinct moments in time. By this reading, the civil rights movement of local demonstrations and grassroots organizing is not central to how public views are activated and transformed. Instead, such movement activism becomes an exogenous shock to a relatively self-contained political system comprised of political elites.

Our abridged account of the protest at Selma is animated with details that suggest that mass opinion is not always transformed at synchronic moments in history or exclusively in response to political elites. Legislative and electoral events like the 1965 Voting Rights Act do not occur without their historical footprints—whether proximate events, like the conflict in Selma or the 1964 presidential election, or longer-term antecedents, like the prior decade of movement activism and elite responses to this activism. Moreover, in the case of Selma there is a discernible sequence of events and interaction of elites and non-elites prior to the activation of opinion that leads individuals such as John Lavine to write an impassioned telegram to his senator or George Leonard to drop everything and catch the next flight to Alabama. As the historian David Garrow intimates,

> The story of how southern blacks finally won equal voting rights cannot be fully appreciated without an understanding of how the dynamics of protest helped them to achieve the remarkable gains that they made. The reason why the voting rights story cannot be understood without an appreciation of the dynamics of protest can be summarized in one word: Selma. (1978, 1)

In this case, the mobilization of black resistance and insurgency begins the sequence, which then provokes a reaction of southern whites and both local and national political elites, which in turn activates mass audiences throughout the land.

In the most general terms, the elite opinion theories of political scientists are problematic because they are at odds with well-established sociological and historical accounts of the civil rights era. This is so because elite interpretations either neglect or misconceive the principally bottom-up dynamics of social movements. Protest politics like the civil rights movement, almost by definition, are sustained challenges to the political status quo that entail the activation and mobilization of ordinary individuals, from the bottom up. By isolating the "political evolution of racial issues" to the mid-1960s and to elite influences on mass opinion, then, elite opinion theories diminish the significance of the prior period of black insurgency and effectively relegate the purposive agency of movement activists to a lesser if not negligible role. As we shall see in this book, this defining feature of social movements applies not only to movement activists but to the mass audiences who observe and respond to the unfolding movement as well.

More pointedly, the dynamics of social movements matter especially to elite opinion theories because the categories that elite theories take as fixed—those of "political elites" and "the mass public"—constantly shift and evolve. During periods of relative political quiescence, the divide between elites and ordinary individuals are fairly impermeable and bridged by a relatively stable set of mediating institutions and politically active citizens. At such moments, top-down accounts that examine the conventional (that is, legislative and electoral) dimensions of politics are likely to suffice. During sustained social movements, however, the divide between elites and ordinary individuals will erode under waves of mass insurgency that activate individuals and mobilize organizations within civil society to demand a place on the political stage. In this process, movement insurgents vie for influence in defining what we know and how we interpret the ongoing events and the issues at stake. To the extent that movement-based actors and organizations succeed in this endeavor, elite opinion theories are less likely to give us a sufficiently accurate account of mass opinion.

The main story in this book thus lies in how public views on race are altered and activated during a social movement and the roles that elites and non-elites play in that transformation. There is also, however, a parallel story. This book is about our durable habits of studying public opinion—how we measure public views and what we assume about these views in the process. In terms of measurement, in the last several decades we have grown accustomed to thinking of public opinion almost exclusively in terms of what poll data have to say. What is lost in this convention are the myriad other possible modes of public political expression. Modes such as public demonstrations and letter writing are very rarely examined by social scientists as instances of public opinion. Such alternative modes cannot claim scientific standing equal to that of opinion polls as a representative sample of public opinion writ large, but they often link opinions more directly to actions and, as a consequence, can be often more politically salient and influential.

Conceptually, elite views exemplify the prevailing objective to aim for social science theories that achieve parsimony and generalizability. John Zaller, for example, strives to derive a common theory of mass opinion that applies across all social groups, historical periods, and political phenomena. As we shall see, Zaller achieves a successful synthesis of the individual-level, cognitively-based, short-term dynamics of mass opinion. The cost of this achievement, however, is a richer, more politically meaningful understanding of the social, historical, and ideological forces that underlie such processes. The upshot is that the nature and dynamics of mass opinion are rendered no differently across distinct or divergent contexts that ought to matter. We shall see that the tools we use and the conceptual foundations we bring to study public opinion have direct consequences not only for how we understand public opinion empirically but also for what normative implications we draw about the role of public opinion in democratic governance.

These considerations—about whether ordinary individuals can challenge and change status quo opinions, about how mass audiences react when such women and men attempt to do so, and about how the ways in which we study public opinion affect the outcome of these questions—are especially urgent and compelling today. By most accounts, public cynicism, distrust, apathy, and alienation are at their highest levels since such opinions have been tracked with poll data. Joseph Nye, Philip Zelikow, and David King (1997) find that by multiple measures—whether the belief that government is honest, responsive, trustworthy, or beholden to the common weal—the American public's confidence in government has declined steadily and sharply over the past few decades.[4] Steven Rosenstone and John Mark Hansen (1993) find that by multiple measures—whether attending local meetings, attending political rallies, serving on a community organization, or working for political parties—political engagement has declined steadily and sharply over the past few decades. And Robert Putnam (2000) contends that by multiple measures—whether joining civic associations, reading newspapers, bowling, or playing cards—"social capital" and civic engagement have declined steadily and sharply over the past few decades in the United States.[5] Ironically, in the victorious aftermath of the Cold War, democracy in the United States increasingly appears to be an unfinished, attenuated, imperiled project. Such troubling circumstances present an especially opportune occasion to revisit a watershed moment of citizen activism in recent history. As we shall see, the civil rights movement is a powerful testament to the capacity of ordinary individuals, under the right conditions, to become attuned to, engaged with, and activated by political conflict.

DEFINING POLITICAL ELITES

Before embarking on our critical reassessment of elite opinion theory, some clarification on how I use the term "elite" is in order. In my use of "elites" I follow John Zaller, who defines them to be "persons who devote themselves full time to some aspect of politics or public affairs . . . these elites include politicians, higher level government officials, journalists, some activists, and many kinds of experts and policy specialists" (1992, 6). This definition is not idiosyncratic to Zaller. Rather, it shares elements with those of earlier thinkers such as Walter Lippmann (1925) and Valdimer Orlando Key (1961) as well as Zaller's contemporaries. Edward Carmines and James Kuklinski, for instance, similarly distinguish between elites, "those whose primary business is governing the nation," and non-elites, "those for whom politics is secondary" (1990, 266).

That said, some imprecision is inevitable in the slippery work of making definitions. It is unclear from Zaller's formulation why "lower level" government officials (who surely also dedicate their full-time labors to politics and public affairs) do not merit the term "elite." For that matter, even Carmines and Kuklinski's parsimonious formulation of "elites" and "non-elites" is likely to unravel into thorny disagreements over what constitutes "primary" and "secondary" spheres of political activity. These ambiguities result, in large measure, from two implicit assumptions we make about political elites. Namely, when we use it colloquially, we are likely to reserve the term "elites" for political actors who wield some legitimating authority and discernible influence over political outcomes. We are also likely to reserve the term for actors who operate within formal, institutionalized political channels. In this book, then, I consider political elites to be individuals who work full-time within formal political channels and institutions and who wield authority and influence over formal political decisions.

The distinction between full-time work within formal political channels and full-time work outside such formal channels and institutions evokes several quite familiar bifurcations of political life: between public and private spheres, between politics and civil society, and to use Habermas's terms, between "system" and "lifeworld."[6] This kind of distinction is pertinent and analytically useful to our present task of describing social movements and non-elite influences on mass opinion. It helps us properly place individuals such as Myles Horton, who ran workshops on political activism for many movement leaders at the Highlander Folk School in Monteagle, Tennessee, or Jo Ann Robinson, who played a pivotal role in the success of the 1956 bus boycott as a leader of the Women's Political Council of Montgomery, Alabama, or Gus Courts, who organized the Belzoni, Mississippi, chapter of the NAACP, or Ivory Perry, a lifelong itinerant foot soldier for social change. Such "counterelites" remind us that in modern pluralist democracies, there are multiple realms of political power and spheres of political influence. Thus persons such as Horton, Robinson, Courts, and even Perry may exert authority and influence within locally bounded and marginalized spheres of political activity. But we surely would not consider them "elites" within mainstream, conventional spheres of political activity. This distinction will be an important one in ensuing chapters.[7]

My proposed refinement of Zaller's definition of "elite" also is slippery because social movements evolve as a dynamic process. That is, the distinction between mainstream elites and marginalized counterelites is likely to be fluid and shifting. At some point in the course of a social movement, especially one that succeeds in mobilizing an issue onto the political stage, non-elite activists and their organizations will become institutionalized and wield influence within formal political channels. The NAACP in its year of founding, 1909, was an organization striving to gain access to formal decision-making channels. By the mid-1950s, the same NAACP was a fully entrenched advocacy organization. Martin Luther King Jr. in 1953 was a freshly minted pastor from Boston University's School of Theology acquainting himself with his new congregation at the Dexter Avenue Baptist church in Montgomery, Alabama. A decade later, the same Martin Luther King became a Nobel laureate and spokesperson for a national movement, sharing his dream to let freedom ring throughout the land before 250,000 fellow Americans on the steps of the Lincoln Memorial. Fanny Lou Hamer, for most of her adult life, was a sharecropper and time-keeper at the Marlowe Plantation outside Ruleville, Mississippi. By 1964, the same Mrs. Hamer addressed the credentials committee of the Democratic Party as a delegate of the Mississippi Freedom Democratic Party.[8]

This slippage and transformation from non-elite to elite, of course, is precisely the point of this book. During periods of mass unrest and political upheaval, elites are best identified not by who they are (that is, by a given professional station in public life) but rather by what they do (that is, by their leadership, their ability to persuade and mobilize, and their flexible adaptation to and exploitation of rapidly changing circumstances). This more fluid conception, linking ordinary individuals to marginalized counterelites to mainstream elites, is what Unita Blackwell describes in this chapter's epigraph. Like Fanny Lou Hamer, Blackwell began as a sharecropper in Mayersville, Mississippi. Blackwell then became galvanized into activism by the mid-1960s and, with her newfound empowerment and experience behind her, successfully gained electoral office as the mayor of her hometown by 1977.

DATING THE CIVIL RIGHTS MOVEMENT

A final prefatory matter is the choice of time span for this book—from 1948 to the mid-1960s. Studies of historical moments often fiercely debate the appropriate start and end points. This is true of the civil rights movement as well. Most commonly, this is a debate over whether to view historical change as top-down or bottom-up and as synchronic or diachronic in origin.[9] In the former case, the point of departure is unfailingly the Supreme Court's 1954 decision in *Brown v. Board of Education of Topeka, Kansas.* In the latter, scholars identify alternate events as divergent in date and significance as the 1953 Baton Rouge bus boycott, the 1955 murder of Emmett Till, the 1955–56 Montgomery bus boycott, and the 1960 student lunch counter sit-ins.[10] And the origins of intensified black resistance could just as well be traced to much earlier historical moments—whether the early 1940s March on Washington Movement, the earlier origins of the National Association for the Advancement of Colored People, the United Negro Improvement Association, the Niagara Movement, or even earlier, the First Reconstruction or the slave revolts.

In terms of public opinion, the radical mobilization of racial attitudes during the civil rights years are likely firmly ingrained in events and institutions dating well before the *Brown* decision. Schuman, Steeh, and Bobo (1988), for example, begin their historical account with the decision in *Plessy v. Ferguson* to uphold the "separate but equal" doctrine in 1896. In restricting my analysis to the span from 1948 to the mid-1960s, I make no rigid commitments on the dating of the civil rights movement. Rather, the choice is taken principally for analytic clarity. By most accounts, both 1948 and the mid-1960s signify focal historical moments in which elites played the primary role. In 1948, President Truman championed his Commission of Civil Rights' recommendations for civil rights reforms and also issued Executive Orders 9980 and 9981, creating a Fair Employment Board to eliminate racial discrimination in federal employment and a Committee on Equality of Treatment and Opportunity in the Armed Services. And the mid-1960s marked the passage of the crowning legislative acts of the civil rights movement (the Civil Rights Act of 1964 and the Voting Rights of 1965) and the 1964 presidential campaign. Choosing such "elite" moments as the temporal bookends thus stacks the deck a priori in favor of elite theory, making evidence for non-elite influences compelling a fortiori.[11]

Of course, picking particular points in history as elite (or non-elite) is precarious work (if for no other reason, because definitions of those terms are so precarious). Even claiming 1948 as a moment of elite advocacy of civil rights can be misleading without some recognition of the opposition and activism at work. Taylor Branch, for example, notes that the walkout of southern delegates from the 1948 Democratic Convention "was treated as something of a menacing joke, as evidenced by the fact that the Southerners accepted their 'Dixiecrat' nickname, and newspaper editors across the South expressed considerable chagrin over the spectacle" (1988, 13). Another historian notes that it was doubtful that President Truman intended any action other than merely supporting his commission's recommendations. That is, Truman hoped that "rhetoric alone would be sufficient to satisfy black demands and that his inaction would appease southern Democrats" (Pfeffer 1990, 124). Such hopes were dashed, however, with mobilized pressure from efforts such as the Congress on Racial Equality's Journey of Reconciliation in 1947 (a precursor to CORE's Freedom Rides in the 1960s) and A. Philip Randolph's formation of the League for Non-Violent Civil Disobedience Against Military Segregation in 1948. Thus even a clarion signal of support for desegregation such as Truman's Executive Orders 9980 and 9981 emerges from Randolph's campaign, Hubert Humphrey's fight on the floor of the 1948 Democratic convention, and Truman's solicitation of the black vote.[12]

OVERVIEW OF CHAPTERS

In chapter 1, I describe the elite view of public opinion in more detail and identify the tensions and contradictions it faces as an account of public views of race during the civil rights movement. I take John Zaller's "Receive-Accept-Sample" model as elite theory's paradigm statement and argue that how aware people are about a given issue and whether and how they voice their opinions about that issue—the inputs and outputs of Zaller's model—depend fundamentally on what the issue is, which social groups and political institutions are invested in it, and how it unfolds within specific historical and ideological contexts. I propose to complement Zaller's individual-level, cognitively-based, short-term account with a more context-specific, group-based account of activated mass opinion. This account argues that the public's views of political matters are often nurtured and activated within multiple spheres of interaction. With respect to an issue such as race, the dynamics of public opinion are rooted in a dominant, mainstream public at the center of political affairs, in marginalized oppositional publics at its periphery, and in the interaction between dominant and marginalized public spheres. This complementary account allows us to consider both elite- and non-elite-based influences on mass opinion. Specifically, the bottom-up insurgency of a black "counterpublic" during the civil rights movement is especially critical in raising the public's awareness of racial issues, mobilizing an active public voice on such issues, and pushing racial policy reforms onto the political agenda.

This context-specific, group-based account is put to the test in chapter 2 using available survey data from 1956 to 1964. The findings presented in this chapter challenge the leading elite account of racial attitudes during the civil rights movement, Edward Carmines and James Stimson's *Issue Evolution*. Carmines and Stimson argue that the transformation of public opinion about race is attributable to elite events such as the 1964 presidential election campaign, in which elite actors (Barry Goldwater, George Wallace, Lyndon Johnson) drew clear partisan lines on racial policy preferences. I model public views on racial policy as a series of "elections" in 1956, 1960, and 1964 between counterelite, movement-based influences and elite, partisan-based influences on school integration, fair housing, and equal employment opportunities. The results show that ties to movement counterelites preceded and predominated partisan elite ties as an influence on racial policy preferences. This primacy of counterelite influences, furthermore, was present well before the mid-1960s. And contrary to Carmines and Stimson's claims that critical linkages between racial egalitarianism, democratic partisanship, and social welfare liberalism were forged during key elite legislative and electoral debates in the mid-1960s, we find ample evidence for such linkages as early as 1956.

Although these survey-based findings offer a compelling corrective to elite theory, they are built on a slender reed of esoteric statistical analysis and ultimately give us a substantively diluted account of the public' views on race during the civil rights movement. In chapter 3 I consider how the virtually singular reliance on survey data limits and prejudices what we know about public opinion. I show empirically that survey data have evolved as the dominant measure of public opinion and consider the historical and ideological trajectory to this sovereign status. Several trenchant critiques of opinion research emerge from this conventional conflation of public opinion and survey data. Most important among these for our purposes, survey data may be particularly ill-equipped to test elite theories of mass opinion during periods of political unrest. Against most detractors and defenders, I argue that the debate over the elite bases of mass opinion and the role of survey data are empirical questions that are best answered with careful attention to theory, hypotheses, and the use of multiple measures and multiple methods to test these hypotheses.

In chapter 4 I propose a framework for considering citizen correspondence as an alternate measure of public opinion on civil rights and racial equality. To set the stage, I first consider the different criteria we might use to evaluate alternate modes of measuring public opinion. In particular, different modes are likely to tell us different things about an individual's incentives to voice an opinion and about the information which that opinion conveys to political actors. I show that by several of these criteria constituency mail is an especially well-suited and valid measure. Letter writing well measures the political awareness of individuals on racial issues and, at the aggregate level, the political salience of an issue to elite actors. Furthermore, letter writing reveals dimensions of political expression that are rarely visible in survey data. In particular, constituency mail conveys the dialogical, narrative, rhetorical, strategic, and affect-based nature of publicly expressed viewpoints. Letters to the president are addressed *to* someone; they are texts that often tell a compelling story and that aim to inform, persuade, even deceive the president; they capture, through style and syntax, an emotional depth and range that is absent from ordinal and interval measures used in survey instruments.

Using a sample of 6,765 letters written to the president concerning civil rights and racial equality between 1948 and 1965, chapter 5 illustrates the dynamics of constituency mail during the civil rights struggle. It outlines changes over time in the racial and regional identity of the correspondents, in the type of correspondences they sent (individual letters, petitions, mass mailings, organizational mail), in the positions they advocated, and in the timing of mailings. The letters are remarkably responsive to specific events (both elite- and movement-initiated) and describe the sequential activation of three key groups—African Americans, southern whites, and racially liberal (mostly northern) whites. Organized appeals from African Americans and northern liberals from the late 1940s through the mid-1950s initiated this activation, which was followed by a striking tug-and-pull between southern white and African American correspondents during the late 1950s, and then crescendoed in a chorus of racially liberal whites who drowned out segregationists by the early 1960s. This sequence is paralleled by a dramatic turn from a steady stream of organizational mail to a deluge of individual letters and mass mailings by the 1960s.

In chapter 6 we move from the broad-brush view of trends in letter writing to a finer-grain analysis of the content of individual letters. A vivid sampling of these letters is captured in three stylized voices—again, of African

Americans, southern whites, and nonsouthern whites. The letters chronicle an evolving, group-based struggle over the public's understanding of racial politics and over the interpretive frames used to shape this understanding. The letters also reveal dramatic shifts in that understanding. For example, African American correspondence that, in the late 1940s, addressed a sprawling agenda of racial grievances were fine-tuned and amplified in the 1960s into an emboldened, racially univocal demand for desegregation and civil rights. For southern whites the letters shifted from unapologetic (even militant) segregationist retorts in the 1950s to reactive references to the violation of whites' rights and deflective references to the president's need to heed the threat of communism (compare racial segregation) in the 1960s. For whites outside the South, the shift was from relative quiescence through the 1950s to an outburst of moral outrage in the 1960s framed around universal rights, police brutality in the South, and the court of world opinion.

In chapter 7 I summarize my main arguments and central findings. Elite accounts of mass opinion and theoretical critiques of survey research are reconsidered in light of these findings. I argue for an interactive, processual view of elite *and* non-elite (counterelite) influences on mass opinion and propose a typology that specifies the conditions—with respect to other issues and across different social groups, institutional settings, and historical periods—under which non-elite influences on mass opinion are likely to matter. Furthermore, I consider the implications that these findings hold for contemporary debates over race relations and racial policy. I conclude by highlighting the contrasting normative views of democratic politics that are at stake in the question of the elite or non-elite dynamics of mass opinion.

ONE

ELITE OPINION THEORY AND ACTIVATED MASS OPINION

It is not the kings or generals that make history but the masses of the people.

—Nelson Mandela

We have the record of kings and gentlemen *ad nauseam* and in stupid detail; but of the common run of human beings . . . the world has saved all too little of authentic record and tried to forget or ignore even the little saved.

—W. E. B. Du Bois

Every fight consists of two parts: (1) the few individuals who are actively engaged at the center and (2) the audience that is irresistibly attracted to the scene. The spectators are as much a part of the overall situation as are the overt combatants. The spectators are an integral part of the situation, for, as likely as not, the *audience* determines the outcome of the fight. . . . To understand any conflict it is necessary therefore to keep constantly in mind the relations between the combatants and the audience. . . . This is the basic pattern of all politics.

—E. E. Schattschneider

According to E. E. Schattschneider, politics is performative, with a central cast of characters onstage playing to audiences before them. The observation is trenchant because we all too often gaze solely on the key actors onstage. Schattschneider reminds us that the relations between actors and audiences—how the spectators are engaged and whether they can be drawn into the fray—are critical to understanding the outcome of events. This is what distinguishes a performance from a rehearsal. When the central actors can engage an audience successfully, they can control its response like puppetmasters do a marionette, evoking comedy, tragedy, or a sober moment's pause with the faintest of gestures. When the central actors fail to engage an audience—when the performers bungle their lines or otherwise hoodwink, patronize, and misjudge the crowd before them—the spectators may upstage the act in shower of boos, hisses, catcalls, and rotten fruit, or worse yet, throw the rascals unceremoniously off the stage. Ultimately, it is this intimate liaison between actors and their audiences that gives meaning to a performance, political or otherwise.

Political scientists have not ignored this fact. The study of political behavior and public opinion comprises a substantial portion of academic research on politics. As we shall see in this chapter, however, political scientists are prone to take a particular, peculiar view of political audiences. Specifically, the actor-audience liaison is most often characterized by a one-way, top-down flow of political communication from elites on center stage to spectators in the audience. How this communication is received and processed and how it motivates or deters political action is then examined primarily in terms of individual-level, cognitively based, short-term influences using survey data. This is a needlessly restrictive approach. It neglects instances in which political communication flows laterally between audience members or bottom-up from the audience to center stage. It reduces citizens to passive repositories of elite messages, incapable of forming autonomous political beliefs and powerless to alter their political destinies. And, as noted in the introduction, it renders a peculiar interpretation of how public opinion is voiced during episodes of social movement insurgency such as the civil rights era in the United States.

In this chapter, I examine the limits of this approach to public opinion and consider how we might enhance such an approach. I begin by situating the elite approach in the central question of whether democratic citizens are fit to govern. The research on this question suggests that they are not. The American electorate appears inattentive, ill-informed, inconsistent, and inchoate in their political reasoning and judgments. Elite opinion theory is one means of consoling this finding with the normative democratic ambition of popular rule. I thus look more closely and critically at a paradigmatic example of elite opinion theory, John Zaller's "Receive-Accept-Sample" (RAS) model. In the RAS model, the elite origins of mass opinion turn out to reflect theoretical priors more than they do inferences sanctioned by empirical analysis. What's more, the model places some strong restrictions on how mass opinion is conceived and measured, in a way that biases any empirical analysis to favor an elite account. The consequence of these restrictions and simplifications is an account of mass opinion shorn from the political, social, and historical contexts in which our political opinions are nurtured and voiced.

I propose a more group-based, historically grounded, issue-specific account of "activated mass opinion" that complements the general framework of a model like Zaller's. This more contextual account foregrounds how issues are defined, which groups are mobilized, and what roles elites and non-elites play in these matters. According to this view, there are multiple mass publics whose political opinions are formed, sustained, and activated in a matrix of intersecting interests, identities, institutions, and ideologies. In a stratified society such as the United States, these sometimes confluent, sometimes contradictory forces are characterized by a dominant public at the center of political affairs and multiple oppositional publics at its margins. Oppositional counterpublics are critical sites for the emergence of non-elite influences on mass opinion. In the case of the civil rights movement, a black counterpublic sphere and black counterelites are critical to the formation and activation of public views on race that challenge the prevailing racial attitudes of the day. When black insurgency successfully mobilizes a groundswell of protest, a sequence and process are set in motion that move racial attitudes out of relative quiescence into activated mass opinion. I conclude the chapter with some empirical expectations about how this proposed account improves our understanding of black insurgency and racial attitudes during the civil rights era.

A BLOOMING, BUZZING CONFUSION AND ELITE INFLUENCE

Everyday politics, to borrow William James's apt phrase, is a "great, blooming, buzzing confusion." Little surprise, then, that one of the most frequently lamented and thoroughly documented facts about democracy in America is that its citizens hold dismally ill-formed and ill-informed political views.[1] There is a deafening chorus of public opinion research showing, for instance, that Americans are more likely to correctly identify celebrity judges who dole out matinee justice on television than they are to identify the justices of the Supreme Court of the United States. In a classic panel study fielded in 1956, 1958, and 1960 by the University of Michigan's Survey Research Center, Philip Converse found that only about 10 percent of the public could meaningfully define the terms "liberal" and "conservative" (1964). Worse yet, asked about government's role in public utilities and housing, only one in four Americans gave a consistent answer to an identically worded question across the three years of the panel study. The consistency of public opinion rises only modestly to 37 percent when people are asked about government's role in desegregating schools. No wonder then, that Converse concludes that non-elites responded to survey questions "as though flipping a coin" (1964, 243).

This empirical finding about the American public is often interpreted as a realist's antidote to Pollyanna-ish hopes for more participatory and deliberative forms of democracy. Perhaps deservedly so, for an inept electorate would be a treacherous foundation for a democracy. If the public pays little heed, keeps barely informed, and capriciously switches positions on political matters, then it is hard to interpret public opinion as an authoritative and meaningful expression of what citizens want government to do. As Walter Lippmann makes the case, "[t]he notion that public opinion can and will decide all issues is in appearance very democratic. In practice it undermines and destroys democratic government. For when everyone is supposed to have a judgment about everything, nobody in fact is going to know much about anything" (Rossiter and Lare 1963, 98–99). There is little reason, moreover, not to expect better-informed, instrumentally motivated, institutionally rooted, and ideologically disposed political elites not to exploit this situation to their private advantage.

Political scientists generally marshal two lines of empirical defense to salvage a more sanguine view of democratic decision-making.[2] The first recourse lies in the magical properties of statistical aggregation. By this reasoning, although individual citizens may be disquietingly ignorant, inattentive, and incompetent, an electorate can exhibit a remarkably stable and secure level of wisdom about political matters. The basic intuition here harks back to the Marquis de Condorcet's "jury theorem" (1785). Condorcet's basic insight was that the likelihood of a collection of individuals, under majority rule, arriving at a socially "correct" judgment rises exponentially as the number of decision-makers increases. When groups are sufficiently large, the likelihood of a socially just or optimal decision by an evenly modestly competent collectivity is greater than the likelihood of such a decision by any member of that collectivity, no matter how Solomonic that individual.[3]

This defense, however, does not take us very far. For one thing, aggregation is not always so magical. As Kenneth Arrow proved in 1951, in some cases aggregation is an impossibility because majority preferences among competing proposals may cycle incoherently. Under Condorcet's parsimonious framework, the ability of aggregation to result in collective wisdom is more a feat of statistical legerdemain than it is a deep fact about demo-cratic decision-making. Optimism about collective wisdom under majority rule teeters on a knife's edge around the basic parameters of the model, like the ability of citizens to form competent political judgments.[4] As we have just noted, empirical studies of public opinion are quite clear that we should be wary of what we assume about the judgmental competence of the mass public.

Furthermore, the evidence that is harnessed to bolster this aggregative defense is somewhat shaky. The best such evidence of the "collective ratio-nality" of the democratic public is based in statistically significant correla-tions between (changes in) mass policy preferences and (changes in) elite policy responsiveness.[5] The first problem with this evidentiary basis is that the strength of this relation changed between the 1960s and the 1980s, leaving us to puzzle about why collective rationality or the power of aggre-gation should vary over time.[6] Worse yet, simple statistical associations are notoriously suspect because they can sustain multiple, even mutually con-tradictory causal stories. Importantly, it is entirely plausible that public opinion correlates with policy outputs because elites have the foresight and influence to craft and coax public opinion toward a particular aggregative outcome that suits the policy preferences of elites, not their constituents. Rather than mass opinion guiding elite policies, elites may instead be guid-ing mass opinion.

Another perhaps more promising defense of the democratic public is rooted in cognitive psychology. Elite actors and their mass audiences, ac-cording to this view, simply allocate the work of politics in a sensible, effi-cient manner. Individuals appear capricious and ill-informed not because they are incompetent but because their complex lives are filled with com-peting demands on their time and attention. Far from the ideal of Athe-nian democracy, politics in present-day America is professionalized and specialized. Ordinary citizens are not the "political animals" Aristotle de-scribes but rather fragmented individuals whose political obligations are often trumped by countervailing demands at work, at home, and within embedded social ties. Walter Lippmann once again minces no words as he observes that "I cannot find time to do what is expected of me in the theory of democracy; that is, to know what is going on and to have an opinion worth expressing in every question which confronts a self-governing com-munity. And I have not happened to meet anybody, from a President of the United States to a professor of political science, who came anywhere near to embodying the accepted ideal of the sovereign and omnicompetent citi-zen" (1925, 20–21).

Thus, by this line of reasoning neither completeness of information nor constancy of attention nor consistency of revealed preferences is a fair criterion by which to judge the competence of democratic citizens. Rather, the proper criterion ought to be whether individuals, in a given situation, can draw reasonable inferences and make fair judgments about political affairs given the level of information and attention they have.[7] Thus, a competent citizen does not need a doctorate in environmental sciences or decision theory to bear reasoned judgments about global warming and automobile emissions policy. She may simply need to know where elites whose judgments she trusts (or distrusts), such as Albert Gore Jr. or the Natural Resources Defense Council or the National Association of Manufacturers, stand on these issues. As this example suggests, an ample body of research shows that ordinary individuals are able to develop reasonable political views by making judicious use of cognitive shortcuts and interpretive simplifiers available to them through political communications.[8]

This cognitive defense of the democratic public, however, is also not without its limitations. The use of heuristics in itself is no guarantee of judgmental competence. The cognitive shortcuts and interpretive filters on which we rely may be difficult to comprehend, misleading, or otherwise ill-suited to our needs. As a consequence, we are unlikely to benefit from heuristics without some quality control. As disinterested and preoccupied as we are in our daily lives, we are unlikely to look to simpletons, sophists, or scoundrels for our political information. As our example in the previous paragraph suggests, the idea that ordinary citizens rely on cognitive shortcuts is intimately tied to the idea that political elites are the source of such information and influence. Edward Carmines and James Kuklinski, for example, argue that

> [c]ontrary to populist conceptions of political representation, American politics is elite-driven. The division of labor between those whose primary business is governing the nation and those for whom politics is secondary dictates that the former will, under most circumstances, set the agenda, define the parameters of major debates, and bring deliberations to their conclusion . . . "insiders," be they in politics or business, occupy the driver's seat. (1990, 266)

This view of the "rational ignorance" of ordinary citizens and the efficient allocation of democratic work dates back to Anthony Downs (1957) and Paul Lazarsfeld and his colleagues (Berelson et al. 1954). Today, the elite foundation of mass opinion is virtually orthodoxy. One aim of this book, of course, is to challenge this orthodoxy. But even granting it for the moment, the power of political elites over public opinion is no assurance that citizens' judgments will be reasonable or faithful to their personal preferences. Note that the cognitive defense of the democratic public succeeds in large part because it demands so little of citizens. The effect of this defense is to shift the burdens of knowledge and competence from ordinary individuals to political elites. Presumably, such cognitive burdens can be confidently delegated to professional politicians because we trust them to do their jobs ably and with the public's best interest in mind.

Hence, as with the aggregative defense, the cognitive case for the democratic public hinges vitally on the biases and incentives of political elites, how they influence and inform the public, and whether ordinary citizens have any autonomy over their political judgments. If elites are selective in the information they share, disingenuous about the policies they favor, or otherwise manipulative, then we are no better off for leaving the cognitive work of politics to professionals. The question of elites' biases and incentives is not mere idle conjecture. It is almost routine for political scientists to describe political elites as strategic (rather than sincere) actors with incentives to maximize private profit and exploit private information to move the electorate's preferences to their advantage.[9]

In addition to elites themselves, the fate of the cognitive defense also rests on the relation between elites and the public. Put bluntly, if the public has no autonomous (from elites, that is) means of forming political judgments, then elites can manipulate and craft the public's views on political matters (even the choice of whom to vote for) with impunity. Ultimately, this question hinges on an underlying account of how we receive and interpret information about the political world, whether and when that information animates or deters political action, and the role that elites play in that process. This is chiefly an empirical question, but it is one with decisive normative consequences.

To this end, I turn next to the main focus of this chapter: a close, critical look at elite opinion theory. I do so by focusing the analytic scrutiny sharply on an exemplary rendition of elite opinion theory. The strategy is to unearth some deep assumptions and tensions in this (elite) paradigmatic approach to mass opinion by poring over the details of a single account with a fine-toothed comb. We shall see that the elite approach sets needlessly exorbitant and theoretically motivated criteria by which to judge the democratic public. I propose instead to reconsider the democratic public on more empirically driven grounds. To wit, I specify amendments to the elite approach that permit us to better understand a particular episode of recent U.S. political history in which the public's views on an issue are powerfully engaged, informed, and activated.

RECEIVE-ACCEPT-SAMPLE

John Zaller's *The Nature and Origins of Mass Opinion (TNOMO)* is the closest thing to a "paradigm statement" among contemporary accounts of mass
opinion.[10] This paradigmatic feature is evident both in the research tradition with which Zaller identifies his work and in the welcome his work has
received from leading opinion scholars of our time. With regard to research
tradition, Zaller describes his work in the preface to *TNOMO* as "simply an
elaboration" of William McGuire's (1966, 1968) model of attitude change
and "essentially a synthesis and extension" of Philip Converse's landmark
papers (1962, 1964) on elite influences on mass opinion.(Both McGuire
and Converse, for those unfamiliar with these names, are pioneering figures in the behavioral tradition of social science research from the 1960s.)
In the judgment of leading opinion scholars, *TNOMO* has received extraordinary critical acclaim. In political science's flagship journal, the *American
Political Science Review,* James Stimson reviews this work as "perhaps the
best book ever written about public opinion" (1995, 182). Larry Bartels, on
the book's back cover, glowingly characterizes it as "the most significant
contribution to the scientific study of public opinion in almost three decades" (making indirect reference to Converse's and McGuire's landmark
works in 1960s). Philip Converse himself, also on *TNOMO*'s back cover,
hails the book as a "giant step forward in the development of a systematic
understanding of the dynamics of public opinion."

The paradigmatic feature of Zaller's book, of course, is best evidenced
in the work itself. As Converse's comments suggest and as Zaller himself
declares, *TNOMO* aims for a systematic and generalizable account of how
public opinion works. For John Zaller, there is a basic cognitive architecture
to mass opinion that he designates the "Receive-Accept-Sample" model. In
this account, the political world is a stage filled with elite actors who construct the political reality to which the audience of ordinary individuals attend. This reality is conveyed through the flow of political messages, received through institutional informational sources such as the mass media.
Professional political elites play the protagonists in this story because the
political world is, to borrow Walter Lippmann's phrase, "out of reach, out
of sight, out of mind" to the general public (1922, 18). Ordinary individuals
generally do not walk around with fully formed, well-ordered opinions in
their heads. Rather, the opinions we express depend heavily on information
we receive through media coverage of political events and whatever cues,
shortcuts, and interpretive frames accompany such coverage.

Political messages represent inputs into the RAS mechanism, depicted

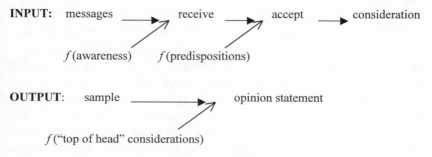

Figure 1.1   Receive-Accept-Sample Model

schematically in figure 1.1. At the input end, "receiving" information is primarily a function of an individual's level of political awareness (the "Reception Axiom"). Zaller defines political awareness as "the extent to which an individual pays attention to politics *and* understands what he or she has encountered" (21). "Accepting" any of the received messages as a relevant consideration regarding a given issue is primarily a function of an individual's prior political predispositions (the "Resistance Axiom"). To keep Zaller's terminology clear, political predispositions are defined as "stable, individual-level traits that regulate the acceptance or non-acceptance of the political communications the person receives" (22), and considerations are defined as "any reason that might induce an individual to decide a political issue one way or the other . . . a compound of cognition and affect" (40).

At the output end, considerations that have been more recently jogged in one's mind are more easily retrieved from one's memory ("the Accessibility Axiom"). As a result, the "sampling" of an individual's "opinion statements" about an issue is the function of an average of the considerations at the "top of one's head" when that individual is asked about that issue ("the Response Axiom"). How an individual responds to a poll question, for example, depends primarily on what that person has been thinking about just prior to being polled. Thus Zaller writes: "Opinion statements, as conceived in my four-axiom model, are the outcome of a process in which people *receive* new information, decide whether or not to *accept* it, and then *sample* at the moment of answering questions" (51, emphasis in original).

My description of RAS skimps on key details, and much of the ingenuity and insight in Zaller's analysis is in the details. Even abbreviated, the power and parsimony of the model should be clear.[11] In particular, it gives a clear rendering of the cognitive and elite-based defense of the democratic public. Unlike Converse, Zaller does not view the "response instability" of ordi-

nary individuals as evidence of an antidemocratic lack of citizen competence. Nor does Zaller reduce it principally to measurement artifact and
statistical noise, as Chris Achen and others have done.[12] Rather, the RAS
model conceives of response instability as characteristic of the ambivalence
of mass belief systems, given the contingencies of our daily lives. Unlike
political elites, who are attentive and knowledgeable as a matter of professional obligation, Zaller argues that ordinary citizens appear ill-formed and
ill-informed in their opinions because we do not always have politics on our
minds. Our levels of political awareness and attentiveness vary, our prior
political predispositions vary, and the considerations that rise to consciousness at the moment we voice our opinions vary.[13]

This leaves the public dependent on political elites for packaged political
information in the form of digestible stereotypes and interpretive shortcuts.[14] Zaller thus notes, "To an extent that few like but none can avoid,
citizens in large societies are dependent on unseen and usually unknown
others for most of their information about the larger world in which they
live. . . . The 'others' on whom we depend, directly or indirectly, for information about the world are, for the most part, persons who devote themselves full-time to some aspect of politics or public affairs—which is to say,
political elites" (6) There is no mistaking the hypothesized role of elites as
the primary source of political information and interpretation in *TNOMO*.
Zaller presents a very nearly mechanical relationship in which "[W]hen
elites uphold a clear picture of what should be done, the public tends to see
events from that point of view. . . . When elites divide, members of the
public tend to follow the elites sharing their general ideological or partisan
predispositions" (8–9).

In its commanding simplicity, Zaller's RAS model succeeds in synthe-
sizing more than four decades of research into a "cohesive theoretical system" (1). The model delivers a uniform and unitary account of how we
come to form and voice our political beliefs. Such parsimony and generalizability comes at a price, however. Zaller himself observes that "the
breadth and generality for which I aim in this book has been achieved at
the expense of strong assumptions and some important simplifications. . . .
Broad social theory and strong results require strong assumptions and significant simplifications, and it is foolish to pretend otherwise" (2). We shall
see that the "strong assumptions and significant simplifications" of RAS
can lead to an inaccurate or at least incomplete view of the elite or non-elite
foundations of mass opinion. Zaller's assumptions and simplifications reflect theoretical priors. These priors effectively bias how we conceive of and
measure awareness and predispositions in favor of an elite account. They

also obfuscate key variations in mass opinion in contexts other than short-term, individual-level, cognitively based changes in survey responses. Elite opinion theory—as reflected in the RAS model—may rescue the spirit of the democratic public but at great cost to the agency of individual citizens and to our substantive understanding of public opinion during momentous political events such as the civil rights movement.

THE LIMITS OF RECEIVE-ACCEPT-SAMPLE

The first limitation of RAS is that the influence of elites is fundamentally a theoretical presumption. Zaller's case for elite influence is based on plausible but undiscriminating anecdotal and inferential evidence. To illustrate the elite origins of opinion change, Zaller points to the sea change in racial attitudes in the twentieth century—from majority support for segregation and principles of racial superiority to majority support for integration and principles of racial equality.[15] The clear inference is that "racial equality is not some sort of amorphous trend, but a new norm created by various elites and transmitted to the public via the political media" (173). Notably, this thesis is not supported by the kind of meticulous, multivariate analysis of survey data found in the rest of *TNOMO*. Rather, the case is made through selective references to several putatively elite-driven events in twentieth-century history. The key moments Zaller cites range from Herbert Hoover's failed attempt to nominate John Parker (an alleged racist) to the Supreme Court in 1930 to a more general "revolution in elite discourse" (11).

I consider the merits of Zaller's historical argument in detail in chapter 2. For now, it is sufficient to note that Zaller's account of these events is incomplete and far from decisive. At minimum, as I show in chapter 2, there is a wealth of countervailing historical evidence of the critical role played by non-elites. In addition, when the analysis turns from historical texts to survey data, Zaller himself notes that "strictly speaking, one cannot use the results of my modeling to support even a weak argument for elite influence" (272). The reason, Zaller recognizes, is that RAS is neutral about where the public gets its political information from. Recall that political messages are the key inputs to RAS. If we cannot discriminate whether these messages come from elites or non-elites, then we can say little—within the RAS framework—about whether changes in considerations, predispositions, or voiced opinions result from elite or non-elite influences. As a result, the best that Zaller can claim is that "the shift in mass attitudes *roughly coincides* with the shift in elite attitudes" (11, emphasis mine).

Moreover, if we look more closely at Zaller's discussion of political messages, it turns out that RAS selects for elite sources of information and a cognitively based, generalized conception of political awareness. Political awareness, the gatekeeper to political information, is operationalized as knowledge about a "neutral" set of issues. Yet two of the three questions Zaller uses measure factual knowledge limited to the sphere of elite political actors and institutional politics.[16] When Zaller controls for the transmission of political messages, he examines only mainstream media sources such as the *New York Times, Newsweek,* and *Time.*[17] In this respect, although Zaller may be agnostic about where political information comes from, he is decidedly *not* agnostic about what constitutes political information.

Zaller may be justified in measuring awareness thus. Knowledge measures may simply outperform alternatives (such as one's educational attainment, media consumption, level of general political interest, and knowledge of a specific issue). Yet by Zaller's own estimation, the case is less than resounding.[18] This is especially true when the alternative measure of knowledge and awareness is issue-specific. On this comparison, Zaller concludes that "[t]hese domain-specific knowledge scales *outperformed* a general knowledge scale in predicting relevant criterion variables (such as attitude stability), but never by margins that approached statistical or substantive significance" (336, emphasis added).

On a more speculative note, it is quite likely that the general knowledge items that Zaller uses and issue-specific knowledge items that he excludes measure quite different dimensions of political awareness. Expressly, general knowledge items are perhaps likelier to measure individual-level cognitive capacity, whereas issue-specific knowledge items are perhaps likelier to capture cognitive capacity articulated through the group dynamics, social processes, institutional mobilization, and information networks, inter alia, that characterize the issue under consideration. I broach no argument here about which of these is better. The point, rather, is that how we measure political awareness is a choice with consequences. In the present case, Zaller's particular choice favors an elite-driven, individual-level, cognitively based, nonspecific conception of awareness, to the exclusion of alternative conceptions.

This kind of theoretical bias also limits RAS's description of our primary political predispositions. In particular, RAS is demonstrably silent about where they come from and what counts as a political predisposition. Zaller's agnosticism about the origins of our primary predispositions is justified on the grounds that "this book is a study of opinion formation and change in particular *short-term* situations, and for this purpose, the long-term influence of elites on predispositions, to the extent that it exists, may be safely neglected" (23, emphasis added). The point is a valid one, but Zaller does appear to aim for more than a short-term account elsewhere in *TNOMO*.[19] In part, this is because if RAS is confined to giving us a short-term account, then its achievements fall shy of rendering a "unified theory" of public opinion.

The limited ambit of Zaller's discussion of predispositions is further compounded by his justification for what counts as a "central" predisposition. To wit, the rationale once again appears data-driven. Zaller argues that political values (most often, liberal-conservative ideology, and sometimes, political partisanship) are the primary predispositions that anchor mass opinion. This choice is defended on the grounds that political values "seem to have a stronger and more pervasive effect on mass opinions than any of the other predispositional factors" (23). As with political awareness, Zaller opts for a specification of primary predispositions that performs well across all possible contexts. This again is a choice with consequences for how we understand public opinion on particular issues, among particular groups, and in particular historical circumstances.

For my purposes, it is germane that Zaller excludes race as a primary political predisposition, even when considering racial attitudes. The justification for this is left to a footnote, and the argument is again data-driven. Zaller claims that "there is little variance to race—that is, the population is too one-sidedly white—to permit making race a central predispositional factor in this study" (23n). On the face of it, one can debate whether the population of blacks, Latinos, Asian Americans, and other nonwhites constitutes sufficient variation. At the time this book is being written, whites comprise roughly 70 percent of the U.S. population, and the Census Bureau projects that the proportion of whites will diminish to one of two sometime between 2050 and 2060.[20]

Moreover, this claim in itself reduces predispositions to demography. The low variation in demographic "race" is thus conflated with the psychological and sociological bases of "race," for which significantly greater variation exists. For that matter, one's demographic race per se fits uneasily under Zaller's own notion of predispositions as the enduring tendencies that regulate the acceptance or rejection of political messages (22). Understood thus, predispositions are described by "race" as a social construction and an organizing principle.[21] According to this constructivist and ideological view of race, there is ample research to support the significance of race as a primary predisposition in the domain of racial attitudes. Michael Dawson and his colleagues show, for example, that race-based schemas and a racial group calculus are defining characteristics of African American mass

opinion (Dawson 1994a; Allen, Dawson, and Brown 1989). A clear implication of this work for RAS is that, for African Americans, one's racial predispositions define which political messages count as relevant considerations.[22]

Public opinion is thus likely to be organized by a greater number of primary predispositions than Zaller allows, especially when we consider mass
opinion in contexts that are issue-specific (for example, racial attitudes),
group-specific (for example, African Americans), and historically specific
(for example, the civil rights era). This multiplicity and contingency are likely
beyond matters of race. For that matter, our predispositions are not likely to
work in isolation. Take political values, which Zaller identifies primarily with
liberal-conservative ideology.[23] Political theorists have recently challenged
the notion—attributed to Alexis de Tocqueville, Gunnar Myrdal (1944), and
Louis Hartz (1955)—that political ideology in the United States is best defined by a single tradition of liberalism.[24] Rogers Smith (1993), for one, contends that political ideology is more faithfully defined by multiple traditions—among them, liberalism, republicanism, and ascriptive ideologies
that sustain racial and gender hierarchies.[25] The diversity of ideological traditions proliferates further within distinct sectors of the public. In this respect
Michael Dawson (2001) proposes that African American political thought is
best mapped on six ideological dimensions: two varieties of liberalism ("disillusioned liberalism" and "radical egalitarianism"), black conservatism,
black feminism, black nationalism, and black Marxism.[26]

Finally, the fact that RAS is agnostic about where predispositions come
from and restrictive about what counts as a predisposition may once again
incline RAS in favor of an elite account of mass opinion. Zaller explicitly
claims that elites "are *not* assumed to have an important role in shaping
individuals' political predispositions . . . predispositions are not in the *short
run* influenced by elites" (23, emphasis added). Yet by limiting what counts
as a central predisposition to a single, dominant ideology (liberalism) and
to formal political institutions (partisanship), RAS presents a more or less
closed system in which other ideological beliefs or institutions in civil society play no appreciable role in shaping mass opinion. Much of the story
about racial attitudes in the civil rights era, as I shall demonstrate in the
ensuing chapters, is told outside such a hermetic framework. Challenges
to liberalism as a dominant ideology and mobilization from non-elite institutions—the black church, the black press, historically black colleges, labor
unions, women's clubs, and other voluntary associations—are key factors
in articulating public views on race.

ACTIVATED MASS OPINION

We have scrutinized elite opinion theory through the lens of John Zaller's RAS model. The brunt of this assessment has been to highlight Zaller's implicit and explicit choices about how to conceive of public opinion, and the limitations that follow from those choices. Sharply put, if the way we measure political awareness selects for elite information inputs and the way we define political predispositions selects for mainstream ideological and institutional forces, then an imposingly high deck is stacked against the possibility of non-elite influences as a matter of initial theoretical specification. The details of our critique belong to Zaller's particular rendition, but its broad strokes reach to elite theory writ large.

At risk of waxing too general, there is an essential tension in the social sciences between minimalist and maximalist approaches to theorization. The RAS model is a prime example of a minimalist account: it reduces the complexity and specificity of a phenomenon to the smallest number of analytic components in order to achieve the greatest possible parsimony and explanatory power. In this section, I specify a more maximalist account that retains as much meaningful complexity and specificity as possible while still retaining a sufficiently generalizable analytical framework. I develop the account from the complexity and specificity of a particular political episode in which the democratic public is manifestly attentive and activated and in which particular, non-elite sectors of the public mobilize to help shape the political agenda and influence mass opinion.

This account of "activated mass opinion"—that is, beliefs and sentiments that are at once *salient* in the mind and *impel* one to political action—incorporates the historically contingent, group-based, and issue-specific contexts within which our political opinions are formed and out of which they are voiced. Activated mass opinion implies a high level of political awareness at the input end and a strong likelihood of voicing one's opinions at the output end. It takes seriously the critical linkage between cognition and action, inputs and outputs. The idea is directly analogous to V. O. Key's notion of "activating latent opinion." [27] As with Key's latent opinion, activated mass opinion is both a process and a tendency. Inert opinions become voiced as action during the evolution of a political conflict, and not all inert opinions are equally likely to be activated.

The civil rights movement is an especially well-suited context for examination of these characteristics of activated mass opinion. As noted in the introduction, grassroots social movements pose a fundamental challenge to top-down theories because they usually entail the activation and mobilization of collective grievances among non-elites onto the political agenda. Sometimes organized protests will only engage the attentions of a limited few. At other times, such protests will mobilize a sizeable, sustained response. And as E. E. Schattschneider notes, "the central political fact in a free society is the tremendous contagiousness of conflict . . . the outcome of every conflict is determined by the *extent* to which the audience becomes involved" (1960, 2, emphasis in original). What makes political conflicts special for Schattschneider is that "the relations between the players and the audience have not been well defined and there is usually nothing to keep the audience from getting into the game" (1960, 18). Moreover, it is the uncertainty about whether, when, and to what degree mass audiences will become activated that makes latent opinion, as V. O. Key observes, "about the only type of opinion that generates much anxiety" for political elites (1961, 263).

One consequence of this processual and infectious quality of activated mass opinion is that the usual boundaries between "elite" and "mass" become permeable and transitory. This is especially likely during extended episodes of conflict such as the civil rights movement. As noted in the introduction, when social movements are successful, active individuals who begin as non-elites (or leaders in a nonpolitical realm) emerge into an elite leadership position as the movement gains momentum and becomes institutionalized. Many prominent African American political leaders today—John Lewis, Harvey Gantt, Jesse Jackson, and Angela Davis, to name a few—began their political training as foot soldiers for the civil rights movement.

Of course, not all people who become mobilized and activated during a social movement make a career of it. Nor are all individuals lumped together under the category of "mass public" equally likely to participate in, identify with, or care to follow the course of a political conflict. The RAS model suggests that an individual's likelihood of becoming activated will depend on her institutional sources of political information, her attentiveness to politics, and her bundle of predispositions. Each of these constituent factors, however, is nurtured within issue-specific, group-based, and historically contingent spheres of shared interactions, interests, identities, ideologies, and institutions. With respect to public views of race during the civil rights movement, the activation of public opinion is principally defined around racial and regional group dynamics and initiated by the grassroots insurgency of African Americans in the South.[28] The "mass public" should thus properly be conceived of as *multiple* mass publics, contingent on the issue dynamics, political groups, and historical period in question.[29]

Thus, to understand the process by which mass opinion becomes activated, we need to first understand the prior tendency for collective grievances to become mobilized within the instigating, insurgent public. As suggested in our earlier discussion of the RAS model, mainstream (liberal-conservative) ideology and partisanship (Democrat-Republican) are unlikely to engender the kind of predispositions or maintain the kind of attentiveness that generate mass movements for social change. Yet the fact that social change does happen means that the tendencies that activate latent grievances come from somewhere. For African Americans in the civil rights era, the wellspring for such attentiveness and predispositions was a distinct "black counterpublic sphere" and a cadre of black counterelite actors and their institutions.[30]

The term "counterpublic" is used to evoke Jürgen Habermas's (1989) idea that public opinion is formed within a "public sphere." Habermas conceives of a single institutionalized site for critical and rational deliberation among free and equal individuals. This is an idealized conception that is limited in much the same way as Zaller's self-contained, short-term account of mass opinion. Accordingly, the criticisms drawn against Habermas by Nancy Fraser (1992) and others are apropos to my claim about multiple mass publics.[31] Counterpublic spheres are thus institutionalized and indigenous safe harbors that generate countervalent political information and sustain oppositional political ideologies. They sow seeds for social change that are harvested through the mobilization of social movements and the activation of mass opinion. As scholars such as Doug McAdam (1982), Aldon Morris (1984) and Charles Payne (1995) show, such indigenous sites are critical to the emergence of the civil rights movement. Morris notes that "[t]he basic resources enabling a dominated group to engage in sustained protest are well-developed internal social institutions and organizations that provide the community with encompassing communication networks, organized groups, experienced leaders, and social resources" (1984, 282).

With respect to elite theory, distinguishing counterpublics from a dominant mass public allows us to transport (or perhaps more accurately, proliferate) the core RAS framework—how we receive messages, whether we accept them as considerations, and how our considerations are "sampled" as expressions of our political opinions—to peripheral, parallel sites of opinion formation and activation. We can accept Zaller's cognitive blueprint without being constrained by a limited conception of political awareness, predispositions, and their linkage to political action and social change.[32]

The process of opinion formation and change in these parallel, peripheral sites may yet be top-down, but the top is occupied by counterelites. Thus the African American mass public of the 1940s and 1950s relied on black counterelites from nonpolitical (or pre-political) institutions—individuals such as Mary McLeod Bethune (founder of the National Council of Negro Women), Elijah Muhammad (founder of the Nation of Islam), John Sengstacke (founder of the *Chicago Daily Defender*), and Benjamin Mays (president of Morehouse College)—for their political messages and opinion cues. Note that influences on mass opinion may not be "either-or" between mainstream elites and counterelites but rather "both-and."

This notion of counterpublic spheres illuminates how the dynamics of mass opinion within marginalized groups differ from that within the general public. The rest of the story hinges on how successful oppositional counterpublics are at engaging the general public. In our processual account, the activation and mobilization of a black counterpublic—and the elite response—should spur the activation and mobilization of at least two other definable sectors of the mass public: a reactive public that staunchly resists attempts to alter the status quo and an adjuvant public that is empathetic to change and allies with movement activists. With respect to the civil rights movement, I will examine southern whites and racially liberal whites as such companion publics, begging the indulgence of some glaring simplifications.[33] The sum total of "public opinion," then, is the resultant of the vector of forces that shape mass opinion within these multiple publics. As Herbert Blumer described it more than fifty years ago, public opinion is

> a collective product . . . a composite opinion formed out of the several opinions that are held in the public; or better, as the central tendency set by the striving among these separate opinions and, consequently, as being shaped by the relative strength and play of opposition among them. In this process, the opinion of some minority group may exert a much greater influence in the shaping of the collective opinion than does the view of a majority group. . . . Public opinion is always moving toward a decision even though it is never unanimous. (1946, 191)

SPECIFYING EMPIRICAL PROPOSITIONS

The implications of these propositions for RAS are elaborated in the three stylized stages of the civil rights movement shown in table 1.1. These stages are described to illustrate the process and sequence of activation, rather than to defend a particular chronology of the movement. The intuition underlying these stages is that democratic politics and the role of ordinary citizens differ depending on whether the forces defining public opinion are in equilibrium or nonequilibrium. Under equilibrium conditions, we are likely to witness relative political quiescence and stability, whereby political conflict is voiced through conventional political elites and formal channels of accountability and representation. Under nonequilibrium conditions, we are likely to witness tumult, transition, and transformation, whereby political conflict is engaged, mobilized, and transformed on terms set by movement insurgents. Table 1.1 thus describes this evolution from equilibrium conditions to fully activated mass protest in three stages: (1) the equilibrium period of relative quiescence (roughly, from 1948 to 1955), during which the dynamics of mass opinion for the dominant public generally follow the top-down dynamics described by elite theories; (2) critical moments during which an insurgent, oppositional sector of the mass public begins to mobilize onto the political stage and to challenge the conventional political elites over the staging and interpretation of political events (roughly, 1956 and 1957); and (3) periods of protest politics during which the categories of "elite" and "mass" are fluid and shifting as the insurgent counterpublic, other activated publics, and conventional elites struggle over the staging and interpretation of political events (roughly, from 1958 to 1965).[34] The choice of years is simply meant to illustrate the process of activating mass opinion, rather than to stake a strong claim about stages of the civil rights movement.

Through each of these stages, table 1.1 hypothesizes variations in the political awareness and primary predispositions across three more or less distinct publics: the oppositional counterpublic (African Americans), the reactive public (southern whites), and the dominant mass public (all oth-

Table 1.1 Adapting the RAS Model to the Civil Rights Movement

	c. 1948–55	c. 1956–57	c. 1958–65
African Americans (counterpublic)			
Awareness	moderate/high	high	high
Predispositions	group-based	group/movement	group/movement
Southern whites (reactive public)			
Awareness	moderate	high	high
Predispositions	mainstream/group	group/movement	group/movement
Nonsouthern whites (dominant public)			
Awareness	low	low/moderate	moderate/high
Predispositions	mainstream	mainstream	mainstream/ movement

ers).[35] At the level of receiving messages, individuals within the dominant
public should exhibit relatively low levels of awareness (and, accordingly,
receive low levels of political information) about racial politics in the initial
period from 1948 to the mid-1950s. This is primarily because civil rights
and racial inequality were not very central to the political agenda of most
elite actors and institutions at this point.[36] Southern whites were apt to be
more attentive to racial politics. This was especially so in the wake of the
showdown between President Truman, who advocated civil rights legislation in 1948, and southern Democrats, who responded by forming a States'
Rights party. As the group directly bearing the cross of racial domination,
African Americans should exhibit the highest level of awareness. As we
have noted, indigenous institutions (such as the black press) and informal
information networks played a key role in sustaining this high attentiveness by supplying a steady stream of countervalent messages. With the
critical events in the late 1950s that begin to push civil rights onto the national agenda, the level of awareness should further intensify for blacks and
southern whites. Once the movement is fully mobilized in the 1960s, the
attentiveness of the dominant public should intensify as well.

At the level of the accepting messages, the role of predispositions should
vary by the predispositions that are evoked, when they are evoked, and in
which groups they are evoked. Mainstream predispositions such as partisanship and liberal ideology are likely to be more central with respect to
matters of race within the dominant public than among African Americans or southern whites. In these other publics, group-specific predispositions—racial group interests and identity in the case of African Americans,
racial and regional group threat and animosity with southern whites—are
likely to prevail, especially when mass opinion becomes mobilized and activated. With African Americans, racial group interests and identity are deeply
rooted in their shared experience of racial domination and resistance to
such domination. Group-specific predispositions are similarly rooted in
shared history among southern whites and are likely to manifest themselves as perceived threat and outward animus as the challenge to the Jim
Crow South intensifies.

Table 1.1 thus illustrates how our expectations about levels of awareness
and types of predispositions are likely to vary across social groups and during the course of a social movement. These expectations are limited to the
"receive" and "accept" stages of the RAS model. There are other important
expectations, beyond RAS, to consider in the "sampling" of mass opinion:
how our political opinions are voiced and what role institutions play in activating those opinions. We shall elaborate these expectations in greater de-

Table 1.2   Activated Opinion, Insitutions, and the Civil Rights Movement

	c. 1948–55	c. 1956–57	c. 1958–65
African Americans (counterpublic)			
Modes of expression	conventional	more diverse	highly diverse
Institutional role	indigenous	indigenous/movement	indigenous/movement
Southern whites (reactive public)			
Modes of expression	conventional	more diverse	more diverse
Institutional role	formal	formal/indigenous	formal/indigenous
Nonsouthern whites (dominant public)			
Modes of expression	conventional	conventional	more diverse
Institutional role	formal	formal	formal

tail in chapters 4–6. For the moment, table 1.2 illustrates (again, in stylized form) how the expression of public opinion is likely to vary across groups and stages of movement activism.

The RAS model simply tells us that public opinion is a function of the considerations on the mind of an individual at a moment in time. Yet when we consider how African Americans, southern whites, and the general public are likely to follow and respond to the civil rights struggle, one's awareness and considerations are likely to be intimately linked. Individuals who are highly invested in an issue, all things being equal, should entertain a greater number of considerations. We might expect, then, that the number of considerations should vary across groups and stages of movement activism in the same manner that awareness varies in table 1.1.

In addition, all things being equal, individuals who are highly invested in an issue should also be more likely to voice their opinions actively and in a diversity of forms of expression. The intensity of an individual's opinions should also vary across groups and stages of movement activism in the same manner as awareness and considerations. And with this variation in intensity, we should expect variations in one's willingness to engage in a diversity of modes of public expression. These individual-level traits (awareness, predispositions, considerations, intensity of preferences) in themselves may be insufficient to activate mass opinion on a meaningful scale. Institutions, in particular, play a key role in defining issues and linking individual preferences and predispositions to political voice and action. Thus table 1.2 also shows how this organizing and mobilizing role of institutions is likely to vary across groups and stages of activism.

In the equilibrium period, from 1948 to the mid-1950s, for instance, individuals in the dominant public should express low intensity of preferences regarding civil rights, voiced through conventional modes of expression such as voting or responding to polls. Moreover, formal institutions (political parties, interest groups) should be the primary source of information and mobilization.[37] By contrast, for African Americans in this same period, the role of black counterpublic institutions should be evident even during periods of political quiescence.[38] Absent a coordinated and sustained protest campaign, however, the modes of expression are likely to remain fairly conventional. As movement activism unfolds and black counterpublic institutions begin to mobilize mass audiences, the modes of expression should increase in diversity and we should expect the creation of social movement organizations such as the Southern Christian Leadership Conference, the Student Nonviolent Coordinating Committee, and the Mississippi Freedom Democratic Party. For whites in the South during the initial stages of black insurgency, table 1.2 postulates little institutional involvement outside of formal (partisan, interest group) political channels.[39] By the mid-1950s, southern whites too should exhibit a multivocality of expressions and with it, indigenous southern white organizations—from local school boards to White Citizens Councils to state, local, and national government—should increasingly jump into the fray.

At the risk of redundancy, the upshot of these propositions is that in the equilibrium state prior to the civil rights movement, the dynamics of mass opinion for the dominant and southern white publics should faithfully follow the elite dynamics expressed in RAS. African Americans, by contrast, should be attentive to dual processes of informational inputs and institutional involvement: from the center stage of elites and from a side stage of black counterelites. As mass protest begins in the South around the mid-1950s, we should expect a web of elite and non-elite interactions to activate and sway mass opinion. Movement activists should begin contesting the staging of focal events on the national stage and, through their actions on this stage, shape the information and interpretive framing of movement events to which mass audiences attend. Moreover, southern white institutions are increasingly likely to play a role in contesting these information flows and interpretive frames. By the 1960s, any pre-existing boundaries between elite actors and mass audiences should be fluid and shifting as movement activists and southern white resistance become fully mobilized on the political stage.

To summarize this discussion in terms of general expectations, black insurgency in the 1950s and 1960s should modify the dynamics of mass opinion in at least six ways: (1) aggregate changes in opinion during the course of a social movement should differ by race and region; (2) these differences should be interpretable in terms of ongoing movement events

and discourses; (3) these differences should be captured at the level of reception of political inputs, accepting those inputs, sampling of public expressions, and, bridging all three levels, the degree of institutional engagement; (4) the activation of African American mass opinion should precede
that of white American mass opinion; (5) the *determinants* of shifts in mass
opinion should differ by race and region; (6) these determinants should
spring from elite and non-elite contestation over the information about and
interpretive framing of ongoing movement events to which mass audiences
attend.[40]

ELABORATIONS AND LIMITATIONS

Our focus thus far has been to specify an account of mass opinion that is
faithful to the diverse contexts in which our political views are formed and
expressed. In doing so, we risk falling prey to precisely what RAS so successfully avoids. That is, the cost of specifying such detail and nuance is the
potential loss of power and generalizability. The story of activated mass
opinion says little about elite or non-elite influences on mass opinion on
other issues, during other historical periods, involving other sets of actors.
Put sharply, if the civil rights movement turns out to be *sui generis* as a
period of U.S. history in which non-elite influences on mass opinion are
salient, then the proposed account of activated mass opinion is of limited
relevance to opinion research writ large.

Strictly speaking, I cannot argue against this possibility, since this book
only examines public views on race during the civil rights movement. That
said, I strongly suspect that activated mass opinion has the explanatory
"legs" to go beyond this specific historical episode. In this section, I specify
the general conditions under which we might expect a more activated, non-
elite voice in mass opinion. The basic intuition is captured in the distinction between politics in equilibrium and politics under rapidly changing
conditions and sustained mass insurgency.[41] The shift from equilibrium
politics and the politics of mass movements, moreover, is likely to be a
change that occurs in degrees.

Here it is helpful to differentiate at least four potentially discernible levels of mass activation: (1) conventional politics in which mass opinion plays
a negligible role in democratic decision-making;[42] (2) conventional politics
in which mass opinion plays a salient role in democratic decision-making
but is limited to activation through formal, institutional channels (for example, political parties, lobbyists, interest groups) and to demands for on
specific legislative reforms or electoral contests; (3) insurgent politics, in

which mass opinion is salient, activated through both conventional and nonconventional channels, and aims to define the political agenda and oust an existing political regime; and (4) insurgent politics, in which mass opinion is salient and activated to further undermine the legitimacy of the status quo by redefining the boundaries of politics and by transforming existing social norms, economic relations, and cultural meanings. Put in Zaller's terms, insurgent politics at the fourth level aims explicitly to challenge, change, and reconfigure our primary predispositions.

These four levels of mass activation overlap with four common ways in which political scientists define power (and resistance to power). Thus the equilibrium state wherein elites govern without any active channels for mass-based demands parallels Floyd Hunter's (1953) conception of power as elite domination. The equilibrium state wherein mass mobilization occurs through institutionalized channels in specific electoral and legislative contests parallels Robert Dahl's (1961) conception of power as political pluralism. The level of insurgent politics wherein mass mobilization aims to define the legislative agenda and reconfigure the balance of electoral power parallels Peter Bachrach and Morton Baratz's (1962) conception of power as agenda control. Finally, insurgent politics in which non-elites struggle to reconfigure social norms, economic relations, and cultural meanings in civil society conforms to Marxist and postmodern conceptions of power.[43]

The extent to which elite opinion theories are challenged by activated mass opinion, then, depends on how these levels of activism correspond to particular episodes of political conflict. Specifically, elite-driven accounts will likely remain robust in instances in which mass mobilization is expressed through formal institutional channels such as elections and interest group politics. In insurgent movements that seek to displace an existing political regime and capture agenda control, there is a greater likelihood that specifying non-elite influences on activated mass opinion will be important. A recent example of this kind of insurgent politics might be the explosion of popular referenda at the state level or the Christian Coalition's role in the Republican capture of both houses of Congress in November 1994. Finally, an understanding of non-elite influences will be critical in insurgent movements that further seek to displace political predispositions by challenging our prevailing social, economic, and cultural rules and relations. Possible examples in recent U.S. political history are the women's movement, the environmental movement, the gay rights movement, and most recently, the multiracial movement.[44]

I have intentionally described these four scenarios as "levels" of mass activation rather than as "stages" of mass activation. Although I expect a more activated, non-elite-based public voice to be more likely at each level, the four scenarios clearly do not constitute a linear, hierarchical, developmental account of mass activation. In large part, this is because the boundaries of politics often vary with context, and the political relevance and salience of particular mass beliefs and sentiments also vary with context. For instance, cultural beliefs in one context may be a central political predisposition in another, and "technical" policy matters in one context may be highly contested political movements in another. With respect to the former case, the question of racial group identity for African Americans during the 1920s Harlem Renaissance is a much less explicitly political conception than during the 1960s Black Power movement. With respect to the latter, the decennial administration of the U.S. Census in the early part of the twentieth century was a decidedly bureaucratic and technocratic affair; by 2000, the census was a hotly contested political issue, subject to partisan conflicts over statistical sampling and to political activism concerning a multiracial category.

Finally, let me offer some clarifying points about what I am *not* attempting to do here. I am not attempting to present an account that captures the full universe of cases in which public views on political matters are shaped by non-elite forces. Rather, my account of activated mass opinion aims to capture the cases of non-elite opinion dynamics in which mass insurgency taking center stage is the primary narrative. In particular, activated mass opinion poorly explains two other kinds of non-elite opinion dynamics.

In some cases, we know that non-elite forces are at work because the general public is stubbornly unresponsive to proactive attempts by political elites to manipulate (or mass media to frame) mass opinion. A notable recent example of this, described by John Zaller, is the stunning upsurge in President Bill Clinton's job approval rating in the first weeks after rumors of his sexual affair with Monica Lewinsky began to surface.[45] This occurred despite overwhelming anti-Clinton media coverage and signals from elites. In other cases, we know that non-elite forces are at work, *res ipso loquitur*, when the beliefs and actions of individuals are defined in explicit opposition to government. Adherence to political conspiracy theories is the most obvious case in point. A notable recent example of this is the belief among many African Americans that the AIDS epidemic and the "war on drugs" are part of a genocidal antiblack government conspiracy.[46]

Furthermore, I am not attempting to present a positive "bottom-up" account of mass opinion formation and change. For one thing, the opposition of "bottom-up" to "top-down" is empirically slippery. It is unclear whether the responsiveness of ordinary African Americans to a black counterelite and to conventional party elites is evidence of bottom-up or top-down processes at work. For another, several scholars—among them Susan Herbst (1995), Nina Eliasoph (1998), Katherine Cramer Walsh (2000), and Jane Mansbridge (2000)—come much closer to describing what social theorists would term public opinion in the realm of "everyday life" and "ordinary talk."[47] In part, these scholars describe everyday dynamics more faithfully because they do not directly or critically engage elite opinion theory. Rendering a positive account of bottom-up opinion dynamics and taking critical aim at top-down opinion theories are perhaps better left as separate projects.

Trying to do both at once would be a prodigious ambition. What's more, the epistemological positions and evidentiary standards for the two projects are likely to be incompatible and incommensurate. Econometric analysis of survey data is quite a distinct undertaking from ethnographic study or discourse analysis. For reasons that will be clear in chapters 3 and 4, survey data (the most commonly used evidentiary basis for opinion research) are well-suited to capture many dimensions of mass opinion, but not all. In particular, survey data are ill-equipped to measure bottom-up opinion dynamics because survey instruments are unlikely to anticipate or mirror groundswells in mass opinion. Moreover, polls rarely ask respondents about their sources of political information (and more rarely about nonelite information sources such as alternative media or informal social networks). For the moment, survey data are reasonably well-suited to a more limited, Popperian task: to show that strict elite-driven accounts of racial attitudes during the civil rights era are false. This is the task that I undertake in the following chapter.

TWO

BLACK INSURGENCY AND THE DYNAMICS OF MASS OPINION

> Just how long can Negro citizens retain this [deep faith in the Federal Government and constitutional democracy] as they daily watch the power structure of the South openly defy the government and select the laws it wishes to obey while ignoring others? Both political parties must be made to face this question, and the only way to do it is to beat them at the old game of playing politics with civil rights.
>
> —Ella Baker

> The public copes with new and great events and questions without the comforting guidance of grooves in the mind . . . governments confront great uncertainties, for the ultimate crystallization of dominant opinion may be governed by an appraisal of events over which government has no control and the response to which is utterly unpredictable. This may be one of the reasons why governments so often temporize and mouth ambiguities as they await the appearance of a crytallization of opinion before they act.
>
> —V. O. Key

The conventional view of public opinion scholars, we noted in chapter 1, is that our political views are shaped primarily by what elites say and do. It should by now be ironic that some of the leading exemplars of this view stake their claim on analyses and arguments about racial attitudes. In this chapter, we will examine one especially prominent work in this vein in which profound transformations in the American racial and political landscape since the civil rights era are explained as the result of key legislative and electoral outcomes in the mid-1960s. The work is Edward Carmines and James Stimson's *Issue Evolution* (1989). We shall see that by isolating the significance of the civil rights era for mass opinion in elite acts in the mid-1960s, Carmines and Stimson effectively diminish the prior period of non-elite, mass protest that propelled civil rights onto the legislative and electoral agenda by the mid-1960s.

According to such an account, the explicit struggle to upstage and contest existing racial attitudes is thus rendered irrelevant or at least exogenous to our system of democratic politics. Movement activists may seek to try their case before the court of public opinion, but if elite theory is correct, mass audiences will not hear their plea until political elites first choose to act upon it. As a result, elite signals and opinion cues take center stage, to the exclusion of context-specific variations—across social groups, historical periods, and political phenomena—in the activation and expression of mass opinion.

In this chapter I re-examine the dynamics and determinants of racial policy preferences during the onset and evolution of the civil rights movement. The analysis uses survey data from 1956 to 1964 and models racial attitudes during the civil rights years as the result of dynamic competition between elite (partisan) and non-elite (movement-based) signals and attachments. In specifying non-elite signals and attachments, the model confers a central role to racially and regionally defined and historically situated group bases of public beliefs about racial equality and integration. The fruits of such a model are quite bountiful. There is ample indication that movement-based opinion influences preceded and took primacy over elite influences during the formative stages of the civil rights movement. Moreover, linkages between racial issue positions, social welfare liberalism, and partisanship are prominent well before the putatively (per Carmines and Stimson) critical mid-1960s. In fact, the evidence in this paper argues quite strongly that as early as 1960, partisan issue positions on racial policies mattered vitally to how ordinary individuals conceived of racial equality and, more broadly, political partisanship itself.

I begin by examining two especially prominent, elite-based contemporary accounts of how racial attitudes have been transformed over the past half-century. Some key tensions in these accounts are highlighted. These tensions are then elaborated as a more formal model of racial attitudes. This model is then specified in two racial policy domains: whether government should actively ensure fair opportunities for jobs and housing for blacks and whether government should actively pursue desegregation of public schools. I conclude by arguing for a more complex, contextualized understanding of the nature and dynamics of racial attitudes during the civil rights era and beyond.

THE MACRO- AND MICRO-DYNAMICS OF RACIAL ATTITUDES

There is an uneasy balance in what we know about racial attitudes in the modern era of opinion polling. At the aggregate level, we now have an abundance of more than fifty years of longitudinal data. These data trumpet a profound shift in public beliefs from the persistence of racial segregation and inequality to the public embrace of racial integration and egalitarian principles.[1] At the individual level, there is an emerging consensus of perhaps equal standing that public opinion is shaped primarily, if not exclusively, by political elites. Linking the macro to the micro, there is a clear implication that political elites have been at the helm of this transformation in mass beliefs. Accordingly, many of the empirical grounds for such elite accounts are studies of racial attitudes during and since the civil rights era.

The chief findings from aggregate and individual-level studies in fact hang together in an uneasy balance. One important reason for this is that our substantive knowledge about the dynamics of racial attitudes during the formative civil rights years is limited by the absence of adequate and appropriate survey data. As Schuman, Steeh, and Bobo (1988) note, although the prescient National Opinion Research Center/Office of War Information surveys in 1942 and 1944 established an early benchmark of poll data on racial attitudes, there was a yawning gap of almost twenty years before questions about racial differences and racial equality gripped the attention of pollsters again.[2] Furthermore, most survey questions on race between 1944 and the early to mid-1960s are single items, generally not repeated over time, asking respondents about specific legislative proposals or elite actions.[3] Specifically, Schuman, Steeh, and Bobo (1988) point to four problems in pinpointing aggregate changes in racial attitudes: (1) pollsters (the NORC/OWI polls excepted) were late to ask about racial attitudes; (2) repeated questions are asked over uneven and different time periods; (3) the functional relation between survey marginals over two time periods is indeterminate (that is, can be linear, convex, concave, or some other pattern of change); and (4) on some critical racial issues, such as voting rights, there are no data to speak of from different time periods.

Thus, although it is clear to macro-level researchers that there was a sea change in racial attitudes between the 1940s and the 1960s, it is less obvious, given the gap in available data, when these changes took place and to what they responded. As Page and Shapiro put it, "The heart of the opinion change, the sweeping liberal trend encompassing many specific issues, is difficult to account for with precision because early survey data are sparse and because the movement of public opinion has generally been so slow and steady" (1992, 76).[4] In most of the issue domains on which we have longitudinal data—residential integration, integration of public accommodations, interracial partnerships, equal employment opportunities—survey items do not appear or reappear until 1963. As a result of this sporadic and incomplete data, then, there is no compelling way to discriminate between competing accounts of how racial attitudes shifted between the 1940s and the 1960s.

Micro-level theorists, however, have boldly staked a claim in the terrain where macro-level scholars have feared to tread. The incompleteness and potential inadequacy of opinion data notwithstanding, the dynamics of racial attitudes are quite clear to elite opinion theorists. John Zaller's RAS model, as we have seen, is one prominent example in this regard. As noted in chapter 1, one of the less convincing aspects of the RAS model is the proposition that attitude change is elite-driven. In particular, to support his account, Zaller weaves together a plausible but ultimately undiscriminating anecdotal and inferential discussion of the unfolding consensus on racially egalitarian principles in the twentieth century.

Notably, Zaller marshals his evidence from a few selective historical references in support of focal elite events. One such event is President Herbert Hoover's attempt to nominate John Parker for the Supreme Court in 1930. Hoover's nomination failed in large measure because of a ten-year-old speech in which Parker deemed African Americans' political participation "a source of evil and danger to both races" (cited in Zaller, 1992, 9). As Zaller notes, "That a single racist speech, of a type that was entirely conventional throughout the nineteenth and early twentieth centuries, could become a basis for the rejection of a Supreme Court nominee by the Senate was an indication that attitudes toward race were undergoing a historic shift" (ibid.). Zaller also cites Gunnar Myrdal's "extraordinarily prescient" 1944 study, An American Dilemma, as representative of a "revolution in elite discourse" (11). This revolution, as Myrdal saw it, grew out of the evolution within elite intellectual circles away from a biological, essentializing view of racial inferiority.

Events such as the Parker nomination and the publication of An American Dilemma, though suggestive, ignore the presence and persistence of distinctly non-elite challenges to prevailing racial beliefs, norms, and rules throughout the century. Parker, the Fourth Circuit Court judge from North Carolina, was defeated in his bid for the Supreme Court by a margin of just two votes. Opposition to Parker stemmed from the judge's racist statements about, among other things, the suitability and capability of African Americans for equal political citizenship. The successful defeat of his nomination resulted in large measure from direct pressure by African American groups and labor organizations, most notably Walter White and the NAACP.[5]

This presence of non-elite or counterelite efforts to resist and replace prevailing racist laws, practices, and beliefs goes well beyond the efforts of the NAACP. The story of active resistance of African Americans against the existing racial regime in the twentieth century begins with the epic numbers of southern blacks who "voted with their feet" and migrated out of the Jim Crow South.[6] This outmigration into the Northwest, Midwest, and West increased the degree of direct contact between black and white Americans outside the South. In urban areas, it also gave blacks sufficient political clout to extract political patronage, if not win a place in representative government.[7]

Also, the early decades of the twentieth century saw the emergence of a thriving, diverse black counterelite and the genesis of organizations formed to advocate the interests of African Americans. Prominent examples include Mary Church Terrell and Ida B. Wells-Barnett's anti-lynching crusade at the turn of the century, W. E. B. Du Bois and the Niagara Movement (founded in 1905) and the NAACP (1910), Marcus Garvey and the United Negro Improvement Association (1911), George E. Haynes and the National Urban League (1911), Cyril Briggs and the Women's Political Association of Harlem (1918), and A. Philip Randolph and the Brotherhood of Sleeping Car Porters (1925).[8] Even in the Deep South, early incarnations of opposition to the racial regime could be found. Examples include Hosea Hudson's efforts to form the Alabama Communist Party in the 1930s and in biracial organizations such as the Southern Conference for Human Welfare and the Southern Conference Educational Fund in the 1940s.[9]

Importantly, the period surrounding the "revolution in elite discourse" to which Zaller points is characterized by the uprise of a black counterelite that played a pivotal role in both intellectual and cultural production that challenged prevailing views of race. Culturally, the Harlem Renaissance of the 1920s—led by Claude McKay, James Weldon Johnson, Langston Hughes, Zora Neale Hurston, Alain Locke, and numerous others—articulated a self-defined and empowered "New Negro" through literary and

artistic expression.[10] Intellectually, the groundwork for a challenge to prevailing racial injustices was set through the founding and flourishing of a
profusion of black colleges and a black press. Black colleges began to establish themselves just after Emancipation, with Fisk University in 1866 and
Atlanta University, Howard University, and Morehouse College in 1867.
Later in the nineteenth century, numerous black presses began to emerge,
such as the *Chicago Conservator* (1878), the *New York Age* (1886), and the
Indianapolis Freeman (1888). And with the onset of the twentieth century,
some of the most prominent black newspapers today, such as the *Boston
Guardian* (1901), the *Chicago Defender* (1905), the *Amsterdam News* (1909),
and the *Pittsburgh Courier* (1910), began publication.[11]

The intellectual challenge to racist stereotypes and racial inequities also
grew out of a black counterelite and its institutional sites, such as Alexander
Crummell's American Negro Academy. This black counterelite actively challenged, through personal example, scholarship, and persuasion of white
elites, the prevailing essentialist stereotypes that whites held of African
Americans.[12] And it is this black counterelite that enabled Gunnar Myrdal's
celebrated analysis of racial inequalities to achieve its insights. As numerous historians have noted, Myrdal relied heavily on forty-four monographs
by scholars outside his staff, many of them African American scholars
such as Ralph Bunche, St. Clair Drake, Charles S. Johnson, and E. Franklin
Frazier.[13]

These points, taken together, argue against Zaller's reading of racial history. Just to be clear here, I am not proposing that the sea change from
essentialist, biological views of race to more a constructivist, situational
view resulted from a strictly bottom-up, non-elite phenomenon. Minerva's
owl is rarely so discerning. Rather, my main assertion is that a selective,
linear rendition of historical change such as Zaller's is apt to miss a significant part of the story. As Zaller himself notes, "[o]wing to the lack of opinion data until the late 1930s, the effects on public opinion of this revolution
in elite discourse cannot be fully documented" (1992, 11).

Also, as noted in chapter 1, even the survey evidence to which Zaller
points is not based on the kind of careful multivariate analysis that make
much of the book so compelling. Instead, Zaller offers three stylized points
from existing research. First, from Schuman, Steeh, and Bobo (1988) and
others, we know that public support—at least for the principles of racial
equality—has undergone a fundamental shift. Second, we know that such
support is especially strong among the most highly educated. Zaller concludes from this that the contemporary elite consensus on racially egali-

tarian principles is greatest among those "most heavily exposed to the new elite discourse on race." And finally, Zaller points to evidence from Edward Carmines and James Stimson's influential *Issue Evolution* (1989) that "the public has been responsive to partisan elite cues" (1992, 11) on racial matters.

The evidence from *Issue Evolution*, as Zaller notes, merits a detailed examination. In fact, for the remainder of this chapter, I take a critical look at Carmines and Stimson's account of elites' influence and put it to an exacting multivariate empirical test. Carmines and Stimson also take a strong view of when opinion change takes place and in response to what. According to their account, there was a punctuated equilibrium shift in mass partisanship sparked by the Senate elections of 1958 and reaching full light during the presidential campaign of 1964.[14] Furthermore, the clarion elite opinion cues signaled during this election orchestrated nothing less than a radical transformation in mass political and ideological preferences.

The distilled argument, for those unfamiliar with it, is that eleven racially liberal Republicans were replaced in the Senate by Democrats, ten of whom were racially liberal. It is, according to Carmines and Stimson, this recomposition of the Senate that set the stage for Barry Goldwater's inflammatory rhetoric of racial conservatism during the 1964 election and instigated the popular alignment of the Democratic party as the party of racial liberalism by the mid-1960s. Thus they contend that

> [w]e did not know it then but the 1958 election was a turning point, an irreversible event that was to help launch a decade of racial politics and thereby reshape American politics for the remainder of the twentieth century. . . . The black civil rights movement that was to erupt so dramatically in the early 1960s can be understood as an event rooted in the rural South, a product of racial oppression, black religion, and charismatic and innovative leadership. But to understand why civil rights became a decisive political movement, not limited to blacks, not limited to leaders, not limited to the South, we need to come to terms with why a party system was ready for the revolution when it came. (xii)

In addition to the fact that this account places a heavy burden on historical accident (the 1958 Senate elections), it is quite revealing that civil rights activism does not enter Carmines and Stimson's historical account in chapter 2 until February 1963, the time of Kennedy's proposed civil rights legislation. Social movement activism, then, is treated as an exogenous shock, rather than as a constituent component of democratic politics. Thus the critical precursors to the movement activism of the mid-1960s, such as the Montgomery bus boycott of 1956, the student lunch counter sit-ins of 1960, and James Meredith's effort to desegregate "Ole Miss" are negligible factors.

> [i]ssues of race were not partisan issues as recently as the early 1960s. . . . The mid-1960s witnessed a fundamental change in this situation. Racial concerns gained a prominent foothold on the national political agenda, and in the process, they took on a clear partisan meaning. . . . Partisanship, the emerging issues of race, and the social welfare issues of the New Deal were now mutually reinforcing. . . . The key event in this transformation no doubt was the 1964 presidential election. (116–17)

To be fair, Carmines and Stimson's objective is to explain the transformation of partisanship and the attitudinal correlates of partisanship, rather than to present a theory of how public opinion works or even how racial attitudes are formed. Moreover, issue evolution is a story about the transformative role of racial politics at the level of *both* elites and the mass electorate (and thus not restricted to an account of mass opinion).[15] Yet the authors are fairly insistent that the chain of events is elite-driven. It is not surprising, then, that the authors argue that "[p]artisanship, the emerging issues of race, and the social welfare issues of the New Deal were now mutually enforcing . . . [t]he key event in this transformation *no doubt* was the 1964 presidential election" (117, emphasis added).

The contentious matter here is not whether 1964 was a critical year for voters to clearly identify one party as the party of civil rights and another as opposing them. Carmines and Stimson's evidence on this matter is quite convincing. Nor is it that racial politics took on clear and enduring partisan meaning after the 1964 election. Rather, the contentiousness comes from their claim that 1964 stands alone as the historical marker of change in racial attitudes and that, as a singular turning point, takes only the 1958 Senate election as its precursor. Ultimately, they also fail to test for nonelite, movement-based influences on racial attitudes and mass partisanship. As a result, the exclusively elite basis of public views of race are once more a theoretical predisposition on Carmines and Stimson's part, rather than an empirically supported proposition.

MODELING THE DYNAMICS OF RACIAL ATTITUDES

Our assessment of whether mass opinion responds to elite or non-elite dynamics—be they Zaller's RAS model or Carmines and Stimson's issue evolution model—has thus far been largely based on argument, rather than a systematic analysis of evidence. In this section, I develop a model that allows us to directly test the influence of elite, partisan signals and non-elite, movement-based signals on racial attitudes. This model attempts to capture the dynamics of social movement politics as endogenous to the dynamics of mass opinion and democratic politics, rather than exogenous to it. As noted in chapter 1, politics is sometimes in stable equilibrium (and at such times public opinion is relatively quiescent) and sometimes undergoes rapid flux (and at such times public opinion becomes activated and transformed).

To reiterate, social movements challenge elite accounts of mass opinion because they entail activation and mobilization from the masses to the elite political stage. With black insurgency in the 1950s and 1960s, I presume that there is an important group basis to this mass engagement and activation. In particular, I juxtapose movement-specific, group-based influences with conventional partisan influences on mass opinion. The significance of these competing influences is likely to vary across mass publics.

Within the general, inactive "mass public," the conventional determinants tested in elite theories (partisanship, liberalism) will likely remain persistent whether or not an insurgent movement is ongoing. Within more activated sectors of the public—African Americans, southern whites, and by the 1960s, white liberals outside the South—however, group-based determinants are likely to matter equally, and possibly more, in shaping racial and political preferences during the course of the civil rights movement. With African Americans, racial group interests and identity are especially likely to matter given the shared history of racial domination and resistance to such domination. With southern whites, the emergent threats to the Jim Crow South should evoke heightened group-based (racial and regional) conflicts and animosity.

This juxtaposition of partisan (elite) and group-based, movement-specific (non-elite) forces describes a competitive "election" to determine what the public supports. On this point, there is a long tradition of modeling competitive elections in political science upon which we can draw. Specifically, we adapt a key insight from spatial voting models that use mathematical representation and axioms of rational choice.[16] This simple but nonetheless powerful insight is that individuals who perceive their underlying preferences as closer to those of one of the two "candidates" will be likelier to form opinions that align with the "issue positions" of that candidate. So individuals who view their politics as closer to the Democratic (or Republican) Party's will be likelier to align with the Democratic (or Republican) Party's issue positions. Similarly, individuals who view their preferences as closer to those of movement activists (or movement opponents) will be likelier to align with movement activists' (or movement opponents') issue positions.[17]

In the present case, the candidates are elite (partisan) and non-elite (movement-based) influences over the issue domain of racial policy preferences. As the conflicts surrounding racial equality and desegregation are mobilized on the political agenda, ordinary citizens will have to determine where they stand. And they will likely look to conventional elite signals or movement-based counterelite signals to form their opinion. The question here, vis-à-vis Carmines and Stimson's issue evolution account, concerns the centrality of the mid-1960s in the formation of public opinion on these issues. Thus, within the framework of spatial voting models, we are less concerned with partisanship or likely vote choice per se than we are with the dynamics of issue positions themselves.

In the standard spatial voting framework, the individual's "vote choice" (conventionally, between two competing candidates) is represented as the "quadratic loss" between the individual's "ideal point" on an issue dimension (or vector of issue dimensions) and that of the two candidates. A quadratic loss function is simply one way to represent a nonlinear relation between ideological distance (how close an individual perceives her politics to be to a particular candidate's) and likely vote choice. Other things being equal, if candidate θ is closer to the individual's policy preferences that candidate ϕ the individual will prefer θ.[18]

Optimally, such models aim to capture how vote choice changes over time and in response to changes in candidate positions. In the present case, there are insufficient data to adopt the kind of Bayesian "adaptive utilities" framework that would be best suited to testing for dynamic change in mass opinion. As a next-best substitute we are left with measures of relative ideological distance between the respondent's ideal position and that of the competing parties. When we use survey data, of course, this relative distance (or proximity) measure is subjective.

Preferences with regard to racial policies and principles, then, are modeled as the result of prior issue position, a vector of exogenous factors (sociodemographic and economic variables), and the relative distances between respondent issue position and the issue positions of elite political actors and movement actors. This is represented in the equation below.

$$Y_{it} = Y_{i,t-1} + \beta_1 X_{it} + \beta_2[\Delta_i(\theta_i - \theta_{PID})] + \beta_3[\Delta_i(\phi_i - \phi_{RID})] + \varepsilon_{it} \qquad (1)$$

In equation (1), $\theta_i - \theta_{PID}$ and $\phi_i - \phi_{RID}$ represent, respectively, the relative distance between the individual's ideal point on racial policy issues and the perceived ideal point of elite partisan actors and movement actors on those same issues ("ideological distance"). Furthermore, $\Delta_i(\theta_i - \theta_{PID})$ represents the change over time in ideological distance between the individual and elite partisan actors, and similarly, $\Delta_i(\phi_i - \phi_{RID})$ represents the change over time in ideological distance between the individual and movement-specific actors. Note that unlike electoral voting models, θ in this case represents partisan attachments and ϕ represents movement-based attachments. Thus Y_{it}, an individual i's stance on a particular policy issue at time t, is a function of (a) that same person's prior stance on that policy issue, $Y_{i,t} - 1$; (b) the change over time in the ideological distance between that individual's ideal point on racial policy matters and the perceived ideal point of partisan elites; and (c) the change over time in the ideological distance between that individual's ideal point and the perceived ideal point of movement activists.

This model is comparable to existing dynamic models of preference change such as Gerber and Jackson's (1993).[19] As their discussion of model specification suggests, however, short of ideal panel data for such a dynamic model, estimating such an account of attitude change involves some theoretical short-changing, methodological leaps of faith, and empirical shortcuts. With the dynamics of racial attitudes during the civil rights era, the 1956–60 CPS Panel Study will permit a rough estimation of such a model, but only for $t=1960$ and $t-1=1956$. This limitation, critically, doesn't get us as far as the period of interest vis-à-vis elite opinion theories, namely, the mid-1960s. Taking all these factors into consideration, I specify cross-sectional models at three different time periods: 1956, 1960, and 1964. This analysis is used to draw inferences about dynamic change from shifts in the significance and magnitude of parameter estimates. The stripped-down version of this model, then, is the following:

$$Y_{it} = \alpha + \beta_1 X_{it} + \beta_2(\theta_{it} - \theta_{PIDt}) + \beta_3(\phi_{it} - \phi_{RIDt}) + \varepsilon_{it} \qquad (2)$$

This model is applied to test four specific hypotheses against Carmines and Stimson's version of elite opinion theory. First, I expect to find that movement-based attachments are a significant influence on racial policy preferences. Second, I expect to find that movement-based attachments influence racial policy preferences earlier and more forcefully than do partisan-based attachments. Third, I expect to find that the kind of linkages that Carmines and Stimson discuss—between social welfare liberalism, partisanship, and racial policy preferences—existed prior to the mid-1960s. Finally, I expect to find that racial policy preferences are a significant determinant of change of partisanship itself prior to the mid-1960s. With each of these hypotheses, I expect race and region (and their interaction with partisanship) to be crucial determinants of the issue evolution of racial politics. According to this alternate model, then, what is more likely novel and momentous about 1964 was that by the mid-1960s, both the Democratic and the Republican Parties were keenly aware of the political salience of race *as a result of* movement activists' successful mobilization and activation of public views of race. As a consequence, both parties began to develop unambiguous positions on racial policies, embracing certain linkages and rejecting others. Political elites knew that race was on the public's mind and responded clearly and strategically in 1964.

MODEL SPECIFICATION AND RESULTS

These hypotheses are tested using data from the 1956 – 60 Center for Political Studies Panel Study and the 1964 American National Election Study. The two surveys allow us to examine two domains of racial policy: public support for government's role in ensuring fair housing and employment opportunities for African Americans and public support for government's role in ensuring school desegregation. The distribution of responses to these dependent variables is shown in figure 2.1.[20]

The two measures show different patterns of support over the period from 1956 to 1964. With respect to fair employment and housing for African Americans, figure 2.1 shows strong support among a majority of respon-

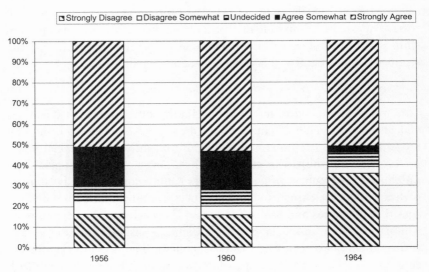

Figure 2.1   Support for Fair Employment and Housing, 1956 – 64

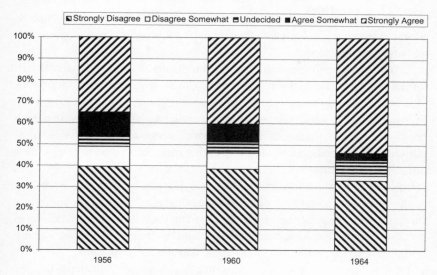

Figure 2.2   Support for School Desegregation, 1956–64

dents (between 51 and 53 percent) across all three time periods. The level of modest support for employment and housing, however, declines markedly (from 19 percent in 1956 and 1960 to 3 percent in 1964), and this shift in support is almost fully picked up by strong opposition to fair employment and housing (from 16 percent in 1956 and 1960 to 36 percent in 1964).

With respect to school desegregation (fig. 2.2), there are two discernible changes over time that merit attention. First, the levels of strong support for school desegregation grows markedly over the eight-year period from 35 percent to almost 54 percent. Second, opinion—regardless of whether one is supportive of or resistant to racial integration—becomes markedly polarized. In 1956, more than one of every four individuals opted for a weak position ("disagree somewhat" or "agree somewhat") or were undecided on school desegregation. By 1964, this proportion diminished to one of every eight individuals.[21]

For both questions, a respondent's vote choice concerning civil rights policies is modeled as the function of the distance between her ideal position on these policies and her perceived ideal position of elites (political parties) and non-elites (movement organizations) on these policies. The operationalization of this ideological distance measure is somewhat counterintuitive and worth elaboration. As is often the case, translating formal abstractions into meaningful empirical measurements is tricky work, fraught with measurement error. With ideological distance, the difficulty is compounded because ideological distance can be captured by distinct, even contradictory, dimensions.

Take the most commonly described dimension of ideological distance in formal voting models: the perceived proximity between the respondent's ideal position and the party's (or movement organization's) ideal position. This perceived proximity depends vitally on the signal clarity of the party's position on a given issue. If the signals that elites or movement activists transmit are ambiguous, too many, or otherwise obfuscated in the public's mind, then the influence of ideological distance on one's policy preferences is likely to be weak or uncertain. That said, signal clarity is also in the eye of the beholder. To take an obvious example, an African American and a southern white may both view the Democratic Party as closest to their ideal point on school desegregation, but their ideal points on school desegregation or fair employment practices can be diametrically opposed.

How we measure ideological distance is further complicated when we consider the likely influence of political parties. The explanatory power of ideological distance will likely depend on whether the party to which one feels closest is the same party with which one generally identifies. For example, the likely effect of ideological distance on support for an active government role in desegregating schools in 1957 will differ for a black Democrat from Harlem and a white, racially segregationist Republican. Both may perceive the Democratic Party as closest to their ideal point on school desegregation, the black Democrat because Congressman Adam Clayton Powell signals the Democratic Party's ideal point, the white Republican because President Eisenhower's intervention in the Little Rock crisis signals the great ideological distance of the Republican Party's ideal point.[22] As this example suggests, ideological distance to elites should have the greatest effect on one's opinion when perceived proximity of ideal points is consonant with one's party identification. Once issue-specific proximity and party affiliation conflict, it becomes a fuzzier matter.[23]

Perceived proximity to party position is thus measured as the interaction of an individual's party identification and the party she views as closest to her ideal position on each of the dependent variables. A high value implies consonance between the perceived proximity to a party and the respondent's partisanship; a low value implies dissonance. For just the reasons I have noted, this measure is likely to be rather subjective. Furthermore, the effect of consonance or dissonance is likely to differ for Democrats and Republicans. Therefore, I use three separate measures of proximity to party position:[24] (1) perceived proximity to the Democratic Party's ideal point on racial policy, given one's partisanship; (2) perceived proximity to the Republican Party's ideal point on racial policy, given one's partisanship; and (3) perceived proximity to the Democratic Party's ideal point as before, for southern whites.[25]

The measure for proximity of respondents' ideal positions to those of movement activists is less abstruse by necessity. The 1956–60 CPS Panel Study asks only a few questions pertaining to African Americans or to the civil rights movement, especially of its white respondents. The closest available measure asks respondents whether whites feel they can trust black organizations. On this measure, there is almost no statistical variation to work with for African Americans, and a separate measure is developed for them. For blacks, we combine the trust measure for whites with two additional items that measure support for black organizations' mobilization in legislative and electoral politics.[26]

In the 1964 ANES, there are no directly comparable measures of proximity between respondents' and the movement activists' ideal positions. For whites, a measure of relative affinity for civil rights movement organizations is used that draws specifically on three feeling thermometer questions. This measure is calculated as the difference between respondent warmth toward two movement advocacy organizations (the NAACP and CORE) and one organization antagonistic to movement aims (the Ku Klux Klan). For African Americans, the 1964 ANES again does not include any comparable measures of proximity to black movement organizations. As a result, we use Charles Franklin's (1991) "two-stage auxiliary instrumental variables" method to construct a variable as if the question were asked in 1964.[27] Franklin's method, with a small statistical leap of faith, enables us to extract a question of interest from a *different* (that is, auxiliary) survey and use it in the survey containing all other measures of interest.[28]

What we expect from these ideological distance measures is fairly straightforward. To the extent that partisan attachments and elite opinion cues matter, then the perceived proximity to party ideal positions should predict racial policy preferences. If party positions on civil rights and racial equality are not, as Carmines and Stimson claim, clearly staked out prior to 1964, then we should not expect perceived proximity to party position to influence racial preferences in 1956 or 1960. Similarly, to the extent that attachments to movement-based groups matter, then the perceived proximity to movement groups' ideal positions should predict racial policy preferences.

To control for the separate influence of partisanship itself (that is, beyond its influence vis-à-vis perceived ideological distance), party identification is

Table 2.1   Determinants of Support for Fair Housing and Employment

Variable	1956	1960	1964
Proximity to Democratic Party, given PID	0.32^	0.74**	0.59**
	(.19)	(.14)	(.17)
Proximity to Republican Party, given PID	0.35*	0.42**	0.45^
	(.17)	(.15)	(.26)
Proximity to Democratic Party, given PID	−1.31**	−.52*	0.21
(southern whites)	(.28)	(.23)	(.21)
Proximity to movement	1.36**	1.17**	2.32**
(whites)	(.32)	(.27)	(.34)
Proximity to movement	0.89**	0.71**	2.15**
(blacks)	(.19)	(.12)	(.26)
Partisanship	0.12	−.24^	−.26
(Democratic)	(.18)	(.14)	(.21)
Activist government, social problems	1.95**	1.29**	1.78**
	(.25)	(.19)	(.21)
Age	0.33	−.08	−.94**
	(.36)	(.29)	(.28)
Family income	−.48*	−.04	−.47*
	(.22)	(.18)	(.22)
Educational level	0.30	−.09	0.54
	(.21)	(.20)	(.46)
$\mu 0$	−.82	−.16	−1.72
	(.39)	(.33)	(.39)
$\mu 1$	0.29	0.19	0.12
	(.04)	(.03)	(.02)
$\mu 2$	0.56	0.48	0.40
	(.06)	(.04)	(.04)
$\mu 3$	1.16	1.06	0.52
	(.07)	(.05)	(.05)
Number of observations	594	908	727
Restricted log likelihood	−787.75	−1161.16	−813.19
McFadden's pseudo-R^2	0.11	0.08	0.22
Goodness of fit $(\chi^2_{df=9})$	167.84	180.52	362.23

DATA: 1956–60 CPS Panel Study, 1964 ANES. The instrumental variable for proximity to black movement organizations in 1964 is reconstructed from the 1960 CPS Panel Study. Cell entries are maximum likelihood ordered probit estimates; corresponding standard errors are in parentheses.

^ $p < .10$ * $p < .05$ ** $p < .01$

included. Shorn of the influence of ideological distance, the partisanship measure most likely will capture the influence of social, psychological, and ideological attachments to political parties. Put otherwise, elites (parties) may still play a critical influence on racial opinions, but simply not in the rational, information-processing manner described by elite theories. That influence should be reflected in the ideological distance variable.

In tables 2.1 and 2.2, partisanship, age, family income, and educational level are included as controls. Schuman, Steeh, and Bobo (1988) well establish the influence of age and education on racial attitudes: older and less educated Americans are more resistant to egalitarian, integrationist principles. Finally, we also test Carmines and Stimson's proposition that the linkage between partisanship, social welfare liberalism, and racial opinions

Table 2.2 Determinants of Support for Desegregated Schools

Variable	1956	1960	1964
Proximity to Democratic Party, given PID	0.30^	0.20	0.86**
	(.16)	(.16)	(.16)
Proximity to Republican Party, given PID	0.32*	−.38*	−.32
	(.16)	(.18)	(.27)
Proximity to Democratic Party, given PID	−.95**	−1.15**	−.09
(southern whites)	(.21)	(.29)	(.19)
Proximity to movement	1.27**	1.53**	2.10**
(whites)	(.27)	(.26)	(.30)
Proximity to movement	0.40**	0.70**	1.09**
(blacks)	(.10)	(.11)	(.20)
Partisanship	−.01	−.30*	−.51**
(Democratic)	(.17)	(.13)	(.18)
Activist government, social problems	0.72**	0.91**	1.30**
	(.22)	(.19)	(.21)
Age	−.98**	−.64*	−.52
	(.34)	(.31)	(.27)
Family income	0.03	0.01	−.14
	(.20)	(.19)	(.22)
Educational level	0.36^	0.78**	0.91**
	(.19)	(.22)	(.40)
$\mu 0$	−.57	−1.01	−1.68
	(.36)	(.34)	(.35)
$\mu 1$	0.26	0.22	0.08
	(.03)	(.03)	(.02)
$\mu 2$	0.41	0.37	0.33
	(.04)	(.03)	(.04)
$\mu 3$	0.71	0.60	0.43
	(.05)	(.04)	(.04)
Number of observations	634	859	727
Restricted log likelihood	−858.09	−1112.06	−798.29
McFadden's pseudo-R^2	0.05	0.06	0.13
Goodness of fit ($\chi^2_{df = 9}$)	80.64	133.25	215.06

DATA: 1956–60 CPS Panel Study, 1964 ANES. The instrumental variable for proximity to black movement organizations in 1964 is reconstructed from the 1960 CPS Panel Study. Cell entries are maximum likelihood ordered probit estimates; corresponding standard errors are in parentheses.

^ p < .10   * p < .05   ** p < .01

did not occur prior to 1964. The specific measure used here is an additive scale of support for government activism in three nonracial social policy domains—school aid, medical care, and job guarantees. Our primary expectation is quite simply that these linkages were significant prior to the mid-1960s. As we shall see in chapter six, furthermore, these linkages were an important resource for movement actors to draw upon in activating public support for civil rights and racial equality.

The results strongly support our expectations about the influence of black insurgency on racial attitudes. Regarding views on government's role in fair housing and employment and in desegregating schools, proximity to African American groups is an early, strong, and persistent predictor of support. Perceived proximity to party position also plays a significant role in views on both racial policy items, even as early as 1956. This influence, however, varies across the three measures of perceived proximity to party position. In 1956 and 1960, remarkably, the perceived proximity to elites measure is strongest and most significant for southern whites.

The relative balance between elites and non-elites is solidly in favor of movement-specific influences on racial policy preferences. For one thing, except for southern whites the statistical significance of the proximity to party position measures is less impressive than that for proximity to movement organizations. For another, the magnitude of influence for one's proximity to movement organizations is much more sizeable than that for one's proximity to political parties. Since our two measures of racial policy preferences are categorical variables—ranging from strong agreement to strong disagreement—the magnitude of the relationships cannot be read directly from tables 2.1 and 2.2. Rather, the strength of the significant effects must be extrapolated from the results. This kind of extrapolation is commonly done by estimating how an individual's probability of expressing one of the dependent variable's response categories is likely to increase or decrease as a function of change in a particular explanatory variable of interest. Figures 2.3 and 2.4 present such estimates of magnitude of effects where the dependent variable's response category is strong support for fair employment and housing (fig. 2.3) and strong support for school desegregation (fig. 2.4) and the variations in explanatory variables are minimum-value to maximum-value shifts (for example, from closest possible ideological proximity to the Republican Party to greatest possible ideological distance to the Republican Party). Figures 2.3 and 2.4 examine such "min-max" shifts for six key explanatory variables: the three measures of perceived proximity to party position (for Democrats, Republicans, and southern white Democrats), the two measures of perceived proximity to black groups (for whites

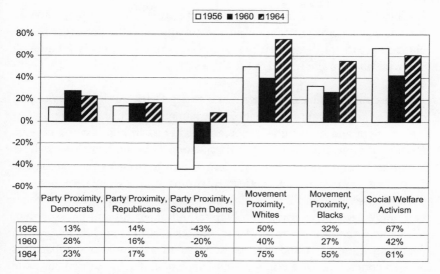

	Party Proximity, Democrats	Party Proximity, Republicans	Party Proximity, Southern Dems	Movement Proximity, Whites	Movement Proximity, Blacks	Social Welfare Activism
1956	13%	14%	-43%	50%	32%	67%
1960	28%	16%	-20%	40%	27%	42%
1964	23%	17%	8%	75%	55%	61%

Figure 2.3   Effect of Min-Max Shifts on Strong Support for Fair Jobs and Housing, 1956–64

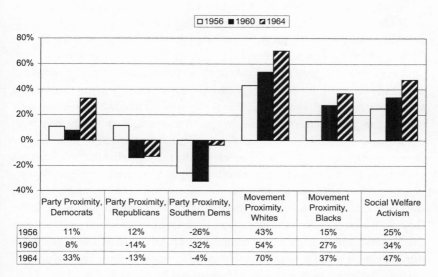

	Party Proximity, Democrats	Party Proximity, Republicans	Party Proximity, Southern Dems	Movement Proximity, Whites	Movement Proximity, Blacks	Social Welfare Activism
1956	11%	12%	-26%	43%	15%	25%
1960	8%	-14%	-32%	54%	27%	34%
1964	33%	-13%	-4%	70%	37%	47%

Figure 2.4   Effect of Min-Max Shifts on Strong Support for School Desegregation, 1956–64

and blacks), and the additive index of support for social welfare liberalism. As is standard protocol for such extrapolations, the predicted probabilities for each of these variables of interest are calculated by holding all other variables in the model at the values for a hypothetical mean respondent.[29]

For example, figure 2.3 shows that a strong Democrat in 1956 who perceives the Democratic Party to hold the same preferences as hers on fair employment and housing is 13 percent likelier to strongly favor a government action on these issues than is a strong Republican in 1956 whose preferences on these issues are far removed from those of the Democratic Party. This is a rather modest effect. By comparison, a white respondent in 1956 who is very trustful of black organizations is fully 50 percent likelier to strongly favor a government role in fair employment and housing than is a white respondent in 1956 who is very distrustful of such black groups. Scanning figures 2.3 and 2.4, we see that these min-max comparisons make a compelling case that non-elite, movement-based opinion cues and support for social welfare liberalism have a more powerful effect on one's racial policy preferences than do elite, partisan opinion cues.

Southern whites are a prominent exception in this regard. In 1956, southern white Democrats whose issue positions on fair employment and housing and school desegregation are perceived as in line with the Democratic Party's are 43 percent and 27 percent, respectively, less likely to strongly support a government role in these issues. This effect of perceived proximity for southern whites remains quite potent in 1960 but diminishes substantially on both racial policy issues by 1964. This decrease most likely reflects the internecine strife within the Democratic Party over racial integration and states' rights.[30] Recall our earlier expectation that the influence of perceived proximity is likely to vary with the signal clarity of a party's issue position and whom the respondent chooses to identify with the "party position." Southern whites prior to the mid-1960s could comfortably view the Democratic Party of Strom Thurmond, Marvin Griffin, James Eastland, George Wallace, and Orval Faubus as *their* Democratic Party—so long as Democratic leaders outside the South such as Adlai Stevenson and John F. Kennedy were willing to publicly equivocate on civil rights for the sake of party unity. By 1964 this was no longer possible.

This same dynamic also helps explain the dramatic shift in the influence of ideological distance to the Republican Party on support for school desegregation over time. Perceived proximity to the Republican Party for Republicans appears to predict greater support for desegregating schools in 1956 but greater opposition in 1960 and perhaps 1964 as well. These effects are modest but statistically significant. One possible explanation is that by 1960, ordinary individuals begin to discern a shift in partisan signals concerning school desegregation.[31] One commonly cited example is the signal sent by candidate John F. Kennedy in the 1960 presidential campaign against Richard Nixon. As the story goes, sensing a potential photo finish, Kennedy sent a well-timed and well-publicized signal to black voters by calling an anxious Coretta Scott King after Martin Luther King Jr. was jailed in rural Georgia.[32] If this explanation is correct, then 1960 marks a turning point in the issue evolution of mass opinion on racial policies. Kennedy squeaked by with a margin of less than 1 percent of the vote in 1960. As one historical account of the election notes, "Civil rights were not a critical issue as the 1960 election got under way, but they became a major issue as the election moved to its conclusion. And John Kennedy did well for himself as he and his team advanced the issue" (Stern, 1992, 39). It was in 1960 that racially liberal Americans felt an ideological breach between their racial policy preferences and the stances of their respective parties on matters of race. Less speculatively, note that with respect to both racial policy items, partisan cues played a significant role well before the mid-1960s. Thus there is ample evidence of an attentiveness to elite opinion cues regarding racial policies well before the critical period suggested by Carmines and Stimson's account.

Just as important as this story about partisanship is the story from figures 2.3 and 2.4 about the importance of the racially and regionally defined group bases of racial policy preferences. Both whites and African Americans with a strong attachment to black movement organizations are significantly more supportive of an active government role in ensuring racial equality. Moreover, the tables confirm our expectations that perceived proximity to the same Democratic Party exerts an opposite influence on racial policy preferences for southern whites than they do for all other Democrats.[33]

Finally, tables 2.3 and 2.4 demonstrate the power of an activist social welfare orientation to explain support for an activist government in racial policy domains. This relationship is significant across all three time periods. As early as 1956, respondents who favor the strongest possible role for an activist government in social policy domains are 67 percent more supportive of a strong government role in ensuring fair employment and housing for African Americans and 26 percent more supportive of a strong role in school desegregation. This result directly bears on Carmines and

Stimson's claims about the centrality of the mid-1960s. Recall their claim that the key event linking partisanship, race, and social welfare issues together in the public mind "no doubt was the 1964 presidential election" (1989, 117). The results here, taken as a whole, offer some weighty evidence to the contrary. Race and social welfare liberalism are forcefully linked, but the evidence of this linkage is visible well before the 1964 presidential election.

BLACK INSURGENCY AND PARTISANSHIP

Thus far, we have seen that movement-based influences on racial policy preferences precede partisan-based influences, and that significant linkages between racial policy preferences, partisanship, and social welfare liberalism precede the mid-1960s. There is yet another claim of Carmines and Stimson's issue evolution account that we have yet to examine: that the partisan realignment they describe is a transformation whose critical juncture dates to the mid-1960s. In this section, I take empirical issue with this claim. Specifically, I examine race and ideological distance vis-à-vis racial policies as a source of change in partisanship itself prior to the mid-1960s. To model this, change of partisanship is represented as follows:

$$\Delta PID = PID_t - PID_{t-1} \tag{3}$$

In its simplest form, the influence of racial linkages on change in partisanship can be modeled as follows:

$$\Delta PID_1 = \beta_1 X_{it} + \beta_2 \Delta \theta_i + \varepsilon_{it} \tag{4}$$

In equation 4, $\beta_2 \Delta \theta_i$ represents $(\theta_{i,t1} - \theta_{P,t1}) - (\theta_{i,t0} - \theta_{P,t0})$, the change in our ideological distance variable from time t_0 to time t_1. $\theta_1 X_{it}$ represents a vector of sociodemographic and other control variables. As before, the linkage between ideological distance and choice of partisanship should differentiate between perceived proximity to the Democrat and Republican Parties and between southern white Democrats and other Democrats.[34]

Figure 2.5 shows the distribution of changes in partisanship from the 1956–60 Center for Political Studies Panel Study. Partisanship is measured in seven categories (from "strong Republican" to "strong Democrat"), and each bar from left to right represents an additional category shift in partisanship between 1956 and 1960. More than half of the respondents show no change in partisanship from 1956 to 1960. Yet almost one in three individuals expressed at least a one-category shift in partisanship (for ex-

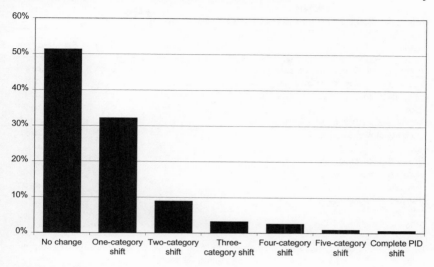

Figure 2.5   Change in Partisanship, 1956–60

ample, from "strong Republican" to "moderate Republican"). The magnitude of partisanship shifts is generally rather modest: four out of five cases of change in partisanship are either a one-category or a two-category shift. There is a full reversal from intense affiliation with one party to intense affiliation to the opposite party in less than 1 percent of cases.

In our actual estimates, we are concerned with change per se and not change from a particular party to another specified party. Thus measures of change are calculated as the absolute value of the difference in scores between our two time periods of interest, 1956 and 1960. The socioeconomic controls are same as before: age, family income, and educational level. In addition, the race of the respondent is included to test whether African Americans—controlling for our issue-specific ideological distance measure—are likelier to shift partisanship. Finally, there are strong a priori reasons to think that prior party identification and intensity of partisanship should affect change of partisanship. The actual model we estimate, then, is shown below:

$$| \Delta PID_i | = \beta_1 X_{it} + \beta_2 | \Delta \theta DEM_i | + \beta_3 | \Delta \theta REP_i | \\ + \beta_4 | \Delta \theta SWDEM_i | \varepsilon_i \qquad (5)$$

The results for this model of partisan change are shown in table 2.3. Contrary to the arguments of Carmines and Stimson, the change in perceived

Table 2.3   Black Insurgency and Change in Partisanship, 1956–60

Variable	Coefficient	Standard error
Δ proximity to Dem. Party on race, given PID	.075	.018**
Δ proximity to Rep. Party on race, given PID	.006	.018
Δ proximity to Dem. Party on race, given PID & southern white	−.075	.025**
Race (1 = African American	.081	.033**
Partisanship, 1956 (high = Democratic)	−.134	.030**
Intensity of partisanship, 1956	−.055	.017**
Age	−.103	.065
Educational level	−.132	.045**
Family income	.019	.039
Constant	.345	.058
Number of observations	406	
Adjusted R²	.143	
SER	.160	

DATA: 1956–60 CPS Panel Study. Cell entries in the middle and right columns are parameter estimates and corresponding standard errors for an OLS model.

** p < .01

proximity between respondent and party ideal positions on civil rights is a significant determinant of change in partisanship. Specifically, perceived proximity to the Democratic Party on fair employment and housing and school desegregation significantly increases the probability of changing partisanship. Perceived proximity to the Democratic Party for southern whites, in contrast, decreases the probability of changing partisanship. As with racial policy preferences, the key to interpreting these effects is that the perception of the Democratic Party's ideal position is likely to differ for southern white Democrats and other Democrats. Thus, southern white Democrats who see the Democratic Party as the party of the status quo will more likely retain their partisanship.

As we might expect, prior partisanship and intensity of partisanship both strongly predict the resiliency of partisanship between 1956 and 1960. Also not surprisingly, individuals who are better educated are less likely to switch parties over time. What is somewhat surprising is that the magnitude of these effects on change of partisanship (which, a priori, ought to be strong) is not hugely different from our key variables of interest: ideological distance from the political parties on racial matters. Although there are better-suited methodological methods for modeling panel data, table 2.3 appears to show that ideological distance with respect to race is a fairly strong influence on change in partisanship. Finally, table 2.3 also shows evidence of a different kind that race and partisanship are linked as early as 1960: African American respondents show a significantly greater likelihood of changing partisanship than do non–African Americans.

THE VARIANCE IN RESPONDENT CHOICES

Taken together, the results offer a corrective to elite-driven accounts of racial attitudes during the civil rights era. To conclude our assessment of elite theory, there is a final unexamined dimension to racial attitudes. Opinion research almost always examines changes in survey responses, and rightly so. But an important yet understudied feature of mass opinion is the underlying variance of responses. For a given set of explanatory variables—such as those in tables 2.1 and 2.2—some individuals may exhibit *systematically* greater unexplained variance in their responses than do others. In this section, I examine whether this possibility is borne out in public views on fair employment and housing practices and school desegregation.

The rationale for examining the unexplained variance in survey responses is conceptual and methodological. With regard to conception, the RAS model tells us that the answers that an individual gives to survey questions are probabilistic responses that vary depending on the type and quantity of considerations "at the top of one's head" at the moment an answer is given. Moreover, some people are simply more attentive to political matters, less reliant on cognitive shortcuts, and able to entertain a greater number of considerations in a given issue. If this is so, we should see some systematic variability in the attitudes we find in survey responses. With regard to method, unequal and unexplained variance across data points can corrupt our results. This phenomenon, known to statisticians as *heteroskedasticity*, is usually either ignored as an arcane technical subtlety or relegated to a footnote on inefficient estimates. But when the question we are concerned with is measured as a categorical, discrete variable, heteroskedasticity can lead to inconsistent estimates and the wrong covariance matrix. If there are reasonable expectations for unequal variances in a model, then heteroskedasticity must be tested for.

Michael Alvarez and John Brehm (1995, 1996, 1997) develop a methodological means to estimate the variance underlying individual responses that is used in their work to reach some striking findings about public views on abortion and race.[35] Alvarez and Brehm identify at least three different sources of unexplained response variance: (1) equivocation, in which respondents might manifest varying degrees of "sociability effects" (that is, anticipating what interviewers expect to hear, especially on controversial issues such as abortion and racial politics); (2) uncertainty, in which respondents might vary in their responses owing to incomplete information; and (3) ambivalence, in which respondents might express varying ability to negotiate the conflict between underlying values at stake.[36]

Public support for school desegregation and fair employment and housing are prime candidates for a heteroskedastic probit analysis. These are categorical dependent variables. And unequal variance is likely to be an issue in public views on race during the civil rights movement. Given the public debate and political mobilization on these issues during a protest movement, public views should be characterized by social pressures to conform to particular norms and beliefs, by an uncertain and shifting information environment, and by a profound clash of core values. Moreover, in the context of a social movement, we might expect changes in the significance of heteroskedasticity over time. Specifically, if social movements succeed in bringing their concerns onto the political agenda, then unequal residual variance should diminish over time as the movement's issues gain salience and clarity in the public mind. Thus, examining heteroskedasticity is not merely vital on methodological grounds but is an important element of what we wish to know substantively about the nature and dynamics of mass opinion during the course of a social movement.

The method of modeling variance in responses is quite straightforward. Essentially, it entails specifying a second-stage "error variance" model along with the primary "choice" model of interest. In the case of public support for fair employment and housing and for school desegregation, I examine educational level and intense partisanship in the variance model. Educational level measures the effect of informational uncertainty and cognitive processing on the variance of respondents' choices. Presumably, to the extent that education matters, it should reduce the variance in individual responses. I include intense partisanship under the hypothesis that strong Democrats and strong Republicans—to the extent that elite theorists are correct—should vary less in their policy preferences, irrespective of party identification.

For the choice model, the results are fundamentally the same for a simple ordered probit estimation (in tables 2.1 and 2.2) and a heteroskedastic probit specification. There are some compelling results in the variance models, however.[37] For both fair employment and housing, there is evidence of significant heteroskedasticity in 1956; education and intense partisanship significantly decreases the error variance. For school desegregation, significant heteroskedasticity is evident in both 1956 and 1960; here education decreases the residual variance while intense partisanship actually increases the residual variance.[38]

Residual variance diminishes during the course of the civil rights movement. By 1964, there is no longer any evidence of significant heteroskedasticity for either public support for fair employment and housing or school desegregation. This fits very well with our substantive expectations about when residual variance ought to matter as a latent issue unfolds during a social movement.[39]

CONCLUDING REMARKS

In this chapter I have examined the dynamics of public opinion during periods of mass mobilization such as the civil rights movement. The results offer an important revision to recent accounts—Carmines and Stimson's issue evolution account in particular—that explain changes in racial attitudes during this period as the outcome of elite influences. The evidence in these pages affirms the critical agency of black social movement organizations and underscores the centrality of racial and regional attachments in the activation of public views about race. Movement-specific, non-elite attachments on the whole have an earlier and stronger impact on the public's racial policy preferences than do partisan, elite attachments. The evidence does not imply that elite influences had no bearing on the public's views on race during the civil rights movement. Elite signals not only influenced mass opinion, but they did so (especially for southern whites) well before the mid-1960s. Finally, the results in this chapter marshal some strong evidence that significant linkages between black insurgency, partisan politics, and social welfare liberalism were present and reconfigured throughout the years examined and not forged at a single synchronic moment in time.

In the interests of streamlining the exposition, I have not discussed additional refinements to the statistical analysis in this chapter. One noteworthy case is the possibility that proximity to elite and movement actors and racial policy preferences are endogenous in a way that casts doubt on the hypothesized causality between ideological proximity and policy preferences. In particular, it is possible that an individual's position on school desegregation or fair employment for African Americans causes her to identify more closely with movement organizations, rather than vice versa. When I test for this possibility, the results from tables 2.1 and 2.2 stand up well, but tests for endogeneity (in this case, two-stage least squares) are often quite sensitive to how our endogenous and exogenous variables are specified.

More generally, the conclusions, solid as they are, are limited by the fact that the theoretical apparatus used in this chapter exceeds the grasp of the available data. In particular, the attempt to model elite and non-elite influences as a competitive election by reference to formal voting models is appealing theoretically but demanding empirically. We cannot, for example, fairly test whether elite or movement-based influences actually transform public views concerning race without panel data that take us from the mid-1950s to the mid-1960s. Also, the availability of data may lag behind the timing of actual political events in a way that makes it difficult to distinguish between elite and non-elite influences on mass opinion.

For instance, group-based interests and conflicts and core political values are central to any account of racial attitudes, both presently and during the civil rights movement. Despite this, the first national academic survey containing a reasonably complete set of questions about racial group consciousness was not available until the 1972 American National Election Study (ANES). The first extensive battery of items on core political values such as equal opportunity and economic individualism did not appear in the ANES until 1984. These years, of course, came well after the height of the civil rights movement. They also came well after the allegedly critical period of opinion change (the mid-1960s) in existing accounts of mass opinion during the civil rights era. Finally, these years came after the tumultuous period of mass uprisings in inner cities and college campuses in the mid-to-late 1960s. Thus data from 1972 and 1984 may well capture important changes in the relations between racial attitudes, group interests, and core values resulting from such tumult. As we shall see in chapter 3, the incompleteness and inadequacy of survey data is a systemic shortcoming of opinion research with troubling consequences for how we evaluate elite opinion theories.

THREE

THE SOVEREIGN STATUS OF SURVEY DATA

> I am invisible, understand, simply because people refuse to see me. Like the bodiless heads you see sometimes in circus sideshows, it is as though I have been surrounded by mirrors of hard distorting glass. When they approach me they see only my surroundings, themselves or judgments of their imagination, indeed, everything and anything except me.
>
> —Ralph Ellison

> The theory of the polls is essentially simplistic, based on a tremendously exaggerated notion of the immediacy and urgency of the connection of public opinion and events. The result is that sometimes we seem to be interviewing the fish in the sea to find out what the birds in the heavens are doing.
>
> —E. E. Schattschneider

We have now seen some compelling evidence of mass audience response to the civil rights movement. In substantial measure—certainly more than recognized by existing elite accounts—racial attitudes in this era were shaped by non-elite, movement-based factors. What's more, the critical linkages between racial policy, partisanship, and social welfare liberalism do not appear *de novo* in the mid-1960s as scholars such as the Edsalls or Carmines and Stimson claim. Rather, these linkages find strong imprints in the prior decade of black insurgency and elite response to that insurgency.

The arguments from chapter 1 and the evidence from chapter 2 thus amount to a strong case against elite opinion theories. We have yet to make a strong positive case for an account of activated mass opinion. As noted in chapter 1, this positive case foregrounds the historically contingent, group-based, and issue-specific contexts in which mass opinion becomes at once salient in an individual's mind and impels that person to actively voice her opinion. Thus the inputs (cognitive) and outputs (behavioral) to mass opinion are viewed in continuity, rather than separately. What makes a person more likely to attend to political affairs makes that person more likely to express coherent views about political affairs and more likely to act on those views. This activated account of public opinion not only bears implications for elite opinion theories but also calls for a reconsideration of how we conceive of "public opinion" itself and how best to measure and test it. In this chapter I undertake such a reconsideration.

I begin by showing that survey data play a predominant role in contemporary opinion research. This sovereign status reverberates in the conceptual, normative, and empirical realms of opinion research: what we imagine public opinion to be, what role public opinion should play in democratic government, and what we can actually discover substantively about the nature and dynamics of public opinion. More pointedly, what we make of elite opinion theories depends vitally how public opinion is conceived and measured in empirical research. Specifically, the ability of survey data to adequately discriminate between elite and non-elite influences on mass opinion depends on whether opinion polls accurately reflect (or even anticipate) the issues that engage the public at a given moment in time. In the case of the dynamics of racial attitudes, this possibility is not merely theoretical: I show in this chapter that the production of survey items on racial attitudes appears—at critical junctures in the evolution of the civil rights movement—to lag behind, rather than anticipate or mirror, the events that engage the public. Survey data, used alone, are thus inadequate to the task of assessing elite theories. I close by arguing that a fuller, substantive account of racial attitudes during the civil rights era must be woven out of opinion data from multiple sources.

FROM PUBLIC OPINION TO SURVEY RESPONSES

The starting point for this chapter is that our academic and practical understanding of the term "public opinion" has come to rest on one point: the opinion poll.[1] Of course, scholars have noted the prevalence of a diversity of alternate modes of public political expression at other historical moments ranging from festivals, strikes, riots, and discussions in French salons and English coffeehouses to straw polls, elections, and revolutions.[2] And with the relentless march of modern technology, ever newer forms of public expression are emerging, from radio and television talk shows to televised "town meetings" and "deliberative polls," and, most recently, to e-mail groups and Internet chat rooms.[3] These active modes of public political expression, however, are generally studied outside the domains of opinion research—usually, under the rubrics of "political participation," "voting behavior," "social movements," "media studies," "mass communications," and the like.

Today, both critics and practitioners of survey research recognize that poll data are singularly sovereign among possible measures of public opinion, and this indicator (poll data) is rather routinely conflated with its underlying construct (public opinion). Among critics, Susan Herbst notes, "These days we tend to believe that public opinion is the aggregation of individual opinions as measured by the sample survey . . . this definition is now hegemonic; when most of us consider the meaning of public opinion, we can't help but think about polls or surveys" (1995a, 90).[4] Among practitioners, Philip Converse notes that "it is exactly this kind of 'one person one vote' tally of opinions as routinely reported today by polls and surveys which has now become the consensual understanding of the world around as to a baseline of public opinion" (1987, S14), and John Zaller writes of "the survey responses that virtually everyone now takes as constituting public opinion" (1992, 265).

This sovereign status is exemplified by the increasing reliance on survey data in social scientific research on public opinion. Stanley Presser (1984) and, building on Presser's data, Jean Converse (1987) show this increase in several social science disciplines between the time before World War II and 1980. Articles in sociology journals that use survey data increased more than threefold from about 18 percent in 1939–40 to more than 54 percent by the mid-1960s. In political science, the proportion of published work using survey data jumped from less than 3 percent in 1939–40 to almost 20 percent by 1964–65, and then to 35 percent by 1979–80.[5] In *Public Opinion Quarterly* (the pre-eminent journal of public opinion research) survey data comprised almost 28 percent of all articles in 1939–40. This proportion doubled by 1964–65 and rose to more than 90 percent by 1979–80. In hindsight, it may appear odd to us that survey data did not comprise a greater percentage of articles in *POQ* even in the 1940s and 1950s. Jean Converse (1987, 402) notes, however, that this progressive rise in the use

Table 3.1   Public Opinion Quarterly Articles on Race, by Type of Public Opinion
Data, 1937–86

Year	Poll data	Interview	Voting	Media	Other	% Poll
1937–46	1	0	2	2	2	14.3
1947–56	2	0	1	2	2	28.6
1957–66	5	2	5	0	1	38.3
1967–76	37	1	1	3	2	84.5
1977–86	17	0	0	1	0	94.3
1987–96	21	0	0	2	0	91.3

of survey data in *POQ* "represented real change. *POQ* was not a journal of survey research at the outset. It had been established for the study of public opinion and thus drew articles on public relations, advertising, propaganda and censorship, radio, film, the press, and public opinion generally, many of which had little or nothing to do with surveys."

The ascendancy of survey data as a measure of public opinion, relative to alternate such measures, can also be shown in the narrower context of racial attitudes.[6] Table 3.1 tabulates research articles in *POQ* on race by different sources of data on public opinion from 1937 to 1996. As with Converse's tabulation of *POQ* articles, table 3.1 shows that, in its first decade, research using survey data constituted only a small fraction (14 percent) of all *POQ* articles on race and public opinion. The remaining articles in this period focused instead on alternate sources of opinion data such as in-depth interviews, voting behavior, and media coverage. By 1967–76, however, almost 85 percent of all research articles on racial attitudes in *POQ* were based in survey data, and by 1977–86 the figure rose to 94 percent.

Table 3.1 also presages two central points in this chapter. First, the rise in the absolute number of research articles on racial attitudes in *POQ* closely parallels the rise in civil rights activism. By implication, the production of survey items on racial attitudes also appears to closely parallel the rise in civil rights activism. Second, a glance at table 3.1 and Converse's findings suggests that the rise of survey research on race lags behind the rise of survey research generally, especially around the period of the civil rights movement. Converse finds that from 1959 to 1960, survey data comprised 58 percent of all articles in *POQ*; table 3.1 shows that from 1957 to 1966, survey data comprised only 38 percent of articles on racial attitudes in *POQ*. These points will be revisited and developed in greater detail later in this chapter.

GOVERNMENT BY PUBLIC OPINION

The exact path to the sovereign status of poll data and their virtual conflation with public opinion is likely contentious, and the purpose here is not
to develop an exhaustive exegesis on how this evolution came about.[7] That
said, the influence of three factors—liberalism, scientism, and technological change—is fairly unequivocal. With respect to liberalism, Sidney Verba,
in a recent presidential address to the American Political Science Association, plainly asserts that what makes poll data so appealing is that "[s]urveys
produce just what democracy is supposed to produce—equal representation of all citizens" (1996, 3). Perhaps the most relevant development in
this regard since the eighteenth century has been the evolution of formal
mechanisms for the expression and aggregation of citizens' political preferences. With the emergence of majority rule, the secret ballot, and liberal
utilitarianism, the "public" came to be embodied in a voting electorate.
Thus the metaphor of polls as instantaneous elections made a clear and
powerful case for what Susan Herbst (1993) terms the "aggregative" view
of public opinion.[8]

These formal mechanisms heralded an important shift in the understanding of public opinion. The move was from the view of public opinion
as a unitary, collective entity in *fin de siècle* France to today's more familiar
view of an aggregation of discrete, anonymously expressed, and equally
weighted opinions. In eighteenth-century France the legitimacy sought
through appeals to public opinion derived from the idea of the public as a
collective entity that spoke with univocal clarity. Mona Ozouf (1988), for
example, notes that the idea of *publique* at the time was counterposed with
particulier (particular, individual). Ozouf also notes that the term *l'opinion
publique* retained the singular form of "opinion" (rather than "opinions") to
embody a univocality of the sort implied in Rousseau's notion of the general will. Thus she writes that *l'opinion publique* drew its "polemic efficacy
from the adjective 'public' and, what is more, from the use of the term in
the singular since Rousseau's public opinions in the plural were short-lived
and returned immediately to the realm of personal prejudices (1988, S3)."
The more familiar juxtaposition to *privé* (private) did not emerge until the
1830s.[9]

Even in the early part of the twentieth century, with the treatises of Ferdinand Toennies (1922) and Wilhelm Bauer (1934), public opinion retained
an organic, unitary conception. And in the United States, nonaggregative
views of the public were present in John Dewey's (1927) unitary ideal of

the public and even Walter Lippmann's (1925) dim view of issue publics. Yet it was the aggregative view—that the sentiments of a polity are best gauged by adding together its discrete, equally weighted, anonymously voiced parts—expressed by James Bryce and then echoed by George Gallup that prevailed. As J. A. W. Gunn colorfully points out, the advent of the social survey served as the linchpin in the ascendance of this aggregative view of public opinion:

> Only when supposedly typical citizens could be confronted individually, and their views related to their electoral behavior and other facts about them, was it in general feasible to contemplate public opinion as a collection of individual responses to particular questions. All of a sudden the prospect opened up of knowing exactly what people thought about public issues. . . . The act of voting may have given to public opinion its modern significance, but it has been survey research that revolutionized how one talked about it. Public opinion came to be what the polls measured. If one still needed elections, as the pleasantry went, it was only to confirm the accuracy of the polls. (1995b, 100)

The easy analogy of surveys to an individualistic, "one person, one vote" model of democracy thus made surveys especially relevant and appealing. It also changed our understanding of public opinion itself. Moreover, this development marked a sea change in the status of public opinion, from being the abstract domain of theorists to being the empirical substrate for practitioners. Leo Bogart writes that "the world of public opinion in today's sense really began with the Gallup Polls of the mid-1930s, and it is impossible for us to retreat to the meaning of public opinion as it was understood by Thomas Jefferson in the eighteenth century, by Alexis de Tocqueville and Lord Bryce in the nineteenth—or even Walter Lippmann in 1922" (1972, 14).

With this shift to an aggregative view of public opinion, the normative appeal to opinion polls also came to presume a particular conception of democratic representation. In Hanna Pitkin's (1967) classic distinction between Burkean trustees, who represent by acting independently but in the best interests of their constituents, and Millsean delegates, who represent by following the direct mandates of their constituents, the appeal of opinion polls clearly nudges us toward the ideal of representatives as delegates.[10] Absent direct democracy of the sort advocated by the Anti-Federalists, Rousseau, or Aristotle, the liberal use of opinion polling was promoted as the best substitute. Polls would provide elected representatives with continuous feedback on their constituents' preferences, and these preferences ought then to shape government output. This implicit normative conception of representation, of course, can be traced back to the "patron saint" of opinion polling, James Bryce, who writes with a flourish that "Towering over Presidents and State governors, over Congress and State legislatures, over conventions and vast machinery of party, public opinion stands out, in the United States, as the great source of power, the master of servants who tremble before it" (1895, 267).[11] Thus early champions of opinion polls such as George Gallup repeatedly alluded to Bryce's skepticism that "the obvious weakness of government by public opinion is the difficulty in ascertaining it" (1895, 354) and used that skepticism to advocate scientific opinion polls.[12]

This form of democratic liberalism is not, however, the only ideological trajectory that impels the ascendancy and legitimation of survey research. Ultimately, opinion polls also prevailed over alternate measures of public opinion because random sampling conferred a scientifically authoritative and descriptively representative means of democratizing public influence on government. Thus Archibald Crossley, an early advocate of the scientific study of mass opinion, writes:

> In the next four years, the country will be faced with many important issues. . . . Will [Congress] be swayed by pressure groups with false presentations of public opinion? Or will it seek by scientific sampling to give American voters the opportunity to express themselves on their views and needs of the day? . . . Scientific polling makes it possible within two or three days at moderate expense for the entire nation to work hand in hand with its legislative representatives, on laws which affect our daily lives. Here is the long-sought key to "Government by the people." (in J. Converse, 1987, 122)

Note that Crossley juxtaposes "false presentations" of public opinion as gauged by interest groups against the verity of scientific surveys. Benjamin Ginsberg thus declares that the "presumption in favor of opinion polls stems from both their scientific and their representative character. Survey research is modeled after the methodology of the natural sciences and at least conveys an impression of technical sophistication and scientific objectivity" (1986, 61).

The rise of survey data must therefore also be understood in the context of academic trajectories. Dorothy Ross asserts that the exceptionalist tradition of inquiry in the United States drew the social sciences toward "scientism" and behavioralism. In particular, social surveys in the late nineteenth century developed, as did social sciences generally at the same time, with the firm "belief that the objective methods of the natural sciences should be used in the study of human affairs, and that such methods are the only fruitful ones in the pursuit of knowledge" (1993, 83n). Social surveys were thus applied to the study of politics in the early twentieth century as a means to eschew value-laden, subjective inquiry and espouse the quantitative, systematic study of political behavior.[13]

It is not altogether fair, however, to view the appeal of opinion polls as a scientific means to gauge the public's sentiments as an entirely ideological or sociological phenomenon. Without doubt the scientific opinion poll outperformed such competitors as the straw poll. The social authority of polls is thus advanced by tangible technological innovations as well, such as the refinement of survey methodology (for example, probability sampling, standardized instruments, computer-assisted telephone interviewing, quasi-experimentation) and the revolutionary progress in computer technology and statistical software. The ability of scientific opinion polls to outperform alternatives depended on such technological innovations, such as advances in market research and sampling theory, from its inception. And this predictive preeminence led to the early acceptance and advocacy of opinion polls by mass media technologies.[14]

Technological change, of course, does not march through history in a linear, rationalized manner. I would be remiss not to mention the hand of historical accident in the triumph of opinion polls. Most famously, in the presidential election of 1936, a prominent *Literary Digest* straw poll inaccurately predicted a sweeping victory for Alf Landon, while randomly sampled polls correctly predicted an easy victory for Franklin Delano Roosevelt. Gallup and Rae, in deliberately revealing language, note that "[t]he 1936 presidential election made possible the first experimental test of this new method [of randomly sampled polling] in a nation-wide laboratory" (1940, 77). The spectacular results of this "experiment" and the dramatic failure of the straw poll as a predictive tool contributed to the rapid demise of the *Literary Digest*. Pioneers such as Crossley, Gallup, and Elmo Roper achieved overnight success and began to conceive a new science of opinion polling out of market research methods and the journalistic demand for election forecasts.[15]

This discussion of the likely influences on survey data's ascendance has been more speculative than exhaustive. Many critics of survey research implicate other forces, such as the logic of social control and the need to engineer democratic consent.[16] That said, the trajectories of liberalism, scientism, and technological change give us the rudiments of an account of how opinion polls achieved their pre-eminence over the course of the past six decades. In the remaining sections of this chapter, I examine some of the reverberations of this dominant role of survey data. Ultimately, I argue that the presumed authority of survey data limits what we understand public opinion to be and how we evaluate elite opinion theories. This limitation, especially in the domain of racial attitudes during the civil rights years, is addressed by undertaking an examination of alternate measures of public opinion.

THE LIMITS OF SOVEREIGNTY

The fact that opinion scholars almost exclusively use poll data does not in itself undermine the survey research program. The sovereign status of survey data may simply be a fortuitous historical contingency or, more forcefully, an outcome warranted by the simple fact that polls are the optimal way to measure public opinion. That said, criticisms of opinion polls persist, and in this section I consider three such criticisms—normative, ontological, and conceptual. In normative terms, the sovereign status of survey research threatens the vitality and autonomy of our political life. In ontological terms, the "public opinion" that opinion polls purport to measure simply does not exist. In more general form, essential characteristics of public opinion are lost when the construct is solely identified with one possible measure of it. In conceptual terms, opinion polls render a static, disjunct, and individualistic notion of what is ultimately a dynamic, conjunct, and collective phenomenon.

To begin, critics of survey research note that polls are far from a neutral mirror of society and that their historical origins and present-day dominion pose a sobering threat to fair democratic representation. Jürgen Habermas (1989) and Benjamin Ginsberg (1986), for example, attribute the ascendance of survey research to the bureaucratic necessity of political states to "domesticate" the sentiments of their electorate. In doing so, the argument goes, such states effectively "manufacture" legitimacy and consent that might otherwise not exist.[17] Ginsberg further argues that opinion polling is thus an instrument of political control, made powerful by the aura of objectivity and political neutrality conferred upon it by the public and politicians alike. For instance, in the context of the civil rights era, Ginsberg alleges that the National Advisory Commission on Civil Disorders—which conducted some of the first surveys to focus on African American mass opinion—effectively used the results of their polling to manipulate public opinion and avoid any costly acquiescence to the demands of blacks in urban America. Ginsberg notes that

> [t]hese surveys allowed the commission to identify a number of attitudes held by blacks that were said to have contributed to their disruptive behavior. As a result of its surveys, the commission was able to suggest several programs

that might modify these attitudes and thus prevent further disorder. Significantly enough, the Riot Commission's report did not call for changes in the
institutions and policies about which blacks had been violently expressing
their views. The effect of polling was, in essence, to help the government find
a way to *not* accommodate the opinions blacks had expressed in the streets of
the urban ghettos of the United States. (1986, 72)

So, as Ginsberg's argument goes, when political actors or organized interests need to delegitimate political claims they oppose, opinion polls afford
them a "democratic" means of doing so by molding public sentiment accordingly.[18]

James Beniger further implicates the logic of technological change in
what he calls "the Control Revolution," in which change is driven by and
reinforces the need for information processing and social control (1986).
Opinion polls thus emerge as merely another "control technology." In particular, Beniger sees polls as a form of "market feedback technology" used
to gather information to shape and influence mass consumption.[19] Softer
shades of such sentiments, of course, can be found in earlier theorists such
as James Bryce and Walter Lippmann. Even V. O. Key notes that "[g]ov-
ernments must concern themselves with the opinions of their citizens, if
only to provide a basis for repression of disaffection" (1961, 3). Hence the
same tool that pioneers such as Crossley and Gallup praised as enabling
democratic representation can also be seen as undermining it.

More pointedly, other critics question the ability of opinion polls to
meaningfully measure public opinion at all. Herbert Blumer, an early and
steadfast critic of opinion polls, warns against "the narrow operationalist
position that public opinion consists of what public opinion polls poll. . . .
What is logically unpardonable on the part of those who take the narrow
operationalist position is for them to hold either wittingly or unwittingly
that their investigations are a study of public opinion as this term is conceived in our ordinary discourse" (1948, 543). The fatal flaw, according to
Blumer, is that pollsters equate the findings of survey data—merely an
instrument used to measure public opinion—with the object of inquiry
itself.

Perhaps Blumer's contemporary on this point is the French sociologist
Pierre Bourdieu, who makes the deliberately provocative claim that public
opinion, in the "sense of the social definition implicitly accepted by those
who prepare or analyze or use opinion polls, simply does not exist" (1979,
130). Bourdieu indicts survey researchers on three counts of problematic
assumption-making: that everyone's opinion is equal; that, on a given issue,
everyone actually holds an opinion; and that a consensus exists about what

questions merit asking (and, by corollary, that surveys can know what that consensus is).[20] Thus survey data—all other possible caveats notwithstanding—adequately measure mass opinion only if they accurately survey what ordinary individuals are actually thinking about at a given moment.

Finally, the study of public opinion through survey research is impugned by critics because it allegedly captures only a static, disjunct, cognitively based, individualistic dimension of mass opinion that is at best tenuously linked to political action and social processes. Ginsberg boldly asserts that "polling has contributed to the domestication of opinion by helping to transform it from a politically potent, often disruptive force into a more docile, plebiscitary phenomenon" (1986, 60). The evidence on which critics draw to support this claim is that legislators who once relied on a diverse range of expressions of public opinion—local newspapers, visits with their constituents, letters from their districts, and interest groups—were now increasingly looking to opinion polls.

In an analysis of emergence of the straw poll, Susan Herbst (1995) demonstrates that this shift is emblematic of a deeper shift in underlying conceptions of public opinion. In particular, Herbst notes a critical shift from public opinion as the product of groups (especially, political parties) to public opinion as "an aggregation of atomized, anonymous individuals" (99). The paradoxical result is that public opinion ceases to be *public*. As Lynn Sanders observes, "because of the analytic and measurement strategies of survey researchers, public opinion has become literally private and only figuratively public" (1999, 263).

Moreover, Bourdieu argues that politics involves conflicts in which citizens must take sides. Hence Bourdieu distinguishes opinion as measured through polls from opinion that influences political action ("mobilized opinion"), and argues that opinion research should focus on how individuals' opinions on an issue become mobilized and activated. These points should not be unfamiliar: they echo the arguments for an active, group-based approach to mass opinion from chapter 1. Recall Blumer's assertion that public opinion is fundamentally a collective product "having its setting in a society and . . . being a function of that society in operation" (1948, 543). As we noted in chapter 1 and, more important, as we shall see in this chapter, such a conception of mass opinion is especially relevant to a study of elite opinion theories and to an understanding of how racial attitudes became activated during the civil rights movement.

The cumulative effect of these critiques is that exclusive reliance on survey data as a measure of public opinion may lead to an impoverished or inaccurate understanding of what public opinion is and what its role in democratic regimes ought to be. The ascendance of survey research is accompanied by a shift in focus from public opinion as the subject of theoretical speculation to public opinion as the object of empirical inquiry. A casualty of this shift is that the normative and conceptual parameters of public opinion largely become presumed, rather than interrogated, to the neglect of alternate parameters of public opinion. And with the growing dominance of opinion polls, pollsters and survey research centers increasingly command authority over the substantive parameters of public opinion as well—over what, when, and how mass opinion is measured, analyzed, and interpreted.

ACCOMMODATING CRITICS AND ELITE OPINION THEORY

Survey researchers are not without rejoinder to these critics. The possibility that our contemporary conception of public opinion may be problematic—whether a bureaucratic invention, an instrument of state control, or simply a captive of the agenda control of survey researchers—does not, in itself, preclude an action or expression from being reliably categorized as an instance of public opinion. Note that Blumer does not argue that public opinion cannot be operationalized, merely that such operationalization should not be conflated or confused with the underlying construct itself. And Bourdieu himself suggests that "polls can make a useful contribution to social science if they are treated rigorously and with certain precautions" (1979, 124).[21]

From the standpoint of the practice of survey research, many of the attacks levied against poll data are capable of being accommodated, and have been. Survey researchers have examined nonrespondents, included open-ended questions, clarified context effects such as question wording and question order, refined sampling techniques, interpreted race-of-interviewer effects, and incorporated uncertainty and heterogeneity of responses.[22] The progress in survey research techniques and the sheer accumulation of knowledge about what the public thinks have been so impressive that Eleanor Singer begins her editor's introduction to the fiftieth anniversary issue of *Public Opinion Quarterly* with the bold proclamation of three words: "Blumer was wrong" (1987, S1).

From the standpoint of theory, practitioners themselves have engaged in ontological skepticism about what opinion polls really measure. Recall from chapter 1 that public opinion, as measured by surveys, provokes some thorny questions about the competence of the democratic public. John Zaller and his contemporaries respond to this challenge by revising our traditional view that polls measure stable and coherent underlying attitudes.[23] Zaller abandons "the conventional but implausible view that citizens typically possess 'true attitudes' on every issue about which a pollster may happen to inquire" (1992, 35). In its place, he presents a more situational account of how people respond to polls and proposes that we use the more fitting terminology of "opinion statements" (instead of "public opinion") to describe what polls measure. Ordinary individuals may not necessarily have the topics in which pollsters are interested at the top of their minds. And for this reason, not all individuals will express informed, intelligible responses to survey questions.

These methodological and theoretical refinements surely yield a more apposite, adaptable view of how to use opinion surveys and what they tell us about public opinion. Yet accommodating such a revised view is not without peril. This is particularly so when we juxtapose the potential pitfall of relying exclusively on survey data with the critical consideration of elite opinion theory from chapter 1. If "true attitudes" are acknowledged not to exist, then we invariably broach the possibility that Ginsberg correctly implicates opinion polls as a tool for state control or that Habermas correctly diagnoses mass opinion as the product of elite manipulation.[24] Zaller himself notes that one consequence of his modified view of "opinion statements" is that citizens "pay too little attention to public affairs to be able to respond critically to the political communications they encounter; rather, they are blown about by whatever current of information manages to develop the greater intensity" (1992, 311).[25]

On this point, accepting a more adaptable view of "opinion statements" has consequences for whether we think that poll data can comprehensively measure the full gamut of public opinion. Opinion surveys hold de facto agenda control over what questions to ask, and when and how to ask them. Thus the potential slippage between public opinion and survey data is negligible only if polling centers produce surveys that ask about the issues that are actually engaging the public at a given moment. In particular, if citizens do not always possess "true attitudes" on the questions that pollsters ask about, then it is also likely that there are matters on which citizens do hold informed and intelligible opinions that pollsters *do not* ask about. As Beniger observes, "survey research does not arise from a need to speak one's mind . . . but rather from the need to find out what is on people's minds— whether they intend to speak them or not" (1983, 482). In short, "public opinion" as gauged from survey responses may differ crucially from "public opinion" as revealed through political action.

Furthermore, the validity and reliability of opinion polls may depend not only on *whether* they ask the questions that are actually on the minds of ordinary individuals, but also on *when* they ask them. If Roosevelt's victory in the 1936 election boldfaces the spectacular success of opinion surveys, then Truman's unexpected victory in the 1948 election footnotes the dramatic failure of opinion surveys. In the latter case, the media and the pollsters on which they relied took Dewey's reasonably strong lead (five percentage points) into mid-October as sufficiently decisive to render a prediction in Dewey's favor. Yet they were caught off guard precisely because they failed to survey voter sentiments at a time when public momentum was actively shifting from Dewey to Truman.

The consequence of this potential mismatch between survey responses and the public's underlying "true" opinion is that polls, used exclusively, may be insufficient to adequately discriminate elite from non-elite influences on mass opinion. Barring foresight or serendipity, pollsters may view an emerging issue as worth asking about *only after* receiving cues (elite or non-elite) that the issue is significant and salient at the level of mass publics.[26] In fact, if polling centers themselves depend on elite cues to decide which issues to ask about, this will predispose opinion research to confirm elite theories. Moreover, even if foresight and serendipity are forthcoming, survey research centers are often constrained by periodic administration (for example, the biennial American National Election Studies), by fiscal constraints, and by the production time required to develop a survey instrument, pretest it, and send it out to the field. Except in experimentally designed survey settings or under fortuitous circumstances, surveys may well tap into the public's mind only after its gaze on a particular issue is engaged and transformed. Thus, surveys may fail to capture non-elite influences on mass opinion (even if they exist) at precisely the time they occur.[27] This possibility is not just a methodological point, but one that bears important substantive implications.

THE PRODUCTION OF RACIAL ATTITUDE ITEMS

Take the current subject of racial attitudes. The question of whether opinion research leads or follows opinion change is embedded in a troubled history of academic research on race. In the nineteenth century, such research by biologists and social scientists (under the rubric of phylogeny, craniometry, and the like) effectively legitimated and perpetuated racist views of nonwhites and segregationist regimes such as the Jim Crow South. Until recent decades, moreover, social scientists either left race off their agenda or continued to examine it within revamped but equally discreditable frameworks of analysis.[28] Along these lines, Hanes Walton and his colleagues argue that

> American political science responded to this concatenation of developments with its own hands-off policy; and when political scientists . . . did take up the issue of race, they usually did so in terms that one can only describe as racist. Moreover, the solutions they sought for the race "problem" often turned out to be little more than justifications for segregation. In other words, political science was responding to realities and reflecting ideologies outside the walls of the academy. (1995, 146) [29]

Thus they implicate political science research on race as emblematic of the historical and political currents of its time, such as social Darwinism and Jim Crow. "The sad fact," add Michael Dawson and Ernest Wilson, "remains that the study of African-American politics still is the stepchild of the discipline" (1991, 192).

This "invisibility" of African Americans has been noted with survey research as well. Despite such early bellwethers as Gunnar Myrdal's *An American Dilemma* (1944) and surveys conducted by the National Opinion Research Center (under the auspices of the Office of War Information) in the 1940s, the polling community has been slow to conduct surveys on race relations. As Wade Smith notes, Myrdal's juxtaposition of the egalitarian principles of "the American creed" with inegalitarian, racist practices toward African Americans largely set the agenda for the survey research. Thus researchers for the most part came to focus on the racial attitudes of white Americans, with the presumption that "blacks' opinions on racial matters were obvious" (1987, 443). Or, when the attitudes of African Americans were examined, it was done primarily *in relation to* the attitudes of white Americans. Thus it is only recently, with surveys such as the 1984 and 1988 National Black Election Studies and the 1993–94 National Black Politics Study, that there has been significant scholarly interest in the attitudes of racial minorities in themselves.[30]

Ira Katznelson (1971) and others controversially allege that the study of African American politics was pursued with a seriousness of purpose only after black insurgency in the 1950s and 1960s successfully pushed race onto the American political agenda. This suggestion—that the production of data and research on racial politics lags behind and responds to actual political events—lies at the heart of our skepticism concerning survey data's ability to adequately test theories of opinion dynamics. We have already seen some faint evidence for the possibility that survey research on racial attitudes actually follows important shifts in mass opinion, rather than mirrors or anticipates them. Recall from earlier in this chapter that the percentage of increase in research on race in *Public Opinion Quarterly* using survey data appears to lag behind the increase in all *POQ* articles using survey data across comparable time periods. Also, we noted at the end of chapter 2 that survey questions on race and racial policy during the civil rights movement are somewhat incomplete and inadequate to the empirical tasks we want them to perform. Recall that the American National Election Study—perhaps the most important source of survey data on U.S. politics—did not contain good measures of racial group consciousness or racial animosity until 1972, and the first extensive measures of "core values" did not appear until 1984. As we shall see in chapter 6, racial group interests, group conflict, and cherished political values are critical influences on the public's views about the civil rights movement. Questions on these critical dimensions of racial attitudes thus appeared only after the height of movement activism and after the allegedly critical period of opinion change (the mid-1960s) in elite accounts of racial attitudes.

That said, at the micro-level of individual questions, the production of poll data on racial politics appears to mirror events fairly well, at least at first blush. The earliest poll data on race are found in January and then again in October–November 1937, when the American Institute of Public Opinion (AIPO, subsequently Gallup) asked the public about whether Congress should make lynching a federal crime.[31] The AIPO then asked the public in February 1941 whether the poll tax should be abolished. Then, on three separate occasions in 1948 (March, late November, and early December), the AIPO polled the public about their views on President Truman's proposal to pass sweeping civil rights legislation. The poll question that marks the onset of what we generally consider the civil rights movement was asked in May 1954 (again, by the AIPO) and concerned the Supreme Court's ruling on segregated schools, *Brown v. Board of Education of Topeka*. The AIPO asked this question again in April 1955, November 1955, December 1956, April 1957, December 1957, May–June 1959, and May–June 1961.

Two features characterize these early polls on racial politics. They all concern legislative issues and, by corollary, all such poll items are framed around elite politics. Thus there are no questions to be found on the Montgomery bus boycott. Even with events such as the Little Rock crisis in 1957, the two poll questions concern public views on the actions of President Eisenhower and Arkansas governor Faubus. Even in the 1960s, most of the questions ask about the actions of political elites, such as President Kennedy's decision to send U.S. marshals to Montgomery and the Supreme Court's decision that public accommodations (trains, buses, public waiting rooms) must be integrated. Thus the timing of poll questions may closely parallel actual events prior to the onset of civil rights movement activism, but they do so primarily in response to elite politics.

There are some exceptions, but not until the 1960s. The AIPO poll in May–June 1961 also asked whether respondents had heard of the Freedom Riders and, if so, whether or not they approved of their actions. The same AIPO poll asked whether respondents believed that black insurgency through acts such as lunch counter sit-ins and freedom rides were helping the cause of integration. An AIPO poll in August 1963 asked whether respondents had heard of the planned March on Washington and, if so, whether they supported or opposed such a public demonstration.[32] Note that in each of these cases, polls were asking about events staged by movement activists *once the civil rights movement was well under way.* A similar relation persisted as the activism proliferated into northern cities and exploded in urban uprisings in the mid-to-late 1960s. Polls by Harris (Brink and Harris 1964, 1966), the Survey Research Center (Campbell and Schuman 1968), and others followed quickly on the heels of these changes, but they were ultimately *reactive* to them.

Thus the suggestion that the production of poll data on racial politics lags behind the actual course of political events remains. To examine the relation between survey research into racial attitudes and the course of racial politics itself more closely, I enumerated all poll questions on race from 1937 to 1972. Figure 3.1 presents the results of this count aggregated over time.[33] These results strongly point to a time-dependent relation between the rise of racial attitude items and the rise of civil rights on the national agenda. Racial attitude items, notably, track closely the unfolding civil rights movement—with the early rise of survey items in the mid-to-late 1950s and an explosion in survey items by the early 1960s.

The production of poll questions on race do not always exclusively follow the insurgent activism of African Americans. Figure 3.1 prominently shows a significant number of racial attitude items in 1942 and 1944, well before the putative onset of the civil rights movement. This anomaly is almost entirely the result of two surveys conducted by the National Opinion Research Center under the auspices of the Office of War Information's Surveys Division. Credit for these early polls goes to the OWI, which needed to have accurate surveys of civilian sentiments and military morale, and to NORC founder Harry Field, whose mission was to conduct academic research on issue domains that, left to the private sector, would be neglected.[34]

Figure 3.2 compares the rise in survey items on race to the number of events initiated by civil rights movement activism from 1948 to 1965. Here

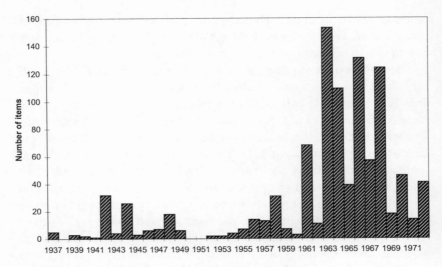

Figure 3.1   Number of Survey Items on Race, 1937–72

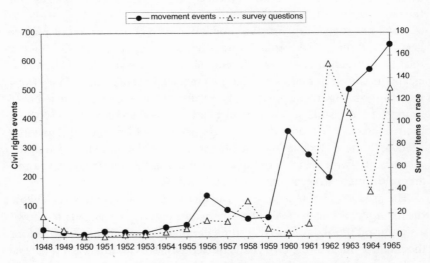

Figure 3.2   Movement-Initiated Events and Survey Questions, 1948–65

the visual evidence more directly demonstrates that opinion research followed the mobilization of mass politics vis-à-vis the civil rights movement. Note that jumps in movement activism between 1955 and 1956 and 1959 and 1960 are followed by jumps in survey items between 1957 and 1962. With respect to elite opinion theories, it is important to note that the time series of civil rights events chosen is deliberately a *non-elite* measure of political events. [35] And the two events that appear to galvanize interest in polling on racial attitudes are clearly movement-initiated: the Montgomery bus boycott from late 1955 through 1956 and the lunch counter sit-ins throughout the South in the spring of 1960.

If (very generous) allowances for the small number observations are permitted, this visual evidence can be put through a more rigorous statistical test. Specifically, the relation between survey questions on race and civil rights movement–initiated events over time can be estimated by a simplified time-series (autoregressive distributed lag) model.[36] Put plainly, such a model estimates the number of racial attitude items in a given year as a function of the number of movement-initiated events in previous years—in this case, one, two, and three years prior—controlling for the carryover effect of racial attitude items from previous years. The results of such a test are unambiguous. The number of movement-initiated events in a given year strongly predicts the number of racial attitude items the following year, controlling for the number of racial attitude items in the initial year. Although this is obviously underspecified as a general model of survey production, the number of movement-initiated events in a given year even appears to influence the number of racial attitude items two years later.

TOWARD A PLURALISTIC APPROACH

My purpose in this chapter has not been to distill and defend a particular conception of public opinion as optimal. Rather, it has been to establish the sovereign status of survey data in the measurement and study of public opinion, and then uncover some essential tensions and important limitations that follow from that sovereign status. As I have shown, the claim that survey data are equated with the construct of public opinion is well grounded: more than 90 percent of research articles on public opinion today rely on survey data. Moreover, I have argued that public opinion *qua* survey data bounds our conceptual, normative, and substantive understanding of mass opinion. Conceptually, public opinion *qua* survey data takes the form of the discrete and equally weighted responses of anonymous individuals within the survey setting. Normatively, public opinion *qua* survey data draws its rhetorical authority from an aggregative, majoritarian mechanism of democratic choice and a delegative system of representation. Substantively, public opinion *qua* survey data delimits our knowledge of the public's viewpoints: what they are, how they are formed, and when they are expressed.

These boundaries on public opinion hold some potentially critical reverberations for elite opinion theories. As I have argued, survey data, used alone, may not satisfactorily discriminate between theories of opinion dynamics. Because the production of survey items may follow the activation and transformation of mass opinion (rather than parallel or anticipate such changes), the relevant survey items may merit asking only after the fact. And in fact, racial attitude items do appear to lag behind the mobilization of events in the evolving civil rights movements.

This limitation is especially relevant to a consideration of racial attitudes during the civil rights era in the United States. For one thing, equating public opinion with the political viewpoints of the voting electorate is dubious in a nation in which race and gender have historically been used as the grounds for an exclusionary conception of citizenship.[37] Metaphorically and in actuality, African Americans have been essentially invisible on the punch cards of opinion polls until the 1960s. Significantly, the place for African Americans in the polls (both the voting booth and the opinion survey) was in part won outside of, and as a direct challenge to, the conception of democracy implicit in opinion polls.

Furthermore, because survey data potentially delimit a fairly narrow conception of public opinion (again, as the aggregation of individual viewpoints, measured anonymously and discretely), using survey data alone will rule out the more dynamic, active, and group-based manifestations of mass beliefs and sentiments. Such a broader conception of public opinion is especially relevant to the study of racial attitudes during the civil rights movement. This is most obviously because social movements, as noted in chapter 1, entail the dynamic interaction and mobilization of group interests — at least initially, outside of formal political channels. What's more, a more dynamic, active, group-based conception of public opinion is especially relevant because it more aptly describes African American political life.[38] Taken together, then, these points make a strong case for a pluralistic approach to opinion data and for research that uses alternate conceptions of mass opinion. In chapter 4, I turn to one such alternate conception: letters that ordinary citizens write to the president.

FOUR

CONSTITUENCY MAIL AS PUBLIC OPINION

See for yourself, listen for yourself, think for yourself.
—Malcolm X

The opinion survey would be closer to reality if it totally violated the rules of objectivity and gave people the means to situate themselves as they really do in practice, in relation to already formulated opinions.
—Pierre Bourdieu

In chapter 3, I established the ascendance of survey data in empirical studies of public opinion. One result of this sovereign status is that much opinion research today simply presumes a conception of public opinion, to the neglect of alternative conceptions. This presumption ultimately limits what we know *substantively* about how individuals reason, think, feel, and act with respect to political matters. It also begs the question of whether such a restricted view gives solace or sobriety to the role of public opinion in democratic theory. These points bear directly on what we make of elite opinion theories and how we study racial attitudes. In particular, how we conceptualize and measure public opinion at the outset is critical to our resultant substantive understanding of its nature and dynamics.

In this chapter, I examine constituency mail—specifically, the letters that ordinary individuals write to their president—as an alternate measure of mass opinion that is especially well suited to a study of racial attitudes during the civil rights years. Letters to the president satisfy the precondition of *opinion*, in that these are neither random thoughts nor logical proofs but,

on the whole, reasoned and deliberated expressions of one's personal beliefs and sentiments. Letters also satisfy the precondition of *public* opinion
in that they are political views of some consequence. There is, prima facie,
good cause to believe that citizen correspondence tells us something meaningful about public opinion.

Yet the move away from survey data is still a risky one. Even if one concedes that alternative measures—from letters to public demonstrations to
Internet chat rooms—aptly capture "public opinion," the empirical analysis of such expressions lacks the conceptual clarity or established guide-
lines of inquiry we enjoy with survey research. I begin with a brief overview
of the history and scholarship on political letter-writing. I then examine the
motivations for letter-writing and the information that those letters convey
to political actors, making pointed comparisons to survey response. This
comparison points us to several characteristics that make constituency mail
an especially apt measure of the activation of mass opinion during the civil
rights movement. I describe my database of letters to the president on race
from 1948 to 1965 and show that these letters are a valid indicator of activated mass opinion in the aggregate. I conclude by giving a flavor of the
multiple dimensions of constituency mail as a more proactive form of opinion data in which the correspondent decides what, when, and how to voice
her political views.

LETTER-WRITING IN HISTORICAL CONTEXT

On September 22, 1862, more than three months before his Emancipation
Proclamation would become official (on January 1, 1863), President Abraham Lincoln issued a preliminary version of this monumental decree. The
public's reaction was swift. On September 25, 1862, a Baltimore gentle-
man named George Cassaru sent Lincoln a barrel filled with a half-dozen
hams as a "tribute of respect from one whose Unionism knows no compro-
mise." [1] Two days later, the local officers of the Pennsylvania Anti-Slavery
Society mailed the president a copy of their resolution of "inexpressible
satisfaction" at Lincoln's proclamation. The society's corresponding secretary, J. M. McKim, added,

> The joy which your great proclamation imparts is not a kind that shows itself
> in noisy demonstration, nor is its extent and depth to be judged of by outward
> appearance. The virtuous, the reflecting, the intelligently patriotic, the people
> in whom inheres the nation's life, the people who make—not those who
> speculate in, public opinion, these are they who, as one man, hail your edict
> with delight.

CONSTITUENCY MAIL AS PUBLIC OPINION

In the months and years to follow, this burst of joy and gratitude was complemented by other letters from southern whites demanding the return of their slaves, northern abolitionists urging monetary means of hastening emancipation, and African Americans throughout the states seeking to extend Lincoln's scope to realms such as equal pay for black soldiers and redress for the generally abhorrent material conditions they faced. In fact, in November 1864, a still somewhat obscure German economist named Karl Marx wrote to Lincoln on behalf of the International Working Men's Association, congratulating the president on his re-election and lauding him for his "triumphant" emancipatory position in the "American Anti-Slavery War."

Harold Holzer, the compiler of two volumes of letters to Lincoln, notes that the president found great value in such offerings. Lincoln is credited with the observation that "Public sentiment is everything" (1998, xvi), he refers wryly to his twice-weekly office hours with constituents as "public opinion baths," and he also notes that although "many of the matters brought to my notice are utterly frivolous . . . others are of more or less importance, and all serve to renew in me a clearer and more vivid image of that great popular assemblage out of which I sprung, and to which . . . I must return" (xx). No surprise, then, that Holzer concludes from his study of letters to Lincoln that "just as these letters reflect the wide variety of their authors' opinions, interests, priorities, fears, joys, and resentments, they also hold up a priceless collective mirror onto public opinion" (xvi).

Written contact with our elected officials—whether to apply political pressure, to gain favor or fortune, or simply to share intimate insights with a political celebrity—has long been a cherished mode of expressing public opinion. Other examples that harken through history are notable and numerous. Possibly the first successful politically motivated letter-writing campaign in the United States contributed to George Washington's decision to run for a second term. Dwight Eisenhower, 160 years later, also chose to seek the presidency in the aftermath of a deluge of public mail. And an infamous letter from a private citizen, Albert Einstein, to Franklin Delano Roosevelt ultimately changed the course of World War II and immutably altered foreign affairs for the balance of the twentieth century.[2]

Although these letters initially reflected only the voice of a landed, educated, white male elite, constituency mail has since evolved into a more egalitarian, democratic mode of expression for ordinary citizens. Today, constituency mail is handled within the division of White House Operations, in the Correspondence Office.[3] In 1993, the Clinton presidency's

correspondence staff included one assistant to the president for correspondence, two assistants to the assistant, seven letter-writers, sixty sec-
retaries, and about three hundred volunteers.[4] In the type of letters, constituency mail captures a striking diversity of messages from ordinary
citizens ranging from issue-specific opinions, political fan mail, tips on
campaign-strategy, congratulatory messages, and requests for personal services ("casework").[5]

Despite the political significance of letter-writing as a mode of public
political expression, examination of constituency mail is largely absent
from studies of public opinion today.[6] Given the dominance of survey data
vis-à-vis *any* alternative modes of expressing opinions (as we saw in chapter
3), this should hardly surprise. As with other alternatives, letter-writing has
not always been so absent from opinion research. Constituency mail was
an important element of opinion research done through Columbia University's Bureau of Applied Social Research in the 1940s and 1950s, and
the spring issue of *Public Opinion Quarterly* in 1956 included four articles
that focus on letter-writing.[7] What we know about letter-writing from
these early studies is that at least as far back as Abraham Lincoln and William McKinley, presidents have paid attention to constituency mail and attempted to distinguish between mail from privileged acquaintances, from
organized pressure groups, and from ordinary individuals writing on their
own behalf.[8]

The volume of letters (weighted by the number of literate adults in the
population) written to the presidents from William F. McKinley to Ronald
Reagan is shown in table 4.1. In sheer numbers, table 4.1 shows an unmistakable rise in letter-writing over time. Measured as the number of letters
per day per 10,000 literate adults in the general population, the rate of
letter-writing grew from an index of roughly 5 under McKinley to about 12
under Herbert Hoover before the stock market crash, and 111 in the late
1930s during Roosevelt's days. The rate of letter-writing not only grew during these years but peaked and troughed in response to specific crises such
as the Civil War, the Spanish-American War, World War I, and the Great
Depression.

Table 4.1 also shows that letter-writing reached a higher equilibrium
with the advent of the Franklin D. Roosevelt presidency. As others have
noted, Roosevelt was the first modern president to methodically gauge public opinion, and letters from constituents became one measure (alongside
poll data secretly provided by Hadley Cantril) in his repository of public
barometers.[9] As Robert Merton notes,

Table 4.1   Volume of Presidential Mail, McKinley to Reagan

William F. McKinley (1900)	5
Herbert Hoover (pre-Crash)	12
Franklin D. Roosevelt (late 1930s)	111
Harry S. Truman (1948)	104
Dwight D. Eisenhower (1952)	103
John F. Kennedy	99
Lyndon B. Johnson	84
Richard M. Nixon	130
Gerald R. Ford	112
Jimmy Carter	158
Ronald Reagan	245

SOURCE: Sussmann 1963, Patterson 1988, U.S. Census.

NOTE: The volume of letters to the president is weighted as the number of letters per day per 10,000 literate adults in the general population, following Sussmann. Data for McKinley through Eisenhower are from Sussmann (1963); data for Kennedy through Ford are calculated using yearly averages from Patterson (1988) and U.S. Census data for the mid-point of each administration. Neither Patterson nor Sussmann give details on how they estimated the number of letters for these administrations, so there is no way of confirming whether or not these are compatible measures of volume. The metric (volume per 10,000 literate adults) is ungraceful but nonetheless gives us some tracking volume, controlling for demographic change over time. There is some evidence that Ira Smith, the original source of these figures and clerk in the White House from 1897 to 1948, may have exaggerated the volume of mail, at least during FDR's administrations (see Sussmann 1956).

> [J]ust as he reshaped the role of the president during his unprecedented series of terms in office, so, more than any that went before him, he reshaped the practice of using mass mail. He gave it new vigor. He developed it from a statistical resultant of many individual decisions to write him into a complex institution, fitted out with distinctive modes of operation, multiple functions and a diversified personnel equipped to make mass correspondence a device for political action. . . . It was he, more than any other person, who turned mass mail into the functional equivalent of an episodic plebiscite. (Sussmann 1963, xv)

Roosevelt insisted on personally reading a cross-section of these letters, which were then used in his press releases or used as early signals on whether to push more aggressively or retreat on important issues.[10] At times, Roosevelt would even actively solicit letters to garner political capital for a particular policy he wished to promote.

It is perhaps no coincidence, then, that systematic research on presidential mail begins with Roosevelt.[11] And these studies are fairly clear about Roosevelt's decisive imprint on this medium of political expression. Leila Sussman concludes from her analysis of constituency mail during the Roosevelt administrations that "[p]olitical mail is part of the new machinery for quickly converting latent political sentiment into effective political demand. Letter-writing is a sufficiently accepted feature of our political life to be called an institution" (1963, 191). Sussman identifies several factors leading to this institutionalization of letter-writing, such as the sheer magnitude of public need incurred during the Great Depression, Roosevelt's personal popularity, the rising literacy of the American public, the growth of the mass media, and the transformation of the citizen's relationship to the state that resulted from the New Deal.

The methods used to analyze constituency mail in these earlier studies may strike contemporary opinion scholars as somewhere between inappropriate and anachronous. In one study, Rowena Wyant coded for the types of stationery used, complexity of vocabulary, and a "cultural index" drawn from handwriting analysis. These curiosities notwithstanding, the conclusions about constituency mail from these early studies presage more recent, more systematic analyses of letter-writing using survey data. These earlier studies also nicely outline some of the limiting constraints and selective advantages of constituency mail. Wyant and Herta Herzog, for example, write that

> A new way of writing history is to be found in analysis of the content of the letters. . . . Granting that the letter-writing sample is a sample biased for age, economic, educational and other factors, and granting that there is evidence of the power of pressure groups, still the letters represent a more spontaneous integrated reaction to the governmental bill than do the responses elicited by the public opinion polls. Letter analysis . . . points to standards and factual representations rampant in the active, literate part of the populace who indulge in congressional letter-writing. (1941, 590–91)

In current political science research, letter-writing is most commonly examined under the rubric of political participation.[12] Using opinion surveys, these studies consider letter-writing together with a range of other participatory acts such as voting, working on a campaign, joining an organization, attending a political rally, displaying bumper stickers or buttons, contributing money, and attempting to sway someone's vote. Most often, letter-writing is simply indexed along with other nonvoting acts. Studies show that the rate of letter-writing in the general population, when examined separately, has been remarkably consistent over time.[13] A 1946 Gallup poll showed that 15 percent of respondents had written or telegraphed their congresspersons or senators. A 1946 NORC poll showed that 14 percent of respondents had written their congressman or some other government official. When Roper Center data from 1973 to 1990 are pooled together, the rate of letter-writing remains at about 15 percent of the electorate.[14]

The other salient finding from these poll-based studies of letter-writing is that correspondents are not randomly distributed throughout the general electorate. That is, consistent with the earlier Columbia University studies of constituency mail, there is considerable selection bias to letter-writing. Thus Rosenstone and Hansen find that whereas 15 percent of members of the general public write their elected officials, among African Americans, this rate falls to only 5 percent (1993, 43). This racial differential was generally true even during the supposed height of the civil rights movement. Data from the 1964 American National Election Studies show that whereas 14 percent of the total sample wrote to a public official, only 5 percent of African Americans did so.

In addition to race, there are other enduring sociodemographic differences in one's propensity to contact elected officials. As with political participation generally, individuals from the higher socioeconomic echelons (usually measured by family income and educational attainment) write more frequently.[15] Rosenstone and Hansen, for example, find that about 25 percent of individuals in the two highest income quantiles write to Congress, whereas slightly more than 10 percent of individuals in the two lowest income quantiles write to Congress. About 25 percent of individuals with a college education write to Congress, whereas slightly more than 5 percent of individuals with less than a ninth-grade education write to Congress (1993, 46–49).[16]

INCENTIVES AND INFORMATION IN LETTER-WRITING

These differences in who writes and under what conditions they do so reflect tangible differences in incentives, resources, and mobilization between whites and nonwhites and between the well-off and the disadvantaged. For some well-connected citizens, political contact with elected officials may require no greater force than the will to pick up a pen, dial a number, or get online. For others less privileged, such an act may require desperation, heroism, irrationality, or some combination of these. When letters are written under such different circumstances, they reflect different dimensions of public opinion. In this section, I consider more analytically what constituency mail tells us as a source of opinion data, in particular, as compared to opinion polls. Specifically, the discussion is centered on two questions about letter-writing: (1) what motivates an individual to write constituency mail, and (2) what kind of information does such correspondence convey to elite actors?[17]

From the "personal" standpoint of the incentives facing ordinary individuals, political participation of any sort—whether voting, responding to surveys, or writing letters—is a fit of irrationality.[18] Letters to elected officials take time, effort, and literacy, with little prospect of material benefit. Even if one accepts the seemingly antiquated view that citizens are obliged to let their representatives know their mind on political affairs, it is always more rational to "free-ride" and let someone else do the work for you. Yet pollsters keep finding individuals willing to respond to their queries, and the mail rooms of elected officials constantly remain flooded with all manner of correspondence from constituents.[19] Politics may be a mostly instrumental and strategic affair, but rationality alone explains too little of the stuff of politics.

In thinking about what motivates particular expressions of public opinion, then, it is useful to consider both material and nonmaterial incentives. Studies of political participation often distinguish between material, solidary, and purposive incentives.[20] Material incentives are tangible (generally monetary) payoffs; solidary benefits are societal, intangible benefits, such as social standing and friendship; and purposive benefits are processual payoffs that result from the act of participation itself, such as a sense of self-mastery, contribution to a cause, or accomplishment of a task. In a given situation, such incentives must exceed disincentives for a particular expression of public opinion to come to pass. Such barriers include the time, material resources, individual effort, and personal competence that a particular act requires.[21]

Given these incentives and disincentives, how do surveys, letter-writing, and other modes of expressing public opinion compare? First, the very idea of discussing the incentives to respond to surveys may seem odd, since individuals cannot proactively *decide* to respond to a survey without first being (randomly) chosen from a pool of potential respondents. Simply put, survey response occurs when a stranger knocks on the door or rings the telephone and you *don't* decline an interview. Viewed thus, survey response entails some cost (that is, it takes time, effort, competence, trust). It is characterized as much by solidary incentives—social desirability, conformity, norms of cooperation, and the like—not to say no to someone's request for your time, attention, and honest viewpoints as it is by incentives to act.[22] As such, it is perhaps better viewed as an *expressive* form of political action than as an *instrumental* form of political action.[23]

Unlike surveys, letter-writing is a proactive form of political expression. As such, incentives alone do not fully explain whether, when, and how letter-writing occurs. Rather, motivations interact with the resources at one's disposal and the degree to which organizations mobilize one to act. This dynamic is reflected in the diversity of contexts in which letter-writing takes place. For one thing, material incentives sometimes motivate letter-writing, unlike survey response. Individuals occasionally solicit gainful employment or government assistance in personal matters. And organizations or other collectivities sometimes seek material benefits by advocating legislative change, government regulation, or juridical action. In addition, correspondence—co-authored letters, petitions, mass mailing, organizational mail—sometimes results from social interactions that confer solidary and purposive benefits not available from survey responses.[24] And, when letter-writing occurs in the heat of political contest—whether during a political campaign, or a legislative session, or a social movement—ample purposive benefits are likely to accrue.

These differences between survey responses and letter-writing are also reflected in the information that is conveyed to elite political actors. For one thing, different expressions of opinion tell political actors different things about the preferences of the polity. The collective voice of thousands of African American men on the steps of the nation's Capitol during the "Million Man March" tells quite a different story than the collective voice of thousands of Irish Americans parading in green garb across an emerald-streaked Chicago River for a Saint Patrick's Day parade. Similarly, political graffiti scrawled in the men's room of a diner in Bozeman, Montana, tells quite a different story about public opinion than a full-page letter of political dissent written by the "Unabomber" in the *New York Times* and the *Washington Post*.

To be more systematic about it, we might identify differences across modes of public opinion on four dimensions of "publicity" that distinguish the kind of information that is conveyed to elite political actors: (1) size, (2) salience, (3) anonymity, and (4) coordination.[25] Size informs political actors about the sheer magnitude (or potential magnitude) of opinion. A particular act of public expression might voice the sentiments of a lone individual or a sizeable collectivity. An opinion poll, literally, tells elite actors about the opinions of five hundred to two thousand anonymous individuals. Figuratively, when that poll is randomly sampled throughout the country, it speaks for the entire nation as well. With constituency mail, size is a more shifting target. Letters from private citizens only voice the sentiments of a lone individual, whereas organizational mail and collective mail can purport to speak for a much larger "public." A letter advocating women's reproductive rights from the National Organization for Women, for example, speaks not just for the particular NOW representative who penned the correspondence but also for NOW's quarter million members and perhaps an even larger number of individuals who support NOW's position on women's reproductive rights.

Coordination informs political actors about the degree of collective action and organizational mobilization involved in a particular political expression. Letters from isolated individuals, for example, usually do not depend on interacting with others or recruitment by organizations. By contrast, mobilizing voter turnout on election day or collecting signatures for a petition can require a great deal of coordination. Coordination, however, is not simply a function of size. Large-scale acts of public expression such as rioting often require spatial and temporal coordination (that is, rioting occurs at a common place at a common time) but little coordination of incentives or institutional mobilization. With surveys, polling firms expend a great deal of institutional resources to organize interviewers and recruit a sufficiently large response. But there is almost no coordination among respondents.

Anonymity informs political actors about whether or not an expression is visible to others or privately voiced. Forms of expression such as riots and demonstrations are public events that entail social dynamics such as contagion, conformity, and social desirability. Individual letters are generally anonymous (to anyone other than the individual correspondent and her addressee), but some forms of letter-writing, such as organized mail and petitions, are visible in their making. With opinion polls, the interview is conducted in anonymity, with the identity of respondents always kept in strict confidence. The opinions expressed in polls become visible to political actors as an aggregate conception (for example, as the percentage of the electorate who support a particular candidate or policy).

Finally, salience informs political actors about how much weight to give to a particular public expression. To the extent that electoral considerations dominate elite actors' political calculus, political salience should vary as a function of the constituency involved: a politically active public, an issue-centered public, a politically attentive public, the voting public, or the general public writ large.[26] In addition, certain instances of political expression, such as riots and revolutions, achieve political salience without any direct electoral considerations to speak of. Letters from individuals are unlikely to be salient unless the volume is especially high or the correspondent is especially prominent. Individual letters are also, however, often taken as a more valid indicator of what the "average" constituency thinks than "pressure" mail that comes from organizations or groups. That said, political actors can seldom afford to ignore such pressure mail. By contrast, surveys—vis-à-vis their claims to produce instantaneous tribunals from the general electorate—should enjoy a fairly high degree of political salience. That of polls will of course vary with the kind of survey conducted, the reputation of the pollsters involved, how newsworthy the substantive findings are, and the like.

ANALYTICAL ADVANTAGES OF CONSTITUENCY MAIL

This discussion of the incentives that motivate political expression and the information that this expression conveys to political elites gives us some stylized ways of thinking about how letter-writing differs from survey response. There is yet another difference between correspondence and polls that underlies this discussion: polls are a relatively standardized product. Opinion surveys may differ by polling firm, sample size, sampling frame, and the like, but the incentives facing survey respondents and the characteristics of publicity that elites read generally do not vary across polls. With letter-writing, these characteristics are apt to vary with context. When the chorus of letter writers generally sings, it is with an upward bias in socioeconomic status and a white bias in racial representation. Yet for a given issue, certain segments of the general public are likelier than others to care enough to actively voice an opinion. And at certain times, the nation as a whole may become activated and likelier to take up vocal forms of political expression. This context-specificity hints at some distinctive analytical advantages to using constituency mail as an alternative to survey data.

At heart, letter-writing varies with the circumstances because it is a costly undertaking that requires a high degree of personal investment. Thus conceived, public opinion is not, as Walter Lippmann observes, "the voice of God, nor the voice of society, but the voice of the interested spectators of action" (1925, 92). As a result, such correspondence informs elite actors about the preferences of an active and attentive public. Constituency mail exists because ordinary individuals are compelled to voice their beliefs and sentiments on a given issue. To reiterate a central point from chapter 3, this method differs sharply from opinion polls, which arise because pollsters are compelled to identify what mass opinions are, whether or not individuals care to express them, or, for that matter, whether or not individuals hold intelligible beliefs and sentiments to begin with. And in the end, a major reason why we care to understand public opinion per se must be that our opinions make a strong claim on our likely actions. This is, to borrow

V. O. Key's oft-cited definition, the form of public opinion "held by private citizens which governments find it prudent to heed" (1961, 14).

Constituency mail thus captures an expression of activated mass opinion in which an issue is salient in the individual's mind and compels that person toward political action. Thus the issues that motivate correspondence should jointly measure high political awareness, high intensity of preferences, and the impetus to link thoughts to action. Moreover, as we hypothesized in chapter 1, the activation of letter-writing on an issue such as civil rights and racial integration in the 1950s and 1960s should also reflect the role that institutions and group dynamics play in mobilizing mass opinion.

As a measure of activated mass opinion, constituency mail more specifically captures the viewpoints of individuals who occupy a special place in public opinion theories. At least since Philip Converse's (1964, 1970) discussion of issue publics, politically engaged and activated citizens have occupied a middle stratum between conventional political elites and the largely inattentive general public. In that position, they are often conceived of as opinion leaders. So, constituency mail should tell us something about the nature and dynamics of what opinion leaders think. And if these engaged and activated citizens do in fact form a critical bridge between elites and masses, then their letters should also tell us something about *how they lead.*[27]

By inference, constituency mail may also tell us something more generally about the nature and dynamics of mass opinion. What letter writers may have to say may signal the potential opinions of a wider constituency above and beyond that of the correspondent. As such, analysis that tracks change in aggregate opinion among letter writers might offer an informative complement to existing studies of long-term aggregate shifts in mass opinion.[28] For instance, although elite opinion theories require that this middle stratum between elites and mass obey a strictly top-down, elite-driven chain of influence, the dynamics of letter-writing might also be used to test for non-elite influences on mass opinion.

The test implication here is fairly clear. If this middle stratum becomes activated or transformed concerning a particular issue in the absence of any elite cues to do so, non-elite influences are suggested. The nuances of such a test are detailed and developed in chapter 5. An important part of such a test, returning once more to the propositions in chapter 1, will be the extent to which elite and counterelite institutions mobilize opinion in these middle strata. If letter-writing is unmediated or results from counterelite mobilization, then mass opinion formation must to some extent be autonomous from elite influences. Moreover, such mobilization and activation in the absence of elite cues can also indirectly show how the categories of "elite" and "mass" become blurred during social movements as previously inactive, disinterested, or unmobilized individuals become mobilized and enter careers of activism and political engagement.

Finally, as data, constituency mail is an especially rich and informative alternative to opinion polls. Letters tell us more than merely that correspondents feel sufficiently invested in a given issue to contact their elected officials. In addition to the act of letter-writing, the content of the letters themselves offers an abundance of textual and contextual information about the correspondents' opinions and how they choose to express them. Thus constituency mail tells us more than do other active modes of public political expression such as attending political rallies, riot participation, and voting. Writers' preferences are revealed both through political action and through the content of the letters.

Letters can make no claims to surgically probe the sincere "attitudes" of the general public. We cannot infer that letters reflect true, underlying beliefs as expressed in the text of the letters per se, since the correspondents often write strategically. Strategic writers may choose metaphor, irony, hyperbole, even dissemblance in order to persuade, rather than sincerely translate thoughts and emotions into words. Opinion polls clearly hold a methodological advantage on this point. As discussed in chapters 1 and 3, there are ample grounds for skepticism as to whether surveys themselves can faithfully capture "true" attitudes and whether such a demanding notion as "attitudes" is sustainable.

This matter notwithstanding, constituency mail clearly offers a qualitatively different kind of opinion data than that found in surveys. Poll questions are typically closed-ended. By contrast, letters are an open-ended mode of expression, and there are few bounds to what a person says and how she says it. Survey response is essentially negative and reactive. Individuals act by *not* declining an interview (often after multiple call-backs) and *respond* to a fixed agenda of (usually) closed-ended questions. Letter-writing, by contrast, is more positive and *proactive:* correspondents not only choose to express an opinion but do so publicly and—within the limits of pen and paper—are unbounded in how that opinion is expressed. The supply of opinion polls begins with the interest, organizational capacity, and material resources (among other things) of polling firms. The supply of constituency mail, by contrast, begins with the interests, capacities, and resources of ordinary individuals. Because the letters result in the first instance from a desire to speak one's mind, correspondents hold free rein not only over issue definition and issue position, but also over how to structure that position—what language to use, which frames to conjure, what other issues to link to, and the like.[29]

This proactive mode of expression will animate four dimensions of mass opinion that are especially limited in survey data. Specifically, the letters reveal a dialogical, narrative, and rhetorical structure and an emotional intensity to public political expression. Like dialogue, letters to the president are addressed *to* someone and opinions are shaped by knowledge about one's dialogical partner. Like narrative, these letters tell a story, and that story can be layered in multiple, interwoven justificatory dimensions that unfold before the reader. Like rhetoric, the letters aim to persuade the president of the writer's views about civil rights and racial equality. And, finally, the letters capture an intensity of opinion and emotional pitch not easily and not often measured in opinion surveys. Through these dimensions, letters more closely exhibit how opinion is expressed in ordinary, everyday life than does the structured survey response. Before illustrating each of these elements, however, a short summary of what we already know about letter-writing and a description of the data sampling and collection of these letters is in order.

DATA DESCRIPTION

In the next two sections, I will present figures and findings that show the validity of constituency mail as an indicator of political awareness and issue salience. I also show that letters, as a form of opinion data, reveal the dialogical, narrative, rhetorical, and affective dimensions of public political expression. This is a first look at the letters that form the raw material for the findings presented in chapters 5 and 6. The sample of letters to the president is drawn from the last year of the first Truman administration, 1948, through the first year of the second Johnson administration, 1965. During these years, a total of 6,765 letters are collected and coded. For most years, this is a systematic sampling of one of every twenty letters on racial politics stored by the National Archives. The estimated total number of letters on civil rights and racial equality during this period is 176,550.[30]

The universe of existing letters to the president is archived in presidential libraries in Independence, Missouri (Truman), Abilene, Kansas (Eisenhower), Austin, Texas (Johnson), and Dorchester, Massachusetts (Kennedy).[31] As for the Johnson years, for reasons unknown to current archivists, all letters regarding Selma, Alabama, are archived (February through April 1965), but outside that period only a small fraction of the total volume of letters appears to have been saved. The Johnson White House did, however, keep weekly tabulations of the volume of constituency mail and issue positions from these letters.[32] These weekly tabulations are used for the aggregate analysis of letter-writing in chapter 5.[33]

The letters are coded for two different kinds of information: (1) categorical data on the race of the writer, region, type of correspondence, and issue position expressed; and (2) subjective impressions of the central frames that structure the correspondent's opinion or argument. Race is coded simply as "black," "white," or "other" (cases in which neither racial category can be inferred). The four regions of the United States are North, South, Midwest, and West.[34] The three types of correspondence identified are letters from individuals written on their own behalf, letters from organizations, and mass mailings that result from some form of collective action, such as petitions, mass mailings, and form letters.[35] Finally the issue position is simply coded as being in favor of or opposed to civil rights and racial equality.

Where I could do so unambiguously, letters from political elites are excluded from my sample.[36] As a compendium of data on public opinion, letters to the president offer a fairly complete time series, at least until the later years of the Johnson presidency, when a significant proportion of letters are missing or unavailable.[37] And, compared to letters to most other political elites, letters to the president draw activated voices from the nation writ large and can therefore make bolder claims to being representative.[38] Along these lines, letters to the president enjoy advantages—random sampling, large sample size, longitudinal series—over alternative, open-ended modes of public expression we might examine such as in-depth interviews or focus groups. To the extent that our sample of letters captures public opinion among the politically attentive in issue-specific, historically contingent contexts, it does so fairly representatively.

LETTER-WRITING AS POLITICAL AWARENESS AND ISSUE SALIENCE

As we noted, constituency mail embodies an activated conception of public opinion. Letter-writing should jointly measure the aggregate level of political awareness, intensity of preferences, and impetus to political action on a given issue. In this section, I demonstrate this empirically. Existing studies, to begin with, nicely corroborate such propositions. Rosenstone and Hansen, for example, find that mobilization is a critical precursor to political action and that such mobilization is likelier to occur in response to particular issues and opportunities. Accordingly, people are likelier to write when an issue becomes more salient, when an issue reaches the moment of decision, and when the outcome of the issue is highly uncertain or close (1993, 72–101).[39] These results do not differentiate between issues and use relatively recent data (opinion polls from 1973 to 1990). It is worth asking, then, whether such evidence holds true prior to the early 1970s and in specific issue domains. In the present case, the germane question is: How well does letter-writing capture political awareness and issue salience during the civil rights era and on the specific issue of civil rights and racial equality?

The question can be tested using data from the 1964 American National Election Study. The results show that whether someone writes to elected officials is unmistakably a function of the writer's political awareness. An individual's likelihood of engaging in political letter-writing rises with level of educational attainment, degree of interest in politics, and level of attention to different media outputs (television, print media, magazines, and radio). Thus individuals who are better educated, more interested in politics, and more attentive to media coverage of public affairs are significantly more likely to write their representatives.[40] These relationships hold constant other plausible determinants of letter-writing: age, sex, family income, and employment status. Moreover, when the "partial effect" of each variable in our model is calculated, the three measures of political awareness stand out as the strongest predictors of letter-writing.

These results show a convincing link between letter-writing and different measures of political awareness during the civil rights era, but we have yet to examine this link vis-à-vis *issue-specific* measures of political awareness (that is, measures of issue salience). This is not simply a detail. Letters are written about specific issues and, as I argued in chapter 1, political awareness and intensity of opinion too should be issue-specific. Here survey data are simply unavailable to test this proposition.

We can, however, test for the validity of letter-writing as a measure of issue salience by comparing our time series for letter-writing against the time series for other plausible issue-specific indicators of awareness. Figure 4.1, for example, compares the volume of constituency mail from 1948 to 1965 to the volume of media coverage (measured as the number of front-page articles in the *New York Times* on civil rights and racial equality) during the same period.[41] The two time series closely parallel each other.[42] This is especially true until 1965; the statistical correlation in the two time series from 1948 to 1964 is gaudy 0.85.[43]

This basic point can also be made using other measures of political awareness and issue salience. In figure 4.2, the volume of constituency mail on civil rights is compared to the aggregate issue salience of civil

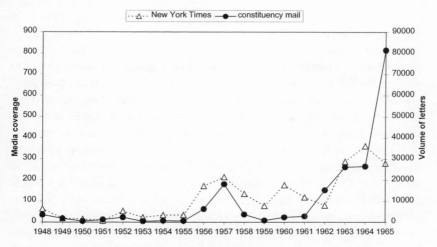

Figure 4.1 Constituency Mail and *New York Times* Coverage, 1948–65

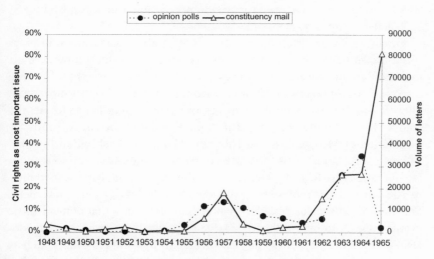

Figure 4.2 Constituency Mail and Issue Salience in Polls, 1948–65

rights from 1948 to 1965. The aggregate measure of issue salience is a commonly used survey instrument that asks individuals to name the "most important problem" facing the nation.[44] Figure 4.2 clearly shows that, with the exception of 1965, both time series track together remarkably closely. The statistical correlation between these time series from 1948 to 1964 is 0.89. At least at the aggregate level, the volume of letter-writing on a given issue thus appears to tell us something about how salient that issue is in the general public's mind.

As an important aside, a skeptic of alternate, non-survey-based measures of public opinion might demur that figure 4.1 undermines our earlier invocations in chapter 3 against survey data. That is, surveys appear to successfully measure the same thing as constituency mail. Thus we need not look beyond poll data to appreciate the dynamic, issue-specific activation of mass opinion, or so the skeptic's argument would run. Here, it is crucial to note that an open-ended item such as the "most important problem" question is the exception rather than the rule in opinion surveys. In fact, in most years of the ANES this question is arguably the *only* such open-ended item.[45] Furthermore, it pairs well with the trend in letter-writing precisely for the reasons described in chapter 2: it allows the respondents to freely interpret and respond to the question at hand. Finally, absent further open-ended follow-up questions, the "most important problem" question only tells us that the activation of mass opinion *is* dynamic and issue-specific. It tells us nothing about *how* this activation occurs and *what* the substance of such activated opinions looks like.

Finally, it is worth noting that letter writers are not equivalent to organized movement activists. The events that move individuals to write their president are not always the same events that make a movement. In some cases, watershed events in historical accounts of the civil rights movement often fail to provoke significant surges in letter-writing. For example, the student lunch counter sit-ins in 1960, the Freedom Rides in 1961, the assassination of Medgar Evers in 1963, the March on Washington in 1963, Albany campaign in 1964, and the campaign of the Mississippi Freedom Democratic Party to seat its delegates at the Democratic Party Convention in 1964 are all key moments in the history of the civil rights movement. We shall see in greater detail in chapter 5, nevertheless, that none of these events appears to have activated a large response from ordinary individuals—as measured by letters to their president. By contrast, events such as the 1958 Supreme Court decision in *Cooper v. Aaron* and white-on-black violence in New Orleans and Tennessee in late 1960 and early 1961 incited a powerful response from citizen correspondents. But these moments are less prominent, if not altogether lost in existing accounts of the movement. This distinction between types of political activism can also be shown through other means. The 1964 National Election Study data show that individuals who report writing letters to elected officials hold distinct racial policy preferences from those who do not.[46]

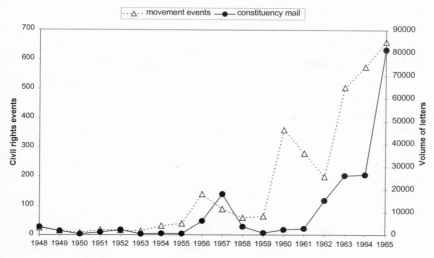

Figure 4.3   Number of Letters and Movement-Initiated Events, 1948–65

We can also illustrate this episodic discontinuity between the events that provoke an outpouring of letters and the actual course of movement activism by comparing the number of letters with the number of movement-initiated events over time. Figure 4.3 shows such a comparison.[47] There is a fairly close coupling between the two trends, especially prior to the Little Rock crisis in 1957. After 1957, however, there are some unambiguous departures, most strikingly the explosion in the number of movement-initiated events with the student lunch counter sit-ins in 1960.

The absence of a documented public response to signal events such as the March on Washington or the Mississippi Freedom Democratic Party may be problematic. Perhaps the public does not see the president as the relevant elite actor in these cases, or constituency mail is incomplete as a measure of activated mass opinion, or there is some other potential explanation. But the fact that other relatively obscure events elicit a demonstrable response suggests that the letters do document modes of mobilizing public expression that are not accessible through alternative sources.

THE STRUCTURE OF CONSTITUENCY MAIL AS OPINION DATA

Constituency mail is hence not merely a valid measure of activated mass opinion. Its real analytic value comes as a textually and substantively rich measure of activated mass opinion. In this section, I preview the kind of window into public opinion that letters permit. People write to their president for a dizzying diversity of reasons. In content alone, letters to the president range from attempts to convey one's policy preferences and propose party strategies to character assessments, congratulatory messages, personal requests, and pen pal mail.[48] Certainly, each of these types of mail is represented in letters sent to the president on civil rights.

Yet this diversity is not a smorgasbord. The letters are unified by a common set of structural elements. Specifically, letters to the president reveal a narrative, dialogical, and rhetorical structure and an intensity of opinion to public political expression. Such letters are carefully crafted texts that convey a story; they speak *to* someone; they aim to inform and persuade that someone; and they capture the intensity and affective timbre of someone impelled from inertia to activism. These characteristics are noticeably lacking from most survey data and more closely exhibit the manner in which opinion is expressed in everyday political discourse as a result.

Like narratives, these letters tell stories, and they are stories that build a meaningful interpretation and understanding out of complex, interwoven circumstances.[49] Unlike surveys, in which beliefs about a particular issue can be isolated and extracted out of the instrument, the opinions contained in letters must be understood in context, as a whole. Of course, research on contextual effects (especially on "question order" effects) does in some sense treat surveys like texts. As we noted, however, the substance of this text is largely predetermined by the survey design. With letters, the construction of the text is uniquely the author's. No single sentence or segment of a letter can be isolated or extracted without risk of betraying the author's intended meaning. Thus a given sentence is meaningful only in the context of the letter as a whole and cannot be compared to a similar sentence in a different letter, or, for that matter, distinguished from a differently worded sentence in a letter espousing a similar overall opinion.

To illustrate this point: many segregationist letters on civil rights base their issue positions in overtly racist and essentialist propositions. Quite a few, however, begin on less repugnant grounds—for example, by avowing one's commitment to a cherished principle or purporting to consider only the realistic conflicts between blacks and whites—before descending (sometimes rapidly) into racist rhetoric. A letter that begins with the remark "I personally am not prejudiced toward Negroes" can either be a prelude to overtly racist views or crescendo to a principled egalitarian position on integration. An example of the former kind of narrative is found in the following letter from an Ohio woman written in March 1965:

I would like to express my opinion on the current racial problems. . . . First I want to make it clear that I think colored should have the opportunity to attend good schools, and other public places, such as restaurants, etc.; of their choice. I am not prejudiced against them in that way. But . . .

1. The rights of white people are being infringed upon in several different ways. We should have the privilege of choosing our friends and the people we want to associate with. It does not bother me to work with colored or eat in public places with them, but, I do not wish to live next door or in the same building. I do not feel better than they are, but, I prefer to associate with my own. Colored in the lower class are vicious, I am even afraid to walk on the street at night. Much as you may not want to admit this, it is true, none the less.

2. How do you know what is really in the back of their minds? These leaders of the colored group! How do you know what will be in store for the whites in a few years? Right now there are as many colored as whites, and they multiply faster! Given complete voting rights, in a few years, we would have total colored government, then what will happen? . . . Some of the lower colored, in the South, and other sections, would sell their votes for $.50, $1.00, or a bottle of wine. This means, we can have almost any kind of government elected!

The author goes on to paint stereotypes of welfare dependency and warns of impending violence if the issue of integration is forced on southern states. This author's narrative thus reveals—in radically different form than multivariate survey analysis—the multidimensional, textured nature of racial attitudes. It also cautions against the hazards of inferring too much from aggregate (univariate or bivariate) analyses of opinion data.

Like dialogue, one's choice of intended recipient can determine or modify the opinion that is expressed. In survey research such responsiveness to a dialogical partner is often compartmentalized as a contextual "interviewer effect" and treated more as a source of measurement error that confounds the clarity of data than as a fundamental aspect of public opinion itself. In studies of racial attitudes, this dialogical dimension is most often found in discussions of "race-of-interviewer" effects, wherein individuals are shown to answer the same survey in distinctly different ways depending on the race (or perceived race) of the interviewer.[50] With survey-based interviewer effects, however, any dialogical contingencies are based on very little information. Most surveys are conducted anonymously, over the telephone, and by a polling firm about which respondents know very little. Respondents might venture reliable guesses as to their interviewer's race, sex, educational level, region of the country, perhaps even age and class. But these are admittedly circumscribed data points.

Correspondents, by contrast, are often favored with intimate, detailed knowledge about the political actors to whom they write. This is especially true with so prominent a figure as the president. The particulars range from knowing the constitutional role of the commander-in-chief and the structural position of the executive branch to knowing the symbolic significance of a particular presidency and the intimate details of a public figure's private life. On this last point, letters to one president often differ in style and content from letters to another. Thus, many letters to President Eisenhower make pointed reference to his penchant for golfing, his military heroism, and his daughter's prospects of attending an integrated school or marrying an African American man. Letters to President Kennedy, by contrast, make ironic references to his book, *Profiles in Courage,* or (as we shall see) launch into ad hominem attacks on his renowned family. Furthermore, since a president's words and deeds are public knowledge (if not a civic responsibility), commentary on the consistency or lack thereof between what a president says and what he does is very often an important rhetorical device. Many letters from staunch segregationists, for example, condemn the president for abetting the overthrow of Jim Crow while leading a socially segregated life. In April 1948, for example, a letter from Florence, Alabama, tells President Truman:

> It is hard for me to believe that a white man would be content to sit by a negro on the train or in a cafe or would like to share the hotels, and most important have his daughter be approached by a negro requesting to call on her at her home. I would like to ask you, Mr. President, would you like for your daughter to arrive at home after one of her night performances with a negro escort? Do you believe in equality of races as outlined above? I will say that you DO NOT. And still this is what you, our President, has requested that Congress pass a law to bring about. Would you welcome a negro man and his wife to your home to have dinner with you and your wife, as your social guest? Mr. President, these are plain questions, and questions that we will be forced to answer if your suggestion should become law. What is your honest answer?

The content of letters, furthermore, is likely to differ not only from other forms of public expression but from letters to other kinds of political actors as well. Hence, we should expect letters to the president to differ in systematic ways from those to state and local officials, judges, members of Congress, newspaper editors, and the like.[51] To draw further nuances of the dialogical nature of letters, correspondents often do not address their letters directly to the president. Many address their letters to First Ladies— Bess Truman, Mamie Eisenhower, Jacqueline Kennedy, and Lady Bird Johnson—as a more personalized means of gaining the president's ear. Given the civil rights movement's powerful initial emphasis on racial equality through legal challenges, many letters are also addressed to attorneys general—notably, J. Howard McGrath, Herbert Brownell, and Robert Kennedy. And many letters by African Americans are addressed to the highest ranking-African American within the White House (for example, E. Frederic Morrow in the Eisenhower administration and Clifford Alexander in the Johnson administration) or within the president's party (for example, Val Washington in the Eisenhower administration).[52]

More generally, correspondents shape and modify their letters in response to the actions and statements of the president. Truman's declared intent to legislate the recommendations of his committee on civil rights in 1948, Eisenhower's order to send troops to Central High School in Little Rock in 1957, and Kennedy's well-publicized telephone call to Coretta Scott King while Martin Luther King Jr. was imprisoned are just a few obvious examples. In some cases (for example, the Truman Commission in 1948), a visible, proactive presidential presence can initiate public response. In other cases, the absence of a visible role by the president (for example, the 1954 *Brown v. Board of Education* decision) can provoke only a tepid public response even to momentous historical events.

In still other cases, the president is compelled to respond to movement-initiated events. Two examples are President Eisenhower's sending federal troops to Little Rock in 1957 and President Kennedy's sending federal troops to Oxford, Mississippi, in 1962. Perhaps the most stirring such example is President Johnson's response to "Bloody Sunday" in Selma on March 9, 1965. On the heels of this brutal act of state-sanctioned violence, Johnson delivered his proposal for sweeping voting rights legislation before a joint session of Congress and before seventy million television viewers on March 12, 1965. The crowning rhetorical moment of this impassioned address was Johnson's purposeful co-optation of the civil rights movement's rallying cry, "we shall overcome." Its electrifying effect is exemplified in the following letter from a New York City man.

> I feel I must express for myself what, I am certain, millions of other people in America are feeling this morning as a result of your history-making address to the nation last night. . . . There were so many high points in your talk, so many moments when the heart was touched by the full realization that the President was saying this, at this time, in this place, so many occasions when the magnitude of the talk's importance struck our consciousness that in our home we all agreed that we had never before experienced such a forty-five minute period so emotion-filled, so gratifying, and so hopeful. . . .
> *At no point in your talk were you so over-powering as when you uttered those*

words—we shall overcome. By using them when you did you touched the very heart of every man and woman of good will within the sound of your voice. In doing so, you immortalized yourself. No one ever will forget listening to you last night and, when all the expressions and descriptions of what you did for people are written and the history books record the impact of your words on your people, the name of Lyndon Johnson as one of the greatest Americans will be recorded for all time. (emphasis added)

It ought to be noted that the use of the term "dialogical" is somewhat misleading, since the conversation in letters to the president is largely one-sided. White House staff do reply to constituents but know little more about the correspondent than what is revealed in the contents of the letter. Moreover, with the exception of mail from privileged voices, few letters actually reach the sight of the president or any other influential personage in the White House.[53] The issue of whether a two-sided exchange of communication takes place, however, is separable from the question of whether correspondents express their political views *as if* engaged in dialogue with someone. Moreover, to the American public, the president is not just a familiar acquaintance but one who is beholden to publicly held expectations of democratic responsiveness and accountability. That is, the dialogical partnership may only be symbolic, but to the citizen correspondent, it is a meaningful one nonetheless.

Like rhetoric, letter-writing aims toward something—namely, persuading and pressuring the president on the matter of civil rights and racial equality. Thus the letters we shall examine often resort to the use of rhetorical devices such as metaphor, hyperbole, irony, and paradox. As such, the content of the letters belie the strategic aims of their authors in addition to the sincere expression of their political opinions. We do not, as a consequence, have the controlled environment of surveys from which to draw exacting psychological inferences about an individual's beliefs. Nonetheless, constituency mail does convey a picture of how individuals attempt to persuade each other in everyday discourse as political events unfold.

One of the most prevalent such devices is the strategic use of paradox, usually in the coupling of a cherished moral or political belief with a state of affairs or personal experience that patently contradicts that core belief. For example, an African American from New York City in February 1954, in the following excerpt, opens by declaring: "As an American citizen and proud of my American birthright, and desiring to enjoy the freedom of a true Democracy such as my wonderful Country grants everyone of its children, I feel it is my patriotic duty to bring to your attention an undemocratic, insulting, and humiliating experience that I was forced to go through while sojourning in the South." This particular correspondent then closes his letter by writing, "I am reporting this to you because I sincerely believe that you are interested in the welfare of the American People, regardless of race, creed, or color, and that you hold dear to your heart the great fundamental American Principles: the Constitution, the Bill of Rights, and the Declaration of Independence."

Correspondents also make pointed use of irony. The following letter from a Canyon, Texas, man, written in response to James Meredith's effort to enroll at "Ole Miss" demonstrates this use of irony:

> Instead of risking another Civil War with Americans fighting Americans over only ONE Negro this time, why not have the UN send in troops from Ethiopia or India, to machine gun a few thousand of the natives of Mississippi, as they did in Katange Province of The Congo. To bring Dixie down to her knees! Or even quicker, just tell Castro its [sic] time to bring his Russian Communists over that short 90 miles to stop this riot against the "Peoples Democracy of the US." Then with your Coalition Government with Castro those extremists Dixiecrats will be easier to handle.

Without explicitly rejecting President Kennedy's intention to integrate the University of Mississippi, this author's views are patently clear.

This particular letter also captures an intensity of opinion and an emotional pitch not found in modes of public expression such as survey data.[54] Opinion surveys do strive to assess intensity and affect with measurement scales. Likert scales, however, limit the continuum of intensity to an arbitrarily set number of categories from "Strongly Agree" to "Strongly Disagree." And thermometer scales constrain our emotional response within the confines of the metaphor of affect as temperature. Further, because survey instruments aim to minimize "measurement error" and optimize valid and reliable indicators, surveys generally avoid using language that is too colorful, inflammatory, idiomatic, or otherwise woolly. Finally, the self-reported nature of survey response renders questions about emotions susceptible to measurement effects, the best efforts to avoid them notwithstanding. Thus "what appear to be substantive differences in the [structure of emotional response] may be due to different choices in methodology" (Markus, Neuman, and MacKuen 2000, 153).

With constituency mail, there are no such strictures. Letters convey a rich, personalized language seldom captured in survey instruments. The expression of anger well illustrates this extraordinary emotional range. For some correspondents, anger undergirds support for racial equality. A

Brooklyn man, for example, responded to the murder of Florida's NAACP coordinator Harry Moore in 1951 by letting the president know that "There is anger and bitterness in my heart today, that such things happen in my country. Unless you act immediately to condemn this outrage and bring the racist murderers to justice, you shame and degrade our government. I do not ask, but I DEMAND that you get off your rear end and do the right thing—NOW!!"

Anger may also be exhibited by opponents to racial equality. An especially vivid example is shown in the following letter from a Bravard, North Carolina, man, signed as "Robert E. Lee's follower."

> Dear Jack(ass), Please don't let the way I addressed you be disturbing, for it is just the beginning. First of all I want you to know that I truly hate you. Please, no offense meant! I mean, just because you like the underdeveloped people (Negroes) it doesn't mean you're not equal to the mill hands, although you're not. Of course, they might have you if you crawl on your hands and beg. By the way, are you trying to kill your wife? It sure appears to be that way. . . . If I didn't know better I'd think our nation was being taken over by a dictator, and his family. Since you're so rich I wish you'd get some braces and a pair of scissors. My horse looks better than the Kennedy clan put together.
>
> I wish you'd take a night off and go to the theater like Lincoln did and then you wouldn't have any more problems, neither would we. If you only had half a mind you'd see that the Negroes don't want to go to school with us to get an education, only to cause trouble. Never fear! The South will rise again! And show you damn Yankees the difference between right and wrong.

Among the other salient emotional categories found in these letters are betrayal, shame, pride, and gratitude. Betrayal is commonly manifested by correspondents who voted for a president based on his position on civil rights only to find the president contradicting that expectation. Many segregationists writing to President Eisenhower during the Little Rock crisis, for example, made note that they voted for him in 1956 because he publicly affirmed the principle of states' rights and disavowed the use of federal troops. Among African American correspondents, betrayal of American principles is a common theme, particularly among black soldiers who do not understand why they are being sent to Korea or Vietnam.

Shame is most often found in letters from nonsoutherners who express their commitment to racial equality and note that segregation and racism diminish their cherished self-conception. Many authors, on this point, report being "ashamed to be white" or "ashamed to be American." In many cases, the author's cherished democratic values are held up against the court of world opinion, as in a missive from a Dearborn, Michigan, native who bemoans the fact that "[t]he United States stands up to this world and says, 'Hey World, look at me!! You should fashion your government after mine! We're a free people and our constitution is for the people, of the people, and by the people.' And the world looks down on us and says, 'Yes, this is true if your skin happens to be white.'" In contrast, shame's counterface, pride, is often manifested (most often among racial liberals) in response to particular acts that make correspondents "proud to be American," "proud of their president," "proud to be black." Finally, gratitude is most commonly found in letters from African Americans, as the following excerpt from a Bronx, New York, man's correspondence in July 1963 illustrates:

> I am a black American. I have been watching your every move. You are, to be sure, our Moses! You are the *sine qua non* of the last half of the 20th century! You are the greatest President ever to be president of these United States of America and history will so record it. . . . God bless you. The world is a better place in which to live because of you. I feel like an American citizen because of you.

As one might expect from the intensity and emotional depth conveyed by these letters, authors occasionally reveal the personal transformation they have undergone vis-à-vis events in the civil rights movement. At the aggregate level, the transformation can be seen in successive shifts in which groups are mobilized to respond to movement-initiated events— starting with African Americans and racially liberal whites outside the South in the late 1940s and early 1950s, then volatile, reactive mobilization of southern whites from the mid-1950s and northern whites by the 1960s. At the individual level, the transformation can be seen in correspondents who note sea changes in their racial attitudes and their political alignments, such as the Mankato, Minnesota, woman who in November 1963 wrote:

> As a political issue I realize that this is a sensitive one, with much beneath the surface. But I cannot believe that a majority of the American people would vote against justice and equality. You may be losing some votes by taking a strong stand for civil rights, but certainly you are winning some as well. Take me, for example: I am a Republican, and in the last few months something very surprising has happened to me. Suddenly I am on your side, and not just on this one issue. Suddenly I resent much of the criticism of you which I used to enjoy. Amazingly (to me) I am hoping that democrats win key elections in Kentucky and Philadelphia. Now when you speak in favor of some-

thing my first inclination is to be in favor of it, too. . . . All of this is a dramatic reversal for as staunch a Republican as I have always been (and probably will be again), and I know that it results from your stand on civil rights.

Among scholars of protest movements, this transformative element is a commonly observed characteristic of "new social movements" that manifests the "cognitive liberation" that predisposes and potentiates a groundswell for mass mobilization and social change.[55]

Finally, many letters evoke the saying "the past as prologue." This is particularly true of what we currently consider novel reconfigurations of racial politics. These letters show that many of the themes ubiquitous in racial discourse today have their precursors during this period. As we shall see in chapter 6, the themes include the linkage of racial antagonism with taxpayer rights, stereotypes of "welfare queens," cries for private education and "school choice," and invocations of reverse discrimination that read like a page out of racially conservative opposition to egalitarian public policies in the 1990s.

ACTIVATED MASS OPINION ON CIVIL RIGHTS PREVIEWED

In this chapter, I have presented an extensive argument for the merits and limitations of looking at constituency mail as a source of opinion data. Clearly, letter-writing differs in illuminating ways from survey data and other potential sources of opinion data, least of all in the incentives that motivate public expression and in the kind of political information contained in that act. Constituency mail is a positive, proactive conception of public opinion that is especially well-suited for examining activated mass opinion. An examination of the conditions under which ordinary individuals choose to express their viewpoints to the president provides a discerning view into how the public reacted as the civil rights movement unfolded. In particular, constituency mail offers important insights into the narrative, rhetorical, dialogical, and affective forms that an individual's political viewpoints take as they are actually expressed in nonsurvey settings.

In the next two chapters, I put these claims about constituency mail to the test. Will letter-writing to the president simply reinforce the elite-driven account according to which ordinary individuals respond primarily to what elite political actors do and say? Or will letter-writing reflect attention to politics generally, including events in which the primary actors—such as Emmett Till, Autherine Lucy, Rosa Parks, Viola Liuzzo, James Meredith, and Fannie Lou Hamer—are distinctly non-elite? Our sample of letters written to the president from 1948 to the mid-1960s will show that, indeed, both elite and non-elite events and discourses activate public opinion. In particular, once black insurgency began to be fomented in the mid-1950s, letter writers were more often than not impelled to write in response to events staged by non-elite and counterelite movement activists and the southern white opposition to such activism. Letter-writing, then, is not only responsive to specific events but also strongly structured around the dimensions of group interests and identity, as well as group threat and animosity. And the substantive opinion expressed in these letters is often the product of a clash between these group dimensions and the cherished values that pervade U.S. political discourse. Let us turn to these letters.

FIVE

THE RACIAL, REGIONAL, AND ORGANIZATIONAL BASES OF MASS ACTIVATION

> I feel that a giant glacier has been started by all this; it's moving onward and there's no stopping it.
>
> —Mamie Till Bradley

> The bill that lay on the polished mahogany desk was born in violence in Selma, Alabama, where a stubborn sheriff handling Negroes in the Southern tradition had stumbled against the future. . . . The nation had seen and heard, and exploded in indignation.
>
> —Martin Luther King Jr.

> There is no Negro problem. There is no Southern problem. There is no Northern problem. There is only an American Problem.
>
> —Lyndon B. Johnson

Chapters 3 and 4 charted a detailed but necessary detour from our original path toward an explanation of what happens to mass audiences when a social movement is under way. We are now at an opportune juncture to look back on what we have achieved in this journey and look to where we are going. In chapter 1, I presented an account of activated mass opinion that specifies the contexts in which our public political views are sustained and activated, and the relative influence that elites and non-elites play in the process. The account distinguishes between multiple publics: a dominant public at the center of political affairs and oppositional publics at the margins. Oppositional "counterpublics" are critical for fostering interactions, interests, ideologies, and institutions that contradict and contest conventional, elite-influenced political information. In the case of the civil rights movement, an insurgent black counterpublic was such a key counter-elite influence on public views about racial equality and policy.

This account of activated mass opinion and the significance of non-elite influences on racial attitudes during the civil rights movement was tested in chapter 2. The evidence from historical accounts and from available survey data challenge strictly top-down accounts of mass opinion. Yet, although the analysis does well in disconfirming the view that opinion change is strictly top-down, it fares considerably less well as a positive account of activated mass opinion. In particular, the survey analysis is incomplete owing to data limitations and, more generally, to the conceptual, methodological, and normative concerns with our general reliance on survey data discussed in chapter 3. And in chapter 4, I argued that presenting such a positive account—of group dynamics, institutional mobilization, actively voiced opinion, and the like—will require looking to alternate sources of opinion data such as written letters to the president.

In this chapter, I present just such an analysis of constituency mail. The chapter begins by contrasting three possible accounts of mass opinion during the course of a social movement: the elite-driven, the movement-driven, and the movement-initiated, movement-elite interactive accounts. The remaining sections describe how the activation of mass opinion unfolds over time and across racial, regional, and institutional contexts. The evidence most closely supports the movement-initiated, movement-elite interactive account. The gist of this evidence is that mass activation occurs as an interactive, sequential process in which particular attentive sectors of the general public become activated with regard to specific issues and in response to specific events.

In the case of the civil rights movement, grassroots activism—of black insurgents in the South and racially sympathetic whites outside the South—is the critical reagent that triggers this process. At the same time, as the insurgency evolved (and opposition to that insurgency unfolded in turn), mass activation clearly resulted from the dynamic interplay of both movement- and elite-initiated events. Organizations—notably, nonpolitical, membership-based voluntary associations—played a critical role in this activation. Taken together, the aggregate view of letters to the president takes us a good way toward a positive account of how mass audiences respond when non-elites begin to upstage the political agenda.

AN INTERACTIVE ACCOUNT OF MASS ACTIVATION

We noted in chapter 4 that citizen activists are particularly likely to play a key bridging role between elites and masses. This bridging role is one that is well noted by scholars of social movements and public opinion alike. Even elite theorists such as Edward Carmines and James Stimson argue that citizen activists "are well-situated to respond quickly to new ideas, to be the carriers of new themes" and that "the structural position of activists, the fact that they move in and out of activity, frees them to be the dynamic element in issue evolution" (1989, 90). Citizen activists are thus a fluid, protean reserve army within the mass public who are highly attentive to ongoing events. They occupy a meso-level between elites and masses and stay informed and interpret the events and actions that much of the mass public are otherwise too indisposed or isolated to follow. As we noted in chapter 4, a proactive and open-ended mode of public political expression such as political letter-writing is especially well suited to capture this meso-level of mass activation.

In Carmines and Stimson's account, active citizens are the key messengers of elites' signals to their less attentive counterparts in the general public and the likeliest targets of institutional mobilization by political elites. We might imagine, however, that during social movements, such attentive individuals might also be key messengers of movement cues and the likeliest targets of mobilization by movement organizations as well. To push the point further, we might imagine at least three plausible ways in which attentive citizens may play a key role in the activation of mass opinion. Figure 5.1 describes these three accounts, which neither exhaust the possibilities nor faithfully capture every nuance and detail about opinion dynamics.

The first account is a strong version of elite theory. The process of activating opinion begins with what elites say and do. Information about what political elites are up to is relayed to the general public by institutions such as the mass media and by active citizens. This flow of information is thus unidirectional. Similarly, there may be some flow between citizen activists and the general public and between activists and elites, but the boundaries between these groupings are, practically speaking, impermeable.

The second account is a strong version of non-elite, movement-driven mass activation. An issue such as civil rights lies dormant until the collective grievances of a sector of the mass public begin to fester and erupt into movement activism. When this happens, movement activists upstage the control of elite actors over the political agenda. What's more, activists inform and influence ordinary individuals through these acts and are in-

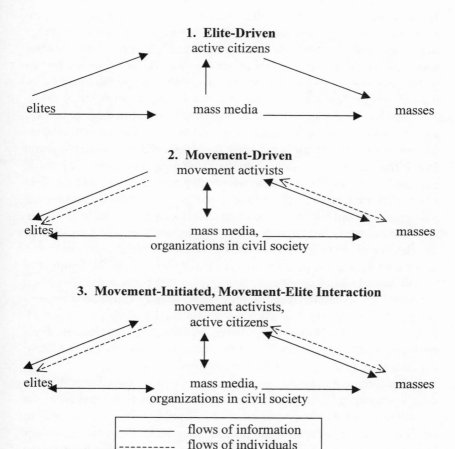

Figure 5.1   Three Accounts of Activating Mass Opinion

formed and influenced in turn by their less active counterparts. The fonts of information are not limited to the mass media but include organizations in civil society—social movement organizations, voluntary associations, informal networks, and the like. Political elites have no direct influence on mass opinion.

The last account combines elements of both accounts. It argues that movement activists and political elites jointly and interactively inform and influence mass publics. There is a bi-directional flow of information between the general public and citizen activists and between activists and elites. There is also a flow of individuals between the general public and activists and from activists to elites. This means that some previously inactive spectators will be spurred on to be participants in a social change movement, and likewise that some movement activists may institutionalize and professionalize their efforts as elite actors. These elements, importantly, start somewhere. In the case of activated mass opinion during a social movement, this dynamic is initiated by movement insurgents.

As we noted in chapter 1, not all individuals from the mass public are equally likely to become activated. Thus Walter Lippmann notes that "[t]he membership of the public is not fixed. It changes with the issue; the actors in one affair are the spectators of another, and men are continually passing back and forth between the field where they are executives and the field where they are members of a public" (1925, 90). Individuals from certain publics are not only likelier to be more attentive to a given issue at a given moment in history but are also more likely to mobilize politically, even in the absence of elite signals to do so. In the case of racial segregation and civil rights during the 1950s, it was African Americans in the South (and racially liberal whites outside the South) who first became mobilized and activated. The dynamic (again, to recap from chapter 1) unfolded sequentially and processually. The insurgency of a black counterpublic and racially liberal whites in the 1950s should, in turn, activate resistance from southern whites, which should in turn incite a wave of activism by African Americans and racially liberal northern whites, and so on.

Political elites, too, are incited to respond. In some cases, rather than being the originating font of political action and information, elites act as the key intermediaries between movement-based publics (for example, African Americans) and other reactive publics (for example, southern whites, racially liberal whites). For instance, NAACP lawyers begin a process by bringing the separate and unequal educational conditions for black and white children to the judicial system. The attorney general's office and the Supreme Court respond, and southern whites react in turn to this elite action.

In other cases, active resistance from southern whites comes first, followed by elite response. For example, when southern blacks such as Autherine Lucy, James Meredith, Harvey Gantt, and nine high school teens from Little Rock, Arkansas, fight to desegregate southern schools and universities, they meet mobilized opposition from southern white locals and elites, and federal elites respond in turn. As an insurgent movement successfully unfolds, the sequence of activism and resistance to activism should crescendo as an insurgent movement rouses attentive citizens, as other latent publics begin to become activated, and as the boundaries between actor and audience become increasingly permeable.

GENERAL AND SPECIFIC EXPECTATIONS

This interactive dynamic involving elites, counterelites, and other activated publics defines the process by which audiences are drawn into and ultimately help decide the outcome of political conflicts. The general expectations from a movement-elite interactive account follow straightforwardly from chapter 1. The responsiveness of mass audiences should vary by racially and regionally defined social groups, by stages in the evolution of the civil rights movement, and by elite and counterelite influences on what we know and how we interpret ongoing events. These dimensions of mass responsiveness should reflect critical differences in how opinion is activated: how political inputs are received and accepted, how public views are voiced, and bridging the two, how institutions manage the mobilization of the public's response to movement events. And, there should be a discernible sequence to this activation, starting with the mobilization of an insurgent black counterpublic.

These general expectations suggest several specific hypotheses about the dynamics and distribution of political letter-writing during the civil rights era. These letters, to recapitulate from chapter 4, are coded for race and region of correspondent, type of correspondence, and issue position of the correspondence. In terms of race, the rate of constituency mail from blacks and racially liberal whites should be disproportionately high, especially prior to the onset of the civil rights movement in the mid-1950s. For African Americans, this rate should diminish as the movement builds in fervor and the relative rate of correspondence from white Americans increases. There are actually two major reasons to expect this decline. Once black insurgency has successfully placed civil rights and racial equality on the national political agenda, a larger number of whites (opponents and proponents alike) are likely to be roused to petition their president. At the same time, the success of movement activism in the South should empower African Americans to voice their beliefs and sentiments in more solidary and purposive modes of public expression than letter-writing.

With respect to regional differences, there is a long-standing tradition in political science of expecting that the South is different. For white southerners, we should expect the level of activation to vary with the perceived level of threat to their status quo for race relations. Thus we are unlikely to see substantial rates of political correspondence from southern whites to their president prior to the mid-1950s for the simple reason that the perceived threat is unlikely to be intensely felt during that time. For African Americans, there are reasonable grounds for expecting the South to be different, but it is unclear a priori in which direction that difference might run. Because the primary stage for movement activism is the South, we might expect southern blacks to be more activated than African Americans elsewhere in the nation. But a large proportion of African Americans "voted with their feet" and migrated out of the Deep South in the twentieth century.[1] For this reason, it may instead be blacks outside the South who hold distinct preferences on racial politics and are likelier to act on their preferences. We might also expect differences between the kind of civic associations and indigenous institutions involving northern and southern blacks to lead to regional differences in mass activation.

The categorization of letters allows us to discriminate between individual, institutional, and collective mobilization and activation related to civil rights and racial equality. Institutional or collective sources of letter-writing should indicate the degree of bottom-up mobilization, and the distribution of institutional and collective sources by race and regions over time should identify a chronology of mass mobilization. Specifically, the distribution of constituency mail over time should support or oppose the thesis that the origins of the civil rights movement pre-date the *Brown v. Board* decision and, more generally, support or oppose resource mobilization and political process theories that stress the role of organizations in mobilizing black insurgency.[2]

Finally, with regard to issue position, the first expectation is for consensus on support for civil rights among African Americans. For whites, the expectations parallel those of volume of mail by region—in particular, periods marked by a high volume of mail from the South should also be marked by high levels of opposition. More generally, the distribution of issue positions should vary with the course of events and discourses.

THE ACTIVATION OF CONSTITUENCY MAIL OVER TIME

Figure 5.2 shows the volume of letters by quarter, from 1948 to 1965, revealing in dramatic fashion how the volume of constituency mail rises and falls with the course of specific elite and counterelite events and speeches. Correspondents are incited to action by key moments such as the Montgomery bus boycott, the Little Rock crisis, and Freedom Summer. As the civil rights movement evolves and heightens in intensity, so too does the reactivity of letter writers in synchrony. Thus citizen activists are responsive to events as early as the late 1940s and early 1950s—for example, in response to President Truman's 1948 speech on civil rights, a 1948 riot in Peekskill, New York, and the 1951 house bombing and subsequent death of

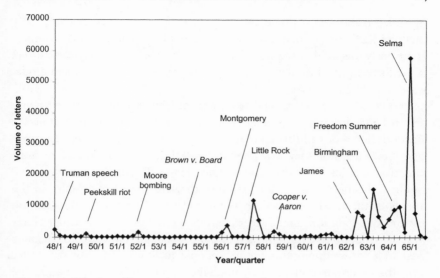

Figure 5.2   Number of Letters by Quarter, 1948–65

Florida NAACP leader Harry Moore. This reactivity, however, is a mere precursor to the striking volatility we see in response to events in the later 1950s and the 1960s—for example, the confrontations in Little Rock in 1957 and Birmingham in 1963. And, as figure 5.2 shows, this event-specificity culminates in an eye-popping response to the campaign for voting rights in Selma. To repeat Martin Luther King Jr.'s words from epigraph, "[t]he nation had seen and heard, and exploded in indignation."

The peaks and troughs in figure 5.2 also give us our first evidence that legislative and electoral moments are not as central to activating racial attitudes as elite opinion theories might claim. For instance, the most striking eruption of letters at the height of the civil rights movement did not come out of the Beltway with the Civil Rights Act of 1964, the presidential election that same year, or the Voting Rights Act the following year. Rather, it came out of Selma, a town of twenty-nine thousand residents far removed from the minds of most Americans but for the protest action of several hundred movement activists. The national outrage over Bloody Sunday in Selma was heightened in the days to follow with the violent killing of Reverend James Reeb and, less than two weeks later, Viola Liuzzo at the hands of southern white segregationists. In the midst of these focal events in the Deep South, Lyndon Johnson delivered an electrifying speech on March 15 before a joint session of Congress and before a television viewing audience of seventy million Americans. The outburst of constituency mail we see in figure 5.2 is the cumulation of this sequence of events. This is a complexity that typifies the movement-initiated, movement-elite interaction account. It is precisely this kind of sequence and interaction between nonviolent direct action, southern white resistance, and elite response that activated a tidal wave of public response.

To take another prominent case in point from figure 5.2, many scholars of the civil rights movement begin with the Supreme Court's *Brown v. Board* decision or call this elite event a decisive moment in the struggle.[3] The *Brown* decision may have been decisive, but not in the minds of most attentive individuals at the time. In fact, Harry Truman's speech on civil rights and other events prior to *Brown* that are relatively obscure in the annals of the movement—such as the riot involving Peekskill locals and patrons of a Paul Robeson concert, and the killing of NAACP leader Harry Moore—mobilized a more forceful public response. The first conspicuous peak in letter-writing occurs not in response to *Brown* but a few years later with the concatenation of local, non-elite events in the Deep South: the brutal killing of Emmett Till, the enrollment of Autherine Lucy in the University of Alabama, and the Montgomery bus boycott. The significance of these events, especially the Montgomery boycott, will be even more dramatic when I describe the influence of organizations and collective action in activating correspondence.

This seemingly unremarkable impact of *Brown* on mass opinion does not necessarily imply, as legal scholars such as Gerald Rosenberg (1991) have argued in other contexts, that the Supreme Court's decision was less consequential than conventional wisdom would have it. For one thing, we may see so few letters because the public correctly attributed the ruling to the Supreme Court rather than the presidency. Even if letters were directed to the executive branch, Attorney General Herbert Brownell's office might be a more obvious address than the White House. Moreover, historians note that Brownell himself was rather loath to submit the *Brown* case to the Supreme Court and did so only because President Truman's Justice Department filed an amicus curiae brief in December 1952 that led the Supreme Court in May 1953 to request arguments from the attorney general's office.[4]

Consistent with this reading, the data suggest that there was a lag in the political salience of the *Brown* decision vis-à-vis the public's awareness and association of the White House with the Supreme Court's ruling. Presumably, when the executive branch took a more visible role in enforcing the judiciary's ruling on desegregation by the late 1950s, the public both realized the political significance of the *Brown* decision and began to identify the decision with the Eisenhower presidency. Moreover, the Supreme Court followed the *Brown* decision with other significant rulings on segregation such as *Browder v. Gayle* in 1956 (upholding a lower court's ruling on the Montgomery bus boycott) and *Cooper v. Aaron* in 1958 (overruling a lower court's decision to halt school desegregation in Little Rock and ruling against the southern strategy of shifting public educational funds to private schools). Accordingly, we find many letters in the mid- and late 1950s that allude to the *Brown* decision either directly or indirectly through references to the Supreme Court.

Another way to make this point about the relative influence of elite- and movement-initiated events is to survey which events successfully activated a mass response. Table 5.1 isolates twenty-six events that triggered the greatest outburst of constituency mail during the years we examine.[5] The dates of correspondence for each event is noted, as well as whether the event can be considered "elite-initiated" or "movement-initiated." This coding is of

Table 5.1   Activating Events, Elite- and Movement-Initiated, 1948–65

		Type
A.	Truman pro–civil rights speech (Feb.–April, 1948)	elite
B.	Fair Employment Practices Commission legislation (May, 1948)	elite
C.	Paul Robeson concert/riot, Peekskill, N.Y. (Aug.–Sept., 1949)	movement
D.	Fair Employment Practices Commission legislation (Feb.–June, 1949)	elite
E.	white-on-black violence in the South (March, 1951)	movement
F.	Harry Moore's home bombing, Florida (Dec., 1951–April, 1952)	movement
G.	Truman's Howard University speech (June, 1952)	elite
H.	House Resolution 1758 (July, 1952)	elite
I.	*Brown v. Board of Education of Topeka*, Kansas decision (May, 1954)	elite
J.	Montgomery bus boycott (Jan.–June, 1956)	movement
K.	Little Rock, Arkansas (Sept.–Nov. 1957)	elite and movement
L.	*Cooper v. Aaron* decision (June–Oct., 1958)	elite
M.	lunch-counter sit-ins (March–April, 1960)	movement
N.	voter registration drive, Tennessee (July–Sept., 1960)	movement
O.	white-on-black violence, New Orleans (Nov.–Dec., 1960)	movement
P.	voter registration drive, Tennessee (Feb.–May, 1961)	movement
Q.	Freedom Riders (May–Aug., 1961)	movement
R.	James Meredith, Oxford, Mississippi (Sept.–Oct., 1962)	elite and movement
S.	Birmingham police brutality (May–June, 1963)	movement
T.	Kennedy's pro-civil rights speech (June, 1963)	elite
U.	Birmingham church bombing (Sept.–Oct., 1963)	movement
V.	Civil Rights legislation (Oct.–Nov., 1963)	elite
W.	Albany, Georgia Movement (May, 1964)	movement
X.	Freedom Summer (June–Aug., 1964)	movement
Y.	Selma, Alabama (Feb.–April, 1965)	elite and movement
Z.	Watts riot (August, 1965)	movement

course somewhat arbitrary. Events that were primarily staged in a nonpolitical arena and whose primary actors were nonpolitical elites are classified
as movement-initiated. Events that were primarily staged in the political
arena and whose primary actors were political elites are classified as elite-
initiated.

In three cases—Little Rock, Arkansas, in 1957, Oxford, Mississippi, in
1962, and Selma, Alabama, in 1965—events are coded as both elite- and
movement-initiated. In these cases, letters that came in prior to the point
of federal intervention (the ordering of federal troops into Little Rock; the
call of federal marshals into Oxford; Johnson's response to Sheriff Clark's
brutality in Selma) are coded as movement-based, whereas letters arriving
after such intervention are coded as elite-initiated. Note that under this
scheme, letters that result from the responses of southern elites or state
actors to movement-staged events—for example, Governor Orval Faubus's
attempts to stop enrollment of the Little Rock Nine at Central High—are
not considered elite-responsive.[6] Similarly, efforts of local southern white
individuals and organizations to stem the tide of racial integration are also
considered movement-responsive (for example, the bombing of the Six-
teenth Street Baptist Church in Birmingham in September 1963).

The picture that emerges from table 5.1 is consistent with a movement-
initiated, movement-elite interactive account. The earliest period, roughly
from 1948 to the *Brown* decision, is characterized by a sequence of a half
dozen elite events and three relatively isolated "movement-based" events.
The elite events begin with President Truman's efforts to advance civil
rights legislation. The report *To Secure These Rights* led Truman on February 2, 1948, to deliver a message urging Congress to outlaw the poll tax
and lynching, pass fair employment practices legislation, desegregate interstate transportation, and form a civil rights commission. That same year
Truman also issued executive orders to prohibit segregation in the military
and racial discrimination in federal jobs. The "movement" events in this
period are the violent descent of a local white mob on the attendees of a
Paul Robeson concert in Peekskill, New York, in August 1949; an outbreak
of white-on-black violence in the South in March 1951; and the murder of
Harry Moore in Florida in December 1951. These are all cases in which
correspondents were outraged by incidents of white-on-black violence.

Notably, these movement-based events did not yet constitute a large-
scale, coordinated campaign to mobilize grassroots activism and engage
political elites. More generally, letter-writing prior to the mid-1950s took
the form of persistent pressure on the president from entrenched activists
within the African American and sympathetic white oppositional publics.

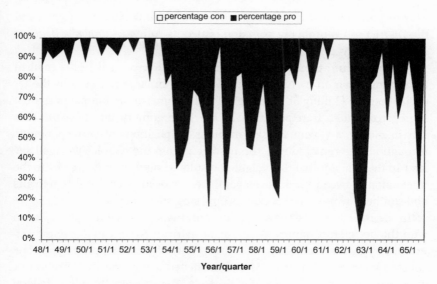

Figure 5.3   Issue Position of Letters, 1948–65

A more broadly based and heightened mass response did not emerge until the mid-1950s. As figure 5.2 suggests, and as we shall see as we disaggregate various dimensions of letter-writing, it was the movement-based
Montgomery bus boycott and not the *Brown* decision that evoked a groundswell of letter-writing. From Montgomery on, the intensifying grassroots
activism in the South played a predominant role in inciting letters to the
president. Eleven of the seventeen primary instigating events, starting with
the bus boycott, are classifiable as "movement" events, three as both elite
and movement-based, and only three as primarily elite-based events.

Finally, before turning to a closer analysis of the racial, regional, and
organizational basis of letter-writing, I illustrate the dynamic elements in
the positions that correspondents voice. Figure 5.3 shows the distribution
of letters when the correspondent's views are classified as, broadly speaking, supportive of or antagonistic to civil rights and racial equality. Across
all years, more than 60 percent of letters to the president came from proponents of civil rights and racial desegregation. In the late 1940s and early
1950s—periods with a low volume of mail and relatively low levels of
movement activism—almost all the mail came from constituents supporting President Truman's efforts to promote civil rights legislation or advocating even greater efforts. The first significant shift in this high level of
support for civil rights did not come until the Supreme Court began its

hearings on school desegregation in Kansas, Virginia, South Carolina, and the District of Columbia in 1953 and issued its ruling in *Brown v. Board of Education* in 1954.

The pendulum then begins to swing back to pro–civil rights mail in tumultuous fashion by 1955 and 1956, incited in large measure by the racially motivated killing of Emmett Till and the grassroots campaign against segregated public transportation in the Montgomery bus boycott. This sets in motion a violent see-saw in the issue positions of correspondents throughout the remainder of the 1950s and into the 1960s.[7] We shall see later in this chapter that this volatility results in significant degree from the interaction between black correspondents advocating civil rights reforms and southern white correspondents opposing such change.

In the 1960s, we see the single most dramatic reversal in mass opinion with the decision of James Meredith, an African American Air Force veteran, to apply for admission to the University of Mississippi in 1962. The court-ordered enrollment of Meredith incited a massive mobilization of southern white resistance and ultimately drew several hundred federal marshals and Assistant Attorneys General Nicholas Katzenbach and John Doar down to Oxford to ensure a peaceful transition. An incendiary speech by Governor Ross Barnett at an Ole Miss football game on September 29, 1962, however, set the stage for a violent stand-off between federal marshals and angry white mobs the following day. By the next morning, 160 federal marshals were injured, 28 by gunshot, and 3 persons killed. As figure 5.3 shows, the net effect of this threat to segregation at Ole Miss, vis-à-vis the activation of attentive citizens, was a massive turnaround from uncontested pressure for racial integration in the spring of 1962 to an almost total demand for racial segregation by late 1962. Ultimately, forces in favor of civil rights regained the upper hand. As Robert Moses was to declare later, if Mississippi was the iceberg that chilled the impetus for change, there was now "a tremor in the middle of the iceberg" (1994, 95).

THE RACIAL AND REGIONAL BASES OF MASS ACTIVATION

These points, in themselves, do not take us far enough in distinguishing between the three possible accounts of mass activation in figure 5.1. To do this, we need to disaggregate these patterns in letter-writing by race, region, and type of correspondence. We begin with race. The race of the correspondent is either explicitly declared by the author or can be inferred from the text of the correspondence in about 47 percent of the cases. Roughly 24 percent of the letters in question are from African Americans.[8] The ra-

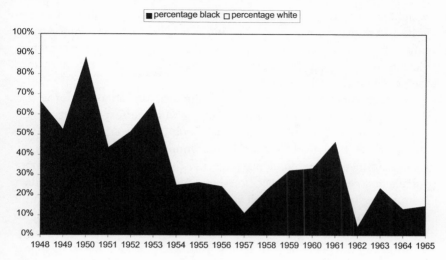

Figure 5.4   Distribution of Letters by Race, 1948–65

cial breakdown is striking not just because blacks are writing at a disproportionately high level (relative to the proportion of blacks in the general
population), but also because of the timing and persistence of their correspondence.

Figure 5.4 shows the racial distribution of constituency mail over time.
African Americans, relative to white Americans, appeared more vigorous
and persistent in their letter-writing during the early stages of movement
activism. It is, in fact, not until 1954 with the Supreme Court's *Brown* decision that we see a pronounced response from white Americans. When we
disaggregate the distribution of letters by race and region, we shall see
that this increase in letters from whites reflects the countermobilization of
southern whites who perceived a threat to the status quo. After the Little
Rock crisis in 1957 subsided, the proportion of letters from whites diminished. Southern whites once again become activated in 1962 with the controversy over James Meredith's enrollment at Ole Miss.

The general pattern of letter-writing over time by race is unsurprising,
but a nice confirmation of our expectations nonetheless. In the early years,
a disproportionate number of letters came from African Americans. As the
movement began to unfold, we find an increasing proportion of whites who
petitioned the president. This salient role of African American correspondence is even more pronounced when we weight the racial breakdown of
letters by the racial distribution in the general population (not shown).

Weighted thus, African Americans were more than twelve times likelier to write a letter to the president concerning civil rights than were white Americans between 1948 and 1953. Even when whites were drawn into the struggle after 1954, African Americans remained about twice as likely to write to the president about the matter.

Another notable finding on racial differences in letter-writing is that there is a strikingly greater variance among white correspondents. Letter-writing by African Americans, although mobilized by critical events, was also anchored by a steady and persistent foundation of pressure across the years examined. Correspondence patterns of whites are significantly more volatile and responsive to specific events. Although the number of letters from white Americans across all years is about three times that of African Americans, the variance across time periods (quarterly) in the volume of letters from whites is about *twenty-seven* times greater than that of blacks.

Surges in the percentage of letters from whites, more precisely, appear to capture three discernible stages of letter-writing. In 1949 and 1951 (the Peekskill riot and the murder of Harry Moore), they reflect the mobilization of northern white liberals in response to high-profile cases of white-on-black violence. With the *Brown* decision in 1954, these peaks reflect the mobilization of a (usually southern) white backlash to federal intervention to enforce desegregation (that, with the *Brown* decision, the 1957 Little Rock crisis, and the 1962 enrollment of James Meredith at the University of Mississippi). And following the Ole Miss crisis, the surge in letter-writing reflects the mobilization of white support for racial integration in response to media coverage of movement activism and local southern responses to that activism.

The pattern of early pressure from African Americans and subsequent activation of other sectors of the mass public is even clearer when we break down the distribution of constituency mail by region. Figure 5.5 shows this decomposition by region for white Americans. We again see roughly three stages of letter-writing: from the late 1940s to the mid-1950s, from the mid-1950s to the late 1950s, and the 1960s. Letters from the late 1940s and early 1950s came predominantly from northern whites who were sympathetic to the plight of African Americans. The main exception to this is the activation of southern whites in 1948, who responded to southern white elites who recoiled in protest against President Truman's public advocacy of civil rights legislation. Thus more than one of every two letters from whites in 1948 was addressed from the South, but by the early 1950s this proportion declined to less than one in every ten letters.[9]

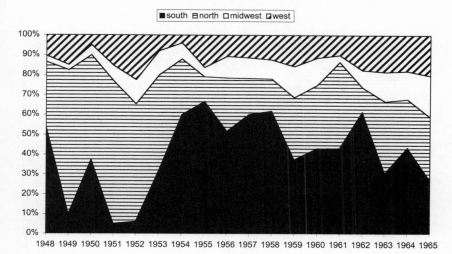

Figure 5.5   Distribution of Letters from Whites, by Region, 1948–65

Southern white voices were then reawakened by the Supreme Court hearings in 1953 and its ruling on school desegregation in 1954. Unlike the rest of the country (recall figure 5.2), southern whites may well have had grounds for viewing *Brown* as a significant threat to their existing segregationist laws and practices. In addition, southern whites had just cause to expect Dwight D. Eisenhower to lend a sympathetic ear to their concerns about the *Brown* decision.[10] More generally, figure 5.5 illustrates the special responsiveness of southern whites to elite events: the prominent spikes in southern correspondence follow Truman's 1948 civil rights speech, the 1954 *Brown* decision, the 1957 Little Rock crisis, the 1958 *Aaron v. Cooper* decision against the southern strategy of "interposition," and the 1962 desegregation of the University of Mississippi. Figure 5.5 also shows the gradual activation of whites from the rest of the nation. In 1955, two of every three letters from whites came from the South. By 1965, only one of every four did so.

We see a markedly different picture with African Americans in figure 5.6. By comparison to the regional volatility of letter-writing for whites, the distribution of letters by region for blacks is remarkably stable. This is particularly so given the modest sample sizes in each year for African Americans vis-à-vis those for whites (recall that across all years, letters from blacks comprise about one of every four letters). The chief exception to this rela-

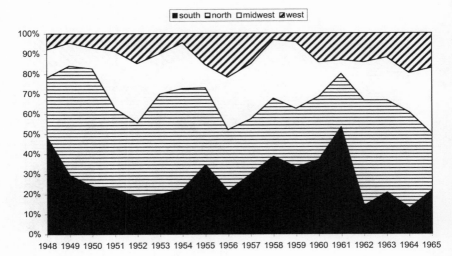

Figure 5.6   Distribution of Letters from Blacks, by Region, 1948–65

tive regional stability is the upsurge in letter-writing among blacks outside the South in the 1960s, perhaps reflecting the rise of black insurgency in urban areas.

The relative stability of letter-writing across regions among blacks is notable not just in itself, but also because southern blacks do not predominate in the distribution of letters by region. This is so despite the fact that the primary arena for movement activism is the Deep South and that southern blacks comprise a majority of all African Americans in the United States. Almost three of every four blacks in the United States in 1940 lived in the South, and, after an extensive outmigration of African Americans in subsequent decades, this proportion remained about one in two as late as 1970.[11] Throughout almost the entire period we examine, only about 20 to 40 percent of correspondence from African Americans come from southern blacks.

This disproportionate representation of African American correspondents from nonsouthern regions of the United States may reflect the interaction of several factors. As we noted above, to the extent that African Americans who "voted with their feet" and left the South are distinct from African Americans who chose to remain in the South, this difference may be reflected in figure 5.6. In addition, the domination of African Americans in the Jim Crow South may have been so total that even the most basic forms of political expression were repressed. And related to these factors, the disproportionate levels of letter-writing by African Americans outside the South may reflect differential literacy rates between southern and non-southern blacks. In effect, this disproportionate representation outside the South—in the face of movement activism staged primarily in the South—bears out the *collective* activation of African Americans during the civil rights era and the salience of racial group interests and consciousness with regard to civil rights and racial integration.

This group basis to the activation of African Americans is perhaps also manifested in their relative lack of a response to the Supreme Court's landmark *Brown v. Board of Education* decision in 1954. Although figure 5.2 revealed that Americans in 1954 were generally inattentive to the *Brown* decision (as measured by letters to the president), we expect certain segments of the general public to be quite attentive to this matter. We certainly see an alarmed response from southern whites in their letters to President Eisenhower. It is likely that blacks simply did not consider the White House the primary address for any comment or celebration in response to the *Brown* decision. Beyond distinguishing the Supreme Court and the White House, African Americans likely understood the *Brown* decision as the culmination of the NAACP's decades-long legal struggle and not a *de novo* jurisprudential affirmation of racial justice. As Leon Higginbotham (1996), Richard Kluger (1976), and others show, the *Brown* decision was the result of a strategic sequence of U.S. Supreme Court precedents, such as *Missouri ex rel. Gaines* in 1938 (the Court ruling in favor of equal education facilities within a state), *Morgan v. Commonwealth of Virginia* in 1946 (the Court ruling against the segregation of interstate bus travel), *McLaurin v. Board of Regents* in 1950 (the Court ruling against segregation at the University of Oklahoma), and *Sweatt v. Painter* in 1950 (the Court ruling that "separate" education facilities are by definition unequal).

Our final view of racial and regional differences in constituency mail is of the support or opposition to civil rights over time. Among African Americans, support for civil rights and desegregation is essentially unanimous and unchanged over time. There are, of course, differences in how the opinions of African Americans are framed, how intensely they are voiced, how radical or accommodationist the demands for change are, and so on. But by the crude measure of pro or con, more than 99 percent of letters are categorizable as "pro."

About 47 percent of white letters in all years favor desegregation and civil rights reform. The primary regional divide for white Americans appears to be a North-South divide. When support levels are correlated with race and region, the percentage of mail from segregationists and the percentage of mail from southern whites correlates at 0.89. The percentage of mail advocating desegregation and the percentage of mail from northern whites correlates at 0.90. There is no significant statistical association between issue position and letters from whites in the Midwest or the western United States.

Finally, the dynamics of letter-writing by whites also roughly parallels figure 5.3. The primary dissimilarities arise when letters come disproportionately from the South—1953–54 for the *Brown* decision, 1957 for the Little Rock crisis, and 1962 for James Meredith's enrollment at Ole Miss—and are marked by high levels of opposition. Along similar lines, periods in which correspondence rises in response to movement campaigns—1956 for the Montgomery bus boycott, 1960–61 for the student lunch counter sit-ins and the Freedom Riders, and 1963–65 for campaigns in Albany, Georgia, Birmingham, and Selma, and Freedom Summer—appear to have activated white proponents of desegregation and civil rights reforms.

THE ORGANIZATIONAL BASES OF MASS ACTIVATION

Thus far, we have seen the striking reactivity of the volume of constituency mail to particular elite and non-elite events. We have also seen evidence of the early, persistent, and collective activation of African Americans and the event- and region-specific activation of white Americans. The activation of mass opinion is thus markedly divided across racial and regional cleavage lines. In describing the racial and regional bases of mass activation, however, we have yet to distinguish between letters written by isolated individuals and letters written on behalf of organizations or collections of individuals. If the activation of mass opinion described in these aggregate shifts corresponds closely with the mobilization of movement activism, then we should expect the rise of institutional and collective sources of mail to rise with this activation. Put otherwise, I asserted above that letter writers and movement activists both reflect a meso-level (that is, a level between elites and masses) of issue-specific attentive citizens. If this is so, then institutional mobilization and collective action should play a vital role in letter-writing, analogous to the role that institutional mobilization and collective action play in movement activism itself.

Figures 5.7 and 5.8 show changes in the type of letters over time for blacks and whites. For the period covered in figure 5.7 the overwhelming preponderance of mail from whites came from individuals. Roughly 90 percent of letters reflected the viewpoints of private citizens speaking for

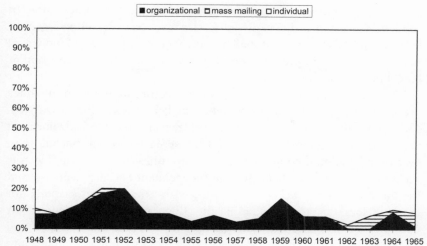

Figure 5.7   Distribution of Letters from Whites, by Type, 1948–65

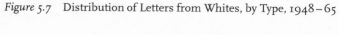

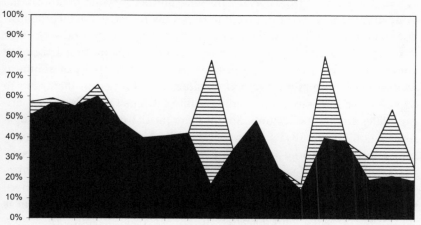

Figure 5.8   Distribution of Letters from Blacks, by Type, 1948–65

themselves. There is not much variation on this dimension over time. In some measure, this is due to the intricacies involved with coding organizational or collective sources of mail by race. Yet the dominance of individual mail is still rather impressive and, if there is a bias here, the direction of bias is not demonstratively clear.[12]

The single largest period of organized pressure in letters from whites occurred during the formative period of the late 1940s to the early 1950s. The organizations were almost exclusively racially liberal, mostly northern organizations. The most common of these were labor groups (including an overrepresentation among relatively obscure unions such as the Electric, Radio, and Machinists AFL-CIO, the Independent Socialist Workers, and the Fur and Leather Workers' Union), Jewish-American associations (for example, local chapters of B'nai B'rith–Hillel), women's associations (for example, the Women's International League for Peace and Freedom and local chapters of the Emma Lazarus Club, a literary club), and progressive partisan groups (for example, local chapters of the American Communist Party, the Progressive Party, and the American Labor Party).[13]

To put this in some numerical perspective, almost 60 percent of all organizational mail from racially liberal, "northern" white organizations came during the period from 1948 to 1955; only 10 percent of all organization mail from southern white groups came during this groundwork stage of movement activism. The relative absence of an organizational presence among southern whites is due in large part to the reactivity of southern whites. Various countermovement organizations formed in the South to oppose racial integration—including White Citizens Councils, the American States Rights Association, Southerners in Alabama, and the National Association for the Advancement of White People—did not play a significant role until the mid-1950s, after the *Brown* decision. Even across all years, letter-writing for northern whites is strongly mediated by organizations, whereas letter-writing for southern whites is not: for Northern whites, the percentage of organizationally affiliated constituency mail is positively correlated with all letters (0.71), whereas for southern whites, only individual mail is positively correlated with all letters (0.79).

Figure 5.8 shows that for blacks the influence of organizations and collective action in activating and mobilizing mass opinion is far more pronounced. Across all years, organizational and collective sources of mail comprise fully 45 percent of all correspondence from African Americans.[14] The level of organizational mobilization is especially striking prior to and during the onset of mass activism from the late 1940s through the 1950s. By 1960, organizational mail somewhat diminishes in influence but mass mailings are much more prominent. Across all years, more than half of the organized mail comes from advocacy groups—that is, groups such as local chapters of the NAACP that explicitly advocate African American interests. But the rest of the mail from black organizations comes from a remarkable melange of associations, most commonly those representing African American women (for example, the Negro Council of Women), historically black colleges (including college organizations such as Alpha Kappa Alpha, a black sorority), religious organizations (for example, local AME-Zion church congregations), and the black press (including the editors of the *Pittsburgh Courier* and the *Chicago Defender*).

When we look closely at which organizations were institutional sources of constituency mail, we do not find, for the most part, the partisan legislative and electorally minded institutions that elite opinion theories might predict. Rather, we find an impressive diversity of nonpartisan voluntary associations. Partisan groups sent only 1 percent of all organizational mail from African Americans. By contrast, fully half of all organizational mail from African Americans came from groups whose primary mission is to advocate for black interests and racial equality. And the next most commonly found source of organizational mail was African American women's groups (roughly one of every eight such items). Thus for African Americans much of the transmission of political information and the activation of mass opinion regarding civil rights occurred outside the dominant, institutionalized sphere of political exchange. And taken together, the range of associations represented strongly confirms theoretical and historical works that stress the institutional diversity behind the black rights struggle.

The comparison of figures 5.7 and 5.8 is especially telling. The clear inference is that mobilized appeals from African American organizations occurred prior to such mobilization among white organizations. For both whites and blacks, as the movement grew and became institutionalized, organizational pressure diminished in salience. This is most likely less a function of a decline in organizational pressure than it is a function of movement activists successfully pushing civil rights onto the national agenda and thus mobilizing a large-scale response among isolated individuals.

Along these lines, the use of mass mailings and collective correspondence as part of a movement repertoire is strikingly more salient for African Americans than for white Americans. Figure 5.8 shows, on this point, the primacy of the period between late 1955 and 1956. This critical period of mass activation in the black counterpublic began with the lynching of Emmett Till, a fourteen-year-old Chicagoan who was brutally beaten, murdered, and mutilated by two white men in Leflore County, Mississippi, in

1955 after Till spoke familiarly with the wife of one of the men. This horrific incident mobilized a response from the black press, national NAACP officials, and African American leaders such as Detroit congressman Charles Diggs Jr., and stirred up a groundswell of letters in the mail room of the White House.

At the same time, just hours away in Montgomery, Alabama, the stage was being set for the first grassroots campaign to successfully engage and activate attentive citizens throughout the nation. Local black counterelites in Montgomery such as E. D. Nixon (a veteran from the Brotherhood of Sleeping Car Porters and leader of Alabama's NAACP) and JoAnn Robinson (chair of Montgomery's Women's Political Council, an association of black middle-class women and a faculty member at Alabama State College, a historically black college) were poised to test the city's segregated public transportation laws when the right case came along. That moment occurred on December 1, 1955, when Rosa Parks famously and with quiet resolve refused to yield her bus seat to a standing white man. After a year's struggle under the aegis of Nixon, Robinson, Martin Luther King Jr. and others, the boycott's unbending tenacity won the day in the "Cradle of the Confederacy" and captured the imagination of citizen activists throughout the nation.[15]

Conspicuously, as scholars of the civil rights movement have documented, this focal event not only incited the first dramatic upsurge in letter-writing, seen in figure 5.2, but in particular it incited an organized response against racial segregation. This occurred with religiously based pacifist (and mostly white) groups such as the Fellowship of Reconciliation and the American Friends Service Committee as well as with black advocacy organizations such as the NAACP and other nonpolitical voluntary associations within the African American community. In figure 5.8, this organized response is seen most remarkably in the rise of mass mailings as a mode of letter-writing and of mass protest. This jagged peak virtually trumpets a clarion call for the civil rights movement.

Moreover, for African Americans this organized response was not simply a southern phenomenon. For example, roughly 740 individually signed cards were mailed by a grassroots organization from Florence, California, a predominantly African American neighborhood in Los Angeles. On one side, the card read: "Walking is a crime in Alabama! Mr. President: The Constitution should be for ALL people. Give Federal protection to civil rights. End segregation." The other side read: "Dear Sir: I urge you to use the full power of the Federal Government to protect the lives, jobs and civil rights of the Negro people in the South. Voting rights of the Negro people should be made a reality in '56."[16] By the 1960s, mass mailings were well established as part of the civil rights movement's tactical repertoire.[17]

Thus Mamie Till Bradley, mother of the slain Emmett, proclaimed the mid-1950s as the critical moment that pushed a "giant glacier" for social change onward without defeat, and the black journalist Louis Lomax declared, "The Negro revolt is properly dated from the moment Mrs. Rosa Parks said 'No' to the bus driver's demand that she get up and let a White man have her seat" (quoted in Robnett, 1998, 262). To restate an important point, scholars such as Aldon Morris (1984) and Belinda Robnett (1997) point out that the Montgomery bus boycott (and its impact on the public's views on desegregation) was not a spontaneous outcry inspired by the isolated heroism of an unassuming, foot-weary seamstress. Rather, Rosa Parks had a "rep" among bus drivers for refusing to give up her seat even in the 1940s and brought to her historic act of civil disobedience a background in community activism from local involvement in the NAACP and the Montgomery Women's Political Council and formal training in organizing at the Highlander Folk School in Monteagle, Tennessee.

MEDIA COVERAGE AND MASS ACTIVATION

The relative sizes of the roles that organizations and collective action played in mobilizing letter-writing confirms our expectations that institutions within an oppositional black counterpublic took the lead in the process of activating mass opinion. There is a yet unconsidered institutional form that is likely to influence the activation of mass opinion. The mass media ought to play a central role in mediating between the primary political actors in the civil rights movement, conventional political elites and movement-based activists, and the general public. A systematic, discriminating analysis of media coverage and its influence on activated mass opinion—in particular, one that compares dominant media institutions (network news, nationally circulated newsmagazines, flagship newspapers such as the *New York Times*) with media institutions serving particular publics (local papers in southern cities or black papers such as the *Chicago Defender*, the *Pittsburgh Courier*, and the *Amsterdam News*)—is beyond the scope of this book.

We can, however, establish a few relationships between media coverage, movement activism, and letter-writing consistent with a movement-elite interactive account. To begin, in contrast to a strict top-down account, if our movement-elite account is correct, we should expect a close correspondence between media coverage and movement-initiated events. This turns out to be the case. When the volume of media coverage is compared with the number of movement-initiated events, the two time series parallel each other very closely: the correlation between these two time series is a healthy 0.87.[18] There are three discernible years in which the volume of media coverage deviated somewhat from movement-initiated events: 1948, 1952, and 1957. These were years, not coincidentally, in which media coverage followed elite-initiated events—Harry Truman and the presidential elections of 1948 and 1952 and Dwight Eisenhower's sending of federal troops to Little Rock in 1957.

In addition, to the extent that mass media coverage informs and activates latent public opinion, we should expect a close correspondence between media coverage and our measure of mass activation, letter-writing. We saw evidence to support the first of these propositions in chapter 4. Figure 4.1, which compares the volume of letter-writing over time with the volume of mainstream print media coverage over time, shows that media coverage increased and decreased intelligibly as the civil rights movement unfolded. Thus, prior to 1956, there was a fairly low level of front page coverage.[19] This coverage then peaked in 1957 with the Little Rock crisis before going through a series of peaks and troughs between 1958 and 1965. When this time-series on media coverage is compared with letter-writing, the parallel movement is quite striking.[20]

This comparison, however, does not consider racial differences in the linkage of constituency mail and media coverage of civil rights issues. Recall from figures 5.4, 5.5, and 5.6 that there is a significantly higher event-sensitivity to letter writing from white Americans and a much greater variance in the volume of correspondence from whites as well. One possible reason is that whites are more restricted in their sources of information about ongoing events. Put otherwise, perhaps even the most attentive white Americans are limited by what mainstream mass media such as the *New York Times* or network news broadcasts present to them. By contrast, we know from our discussion of organizational fonts of constituency mail that African Americans are engaged by alternative sources of political information and mobilization from the black press to indigenous institutions such as churches, colleges, and civic associations. If this is correct, then the parallel between the level of correspondence and the level of media coverage should be quite close for white Americans and perhaps less close (certainly not more close) for African Americans.

This turns out to be partly true. The racial breakdown in number of letters and media coverage is shown in figures 5.9 and 5.10. As in figure 4.1, media coverage is measured as the number of front-page articles in the *New York Times* on civil rights and racial equality, based on the *New York Times*

Index. The volume of constituency mail from both whites and blacks track closely with media coverage. Keeping in mind that this is relatively undiscriminating analysis, we see that letter-writing by whites appears to parallel media coverage more closely than does letter-writing by blacks: the resulting correlation between media coverage and constituency mail from 1948 to 1964 is 0.75 for whites and 0.67 for blacks.

The fact that whites may be more attentive than African Americans to mainstream print media such as the *New York Times* is fairly unsurprising, but it does run somewhat counter to our earlier finding that African Americans *generally* were more attentive to ongoing events than were whites, especially before the rise of movement activism in the mid-1950s. This potential incongruity is mitigated by splitting the sample. If we simply focus on how closely media coverage parallels activated mass opinion from 1948 to 1955, the resulting correlation is 0.18 for whites and 0.37 for African Americans. Thus, in the period prior to the organized campaign for civil rights, media coverage and letter writing were more tightly linked for African Americans, even as measured by mainstream media coverage.

In themselves, these parallels and simple correlations cannot tell us anything decisive about elite versus non-elite influences on the formation of mobilized opinion.[21] Nonetheless, they nicely illustrate the role that institutions such as the mass media play in transmitting information about ongoing events—whether elite or non-elite in origin—and the effect that

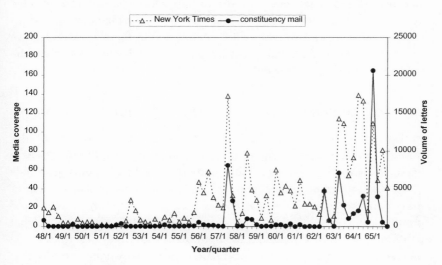

Figure 5.9   New York Times Coverage and Letters from Whites, 1948–65

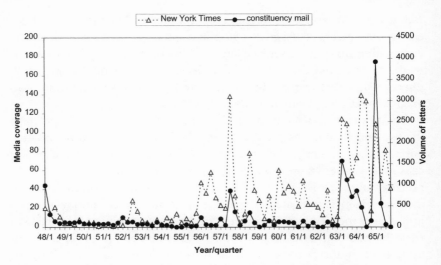

Figure 5.10   New York Times Coverage and Letters from Blacks, 1948–65

such information plays in activating mass opinion. The key assumption underlying the link between the transmission of information about civil rights events and the activation of individuals (for example, through letter-writing) is that the individuals who become activated come out of a sector of the mass public that is highly attentive and for whom civil rights holds an especially high degree of issue salience. And this is not an unreasonable assumption. To borrow Page and Shapiro's (1992) terminology, there is an unmistakable "collective rationality" manifested in the close parallels we see between how often and when people write and often and when the media report on ongoing events.

MASS ACTIVATION AND MOVEMENT-ELITE INTERACTION

In this chapter, I have examined the dynamics of activated racial attitudes through an analysis of changes in letter-writing from 1948 to 1965. These letters illustrate the dynamic, labile nature of mass opinion during periods of mass mobilization such as the civil rights movement. The activation of mass opinion, as measured by letter-writing, is highly time-, event-, and group-specific. In particular, the dynamics describe the activating effect that political events have on latent mass opinion. As V. O. Key describes it: "At one point in time no pattern of interactions may exist among persons (that is, they may not constitute a group) although they may share a particular set of attitudes . . . certain attitudes or opinions may exist in the minds of men without their being activated politically. Given the relevant or appropriate stimulus, the opinion will be triggered into expression or action" (1961, 264). The idea of latent opinion is especially helpful in capturing the tendencies in mass opinion to respond to evolving political issues and events in ways that may take political elites off-guard. Thus Key notes, "[u]ntil the opinion moves by activation from its state of hibernation, one can know neither its form not its direction." Precisely for this reason, "in the practice of politics and government latent opinion is really about the only type of opinion that generates much anxiety" (1961, 263). What makes public opinion so powerful is its unpredictability—about when individuals will be roused to action and whether that activation will be a tempestuous flicker or an enduring glow.

In particular, different events during stages of the civil rights movement activated an upsurge of mail from different sectors of the mass public. In the formative stages, most of the correspondence came from highly engaged African Americans and racially liberal whites. With the onset of elite and non-elite events by the mid-1950s (the *Brown* decision and the Montgomery bus boycott, respectively, the activation shifted back and forth between southern whites opposed to changes in their status quo and African Americans (and whites outside the South) pushing for change. By 1960, there was a crescendo of sympathetic white voices that—with the striking exception of a mounted effort to resist James Meredith's enrollment at Ole Miss—began to drown out voices of opposition to change. And, finally, this crescendo rose to a deafening roar of outrage against state-sanctioned brutality in Selma in 1965.

The findings in this chapter suggest, in addition to this barbed racial and regional divide, the importance for blacks of organizational and collective sources of mobilization, which strongly confirm E. E. Schattschneider's view that "organization is itself a mobilization of bias in preparation for action" (1960, 30). Furthermore, the story of mass activation during the civil rights era told in this chapter is quite consistent with social movement theorists' accounts of the critical role that institutions played in the early stages of black insurgency. This role was not limited to organizations indigenous to the African American community but included a diversity of other organized interests from labor unions and radical political parties to, in particular, Jewish American associations and women's social clubs. And as movement activism began to heighten in scale and scope, we see a striking shift from a heavily organizational component to letter-writing to the mobilization of the masses, as seen in the heavy volume of individual letters and the emergence of mass mailings.

The findings here thus rub against elite-driven accounts that attribute mass-level shifts in partisanship and racial attitudes primarily to elite partisan cues (for example, cues present in moments such as the 1958 Senate elections and the 1964 presidential race). In addition, the organizational sources of mobilization are seldom political parties or conventional interest groups but rather are a rich diversity of civic associations and movement-related organizations. Although the level of analysis here does not conclusively refute strictly top-down accounts, the results do show a more complex, interactive portrait of the insurgent role of a black counterpublic, the mobilization of other sectional publics (that is, southern and northern whites), and the response of government actors at the elite level.

Not all elite-based theories, of course, are equally implicated. Benjamin Page and Robert Shapiro's account of the "rational public" (1992), for example, fully permits—both in theoretical specification and in substantive discussion—a role for non-elite citizen activism as an influence on mass opinion. Theoretically, their specification of causes of change in public opinion cedes a clear role to social movements (albeit lumped together with "organized interests" and "corporations") as an influence on mass preferences (1992, 354). Substantively, Page and Shapiro credit the sway of "broad historical development" for shifting racial attitudes in the twentieth century and point to both elite- and movement-initiated events from the late 1950s to the early 1960s. They note the Montgomery bus boycott of 1956, President Eisenhower's decision to send federal troops to Little Rock schools in 1957, lunch counter sit-ins in 1960, the freedom rides of 1961, James Meredith's enrollment in the University of Mississippi in 1962, and the March on Washington in 1963 (1992, 76–77). The authors place their greatest emphasis, however, on the impact of black migration out of the South, with the influx of African Americans in the urban North politically mobilizing blacks and putatively undermining racist stereotypes among whites. And they note that

> [i]f this account is correct . . . then any opinion-leading roles of the Supreme Court and President Johnson and other political figures were quite secondary, reacting to change, helping mainly to legitimate the evolving egalitarian beliefs and to spell out policy implications. The civil rights movement was more important, forcing attention on the issue and dramatizing the realities of racial oppression, especially in the South. (1992, 80)

The findings presented in this chapter are certainly consistent with Page and Shapiro's understanding of changes in aggregate mass opinion, and perhaps more important, consistent with much existing secondary historical and sociological analysis of the civil rights movement. As with aggregate results generally, the level of analysis in this chapter has generated some inviting but ultimately not fully discriminating results. In chapter 6 we will begin to break through this rarefied air of aggregate changes and "broad historical development" to look quite intimately at the individual articulations of sound, fury, and uplift in the struggle over race relations in the American republic.

SIX

CONTESTED MEANINGS AND MOVEMENT AGENCY

Is this America? Is this the land of the free? Is this the home of the brave?

—Fanny Lou Hamer

The whole history of the progress of human liberty shows that all concessions yet made to her august claims, have been born of earnest struggle. . . . This struggle may be a moral one, or it may be a physical one, and it may be both moral and physical, but it must be a struggle. Power concedes nothing without a demand. It never did and it never will.

—Frederick Douglass

There remains a great and well-understood meaning simply in *the* South; there is, in fact, a sense of oneness here, an identity, a sharing. . . . The Confederacy was, as a matter of law, a state in being; but it was first of all, and still is . . . a state of mind. And running through this state of mind, now loose as basting thread, now knotted as twine, now strong and stubborn as wire, coloring the whole fabric of our lives, is this inescapable awareness: the consciousness of the Negro.

—James J. Kilpatrick

For most ordinary Americans, the look back in time is a stubbornly erring gaze. When we reflect back on the civil rights movement, our memories are shaded and hued by personal experience, nostalgia, stories we have heard from "back in the day," and the freeze-framed images found in textbooks, celluloid, cultural artifacts, and popular media accounts of the era. What shines through even today, however, is the powerful language we remember from the civil rights movement: from Martin Luther King Jr.'s rapturously uplifting "I have a dream" speech and Malcolm X's incendiary demand for equality and freedom "by any means necessary" to George Wallace's defiant vow, "Segregation now! Segregation tomorrow! Segregation forever!" Even today, these words have the power to stir our political imagination, sober our realities, and challenge our habits of mind.

In this chapter, we shall see that the activation of public opinion profoundly involves a struggle over words—their meanings and the forceful interpretive frames they evoke. Our analytic lens shifts from the panoramic view of aggregate changes in letter-writing in chapter 5 to a microscopic, magnified view of the substance and strategic framing of individual letters. The vivid language in these letters further animates the dialogical, narrative, rhetorical, and emotive dimensions of political expression first depicted in chapter 4. More than this, they demonstrate the powerful motivating force of cherished political principles and group-based predispositions in voicing public views about race during the civil rights movement.

Importantly, there is a structure and sequence to how cherished values and group-based predispositions are articulated. This structure and sequence support the movement-initiated, movement-elite interaction account of mass activation. As seen in chapter 5, these letters tend more often to respond to movement-based influences than they do to elite-based influences. This sensitivity to movement events and organizations illustrates the collective "agency" of black insurgency in activating public views of race. Our window into this collective agency is the written narratives of activated audiences, with the clash between civil rights advocates and opponents as the backdrop. As we shall see, the struggle over civil rights reflects as well the struggle over how mass audiences interpreted and understood the unfolding events of the 1950s and 1960s.

I begin the chapter with a discussion about language and its power to influence and to transform the way we think. In particular, political actors (elite and non-elite) can demonstrate their agency in defining public views on race by contesting the meanings of cherished political concepts or rearticulating them in novel contexts. Next I present stylized examples of the voices of each of the three primary attentive publics we have considered in this book: African Americans, southern whites, and racially liberal (northern) whites. The emphasis here is on sketching the kinds of appeals made for civil rights by each group and delineate significant shifts over time in the kinds of appeals made. These stylized descriptions are followed by a more systematic comparison of differences in the expression of four major types of interpretive frames: cherished principles, group dimensions, political considerations, and responsiveness to elite- and movement-initiated events. I conclude with some thoughts on what this more textual, activated voice means for how we study public opinion and for how we understand the role of mass audiences in social movements.

CONTESTED FRAMES AND BLACK INSURGENCY

The quest for social and political change, Frederick Douglass reminds us in the epigraph, entails struggle. Whether in a democracy or a dictatorship, reforms that do not come about through formal, institutionalized decision-making processes must be demanded. And making such demands involves a clash of both physical and moral forces. Thus protest movements demand real outcomes: better material conditions, greater political representation, fairer public policies, fuller legal protection. In most instances, they also involve struggles over the values and meaning that we give to our experiences and to the issues at stake. As a result, insurgent campaigns also entail conflict over the content and contours of mass opinion.

This is a central fact about conflict that the political scientist E. E. Schattschneider understood well. I quoted Schattschneider in chapter 1 as saying that "spectators are as much a part of the [struggle] as are the overt combatants. The spectators are an integral part of the situation, for, as likely as not, the *audience* determines the outcome of the fight" (1960, 2). And in chapter 5, we saw how struggles at the grassroots level in the Deep South and under the glittered dome of Congress are reflected in struggles across racially, regionally, and institutionally defined factions of the mass public. But the view in chapter 5 is rendered in broad, aggregate strokes that tell us little about the substance of this struggle. Surely we are curious about the colors, textures, images, and movements of line and shade that embody this conflict and contestation over public views of race.

Such a detailed and nuanced portrait is drawn with the words and interpretive frames that motivated audiences to voice their political opinions. Language defines the common basis for understanding and interpreting what political actors say and do.[1] "Words are deeds," in Ludwig Wittgenstein's famously economical phrase. Words reveal something about what political actors think, how they communicate their views, and how they persuade other political actors. As Daniel Rodgers observes, under the right circumstances, words also wield an extraordinary power to inform and transform the public's views on an issue at hand:

[T]hough words constrain their users, hobble political desires, nudge them down socially worn channels, they are in other circumstances radically unstable. Let enough persons repeat a cant phrase . . . and there is a chance that they will suddenly charge the words with new meaning. . . . [Words] are all double-edged, profoundly radical or profoundly conservative, depending on who has hold of them . . . words are tools, often weapons; the vocabulary of politics is contested terrain and always has been. (1987, 10–11)

As Rodgers implies, sometimes sheer volume and incantation are what give words such potency. Yet often, contesting the language we use is a crucial pathway to social change. Political actors can change minds and activate beliefs with the specific, strategic words they choose. Survey experiments on question wording and issue framing make this case quite impressively. Data from the 1989 Race and Politics Study, for example, show that fully three out of four individuals will oppose affirmative action in university admissions if asked whether "qualified blacks should be given preference." If instead they are asked whether "an extra effort should be made to be sure that qualified blacks are considered," the distribution of viewpoints skews in the opposite direction, with more than three out of five individuals favoring affirmative action.[2]

The powerful effect of language is echoed in recent racial conflicts involving state- and municipal-level referendum campaigns to eliminate affirmative action policies in California, Washington State, Houston, Texas, and other locales. In each of these cases, the fault lines are drawn not just in terms of the distribution of material benefits and burdens, but also in terms of the distribution of contested meanings of race and racial policy. Opponents of affirmative action in California, for instance, artfully dubbed Proposition 209 the "California Civil Rights Initiative" and framed the text of the proposition with this opening: "The state shall not discriminate against, or *grant preferential treatment to,* any individual or group on the basis of race, sex, color, ethnicity, or national origin" (emphasis added).[3] Thus we can understand political change (or at least a significant aspect of it) by understanding changes in the use of political language. In the present case, I examine the language that activated audiences to express their views as the civil rights movement unfolded and intensified. In particular, I examine whether the language used by the insurgent black counterpublic prevailed in the contestation over meaning and interpretive frames with regard to racial integration and civil rights.

That said, change and change agents are notoriously difficult to pinpoint, especially when the units of analysis are words and discourses. Moreover, the putative agency in this chapter is attributed to a collective, and thus our view of movement agency is indirect. Evidence for movement agency is obtained from the written narratives of activated observers of civil rights history. Thus the actual history of the civil rights movement is not explicitly part of the analysis. Rather, it shadows the analysis. These difficulties are even thornier because the object of change here is a belief system as entrenched and glacially intransigent as racism.

To gain a better analytical foothold on how change is effectuated by a collectivity within such rigid belief systems, we need a workable notion of how "agency" is embedded within "structures" that mitigate against change. The difficulty with finding such a notion is that the theoretical frameworks that explain well how existing conditions are stable and self-perpetuating ("structure") often explain poorly, if at all, the perceptible, sometimes radical transformations that actually occur ("agency").[4] Explanations of stability often rule out change, and vice versa, although we know that both things happen.

One useful resolution to this difficulty comes from William Sewell (1992). Sewell defines social structures as "sets of mutually sustaining schemas and resources that empower and constrain social action and that tend to be reproduced by that social action" (19).[5] For example, a durable and stable racial regime such as the Jim Crow South is sustained and reproduced by the conjoint influence of prevailing schemas about race relations (for example, belief in a "natural" racial order or adherence to the sovereignty of states' rights) and southern whites' control over resources (for example, political offices, economic capital, media institutions, social networks). This conjoint influence engenders certain practices and excludes others, and the engendered practices in turn sustain and reproduce the existing distributions of resources and the prevailing schemas about race relations in the South.

To explain how change occurs, Sewell observes that the resilient, mutually reinforcing relation he describes between social structures and the practices that constitute and reproduce them is "never automatic." This is so for three important reasons: (1) social structures are multiple and interpenetrating; (2) the sustaining schemas are transportable from one context to another; (3) the reproducible resources are polysemous and contingent. Agency thus arises out of the interactive, indeterminate, and contingent relations between structures, schemas, and resources. Specifically, agency entails "the capacity to transpose and extend schemas to new contexts" (18) or "arises from the actor's knowledge of schemas, which means the ability to apply them to new contexts" (20).

The collective agency of black insurgency, then, should be manifest

when correspondents present their viewpoints by transporting schemas—
or, as I shall use the term, frames—from typical contexts into novel ones.
Two varieties of frame transposition are especially prominent in the letters
I examine. The first is the use of contradiction. The power and prevalence
of rhetorical uses of contradiction should not surprise us, given the vital
role of cognitive dissonance in psychological studies of attitude change.[6]
For example, in the letters I examine, movement supporters transpose the
value of patriotism out of its dominant Cold War context and into the context of black servicemen waging war in the name of democracy abroad but
enduring injustice at home. In making such a move, these correspondents
endeavor to frame the issue before the president as a matter of moral contradictions. More generally, proponents of racial integration seek rhetorical
leverage by transposing broadly based principles (justice, equality, universal rights) into material contexts that effectively undermine and contradict
those very principles. The result of such moves, when successful, is to reconfigure the words and frames we use to understand the lived experiences
of African Americans in the South. Prior tolerance of racial segregation
justified vis-à-vis the affirmation of states' rights or southern cultural integrity, for example, might be reconfigured into opposition to racial segregation vis-à-vis the violation of cherished democratic principles.[7]

Black insurgents and their attentive, activated audiences were not, of
course, the only political actors during the struggle over racial equality. Opponents of change and their attentive audiences vied to counter such efforts. The other prominent instance of schema transposition we shall see
is frame-shifting—in the case of constituency mail, redirecting the president's attention from one interpretive frame to another. For example, in the
letters, southern whites react to the use of rights discourse by movement
advocates by appealing to injustice frames of their own. The repeated references by movement advocates to the violation of whites' rights, taxpayer
rights, or property rights reflect an attempt to usurp the normative force
of rights discourse. Thus agency is manifested not only when individuals
strive to transport a particular interpretive frame from one context to another but also when individuals wrestle to transport a competing or diverting frame into a particular context. As we shall see, the former strategy often initiates the sequence of frame contestation, whereas the latter strategy
is often a direct response.

A final point about terminology and concepts is in order before we examine the language and interpretive frames in the letters. I generally use
the term "frames" rather than "schemas" to describe how correspondents
try to articulate to the president a viewpoint on civil rights and racial equal-

ity. A frame is an informational filter, or as David Snow and Robert Benford define the term, "an interpretive schemata that simplifies and condenses the 'world out there' by selectively punctuating and encoding objects, situations, events, experiences, and sequences of actions within one's present or past environment" (1992, 137).[8] Social movements, as Snow and Benford and others powerfully demonstrate, involve a contestation of such frames, with movement participants and their organizations "actively engaged in the production and maintenance of meaning for constituents, antagonists, and bystanders or observers. This productive work may involve the amplification and extension of extant meanings, the transformation of old meanings, and the generation of new meanings" (1992, 136).

In the following analysis, we shall see the discursive residue of such contestation. Activated citizens frame an argument when they put their personal "spin" on a particular matter. When grouped by race and region, they exemplify "collective agency" and the manner in which social movements involve interpretive clashes in which activated publics vie over which amplifications, extensions, transformations, and novel generations of meaning will prevail.[9] Importantly, this endeavor is often provoked by key political actors and events. Sewell (1996) examines such focal moments in the initial stages of the French Revolution, but his central ideas travel well to the context of social movements generally and the civil rights movement specifically. We saw in chapter 5 how attentive publics are activated by particular events and the efforts of movement activists to construct novel contexts, dislodge inveterate practices, and galvanize social change. In the following pages, we see that the way correspondents choose to frame and articulate their views also responds to key events and actors. And they do so in a manner that again supports a movement-initiated, movement-elite interactive account of activated mass opinion.

COLLECTIVE VOICES: AFRICAN AMERICANS

The following letter from Pease Air Force Base in New Hampshire, written in September 1962, at about the time of James Meredith's efforts to enroll at Ole Miss, echoes many of the themes found in letters from African Americans:

> With due respect to you as my Commander in Chief and beloved President, I must let you know that, in the presence of my family, I shed uncontrollable tears last night while viewing the CBS Report "Mississippi and the 15th Amendment." As an American, I am ashamed that such conditions are permitted to exist in our country. As a Negro, I am ashamed of the federal

government's inability or unwillingness to take positive actions which will guarantee *all* Americans—regardless of race, creed, or color—the unimpeded right to enjoy the fruits of democracy. As a member of the Armed Forces, with twenty years of active military service, I ask you; are the conditions which exist in Mississippi, Louisiana, Georgia, Alabama, and other areas of the deep south the conditions which I jeopardized my life to protect? As a father of four small children, I ask you; will my children—as American citizens—be free to live, study, and vote without fear of "Night Riders" or physical harm?

Sir, I am gravely concerned about the welfare and safety of my racial brethren who are undergoing the supreme test of human endurance in the South. While I appreciate the stand you have personally taken in this matter and the genuine concern exhibited by Attorney General Kennedy, I do not believe that positive action is being taken by the Federal Government to guarantee my people their constitutional rights and benefits of first class citizenship. We—as a racial group—do not seek *special* favors, *special* legislation, or other *special* considerations. All we ask is that we be treated as Americans—nothing more and nothing less.

This letter exhibits several overarching themes that recur in letters from African Americans, as well as more general characteristics of constituency mail as a source of opinion data. First, the correspondent manifests the salience and subtle interaction of two dominant frames: racial group identity (in phrases such as "As a Negro," "my racial brethren," and "We—as a racial group") and equal treatment (referred to in the mention of "the unimpeded right to enjoy the fruits of democracy"). The appeal to justice and equal treatment is made by underscoring the paradox and contradiction between the objective conditions of African Americans in the United States and abstract, principled commitments to equality in American political discourse.

Especially common in this regard are appeals that juxtapose one's universal membership ("As an American") or one's patriotic military service ("As a member of the Armed Forces") with the reality of "second-class citizenship." As several scholars have argued, appeals for racial justice and equal citizenship are especially poignant and potent during periods in which the United States is prosecuting a war abroad.[10] This rhetorical exploitation of contradiction is more fully developed in the following letter from a Kentucky serviceman written in April 1952:

I am in the U.S. Army and will soon be sent to Korea to fight for what you might call my country. Do you as an individual think that I or anyone else will enjoy fighting. "No" is right. But I would feel more at ease if I had a reason for fighting. Being a member of the Negro race, I think it is your job to first stop these unrightful actions of hate here in the United States. The Negro people in the South are still living under the spell of the White man. First put out of action such organizations as the KKK and any other organizations against the Negro race. And then send us to Korea to defend this country. Why should I or any other Negro person fight like dogs in Korea and then come home to a country of hate. . . . I know I will go to Korea but believe me, I will be fighting for my life and not for what the Red, White, and Blue stands for.

The prevalence of appeals to cherished principles and to racial group identity is quite impressive when we count the incidence of specific frames. This enumeration is shown in table 6.1. The categorization of interpretive frames used in this chapter is described in appendix 4. The primary categories used are cherished principles, group-based references, symbolic references, issue considerations (partisan, presidential, policy-specific, movement-specific), and affective frames.

Among African Americans, the three most common frames for all years—universal rights, justice and equality, and democratic principles— all appeal to cherished political principles. When we combine all different kinds of explicit appeals (those shown in table 6.1 and not shown), cherished principles are present in about 65 percent of all letters from African Americans. This dominance, furthermore, increases over time. By the 1960s, the focal point for such framing became the appeal to universal rights. Between 1960 and 1965, universal rights frames alone are found in almost 34 percent of letters from African Americans, and explicit appeal to the three most commonly cited cherished principles is found in fully 78 percent of letters.

Several prominent appeals to cherished beliefs not illustrated by the serviceman from Pease Air Force Base are references to religious morality, appropriation of cherished democratic symbols such as the Declaration of

Table 6.1 Most Common Individual Frames, African Americans

	1948–59	1960–65	All years
Universal rights	15.9	33.6	25.2
Justice and equality	15.9	23.5	19.9
Democratic principles	16.1	10.7	13.3
Black identity, interests	11.8	14.6	13.3
Religious morality	9.6	12.4	11.1
World opinion	10.4	11.5	11.0
Political symbols	9.2	11.1	10.2
Number of letters	415	459	874

Independence and the "Founding Fathers," and indirect appeals to antide-mocratic conditions vis-à-vis appeals to the court of world opinion. The re-currence of letters framed in terms of religious morality, democratic sym-bols, and world opinion again underscores the rhetorical force of frames that highlight the contradiction between these normative beliefs and the persistence of anti-democratic, unjust conditions facing African Americans in the South. In each case, correspondents also appealed to an external ar-biter: in the case of religious appeals, to a Supreme Being; in the case of symbolic appeals, to the judgment of history; and in the case world opinion, to the judgment of other nations of the world.

Table 6.1 also shows the prominence of group-based appeals from Afri-can American correspondents. Explicit reference to black identity and inter-ests is found in roughly one out of every eight of letters in all years. When indirect references are included, such group identity and interest frames are present in almost 40 percent of these letters. Such indirect references include viewpoints framed in terms of blacks' rights, military service and "second-class" citizenship of African Americans, historical references to the black rights struggle, promises of blacks' racial bloc voting, and dem-onstration of a "Third World consciousness." The presence of group iden-tity frames, whether direct or indirect, is pervasive and persistent during the course of the emerging civil rights movement.

In addition to these recurrent frames, the letters also manifest a dynamic element of African Americans' racial attitudes during the civil rights era. For one thing, contrary to the common view that the primary objective of black insurgency was school desegregation and that the *Brown* decision set the agenda for the civil rights movement, we find a broader agenda for racial justice for many African Americans in the late 1940s and early 1950s.[11] From 1948 to 1959, some request for economic or social reforms can be found in about 12 percent of all letters. Once movement advocates began to mobilize mass protests for civil rights and racial integration in the 1960s, this incidence diminished to less than 3 percent.

These early demands range from letters that appeal to the importance of economic well-being and self-determination to letters that identify needed reforms in housing, health care, business loans, farming, job training, and community development to still other letters that call for the president to appoint an African American to a cabinet post or to sanction social integra-tion by accepting personal invitations to social functions held by or honor-ing African Americans. Often the appeals for specific policy reforms in this early period, notably, illustrate African Americans' keen awareness of and responsiveness to what political elites were up to. For example, the demands in the petition below from a black sorority in Hampton, Virginia, in May 1948 closely mirror the recommendations of the report *To Secure These Rights,* issued by President Truman's Committee on Civil Rights in the same year: [12]

> We the members of the Gamma Upsilon Omega Chapter of Alpha Kappa Alpha Sorority, and interested citizens of Elizabeth City County, and Hampton, Virginia, do hereby appeal to you as President of the United States of America, to use your influence and power to: (1) Establish a Commission on Civil Rights in the Executive Office *Now* to act until Congress established a Permanent Commission; (2) Issue *immediately* a mandate against discrimination in government employment and create adequate machinery to enforce the mandate; (3) Initiate an internal civil rights campaign for all government employees; (4) Set up integrated units in all branches of the Armed Forces. We believe that as a democratic nation that we have the obligation to all other nations of the world to demonstrate that democracy can work for strengthening the rights and obligations to citizenship and providing equality of opportunity. We believe further, that our deeds, not our dollars will demonstrate to other nations of the world that democracy is the best form of government. May we urge you to take these steps *now.*

Before the 1960s, moreover, the letters disclose an important role of black correspondents: surveillance. Many letters make it a point to document specific cases of discrimination (for example, in the military, in the workplace, and in housing markets), issue detailed requests for federal protection from white-on-black violence, and report instances of racial brutality. In some instances, these are relatively well-publicized cases such as the killings of Harry Moore and Emmett Till. In others, the cases are far less publicized ones, such as the murders of local NAACP activists Lamar Smith, George Lee, and Gus Courts, or even otherwise undocumented incidents, such as the indignity faced by a black soldier from Fort Bragg, North Carolina, who informed his Commander-in-Chief about segregated restaurants in Henderson, North Carolina. Between 1948 and 1959, one out of every ten letters called the president's attention to discrimination within the federal government. And one out of every eight letters in this time period focused on the contradiction of black patriotism in a segregated military and in military bases within the Jim Crow South.[13]

By the 1960s, once movement activism in the South began to be coordinated around segregation and voting rights, the incidence of letters about federal government discrimination dropped to zero, and the incidence of letters about black military service dropped to 6.5 percent. Importantly, letters also began to echo the successful movement strategy of drawing public support through nonviolent direct action: references to the resulting police brutality increase from about 1 percent of all letters from 1948 to 1959 to about 12 percent from 1960 to 1965.[14] Lastly, by the 1960s, we see the emergence of a more confident, more empowered, notably transformed African American voice. This shift, however, is not easily captured using the interpretive frames I have coded, although we do see by this time the first emergence of references to imminent black revolt and militant response, in about 4 percent of letters. Such a transformed voice is rather better captured in the changing tone of address found in letters from African Americans, such as the following New York City male who wrote to the White House in November 1963:

> You're supposed to represent the American way of life and I believed in you for the job ahead and agreed with you mostly because I see what you see with earnest but, when you settle for a weak Civil Rights Bill we part company. . . . I do know that the masses of black people are very much displeased with your action . . . to back down from what you believed and what I thought you believed in—Freedom for all.
>
> How long Mr. President will my people have to wait in bondage? Do you not see what revolution can do to a country? The Negro today are not waiting any longer for excuses. We want action and we want it now. Not word, Mr. President. Action! Or the massive force of the Black Revolution will soon turn to *RED* in *these* United States. I pray for your good health.[15]

COLLECTIVE VOICES: SOUTHERN WHITES

Letters from southern whites exhibit a clearly defensive voice, moved to political action by the imminent threat to their existing social order. This southern white voice, notably, reacts to the perceived threat from black insurgency in three recurring ways. Some letters attempt to recast the issue in terms of alternate frames that might supersede or trump civil rights. Other letters spin a taut web of justifications that belie a distinct segregationist belief system. And yet others seek out novel frames that directly respond to and attempt to usurp the normative force of the framing promulgated by movement proponents.

By far the most common means that southern white correspondents use to attempt to divert the president's attention from movement demands is raising the specters of communism and the Cold War. These diversionary tactics range from general requests that the president concern himself with the communist threat rather than the interests of southern blacks to the specific charge that movement leaders and organizations themselves are communist-inspired. An example of the latter follows in this letter from a Selma woman at the height of tensions in Selma in March 1965:

> Thank you, Sir, for your deliberation and hesitancy to take rash action in the deplorable situation existing in Selma. . . . Every major so-called "civil rights" battle has been simultaneous with a crisis: Little Rock and the Berlin Crisis; the "Freedom Rides"—started just two weeks prior to a schedules conference between Kennedy and Khrushchev; "Ole Miss" and the Cuban Crisis; and now Selma and the stepped up Communist aggression in Viet Nam. These facts need careful and prayerful consideration, for these internal crises have been too perfectly timed to be considered mere coincidence.
>
> I know not what Martin Luther King claims to have sought when he visited Russia, but one thing is apparent—he returned to this country thoroughly indoctrinated in Communist tactics. Just as the Reds bombed their own air strips during the Korean War and blamed US planes . . . so have Negro leaders in the South bombed their own homes and churches and placed the blame on the White southerner. . . .
>
> Regardless of the nature of future grievances and the resulting demonstrations, you can rest assured that they will continue. The only solution is going to be found in exposing Martin Luther King for what he really is—an agitator working hand and foot for the Communist cause in our country. The SCLC he heads could better be termed "Southern Colored Leaders for Communism." I have always said that NAACP stood for "Negro Agitators for the American Communist Party."

In some cases, the charges are quite elaborate and specific; for instance, there are letters that identify Martin Luther King Jr.'s involvement in the Highlander Folk School as "communist" and the work of "northern agitators." [16] The charge of communism is so salient and incendiary that even presidents are not immune to such framing. Harry Truman, who played a critical role by issuing executive orders to eliminate racial discrimination in civil service jobs and in the military, alleged that communists were "engineering the student sit-downs at lunch counters in the South." When asked to provide details to back up such allegations, Truman demurred, "I know that usually when trouble hits the country the Kremlin is behind it." [17] And, as the recipient of such a charge, John F. Kennedy received letters such as the following from a Dallas woman in 1963:

> Dear Mr. President, How would you feel about mulatto grandchildren? Or are you going to move out, after selling this country down the river. But what about the rest of the whites who haven't enough money to get out of this future mulatto nation? You should be ashamed. How can you sleep? *Communist!*

Table 6.2   Most Common Individual Frames, Southern Whites

	1948–59	1960–65	All years
Communism, Cold War	20.6	23.9	22.6
States' rights	17.9	18.2	18.1
Civil rights activists as communists	7.0	16.6	13.1
Whites', taxpayers' rights	1.2	17.3	11.4
Movement leaders, organizations	5.8	13.2	10.5
Religious morality	11.8	8.1	9.5
Religious essentialism	15.0	5.8	8.8
Number of letters	515	892	1407

By the onset of President Kennedy's showdown with Castro in Cuba in the early 1960s, letters increasingly used "the communist threat" in Cuba to divert Kennedy's attention from the South. Several hundred telegrams from southerners in 1962 made the terse demand: "Cuba, Si. Integration, No." Between October and December of the same year, approximately 47,720 note cards distributed in Tennessee were sent to Kennedy with the short but forceful message:

> Please take notice that I respectfully resent the unnatural warfare being waged against the sovereign State of Mississippi and urge that you give more serious attention to facing up to the Communist menace and our Cuban problem.[18]

Table 6.2, which lists the most common individual frames found in letters from southern whites, shows the recurrence of references to communism and the Cold War. This specific attempt to recast the issue of civil rights is present in more than 22 percent of all letters from southern whites, and the specific allegation that the civil rights movement and its activists are communist is found in an additional 13 percent of letters. Interestingly, as the movement activism intensified during the 1960s, the prevalence of linking civil rights activists to communists more than doubled. Table 6.2 shows that in the 1960s, one out of every six letters from southern whites makes this linkage. This increase gives us our first peek into the way in which one collective voice—that of southern whites—responds to movement activism.

The second most prominent and persistent frame found in letters from southern whites is references to states' rights. As Lewis Killian observes, states' rights is an "ancient battle cry," and "[w]hatever it might mean to politicians and voters in other sections of the nation, below the Potomac

this slogan means 'southern rights' and 'freedom from Yankee interfer-
ence'" (1970, 6). The recurrence of defenses based on states' rights limns
the distinct segregationist belief system exhibited by many southern whites.
As George Frederickson (1971) and C. Vann Woodward (1966) and others
document, this belief system is centered around an ideology of *"herrenvolk*
democracy" developed in the latter part of the nineteenth century.[19]

In the text of letters from southern whites, it is manifest in the recurrence of highly specific phrases such as "You can lead a horse to water, but
you can't make it drink," "rammed down our throats," "divide and con-
quer," and "the South shall rise again." Examples include at least one letter
in which the correspondent clearly does not comprehend the meaning of
the phrase "You can lead a horse to water" but feels compelled to include it
in his plea against integration anyway. Another important element of this
segregationist belief system is the power of religious justification. Table 6.2
shows that in the period from 1948 to 1959, one out of every four letters
from southern whites justify segregation on religious grounds. Many of
these letters not only make religious allusions but also quote from a highly
specific, recurrent set of biblical passages. Biblical citations that are especially frequent include Genesis 4:11, Genesis 6:1–7, Genesis 24:3–4, Genesis 9:20–27, Leviticus 9:9, Nehemiah 13:22–28, Deuteronomy 7:3, 7:6,
and Acts 17:26. The following Oklahoman manifested a dramatic example
of this in her plea to President Eisenhower in May 1955:

> After listening to your Monday night speech I am convinced you do not know
> GOD's laws as given in the SCRIPTURES regarding the RACES in this world.
> PLEASE READ Genesis, Numbers, Nehemiah, and Deut[eronomy]. The FLOOD
> in Noahs time was caused by intermarrying; socially with different RACES.
> After the Flood GOD sought to purify the RACES but man again defied HIM and
> brought this SIN upon the WHOLE WORLD. The RACES with their different colors
> of skin was thru the mutation GOD performed. HE placed different RACES geo-
> graphically and forbade by HIS Laws for them to INTEGRATE or FELLOWSHIP
> [sic] and certainly NOT to INTERMARRY at the Tower of Babel. . . . HENCE GOD IS
> THE AUTHOR of SEGREGATION and SATAN THE AUTHOR OF INTEGRATION AND
> DISCRIMINATION and the cause of people drifting into bigtime SIN. . . . Please
> get your BIBLE and read it for yourself. . . . GOD will have the last word with
> you and the people who are rebelling against HIM—Remember that.

Such letters often evince the organized basis of belief systems. A fair number of southern whites' letters to Eisenhower include as an attachment a
commonly circulated pamphlet titled "A Christian View of Segregation," by
one Reverend G. T. Gillespie. This pamphlet identifies its origin as the Association of Citizens' Councils of Winona, Mississippi, and is often accom-

panied by pamphlets on white citizens councils. Interestingly, the biblical references in this pamphlet closely parallel those found in letters from southern whites who have no association with Gillespie, White Citizens Councils, or any other organized group.[20]

This segregationist belief system also equips correspondents with group-based rhetorical artillery to defend the racial order. Many letters thus angrily refer to the violation of states' rights, claim the unconstitutionality of the Fourteenth Amendment, and broadly defend "the southern way of life." The perception of group threat to the existing social order enjoyed by southerners, significantly, is found in about 44 percent of letters. The salience of group threat frames, unsurprisingly, increases with the successful evolution of movement activism (from 34 percent of letters between 1948 and 1959 to 49 percent between 1960 and 1965).[21]

Manifestations of group-based appeals are also present in the paternalist impulse characteristic of the southern *herrenvolk* ideology. For example, a Claxton, Georgia, woman wrote in October 1962, "I know many Negroes whom I have learned to love, but I regard them as children because they have no ambition and often care nothing for an education." Such paternalist and patronizing correspondents often also staunchly defended the southern social order by arguing that African Americans should be "put where they belong" or should "stay in their place." Several of these letters go so far as to draw explicit comparisons to India's caste system to justify segregation as a natural state of human affairs. And southern whites were often unabashedly willing to write on behalf of southern blacks. Not surprisingly, when this happens, the letters point out that African Americans in the South are happy, that they oppose desegregation, and that they are grateful for the efforts of southern whites to "civilize" them. In August 1949, for example, an Alabama man wrote:

> Mr. President why don't you and your followers let the negro speak for himself—I think you would be surprised at their answers. He is proud of his church, even if its not as large and pretty as mine, he is proud of the place he calls home even if its not in pretty section of town and most of all he's proud to be a negro and most of all he knows that he has come a long way in the last 150 years—from the dark jungle of Africa to modern civilization.

Another dimension of such a distinctly southern paternalistic voice is found in the following letter from a Vicksburg, Mississippi, male in March 1948:

> The southern Negroes are satisfied. If not, why are 79 percent of them in the South, only one third of the US? Let the southern Negro vote on it [desegregation]. They represent 79 percent of the Negroes. Why not let them say in-

stead of a bunch of New York whites who are morally no better than the Negroes, and who always vote for a Democratic governor and a Republican president. The idea that the southerner who advocates segregation hates or even dislikes the Negro is absolutely false. We are the best friends they have, and most of them know it. Since segregation, not a Negro has been killed in the South for being black. In this same fifty years, Illinois alone has killed 345, then the thirty at Detroit, etc. . . . This may account for so many Negroes staying in the South. They want to live with white people whom they can "look up" to, and improve their moral condition.

This letter is an especially compelling instance of southern paternalism being expressed jointly with references to regional conflict and relative well-being of North and South. References to relative well-being more broadly recur in assertions that African Americans fare best under existing conditions in the South. Specifically, correspondents claim that black schools are better off than white schools; that African Americans in the South are better off than African Americans in the North; and that African Americans are better off than denizens of African nations.

These often eloquent moral appeals, defenses of southern culture, and claims of relative group well-being should not mask the prevalence of overt racism in many letters. Invidious racial ascriptions are present in about 25 percent of letters from southern whites: sometimes as essentialist claims about the racial superiority of whites, sometimes as dehumanizing racial stereotypes (for example, claims that African Americans are unclean, immoral, uneducated, savage, lazy, or wanton), sometimes as claims about the social, sexual, and physical threat of African Americans (for example, in references to interracial marriages, bi-racial children, black-on-white crime, or black male rape of white females). Where the possibility of racial intermarriage and black male sexuality is condemned, these letters illustrate the extent to which the perceived threat to the racial order in the South is also a perceived threat to the existing sexual order in the South.[22]

Principled defenses of segregation, religious appeals, articulations of southern paternalism, and overt racism (or some combination of these) are often within the same narrative. Thus, a letter that begins with one frame can end with a different frame altogether. For example, the following Dallas correspondent writing to President Kennedy was fully willing to engage in principled appeals to whites' rights, but the full narrative of the letter reveals deeply racist beliefs and the perception of group threat:

To me it seems like you are taking the rights from the whites. If a white person has a business, it is his business to refuse service to anyone. But the way you are getting it, we will be working for the niggers later on like in slave days. How would you like [it] if your wife and kids go swimming with a big black nigger? . . . And niggers are already getting the big head over this integration, flirting and raping white people. . . . When I voted for you, I thought you was for everybody, not just niggers. When you read this letter please consider whites' rights instead of just niggers.

Finally, as with African American voices, the content and framing of southern white voices evolves through the years examined. With racial segregation and the southern social order coming under increasingly critical scrutiny, we see a decline in affirmative defenses of the Jim Crow South manifested in the decline in essentialist claims, negative stereotyping, paternalism, and declarations of southern white militant response. In lieu of these more overt and defiant defenses, we see the rise of attempts to deflect the president's attention onto other issues (most often, communism) and attempts to defend the status quo along other justificatory grounds, such as the need to maintain law and order and avert mob rule. About 10 percent of letters from 1960 to 1965 frame the issue in terms of law and order or mob rule.

With the success of movement activism, southern whites increasingly turned to frames that directly address movement leaders and movement frames. Thus, over time, southern whites increasingly centered on movement leadership and organizations in their correspondence. About 13 percent of letters from 1960 to 1965 framed their views thus; the figure increases to almost 30 percent when the charge that movement leaders are communists is included. In this regard, southern whites also increasingly turned to attempts to warn the president against the growing empowerment of African Americans. Thus letters to Kennedy and Johnson in the 1960s included allegations that African Americans were unfairly seeking special privileges, that social policies favoring African Americans would disfavor poor whites, that the black liberation struggle would turn violent, and that African Americans ultimately sought to take over government.

Furthermore, letters from southern whites increasingly aimed to deflect the normative force of appeals to universal rights by making particularistic references to the violation of whites' and taxpayers' rights. As table 6.2 shows, this is a dramatic reconfiguration of rights discourse that appears to originate during the course of the civil rights movement. Particularistic rights frames are present in only 1 percent of letters from southern whites from 1948 to 1959 but fully 17 percent from 1960 to 1965. The excerpt from September 1962, for example, raises allegations of reverse discrimination that foreshadow the kind of rhetorical framing in racial discourse today.

I, Jimmy Ward Smith, applied for admission to the University of Mississippi in 1959. My application was rejected because I failed to meet the requirements of the University. In order to show that America is a land of equal opportunity I wish to request the same Federal support be given to me as was Meredith. We were both rejected for the same reasons with one exception, I am a white male.

COLLECTIVE VOICES: RACIALLY LIBERAL WHITES

Whereas African Americans and southern whites manifested distinct, group-based beliefs, racially liberal whites overwhelmingly appealed to cherished principles of the American liberal political tradition. The following appeal from a Bronx girl in January 1956 well illustrates this prominence of cherished principles:

> I'll start this letter off by saying that I don't know much about politics; and that I am only ten years old. But I wouldn't have started this letter, if I hadn't been driven to it by a great force. It's this. About every American citizen knows that there's a Constitution and a Declaration of Independence. But what too many of them don't realize is that they're both being violated! And at this very moment! . . . don't *you* ever read about the busses, the hotels and public services that won't serve Negroes? It's a horrible, prejudiced practice. In the Declaration of Independence is a section which says, quote:
> "We hold these truths to be self-evident: That all men are created equal; that they are endowed by their Creator with certain unalienable rights; that among these are life, liberty, and the pursuit of happiness."
> That means everyone! Negroes and white alike! And I ask you as President of the United States of America, to help stop and prevent this prejudice, this violation of the rights of the American people! . . . I hope you understand the knowledge of wrong being done that is in my heart. I write this letter unaided, because I want it to come from my own heart. It does, because I know of prejudiced practices still going on, and they are *completely* unconstitutional!

This letter contains an impressively articulate coupling (for a ten-year-old) of explicit appeals to "American rights" and political symbols (for example, the excerpt from the Declaration of Independence). The incidence of such appeals, as separate frames, is shown in table 6.3. As the table shows, the single most common frame in letters from northern whites is some appeal to universal rights. This appeal, moreover, increased in prominence as the movement evolved: framing one's position in terms of universal rights increased from just 8 percent of letters from 1948 to 1959 to fully 36 percent from 1960 to 1965.[23] Moreover, in the 1960s, we also see the common rhetorical use of frames that underscore moral contradiction in the existing state of race relations.

Table 6.3   Most Common Individual Frames, Racially Liberal Whites

	1948–59	1960–65	All years
Universal rights	8.1	36.1	28.7
World opinion	10.0	18.7	16.4
Police brutality	0.0	19.3	14.2
Justice and equality	14.3	13.2	13.5
Equal protection under the law	2.7	15.0	11.7
Number of letters	259	722	981

Thus letters from northern whites protested the ongoing police brutality in the South in response to movement activism (in about 19 percent of letters from 1960 to 1965) and demanded equal protection under the law for movement activists (in about 15 percent of letters from 1960 to 1965). Correspondents also drew explicit parallels between the American South and Nazi Germany (in about 10 percent of letters from 1960 to 1965). As with letters from African Americans, the prevalence of framing letters in terms of police brutality and equal protection under the law underscores the success of movement activists' strategy of nonviolent direct action. These themes are illustrated in the following letter from Oakland, California, in May 1963 in response to Sheriff Bull Connor's brutality toward demonstrators in Birmingham:

> I am revolted at the timidity and "caution" of our Federal government in its failure to protect the rights and safety of the negro citizens of Birmingham— particularly as it contrasts so sharply with its truculence and boldness in dictating what it will and will not tolerate in all other parts of the world.

Letters from northern whites also increasingly turned to the tribunal of world opinion (about 19 percent of letters from 1960 to 1965). Again, the post–World War II and Cold War context is crucial to correspondents' efforts to underscore the contradictions between U.S. attempts to export democratic principles abroad and the violation of those very same principles with African American citizens at home. The following letter from a Dearborn, Michigan, woman in June, 1963 well exemplifies the force of these appeals:

> Would you care to read the viewpoint on desegregation from an ordinary thirty-four year old white homemaker? I'm not important and perhaps my point of view is also unimportant but I did have to write someone about it. The United States stands up to this world and says, "Hey World, look at me!! You should fashion your government after mine! We're a free people and our constitution is for the people, of the people, and by the people." And the world looks down on us and says, "Yes, this is true if your skin happens to be white."

> Just who do we think we are? God Almighty?? That we can tell the Negro,
> a fellow human being, what store he can go into, where he can eat, what
> drinking fountain he can use, and what school he can go to? . . . We are much
> too great a nation to let integration divide us. We have a wonderful constitu-
> tion and for the most part a conscientious government. And both the consti-
> tution and the government should be for the best for all peoples no matter
> what their creed or color.

It is critical to remember that individuals outside the South were faced, sometimes daily, with images of the interplay between the nonviolent movement appeals to equality and justice and the fire hoses, billy clubs, racial invectives, and murderous animus facing such appeals, often with the full force of state and local government behind it. And the strong reaction to such images bears witness to the powerful influence of mass media coverage and the critical agency of movement activists in staging a riveting drama before the American public. On more than one occasion, historical accident also helped movement activists. The most stunning instance of this occurred with the broadcast of *Judgment at Nuremberg* on the same Sunday night—March 7—as news of police brutality in Selma. The effect was electric: a remarkable number of letters written that night and the following days compared Governor Wallace and Sheriff Jim Clark's police posse to Hitler and storm troopers. The following excerpt from a Minnesota woman's letter illustrates this well:

> I have never before become so alarmed or concerned about anything that I
> actually wrote to The President, although many times I felt I should write to
> express encouragement or concern. But today, I feel compelled to do some-
> thing.
>   Last night I watched the rerun of the movie "Judgment at Nuremberg"
> on our Rochester station. My husband and I were discussing the picture. We
> agreed that Hitler couldn't have done it alone for the people had to be con-
> senting or not caring. My husband was saying it could happen to any na-
> tion—ours included. Just then the news came on with the horrible and un-
> believable police brutality against the Negro people in Alabama. The impact
> of this scene hit both of us and I felt perhaps it would help in a small way if
> we let you know that we do care. It makes us ache within to see the law officers
> in one of our own States act in a manner reminiscent of the days of Hitler.
> I'm sure there are millions of Americans with this same ache who have not
> found the time to write to you this morning. Please do all in your power and
> the power of your office to restore true freedom to all throughout the country.

Finally, along these lines, many letters manifest the degree to which incidents of southern white brutality violently shake the faith of northern liberals in the American democratic system. Thus one New York City woman's cherished political beliefs were betrayed by the Birmingham church bombing in September 1963:

> When four American children were killed while attending church, our nation entered its darkest hour. Remember, this happened under your administration. . . . The conscience of the American white population has been aroused. Like so many others, I am secure, free, well-housed, well-clothed, and well-fed—but I cannot rejoice in the prosperity this nation has brought me when others are denied the right to know even the dignity of having been created men.

On this point, there is a striking increase in the presence of letters in which one of the primary frames is the affect of the correspondent. Affective frames increase in incidence from 1.5 percent of letters from 1948 to 1959 to more than 11 percent of letters from 1960 to 1965. And significantly, the most common such affective frame by far among northern whites is one of shame, as shown by the correspondent from New York in December 1955, who signed his letter, "white, disgusted, and ashamed of his fellow men." Such letters offer a stark testimonial to Walter Lippman's observation that the public does not "rouse itself normally at the existence of evil. It is aroused at evil made manifest by the interruption of a habitual process of life" (1925, 67).

These vignettes, of course, do not exhaust the scope of ways in which opinions on civil rights are expressed. For example, there is an abundant diversity *within* these groups. Among African Americans, some letters (especially in the late 1940s and early 1950s) took a reluctant and pessimistic view of civil rights and attempt to argue instead for state-sponsored resettlement of African Americans (either back to Africa or within the United States). There are also a handful of letters from African Americans who wrote to the president primarily to object to the tactics of the civil rights movement leaders or to offer themselves as the veritable spokespersons for African Americans. And in the following 1950 letter a woman from Detroit was clearly working to uplift the status of African Americans but did so by espousing some rather invidious stereotypes:

> I have started to do missionary work by myself, it is to improve the intelligence of the Negro people and help us make better citizens. Being a Negro myself I feel sure my country and President will approve this wonderful work. . . . My purpose is for better social conduct. More self-respect. More respect for your fellowman. Better moral respect, and to stop talking loud telling all their secrets and stop loafing on street corners, swearing and molesting every woman that walks alone. Stop getting on their jobs talking low about our womens. . . . All these things give the other races the impression

that our people are the worst people in the country and should be left out to themselves.

With southern whites, there is an unquestionable undercurrent of passionate appeals for racial justice and desegregation. Even as early as 1948, support for racial equality is visible in letters from southern whites, such as the following from a New Orleans woman:

> I have just finished reading the report to the President of the Committee on Civil Rights, entitled "To Secure these Rights." I had been aware of some of the injustices and discrimination practiced against our minority groups, particularly Negroes, but I had no idea these injustices were so great in number nor so grave in their effect and implication. I have had my eyes opened, and feel that there are many citizens of the U.S. who, like myself, had not given much thought to violations of civil rights because of ignorance of these violations.
>
> Permit me to congratulate you on the stand you have taken on civil rights. I cannot understand how any American who claims to be a Christian can oppose such a program. I pray that your efforts will be rewarded; that enough citizens will have their eyes and hearts opened so as to bring their thoughts and actions in line with the principles of Christian charity and love for fellow men.

Moreover, the stylized presentation here in no way implies that manifestation of racial group conflict, perceived threat, and invidious racism are uniquely southern white responses to the civil rights movement. Far from it. White opposition outside the South, in particular, increased as the movement began to turn toward urban sites through the country, owing to the growing anxiety that black insurgency might turn violent, move too hastily, or extend blacks' demands in the arena of economic and social rights. Thus, by August 1965, in the aftermath of the Watts uprising in Los Angeles, the following California man wrote:

> As hard-working, law-abiding, tax-paying citizens, may we express to you our outrage at having to pay the bill for the irresponsible criminal negro hoodlums, who, while they sit and wait for their relief and unemployment checks, are looting and burning our city. And why, as a reward for their 200 million dollars worth of destruction, they are rewarded with one million dollars in county relief and $57,00 per day worth of food.
>
> We have a great need for farm labor to harvest our California tomato crop. Is it too preposterous to suggest that they do an honest days' work? We pay large City, County, State, and Federal taxes that the government is spending on welfare that is all out of proportion to what the needy negro deserves. When are they going to stop the welfare payments that reward the mothers of illegitimate children.

This outrage is felt also by many many of our friends, who possibly will not take the time to write. It is high time the negro stop crying and get to work.

The intimation in the last sentence of this letter—questioning the work habits of African Americans—takes us back to a point from chapter 3. Many of these letters evoke themes that are prominent in racial discourse today. Thus they evoke the idea that the past is prologue: the seeds of the Black Power movement in the late 1960s are found in the early 1960s, and the letters also show the germs of white discontent and "racial resentment" that characterize racial politics in the United States today. The following letter from a Garwood, New Jersey, man in May 1963, for example, forged a link between the violation of whites' rights and taxpayer rights that is all too familiar to us today:

> In recent months all I have read in the newspapers or heard on TV or the radio is the Constitutional rights of the Negro. Seeing all of this I begin to wonder what about the Constitutional rights of white people. Don't we have the right to choose who we wish to associate with or not? . . . As a taxpayer and voter when do my rights begin? . . . It is the white taxpayer that is supporting all the Negroes that are on welfare. I read of Negroes getting as much as $900.00 a month welfare. I work for a living and I do not make $900.00 a month.[24]

More generally, letters (even as early as the 1950s) manifested linkages between racial animosity, taxpayer rights, and school financing; invoke "reverse discrimination" frames as a means to oppose racially egalitarian policies; and manufacture odious stereotypes of African American men as criminals and sexual deviants and African American women as "welfare queens." As an example of the last of these evocations, the following letter from a Dallas man in September 1954 urges President Eisenhower not to act on desegregation until African Americans'

> moral record is better. Their five to ten times higher illegitimacy rate is a disgrace to any race. No doubt this condition has been fostered by one of our New Deal laws to pay a mother $15 a month for each bastard child. This law should be repealed. It is known as the Federal and State Aid to Dependent Children.

This emergence of the stereotype of blacks as welfare cheats is striking. Among southern whites, it is found in only 0.3 percent of letters from 1948 to 1959. Between 1960 and 1965, the incidence increases tenfold to about 3 percent. This stereotype is absent from letters from northern whites from 1948 to 1959 and present in less than 1 percent of letters in the 1960s.

CONTESTED FRAMES AND GROUP DYNAMICS

We have seen the archetypical kinds of appeals made by activated African Americans, southern whites, and racially liberal whites. For each stylized voice, certain frames resonate whereas others are seldom heard. This presentation has largely focused on animating these stylized voices, without systematically comparing how these voices respond to each other and to ongoing political events. Even without such rigorous comparison, the characterizations have been suggestive. The interpretive frames that characterize one group appear responsive to the framing of letters by other groups and responsive to the evolution of movement activism. In this section, I compare these letters explicitly. Specifically, I contrast the type and prevalence of values-based and group-based frames used, the type and prevalence of political considerations raised, and the relative responsiveness of correspondents to elite and movement-initiated events across time and across the three primary group voices we have thus far examined.

Interpretive frames that appeal to cherished moral and political principles can be either explicit or indirect (for example, logically implied or symbolic). Explicit references to cherished values are broken down into different types: general political principles (for example, references to equality and justice, liberty and freedom, democracy and majority rule); rights-based appeals (for example, universal rights, particularistic rights—whites' rights, states' rights, taxpayer rights, blacks' rights); and nonpolitical forms of moral suasion (both religious and secular values). Indirect references to cherished values either make direct references to democratic symbols (the Constitution, the Bill of Rights, the law of the land) or point out injustices resulting from antidemocratic conditions at home (police brutality, second-class citizenship, black service within a segregated military, discrimination within the federal government itself) or antidemocratic implications of world affairs (the Cold War, Nazism, recourse to world opinion, charges that movement activism is communistic).[25]

Frames that appeal to group dimensions can likewise be explicit or indirect. Explicit appeals to group dimensions generally fall into three categories: group conflict and threat (social, sexual, political, economic, or physical); group identity and interests (black, white, or southern white identity, Third World consciousness, or claims to group identity based on personal acquaintance); and group superiority or overt racism (essentialist notions of race, dehumanizing stereotyping, or invocations of southern paternalism). Indirect references to group dimensions are primarily contained in references to U.S. racial history (for example, Jefferson Davis, the "South," carpetbaggers, "Yankees," Gettysburg, the Emancipation Proclamation, the Fourteenth Amendment). In some cases, they also include group-based electoral and political considerations (accusations of wooing black votes, pledges of racial bloc voting, requests for minority political representation) and references to movement-specific considerations (movement or southern white leadership, organizations).

A case can even be made that rights-based frames or symbolic references to cherished values can act as indirect group-based frames. In this manner, the boundaries between group dimensions and cherished values are to some extent arbitrary. Rights-based references to particularistic principles such as states' rights, taxpayer rights, or whites' rights clearly also draw the reader's focus to group dimensions. Similarly, symbolic references to blacks' "second-class citizenship" and military service summon the reader's attention not only to the violation of democratic equality but also the interests of African Americans themselves. Moreover, the framing of a letter in terms of values-based or group-based frames is not exclusionary: many letters contain frames that underscore core principles and, at the same time, frames that underscore group-based considerations.

Table 6.4 shows the distribution of values-based and group-based frames for African Americans, southern whites, and racially liberal ("northern") whites. The across-time comparisons in table 6.4 simplify the onset and evolution of the civil rights movement to two stages for ease of exposition, the period from 1948 to 1959 and the period from 1960 to 1965. Very roughly, this split in time periods distinguishes the formative stages of movement activism (1948–59) from the explosion of movement activism that began in 1960 with the lunch counter sit-ins in Greensboro, North Carolina. To use Doug McAdam's words, this split divides the "historical context" and "generation" from the "heyday" of black insurgency.[26]

The first set of rows compares letters that primarily appeal to cherished values with those that primarily appeal to group-specific considerations. In this table, references to cherished values and group dimensions are explicit, although the same comparisons and changes over time can be shown even if indirect references are incorporated. Appeals based on cherished values are about equally prominent among African Americans and northern whites; both groups are much likelier to frame civil rights in terms of cherished principles than are southern whites. Values-based frames are present in 65 percent of letters from African Americans, 66 percent of letters from Northern whites, and only 52 percent of letters from southern whites. Appeals based on group dimensions are most common among southern whites and least frequent among northern whites. References to group

Table 6.4 Comparisons of Values- and Group-Based Frames

	African Americans			Southern Whites			"Northern" Whites		
	1948–59	1960–65	All years	1948–59	1960–65	All years	1948–59	1960–65	All years
Cherished Values and Group Dimensions									
Values, explicit	51.1	77.8	65.1	44.1	56.3	51.8	46.7	73.0	66.1
Group, explicit	26.0	26.8	26.4	47.4	37.2	40.9	16.6	14.8	15.3
Values-Based Frames									
Principles, univ. rights	45.3	70.2	58.4	24.1	24.3	24.2	41.7	66.6	60.0
Nonuniv. rights	2.2	2.4	2.3	19.4	35.3	29.5	8.9	7.5	7.8
Antidemocratic, U.S.	23.6	27.2	25.5	1.9	4.8	3.8	7.3	25.5	20.7
Antidemocratic, global	13.3	14.6	14.0	32.6	41.7	38.4	22.0	32.3	29.6
Group-Based Frames									
Black interests	38.8	40.3	39.4	1.4	2.2	1.9	13.5	20.4	18.6
Perceived threat	2.2	2.6	2.4	34.2	49.3	43.8	11.6	7.6	8.7
White racism	0.2	0.0	0.1	29.1	22.2	24.7	6.6	5.4	5.7

dimensions are found in about 15 percent of letters from northern whites, 26 percent of letters from African Americans, and fully 41 percent of letters from southern whites.

For all three groups, there is an increase in letters framed in terms of cherished values over time. For African Americans, references to cherished values increase almost 27 percent between stages while references to group dimensions remains essentially unchanged. For northern whites, references to cherished values increases fully 26 percent between stages while references to group dimension again change little. For southern whites, the change in values-based frames is more modest, increasing 12 percent. Perhaps more interestingly, explicit references to group dimensions actually decrease about 10 percent. Indirect group-based frames, however, increase, for example, through references to states' rights, whites' rights, and the communist influences on movement leaders and organizations.

The next set of rows in table 6.4 compares different types of appeals to cherished principles. Cherished principles are broken down into four condensed categories: explicit references to general principles (justice, freedom, democracy) and universal rights; explicit references to nonuniversal rights (states' rights and particularistic rights); indirect references to domestic antidemocratic conditions (black military service, police brutality, second-class citizenship, discrimination within the federal government); and indirect references to global and historical antidemocratic implications (Communism, Nazism, world opinion).

Explicit references to general principles and universal rights are by far the most common values-based frames among African Americans (58 percent of all letters) and northern whites (60 percent of all letters). Beyond appeals to general principles and universal rights, African Americans are most inclined to promote civil rights by drawing references to antidemocratic conditions in the United States (about 26 percent of letters). Northern whites, by contrast, are more likely to point the president's attention to the global and historical antidemocratic implications of racial segregation (about 30 percent of letters), largely vis-à-vis the tribunal of world opinion and parallels to Nazi Germany. The most notable increase for both African Americans and northern whites over time is the sharp rise in references to general principles and universal rights. For northern whites, there is also a marked increase in indirect references to domestic antidemocratic practices. Most of this increase occurs as references to police brutality in response to movement activism in the South.

For southern whites, on the other hand, references to general principles and universal rights are far less common (24 percent of letters). Instead, the most common reference is to global antidemocratic implications (38 percent of letters), most of which frame the issue vis-à-vis references to communism and the Cold War. Correspondence from southern whites is also notable for references to nonuniversal rights (almost 30 percent of letters). References to antidemocratic conditions in the United States, not surprisingly, are mostly absent from southern whites' correspondence. The most notable shift over time for southern whites is the marked increase in references to nonuniversal rights (from 19 percent between 1948 and 1959 to 35 percent between 1960 and 1965). The bulk of this increase, as previously noted, comes in references to particularistic rights.

There is, as we noted earlier, a strong and significant undercurrent of letters that appeal to group-specific considerations. The third cluster of rows in table 6.4 compares three different types of group-specific argument: letters that frame their position in terms of blacks' interests and identity, those that frame their position in terms of perceived threat from black insurgency, and those that frame their position in terms of racist appeals. African Americans exhibit a fairly strong degree of group identity and interest. Unsurprisingly, they seldom use the perceived threat of whites or white claims to superiority as a focal frame in their correspondence. For southern whites, there is an equally strong showing of perceived group threat and a high prevalence of defenses based on white superiority and racism. Few frame their arguments in terms of black identity or interests. Northern whites, as a largely sympathetic, adjuvant public, are the least likely to adopt group-based frames. Accordingly, none of the three categories of group-based frames is strikingly common, although the most common of these are appeals to blacks' interests, especially with the evolution of movement activism.

Taking these results together, the attempt to frame ongoing movement events in terms of core principles is quite clearly a strategy of advocates of civil rights. Values-based appeals from southern whites, by contrast, are highly selective and restricted to frames such as states' rights, whites' rights, and anti-communism. With southern whites, moreover, the group dimensions of racial attitudes are much more salient, whether manifested as perceived group threat or as overt racism. Where such group dimensions are evident for African Americans, by contrast, the dominant frame is the affirmation of group identity and interests.

Another, more substantive window into collective agency is through letters that focus on specific considerations. Here four kinds of political considerations are coded for (1) policy-specific considerations, in which the respondent refers to particular policies, rulings, and reforms (Supreme Court decisions, pending civil rights legislation, social and economic reforms, minority political appointments); (2) partisan-specific considerations, in which the respondent discusses the implications of civil rights or racial equality for the Democratic Party, the Republican Party, or more narrowly, southern Democrats; (3) president-specific considerations, in which the respondent refers to a particular presidential speech or act, to the personal electoral implications for the president (promises of votes, regrets of past votes, charges of vote-seeking) or to the undue influence of presidential advisors ("palace guards") and where respondents make personal requests from the president (for casework, money, appearances, public statements); and (4) movement-specific considerations, in which the respondent refers to pro– and anti–civil rights leaders, organizations, or events. The distribution of these considerations across the activated publics considered will give us additional clues about which group is pushing the agenda on civil rights and which group is being pulled into the fray.[27]

Table 6.5 shows this distribution of specific considerations. As suggested by my presentation of stylized collective voices, African Americans are the most likely to place policy-specific considerations at the center of their message. This focus on policy-specific appeals is stronger from 1948 to 1959 (21.5 percent) than from 1960 to 1965 (10.7 percent), when many of the letters attempt to focus the president's interest on social and economic reforms not under legislative consideration. Letters from African Americans are notable for the frequency of president-specific considerations as well. The most common such appeals are promises of racial bloc voting for the president in return for pushing for racial equality, and, mostly from 1948 to 1959, personal requests, such as casework, invitations to attend social functions, and solicitations.

For northern and southern whites, by contrast, fewer letters attempt to gain the president's ear by discussing president-specific considerations and fewer still address policy-specific considerations. Rather, the most striking figure from table 6.5 for these groups is that, once movement activism was fully mobilized in the 1960s, letters from northern and southern whites commonly pointed the president to specific movement issues, leaders, and organizations. Thus from 1960 to 1965, about 20 percent of letters from northern whites and 31 percent of letters from southern whites place movement-specific considerations at the center of their discussion. Although the inference here is indirect, this pattern of political considerations for the three groups suggests that northern and southern whites are drawn

Table 6.5 Comparisons of Consideration- and Event-Specific Frames

	African Americans			Southern Whites			"Northern" Whites		
	1948–59	1960–65	All years	1948–59	1948–59	All years	1948–59	1960–65	All years
Political Considerations									
Policy-specific	21.5	10.7	15.8	2.3	4.0	3.4	5.4	5.3	5.3
Partisan-specific	4.8	3.5	4.1	14.2	7.0	9.6	8.9	2.1	3.9
President-specific	14.0	16.1	15.1	7.6	12.8	10.9	7.7	10.1	9.5
Movement-specific	4.6	11.8	8.4	13.2	31.4	24.7	5.4	19.8	16.0
Elite and Movement Responsiveness									
Elite-responsive	31.1	29.0	30.0	67.4	10.2	31.1	48.3	26.7	32.4
Movement-responsive	7.2	46.0	27.6	8.5	68.8	46.8	29.3	36.7	34.8

into the issue of civil rights through ongoing movement events and discourses, whereas African Americans take a far more proactive stance in vigorously trying to frame the civil rights agenda for the president.

Finally, residues of movement agency should also be evident in the events that provoke ordinary individuals to write to their president. The categorization of events as movement-initiated or elite-initiated in table 6.5 is the same as that used in table 5.2. To remind the reader, events that are staged in a nonpolitical arena and whose primary actors are nonpolitical are counted as movement-initiated. Events staged in a political arena and enacted by political elites are elite-initiated. In three cases events are coded as both elite- and movement-initiated.

The final set of rows in table 6.5 shows the relative responsiveness of letters from each group to elite and movement-initiated events. Of the three groups, the responsiveness of letters from southern whites is strikingly reactive over time. From 1948 to 1959, during the formative stages of the civil rights movement, southern whites were overwhelmingly responsive (67 percent of letters) to elite actions such as Eisenhower's decision to send federal troops to Little Rock or the Supreme Court's affirmation of their *Brown* decision in the 1958 *Aaron v. Cooper* decision. By the 1960s, however, this responsiveness underwent a full reversal. Southern whites were now responding equally overwhelmingly (69 percent of letters) to movement-based events and actions. This general pattern of shifting from elite-responsiveness to movement-responsiveness is evident in letters from northern whites and African Americans as well. Nonetheless, the general impression remains fairly consistent with the evidence on types of values-based and group-based frames and types of political considerations: African Americans appear to be setting the terms of the debate, whereas northern whites follow and southern whites react.

MOVEMENT AGENCY AND MASS ACTIVATION

We have seen a dramatic account of how protest movements involve struggles over the content and contours of mass opinion. This is a drama that unmistakably captivates and activates the voices of audiences that are attentive to the civil rights movement. Nowhere is this truer than in the words we have read in this chapter. "The making of words," Daniel Rodgers reminds us, "is indeed an act, not a business distinct from the hard, behavioral part of politics but a thing people do" (1987, 5). The words in this chapter (and the interpretive frames they conjure) echo the central role that our cherished moral and political values and our group-based interests, identities, and conflicts play in articulating racial attitudes. Some of the activated voices we have heard vied to change public views on race by exposing the harsh contradiction between dearly held beliefs and everyday conditions facing African Americans in the South. Others struggled to maintain support for the status quo by appealing to custom, religious mores, political order, constitutional imperative and by making naked attempts to divert the public's attention to other matters such as communism and the Cold War.

This conflict, critically, is played out on a terrain of racial and regional boundaries. Letters from African Americans reveal a proactive voice that frames the state of racial affairs in the United States as a contradiction of core moral and political principles. African Americans also exhibit a strong sense of racial group identity and interests, push for broadly based economic, social, and political reforms (even in the absence of elite consideration of such reforms), and play a watchdog role by monitoring racial injustices around the nation. Letters from northern whites reveal a sympathetic voice that echoes the move by African Americans to frame civil rights and racial integration in terms of cherished principles. Letters from southern whites reveal a distinctly reactive voice that belies a sense of perceived threat to the existing social order in the South. This reactive voice is manifest in the selective appropriation of core principles, the responsiveness of letters to movement events, leaders, and organizations, and attempts to counterpose alternative frames that directly respond to frames promulgated by African Americans and northern whites.

These findings, taken together, illustrate the collective influence of black insurgency on the viewpoints that activated audiences. In the evocative framing of these viewpoints within the context of the civil rights movement we see traces of Sewell's conception of agency, described earlier in this chapter. For instance, the egalitarian convention of rights discourse is transposed onto the unambiguously inegalitarian context of racial segregation and domination by African Americans. Correspondingly, that same rights discourse is transposed in turn onto the context of states' rights, whites rights, taxpayer rights by southern whites. Similarly, the ideological threat of communism and the Cold War is transposed onto the context of black military service for African Americans. And that same ideological threat is exploited both to identify African American movement leaders as communist and to try and divert the president's attention away from the emergent crisis in the American South.

I conclude with two brief theoretical points of departure from the analysis and findings in this chapter. First, a main theme of this chapter has been to demonstrate the non-elite basis of activated opinion by showing the influence of black insurgency on the specific frames that mass audiences used to inform and persuade their president about the struggle over civil rights. In doing so, I adopted a particular approach to a lively yet open debate over how to conceive of agents of social change given the bedrock social structures that resist such change.

The conception I adopt from William Sewell, however, is not without limitations. In particular, it bears the same limitations that characterize sociological accounts that emphasize the habitual and routinized bases of social action, à la Pierre Bourdieu and Anthony Giddens. Agency "happens" when transpositions of schemas "happen." Absent from this rendition is the role of motivation, choice, reasoning, deliberation, strategy. When we think of the leadership, creativity, inspiration, and heroism involved in manufacturing social change, a radically disembodied formulation such as schema transposition can leave us cold.[28] Yet in this instance, Sewell's conception suffices because our data cannot sustain a more muscular personification of agency. The words and interpretive frames in citizen correspondence, vivid as they are, portray well the cultural, narrative context of social action but are poorly suited to address the psychological or structural contexts.

The second point of departure is the relationship between public opinion and social movements. From the standpoint of social movement theory, mass opinion is seldom examined as an important resource, constraint, or objective. To be sure, there are instances in which the motivations and beliefs of individuals play a central role. Frances Fox Piven and Richard Cloward (1979), for instance, describe three cognitive states that enable movement activism—the perceived illegitimacy of a ruling regime, the rejection of fatalism, and the rise of personal efficacy. William Gamson (1992) describes an analogous typology of injustice, agency, and identity frames. Yet even in these cases, the scholarly gaze is mostly fixed on center stage—the strategic and symbolic encounters between oppositional movement activists and conventional political elites and the material resources, cognitive frames, and institutional arrangements necessary to stage such encounters.[29]

In the context of civil rights movement, the incompletely defined role of public opinion can be shown in Doug McAdam's "political process" model (1982). For McAdam, social movements take flight when three factors converge: when the prevailing political opportunities are predisposed toward social change, when the organizational resources of the counterpublic are strong, and when the insurgent public's cognitive state is liberated.[30] Cognitive liberation occurs as otherwise inactive, disenfranchised individuals imbue their objective circumstances with powerful subjective meanings and transform "hopeless submission to oppressive conditions to an aroused readiness to challenge those conditions" (1982, 34). As a result, cognitive liberation bridges the gap between the "structural potential" for social change (vis-à-vis opportunity structure and organizational strength) and the political action necessary to mobilize demands for such change.[31]

This conception of cognitive liberation is somewhat theoretically and empirically underspecified. Theoretically, it is intended to explain how disempowered and marginalized individuals are inspired to demand better. But it does not satisfactorily explain why some individuals choose to demand a change in their life circumstances and others do not. It also fails to explain variations in the level of cognitive liberation among the privileged who gain from an unjust state of affairs. For that matter, neither is there any account of whether cognitive liberation is principally something that applies to movement participants or whether it is relevant to mass audiences as they witness the developing drama.

Furthermore, although McAdam's political process model is a brilliant account of the civil rights movement, his evidence for cognitive liberation is somewhat thin. Specifically, McAdam compares the aggregate responses of African Americans and white Americans to two Roper Center survey items asked in 1942 and 1947: whether "the average young man" will enjoy more or fewer life chances after World War II and whether the respondent's son will enjoy more or fewer such opportunities in life than the respondent.[32] In addition to being a crude use of survey data, the link between optimism and political empowerment is a decidedly tenuous one. Several studies have shown, for instance, that African Americans who are the least well-off and most politically disengaged tend to hold the most optimistic views about their future prospects.[33]

In this book, I have developed an account of activated mass opinion that extends McAdam's concept of cognitive liberation and gives it a robust empirical foundation. The story here, crucially, is not limited to movement activists but describes the interaction between the general public, active citizens (whether movement proponents or opponents), and elite political actors. Moreover, the evidence brought to bear on the relation between activated mass opinion and social movements draws from multiple sources of opinion data. In this chapter, we have seen that the dynamics of social movements structures the dynamics of public opinion. But the converse— that the dynamics of public opinion should structure the dynamics of insurgent movements—should be true as well. Like theater, the interplay between actors on stage fails as compelling political drama unless it engages and is engaged by the general audience.

In some contexts, the dynamics of mass opinion during a social movement provide organized interests with an additional, valuable resource.[34] Most obviously, this is the case when the passions and principles of inactive publics can be stirred to action and ordinary individuals can be recruited as participants in a social movement.[35] In addition, in democratic societies, inactive individuals represent potential voters. Thus public opinion readily translates into constituency pressures on government, and actors can change the balance of power in a social movement by changing the dynamics of mass opinion.[36]

In other contexts, mass opinion defines the feasible boundaries within which movement advocates and adversaries can maneuver. The dynamics of public opinion is, more often than not, part of the contested terrain in political conflicts. The injustices that motivate mass insurgency are perpetuated not only by the laws, policies, and institutional arrangements of political elites, but also by the beliefs and sentiments of ordinary individuals in everyday social, economic, and cultural transactions. Thus the dissimilarities, commonalities, and interactions we have seen between African Americans, southern whites, and racially liberal whites animate the clash over how the public interprets the unfolding political conflict. This contestation is well recapitulated by the social historian Daniel Rodgers:

> From the beginning the civil rights campaign was a movement of several tongues. But politically its most telling rhetoric worked by exploiting the massive, barely veiled contradiction between the official postwar rhetoric of Freedom and customary practice. . . . The civil rights movement swept up rights and Freedom into a common cry of protest and threw it back at mainstream America in a score of nervy, ingenious ways. . . . Here was no strange political tongue, no language easily turned aside as alien to American politics, as politicians and presidents noted with visible confusion. This was the core rhetoric of the Cold War translated into black vernacular, specified, sharpened into radically destabilizing demands, appropriated by the most marginal of Americans. (1987, 218–19)

SEVEN

TWO NATIONS, SEPARATE GROOVES

Our nation is moving toward two societies, one black, one white—
separate and unequal.
—The Kerner Commission Report

. . . not two, but many Americas, separate, unequal, isolated.
—William Jefferson Clinton

One nation, under a groove, Getting down just for the funk of it.
—George Clinton, Funkadelic

My faltering footsteps toward this book trace back to a particular time and place. On Wednesday, April 29, 1992, a jury of ten whites, one Latino, and one Asian American, in a courtroom nestled in Ventura County's Simi Valley, voted to acquit four white Los Angeles police officers accused of beating a black motorist, Rodney King. Almost instantly, the predominantly African American and Latino residents of South Central Los Angeles reacted to this verdict violently and the City of Angels burst into a raging hellfire. By the time the angry black smoke thinned to a putrescent smog, the conflagration had left in its path 53 dead, 2,400 injured, $800 million in property damage, 25,000 lost jobs, and 10,000 defunct businesses. Over the course of the three-day episode, more than 20,000 officers of the LAPD, county sheriff, California Highway Patrol, National Guard, FBI, SWAT, infantry, and Marines were mobilized to restore order to the scorched earth of Los Angeles.[1]

This civilian act of collective violence and the state's militarized response, which by almost any account reached a scale of destruction unmatched in United States history, quickly became a defining moment for journalists, politicians, and academics to interpret. In its unfolding, the violence was televised live before a shocked and spellbound public as a spontaneous, senseless, self-destructive act of an African American community wounded into a blind rage by the injustice of the King verdict. Conservative scholars such as Eugene Methvin (1992) and Charles Murray (1992), attempting to preempt clarion calls for a national urban policy, were quick to point to the violence and lawlessness as symptomatic of a deeper malaise of the disintegration of family values and social norms and the diminished capacity of the law to straightjacket dangerous miscreants. The title on the cover of the June 8 issue of the *National Review*—"How to Get a Week's Groceries Absolutely Free *PLUS* $600 Million in Federal Aid"—well depicted the conservative's view of the rioting in South Central Los Angeles and the Wilshire District as a freeloader's carnival.

Commentators from the left such as Mike Davis (1992) and Tim Rutten (1992), however, were equally quick to decry these representations of the event and pointed to the strands of purposive action and political significance embedded in the "Los Angeles Rebellion."[2] The destruction, it was proclaimed, was "A New Kind of Riot"—the nation's first multiracial uprising. Of the 17,000 persons arrested, only about 40 percent were African Americans, whereas roughly 50 percent were Latino. Moreover, report Johnson et al., the violent response was "targeted, systematic, and widespread" (1992, 118). Within the first forty-eight hours of the rebellion, 90 percent of all Korean-owned businesses in South Central and the Wilshire District had been burned to the ground (Davis 1992, 744). An anthology of essays by prominent African Americans on the left, in addition, included an itemized and budgeted list of economic, social, and political programs to rebuild South Central articulated by the street gangs the Bloods and the Crips (Madhubuti 1993, 274–82). As Mike Davis poignantly proposed, "the nation's first multiracial riot was as much about empty bellies and broken hearts as it was about police batons and Rodney King" (1992, 743).

Like most Americans, I put my life on hold for three days. I planted myself before the television set, riveted by the unrelenting stream of apocalyptic images out of Los Angeles: a bewildered white man pulled from his truck and set upon by a mob of African American youth, disillusioned Korean merchants perched above their stores brandishing artillery, and continuous reruns of George Holliday's amateur videotape of "L.A.'s finest" assaulting Rodney King with Taser gun and police baton while King lay helpless on the ground. To many who viewed these shocking images, the violent aftermath of the Rodney King verdict and the contested readings of this episode were eerily familiar. These images were an epic remake of the long hot summers of mass unrest and racial tumult in the 1960s. A quarter-century after the Kerner Commission's celebrated report, the United States seemed still a nation divided by color. And Kenneth Clark's comments before the Kerner Commission in 1968 seemed painfully prophetic:

> I read that report . . . of the 1919 riot in Chicago, and it is as if I were reading the report of the investigating committee on the Harlem riot of '35, the report of the investigating committee on the Harlem riot of '43, the report of the McCone Commission on the Watts riot.
>
> I must again in candor say to you members of this Commission—it is a kind of Alice in Wonderland—with the same moving picture re-shown over and over again, the same analysis, the same recommendations, and the same inaction. (National Advisory Commission on Civil Disorders 1968, 29)

Clark's sobering observation emphatically extends beyond the recurrence of urban uprisings and government commissions that investigate their origins. The themes that underscore the unfolding of the 1992 Los Angeles uprising also underscore the central points of this book. For one thing, what the public believes (and how intensely it believes it) is not always well behaved and easily discernible through research tools such as opinion polls. Most of the time, on most issues, we can speak of public opinion by referring to poll results. But sometimes, public opinion does not wait for the pollster. Sometimes, like Langston Hughes's dream deferred, it explodes before us, with unexpected clarity and cogency. When this happens the outcome turns as much on how ordinary individuals interpret and respond to the issue at hand as it does on how political elites interpret and respond to it. Elites, counterelites, and their mass audiences alike will engage in a clash over words, meanings, and motivations.

In this book, we have taken a systematic look at public opinion in action—how an insurgent protest movement can engage and activate citizens' political views. This is a story of two nations—black and white—and of the separate interactions, interests, identities, ideologies, and institutions that define the collective responses of African Americans and white Americans to the unfolding political drama. V. O. Key tells us that "[t]he public copes with new and great events and questions without the comforting guidance of grooves in the mind" (1961, 267). We have seen that the verity of Key's observation depends on which public we are speaking of and what circumstances bring about such "new and great events and questions." With respect to racial attitudes during the civil rights movement, the events and questions arise because of the collective insurgency of an activated sector of the mass public. Thus the grooves are simply separate and multiple, not nonexistent.

The title of this chapter, then, comes in the first instance from an empirical claim about the separate realms of experience and opinion dynamics that characterize public views of race. There is a second, somewhat more oblique, basis for the chapter's title. "Two Nations, Separate Grooves" also refers to competing normative models of democratic politics and the role of public opinion and mass participation within them. By one conception, democracy's ambitions are met when citizens play a limited, institutionalized role in political decision-making and their basis for making political judgments is largely defined, top-down, by political elites. By another, democracy flourishes when its citizens play a more direct, participatory role in political decision-making and their basis for making political judgments is significantly defined, bottom-up, by their interactions and institutional attachments in civil society.

Critically, as social scientists, we often circumvent an explicit choice between such normative conceptions. An important undercurrent in this book has been that such normative inclinations are unavoidable and implicit, despite our best ambitions to sidestep them, in our theoretical and methodological frameworks. In chapter 1, I noted that social science theories can be characterized along a "thin-thick," or minimalist-maximalist, continuum. In the minimalist case, the complexity and specificity of social scientific phenomena are condensed to the fewest possible analytic components, with maximum payoffs in parsimony and explanatory power. In the maximalist case, as much complexity and specificity as possible is preserved to faithfully embody social science reality while still retaining a sufficiently generalizable analytical framework. In this final chapter, I shall argue that minimalist and maximalist approaches to social science theory, and their corresponding methodologies, parallel a minimalist and maximalist conception of democratic politics. Thus we explore the linkages and tensions between the theoretical priors and methodological tools we bring to the study of mass opinion and their substantive and normative implications. But first a summary of central arguments and key findings in this book is in order.

ELITE OPINION THEORIES REEXAMINED

In chapter 1, I began by carefully laying out some of the tensions in elite theories of mass opinion using its paradigmatic contemporary rendition:

John Zaller's "Receive-Accept-Sample" model. In the RAS model, opinions are formed and changed by a process that begins when a person receives new information (as a function of her individual level of political awareness) and accepts or rejects that information as a relevant consideration on a given issue. If the person is then asked about the issue, the "opinion" she gives is an averaging of whichever considerations happen to be most accessible to her ("at the top of one's head") at that particular moment. Zaller's RAS model delivers a parsimonious and powerful look into the common cognitive structure of our political opinions. This model, however, treats the mass opinion formation and change as a unitary, uniform process that generalizes across all social groups, historical periods, and political phenomena. As a consequence, the dynamics of mass opinion during periods such as the civil rights era are rendered no differently than the dynamics during any other period, or involving any other social groups or political phenomena.

How, then, do we retain the insights of elite models such as RAS while incorporating the shifting, contextual dimensions of mass opinion, in particular, during the onset and evolution of a protest movement? In this book, I suggest amendments along two fronts. First, the cognitive states that regulate our political inputs (that is, our awareness) are not so easily dissociable from the mechanisms that regulate how we interpret our political world (that is, the considerations at the top of our heads) and how we express our political views (that is, our "opinion statements"). People characterized by greater awareness about racial politics are not only likely to seek out and receive more information about it, but they are also likely to think more about the issue and express their viewpoints in more active ways than simply responding to opinion surveys.

Second, on an issue such as racial attitudes during the civil rights movement, race is an important, if not *the* most important, political predisposition. During the evolution of a social movement, the particular predispositions, levels of political awareness, and institutional ties at work will depend on how the cleavages are drawn relative to the issue or issues at the heart of the insurgent movement. With black insurgency during the 1950s and 1960s, these cleavages were drawn quite sharply around racial and regional group markers. Thus processes of racial attitude formation and change do not begin and end with political elites but originate within and across racially and regionally specific group institutions and actors as well. And stable, collectively defined predispositions such as group consciousness, conflict, and animosity are an essential part of the story. This is especially so when we consider the non-elite bases of mass opinion. In the case of the civil rights movement, the group-specific dynamics that led to black insurgency in the 1950s and 1960s originated from counterpublic spheres and counterelite actors and institutions within the African American community that enabled alternate modes of political information and nurtured oppositional institutions and ideologies.

These amendments, taken together, suggest a considerably different picture of "activated mass opinion" during the course of insurgent protest movements. In the equilibrium state prior to the onset of the civil rights movement, African Americans should (as a group) exhibit high levels of awareness of and responsiveness to dual informational inputs and institutional attachments (that is, from the center stage of elites and from a side stage of black counterelites). For most white Americans (with the exception of activist, racially liberal whites), racial integration is unlikely to be very salient in the public mind at this stage. With the onset of organized insurgency in the South by the mid-1950s, civil rights should percolate up into the consciousness of the general public and onto the agendas of political elites. As the campaign against Jim Crow in the South intensified, movement activists should increasingly play a role in defining the content and framing of information about civil rights that is transmitted to mass audiences. With this growing challenge to their status quo, southern white actors and institutions should become activated and progressively disseminate their own countervalent information flows and interpretive frames on civil rights. And into the 1960s, at the height of the civil rights struggle, the boundaries between elite actors and mass audiences should increasingly dissolve as greater and greater numbers of civil rights advocates and adversaries become activated and mobilized.

These propositions comprise a "movement-initiated, movement-elite interactive" account of activated mass opinion. The empirical chapters of the book presented evidence in support of this interactive account using multiple methodologies and multiple measures of opinion. In chapter 2, I tested for the hypothesized non-elite opinion dynamics using available survey data from 1956 to 1964. Specifically, I modeled racial attitudes as a dynamic competition between partisan (elite) opinion cues and movement-based (non-elite) opinion cues. The results convincingly showed the influence of non-elite, movement-specific attachments on public views of race during the civil rights movement. We examined public support for government's role in fair housing and jobs and government's role in school desegregation. With both questions, affinity to movement groups (in the case of white respondents) and racial group identification (in the case of black respondents) was an earlier and stronger predictor of support than partisan-specific attachments. Even when party attachments significantly influenced racial attitudes in the 1960s, their influence was contingent on racial and regional markers: the influence of party worked in opposite ways for southern whites and whites outside the South. With just a limited number of available survey items, then, I showed that the influence of movement-specific considerations was significant at an earlier point in time than party-specific considerations and that this influence differed across racially and regionally defined contexts.

More narrowly, the results in chapter 2 offered an important corrective to a leading elite account of racial policy preferences during the civil rights movement, Edward Carmines and James Stimson's *Issue Evolution*. Carmines and Stimson, recall, claim that the mid-1960s was the critical moment during which durable ties between racial attitudes, social welfare liberalism, and political partisanship were forged. The findings showed that support for social welfare liberalism was significantly linked to racial attitudes at least as early as 1956 for both racial policy questions examined. Moreover, partisan considerations influenced racial attitudes as early as 1960. And racial considerations influenced change in partisanship itself as early as 1960; the degree of respondent-partisan affinity on racial issues significantly predicted change of partisanship between 1956 and 1960 (this effect was again diametrically opposite for Southern whites), as did race of correspondent. Again, the import and implication of pushing back these links at least as far back as 1960 is that movement-initiated events and discourses played a significant (if not central) role in forging these links, contrary to the elite presumptions found in Carmines and Stimson's account.

Looking beyond survey data, we found even more persuasive evidence to support a positive account of activated mass opinion from both macro-level and micro-level vantages. In chapter 5, we examined at the aggregate level changes in the activation of mass opinion as measured by the level of letter-writing and the shifting racial, regional, and institutional contexts from which correspondence emerged. The starting observation from this aggregate account is that particular, attentive sectors of the mass public become activated on specific issues and in response to ongoing events. In the case of civil rights and racial integration from 1948 to the mid-1960s, we saw that African American individuals and organizations were activated even prior to the onset of movement activism in the South, with significant support from racially sympathetic whites and organizations with predominantly white memberships. Prior to the onset of movement activism, these activated groups were alert to elite initiatives and to outbursts of white-on-black violence.

Once the story of the civil rights movement began to unfold in the mid-1950s with the *Brown* decision and the Montgomery bus boycott, we began to see successively greater numbers of correspondents and a see-sawing of activated opinion between African American and racially liberal white proponents and largely southern white opponents. With the continued escalation of movement activism and the increased media focus on racial brutality in the South in the 1960s, we saw an eruption of activated opinion, most impressively from sympathetic whites in support of movement activists' objectives and demands. Throughout this period mass opinion was activated by a dynamic interplay between movement- and elite-initiated events and discourses. Once organized activism begins in the South in the mid-1950s, however, it was more often than not movement-initiated events that dictated when correspondents would write to their president. And *contra* elite opinion theories, the peak of letter-writing in the mid-1960s did not respond to elite-initiated moments such as the 1964 Civil Rights Act, the 1964 presidential election, or the 1965 Voting Rights Act, but with the events in Selma, Alabama.

In chapter 6, we revisited the themes from this aggregate level by looking more closely into the structure and content of individual letters. These letters opened a window into a more brightly articulated, passionately held, dialogical, narrative, and rhetorically structured public opinion in which individuals determined which issues and opinions to voice and which words and interpretive frames to use. These individual letters—again, the analytic focus is on the activation of racial attitudes within racially and regionally defined sectors of the mass public—revealed not only the views of correspondents about civil rights and racial integration but also the choices they made concerning the wording and framing of those views.

These choices showed the powerful rhetorical force of dearly held values and the resounding influence of group-based interests, conflicts, and animosity. In the voices of African American correspondents, the most prominent frames were appeals based on moral suasion (universal rights, justice, and equality) and racial group interests and identity. In the voices of racially liberal (most commonly, northern) whites, the primary basis of persuasion was moral: correspondents made their case both in the abstract language of universal rights and justice and through more specific references to police brutality, the lack of equal protection under the law, and the tribunal of world opinion (vis-à-vis the broader political context of the Cold War). And in voices of antagonistic southern whites, the appeals most often belied a perception of group threat or racial animus toward African Americans. When moral frames were used, they appeared as direct attempts to respond to and usurp the normative force of moral arguments used by movement advocates.

Out of these differences emerged an oft-understated dimension of mass opinion and of social movements, namely, that in the public mind, the struggle over civil rights is partly a struggle over meaning. African Americans, racially liberal whites, and southern whites clashed over how the insurgent demands of movement activists ought to be interpreted. African American voices increasingly framed racial integration as a test of the core moral principles in American political discourse. Moreover, they did so with an increasingly confident and empowered tone. Racially liberal white voices were most striking for the degree to which they echoed and embraced this moral rhetorical grounding and for the explosion in the number of letters with the evolution of movement events. And southern white voices shifted from indignation (found in the salience of references to states' rights and the religious grounding of segregation) to a reactive defense of their status quo. This reactive voice was found in attempts to re-cast movement demands in terms of other issues (notably, communism) that might supersede or trump racial equality and in letters that, as noted above, attempted to expropriate the moral force of rights-based and equality-based movement frames (for example, by defending whites' rights or taxpayers' rights).

In these letters, then, the very terms in which correspondents defended their position reflects (albeit indirectly) a sensitivity to the agenda-setting of movement activists. In this responsiveness to movement events and actors we saw the purposive agency of black insurgency. This responsiveness was found more directly as well when we looked at the type of specific political considerations raised and the event-specificity of letters. Whereas letters from African Americans were more directly focused on considerations specific to the president and particular policy options, letters from northern whites and to a greater extent southern whites focused primarily on movement-specific considerations (that is, references to particular movement issues, campaigns, leaders, organizations). And when the particular events that provoked letter-writing were disaggregated by group, we found an impressive shift from responsiveness to elite events prior to the onset of the civil rights movement in all groups to a responsiveness to movement-initiated events with the full onset of movement activism.

The analysis and results in this book are far from exhaustive. In particular, there remain several unexplored ramifications of my critique of elite opinion theories worth noting. First, there is no explicit empirical analysis of the central cast of characters during the civil rights movement. I have described an account of mass activation during periods of political tumult in which the agents of activation and change are shadow players. Similarly, there is no explicit empirical analysis of the information flows between political elites, movement counterelites, and ordinary individuals. Mass media institutions—as well as other sources of political information such as volunteer associations and informal social networks—are presumed to play a key intermediary role in both top-down and bottom-up opinion dynamics, but this aspect too lurks in the background. An illuminating amplification in future studies would thus be to parallel my findings in chapters 2, 5, and 6 with an analysis of the substantive information and strategic framing of elite and counterelite actors, and the transmission of this information and framing vis-à-vis media institutions and communications networks.

In addition to these loose threads in the analysis, this book develops a contextual account of mass opinion without considering the full range of contexts in which the activation of public voices is likely to vary. For starters, I do not consider, conceptually or empirically, the aftermath of mass activation. Specifically, if black insurgency in the period leading up to the mid-1960s exerted a powerful activating effect on mass opinion, what role did the subsequent evolution of the civil rights movement have on mass opinion vis-à-vis the growing voice of the black power movement, uprisings in America's cities, the poor people's movement, the emergence of new protest movements organized around communities of color, gender, culture, and ideology, and the like? The period from the mid-1960s to the early 1970s, notably, was one of mass protest marked by increasing dissensus and divergence within the black counterpublic, growing fear and resentment among sympathetic or otherwise inattentive white audiences outside the South, heightened responsiveness to the demands of African Americans by government actors, and, at the same time, intensified surveillance and infiltration of movement organizations by government actors. Although I have been chiefly concerned in this book with making a case against elite opinion theories and against substantive accounts that make extravagant claims about the mid-1960s, assessing the whole cycle of activation and deactivation is obviously indispensable to a full rendition of activated mass opinion. Along similar lines, we have considered simply one case of mass activation. We might also extend the analysis to other issue domains—movements organized around women's rights, abortion, gay rights, the environment, multiracial identity—in which grassroots activism has more or less of an influence on public opinion.

Finally, the focus in this book has been the non-elite bases of public opinion during mass movements for social change. There are, to be sure, more sporadic, less organized instances in which mass opinion may not follow elite, top-down dynamics. Three unexplored alternative strategies to demonstrating instances of non-elite opinion dynamics are worth noting. The first such strategy is to examine cases in which top-down political information flows push in one direction, but public opinion shifts instead in the opposite direction. John Zaller himself follows this strategy in his description of the Bill Clinton–Monica Lewinsky affair, in which media coverage was unambiguously negative yet Clinton continued to fare remarkably well in his "presidential approval" ratings (1998). Another strategy is to examine the nature and origins of conspiratorial thinking. In particular, where such beliefs are premised on the view that government is the enemy of the people—for instance, when African Americans view AIDS and the war on drugs as manifestations of a government-manufactured genocidal conspiracy—we might expect very little diffusion of information from mainstream political actors or mass media, notwithstanding of one's level of political attentiveness.[3]

The third strategy is to examine individuals who enter a political system with a tabula rasa, without what V. O. Key terms the "comforting guidance of grooves in the mind." For most citizens of the United States, these grooves in the mind are a natural outcome of one's political socialization from childhood to adulthood. With immigrants, however, this is not the case. One approach to this third strategy would thus be to study the massive influx of new citizens to the United States since the Immigration Act of 1965—most visibly, of Asian Americans and Latinos—as a natural experiment to examine the formation of political predispositions and elite partisan attachments.[4]

ACTIVATED OPINION AND SURVEY RESEARCH

These findings are embedded in a broader cautionary tale of the sovereign status of survey data in the study of public opinion. In chapter 3, I described the ascendance of survey data as the dominant mode of expression studied as "public opinion." I then reviewed several possible perils that emerge from this sovereign status. Normatively, the reliance on opinion polls and elections may threaten the vitality and autonomy of our political life and may limit our public imagination with regard to democratic representation and citizenship. Ontologically, essential (perhaps defining) elements of public opinion, properly understood, are left beyond our grasp when we confuse and conflate the construct we seek to understand (public opinion) with one particular measure of it (survey data). We will return to the normative stakes here vis-à-vis elite opinion theories in the ensuing section.

The primary empirical implication of this sovereign status, recall, was that the validity and reliability of opinion polls depends critically on whether the questions that actually engage the mass public are being asked. Barring appropriate insight, foresight, or serendipity, survey researchers may perceive an issue as worth polling about only after that issue has become salient in the arena of politics or the realm of the public mind—that is, only after there has been some prior transformation and activation on that issue. This potential shortcoming is especially keen if the transformation and activation are initiated by non-elites. Thus, poll data may be especially ill-equipped to satisfactorily confirm or disconfirm elite versus non-elite accounts of racial attitudes and mass opinion.

In the case of racial attitudes, the first finding from chapter 2 was the strikingly ubiquitous reliance on survey data in existing research on racial attitudes. Moreover, the historical lapses in political science research on race—either in viewing the attitudes of white Americans as the primary subject of interest, or in being implicitly (and sometimes explicitly) racist in the kind of research conducted, or in simply lagging far behind the actual course of political change—were noted. On the last point, the production of survey items on racial attitudes, specifically, lags behind actual political events: the number of movement-initiated events in a given year strongly predicts the number of racial attitude items the following year.

What is to be done in light of the possible perils of the conflation of public opinion and survey data? One possibility is to throw up one's hands and give up on the ability of survey data to answer questions such as the dynamics of mass opinion, as many critics of survey research have done. Another possibility is to ignore the possible pitfalls and plod ahead with the best kind of evidence that survey data can provide in the hope that sufficiently broad time series and representative panel studies might yield adequate answers in the long run, as many survey research practitioners have done. In this book, I steer a middle course: namely, to use survey data for the discriminating analysis and the broadly generalizable claims it facilitates, but complement and parallel the results with an examination of alternate measures and competing conceptions of public opinion. This is an approach that is increasingly common in recent opinion research from Amy Fried (1997), Susan Herbst (1998), Katherine Cramer Walsh (2000), Lawrence Jacobs and Robert Shapiro (2000), and others.

This middle course, vitally, is more than a catholic embrace of methodological diversity. Rather, it is an acknowledgment of the complexity and multidimensionality of public opinion. Depending on the question or phenomenon at issue, certain alternate measures or conceptions of public opinion will be more appropriate than others, and we lose important information about public opinion by limiting ourselves to just one conventional mode of measuring opinion. In a study of the non-elite bases of mass opinion during the course of an insurgent protest movement, opinion polls are not the most appropriate alternative. Rather, I made the case in chapter 3 for alternative measures that better capture the organic, interactive, and collective dimensions of mass opinion. In particular, I advocated the analytical advantages of modes of expression that permit an individual free rein over the structure and content of her public political expression.

In this book, constituency mail—the letters and other types of correspondence that citizens write to their political representatives—fits this bill. An alternate source of opinion data such as constituency mail opens a window for discernment of how the public (and *which* public) became engaged and activated as the civil rights movement unfolded. Specifically, I argued in chapter 4 that constituency mail reveals the narrative, rhetorical, dialogical, and affective forms that an individual's political viewpoints take as they are actually expressed in non-survey settings. Thus, constituency mail and opinion surveys should rightly be viewed as complementary sources of data on public opinion.

The analyses and arguments about survey research in this book, more broadly, enjoin future researchers to theorize the historical, group-specific, and issue-specific contexts in which public opinion becomes transformed and activated. On this point, I argued in chapter 1 that the degree to which we ought to look for non-elite sources of opinion change will most likely vary with the degree and type of activation of mass opinion. Specifically, I proposed four distinguishable levels of mass activation: (1) routine politics, in which there are no discernible constituent demands made on elite actors concerning given issue; (2) routine politics in which there are such constituent demands but they are mobilized and channeled through institutional means, such as well-established interest groups; (3) insurgent politics, in which ordinary individuals begin to mobilize their demands beyond established institutional channels and vie for electoral power and agenda control; and (4) insurgent politics, in which the mobilization of mass grievances extends into civil society in attempts to undermine and transform existing social and economic relations, cultural meanings, and terms of political discourse. Existing elite opinion theories are likeliest to remain robust in instances of routine, institutional politics. In instances of insurgent movements, however, there is a greater likelihood that public opinion will move without waiting for opinion polls to capture its movement and a greater likelihood that non-elite, insurgent opinion dynamics is at work.

In the case of the activation of mass opinion during the civil rights movement, we saw ample evidence of both insurgent attempts to vie for political office and agenda control and insurgent attempts to dislocate and shift existing racial meanings, practices, and discourses. This conception of insurgent politics and activated mass opinion, to return to themes first introduced in chapter 1, spans the disciplinary boundaries of opinion research and social movement theory. According to this view, insurgent movements can involve not simply a demand for and struggle over material entitlements and legal rules but also a contestation over how ordinary individuals come to understand this demand and struggle. As a result, insurgent movements also involve a struggle over the dynamics and distribution of mass opinion itself, and the shifting contours of mass opinion then act as an important resource for or constraint on a social movement. Thus the enactment of social movements not only structures but can also be structured by the dynamics and distribution of mass beliefs and sentiments. An important consequence of adopting such a view is that the critical agency of movement activism, and of participatory politics more generally, is not submerged beneath the weight of theoretical commitments to political elites or of methodological commitments to survey data.

ACTIVATED OPINION AND DEMOCRATIC CITIZENSHIP

One possible defense of elite opinion theories and of exclusively survey-based opinion research is that, in the end, the substantive and theoretical account in this book is closer to a quibble than a full corrective. John Zaller, for example, himself acknowledges the limitations of the RAS model. This model does a poor job, by Zaller's own admission, of explaining the long-term dynamics of mass opinion and discriminating between (the elite or non-elite) sources of political information and political predispositions. Moreover, even though I suggest that non-elite, activated opinion dynamics may be at work in many different contexts, I have really only made the case for one historically contained case: public views on race during the civil rights movement.

My bias, of course, is that the account in this book is far closer to a corrective than a quibble. But even if that were demonstrably not the case, the stakes here ultimately involve more than trimming the edges of a largely overlapping empirical account. Put bluntly, there is a world of normative difference between an account of public opinion in which the mass electorate merely responds to political elites and a more participatory account of public opinion in which the mass electorate, under certain historical, institutional, and ideological circumstances, can mobilize their collective grievances and play an active role in the crafting of democratic politics. Just beneath the choices we make about which theoretical positions and methodological tools best suit the study of public opinion, and just beneath the substantive account of the civil rights movement that emerges from those choices, lie critical choices about how we view democratic citizenship and representation. In particular, underlying elite, survey-based opinion research such as Zaller's RAS model or Carmines and Stimson's issue evolution model are judgments about the competence of ordinary individuals, *empirically*, to *do* the work of democratic politics, rather than having politics *done for them* by political elites. Also underlying such research are normative judgments about whether we value a minimal conception of citizenship and public life or a more full-bodied, participatory ideal.

A salient consequence of the sovereign status of survey data, I note in chapter 2, is that opinion polls end up, de facto, controlling how the conceptual, normative, and substantive parameters of "public opinion" are defined. Notably, the easy analogy of opinion polls to a "one person, one vote" conception of democracy not only lends special appeal to the use of surveys but also bounds our understanding of what public opinion itself *is* and what its role in democratic politics *ought* to be. In its early formulation—captured most succinctly in James Bryce's phrase "government by public opinion"—it is the regulative ideal of public opinion that makes political representation a fair bargain, for public opinion stands "[t]owering over Presidents and State governors, over Congress and State legislatures, over conventions and vast machinery of party" (1895, 267).

For all the rhetorical flourish that has accompanied it, however, this regulative ideal of public opinion faces a basic tension when coupled with elite opinion theories. Put plainly, there is a contradiction between Bryce's account of democratic representation as "government by public opinion" and elite opinion theory's account of a government that holds controlling authority over what, when, and how the public thinks about political matters. Even if political elites are entirely benevolent or neutral in their dominion over political information and interpretive frames, the authenticity of mass preferences would be suspect. And if political elites are strategic or, worse yet, manipulative in exercising their control over what we know and how we interpret things (as the sizeable literature on game theoretic approaches to politics suggests they ought to be), then we are just small steps

removed from Benjamin Ginsberg and Jürgen Habermas's dismal prognos-
tications of "domesticated public opinion" and "manufactured publicity,"
which were noted in chapter 2. As Ginsberg puts this argument, "Elections
facilitate participation in much the same way that floodgates can be said to
facilitate the flow of water. Elections direct mass involvement into formal
channels, thus removing many potential impediments to participation, but
at the same time diverting it from courses that may be hazardous to the
established political order" (1986, 54).

A key to unwrapping this tension between "government by public opinion" and government control over that opinion rests with what we think
ordinary citizens are capable of. How we view the competence of the mass
public—whether we embrace the will of ordinary citizens as a regulative
ideal or fear the caprice of an inattentive, ill-informed, and always manipu-
lable electorate—is, of course, a deep normative tension within the idea of
public opinion that goes perhaps as far back as democratic rule itself. This
tension is perhaps first articulated in ancient Greece, with Plato's distrust
of the multitudes and his belief that government should rule by rational,
scientific principles *(techne)* juxtaposed against Aristotle's more sanguine
belief in their potential for collective or practical wisdom *(phronesis)* as
judged by citizens in a democratic polity.[5]

The tension persists even with the evolution of a more explicitly normative and regulative "modern" conception of public opinion around the
time of the demise of the *ancien régime* in late eighteenth-century France.[6]
Keith Baker describes this transformation into public opinion as a regulative ideal thus:

> Whereas before its principal characteristics were flux, subjectivity, and uncer-
> tainty, now they are universality, objectivity, and rationality. Within the space
> of a generation, the flickering lamp of "opinion" has been transformed into
> the unremitting light of "public opinion," the light of the universal tribunal
> before which citizens and governments alike must appear. (1990, 168)

As Baker further notes, the legitimacy that comes with these appeals to "the
public" derives from the idea of the public as a collective entity that spoke
with univocal clarity. And thus for Jürgen Habermas (1989), what bestows
such "unremitting light" on *public* opinion and distinguishes it from mere
opinion per se is more than its univocal clarity and more than the fact that
the beliefs of citizens could hold sway over the conduct of the state. What
gives public opinion its legitimating force, Habermas emphasizes, is that
these opinions could be the collaborative outcome of citizens engaged in
critical and rational deliberation.[7]

Note that this idealization of public opinion—most obvious in Habermas's formulation—makes ambitious, perhaps utopian demands on the judgmental competence of democratic citizens. Not surprisingly, Baker finds that even in eighteenth-century France, *l'opinion publique* was a political invention—the last rhetorical resort of an absolutist state facing a crisis of legitimacy. Thus Baker argues that "[p]ublic opinion took form as a political or ideological construct, rather than as a discrete sociological referent. . . . The result was an implicit new system of authority, in which the government and its opponents competed to appeal to 'the public' and to claim the judgment of 'public opinion' on their behalf" (1990, 172). In practice, only the few privileged men of letters (for example, members of academia and parliament) were legitimated as spokespersons for the "public."[8] And skeptics such as Jean-Jacques Rousseau were ever fearful of social factions and mistrusted the capacity of ordinary citizens to achieve the kind of political reasoning necessary for *l'opinion publique* to speak as an organic unity. Even the Marquis de Condorcet—known today for his elegant defense of majority rule—observed that "[w]hen one speaks of opinion, one must distinguish three species: the opinion of enlightened people, which precedes public opinion and ultimately dictates to it; the opinion whose authority sweeps along the opinion of the people; popular opinion, finally, which remains that of the most stupid and most misery-stricken part of the people."[9]

This tension travels across the Atlantic and persists in the New Republic from its very founding. Members of the Philadelphia Convention were at odds over contested views of popular sovereignty and representative government. In particular, the regulative legitimacy of public opinion was contingent on whether that opinion resulted from reasoned, appropriately deliberated, and adequately informed political judgments. Thus James Madison declared, in *Federalist* 49, "It is reason, alone, of the public that ought to control and regulate the government. The passions ought to be controlled and regulated by the government." In fact, Bernard Manin (1997) points out that Madison favored representative democracy not because he viewed representation as the best pragmatic approximation of direct democracy but because he saw representation as a better political system because it ensured that only men of reason and distinction would be given the authority to judge the best interests of the nation.[10]

Even James Bryce, bedrock advocate for the "rule of public opinion," held no illusions about the rationality or stability of this regulative public opinion, noting that "[i]n examining the process by which opinion is formed, we cannot fail to note how small a part of the view which the average man entertains when he goes to vote is really of his own making" (1895, 253).[11] Among elitist skeptics, the language turns downright grisly. Joseph Schumpeter's "competitive elitist" account of democracy is contemptuous of ordinary citizens as "incapable of action other than a stampede" (1976, 283). Walter Lippmann (1922) disparages public opinion as nothing more than the "pictures in our heads" given to us by political elites and the mass media. Crucially, for both Lippmann and Schumpeter, the implication is that citizens ought to bear only the most minimal obligations.[12] And, as I described in chapter 1, with the rise of the era of survey research these dim views of the democratic public gained an empirical foundation as polls that gauged public knowledge about political affairs began to reveal a dismayingly ill-informed citizenry.

ACTIVATED OPINION AND THE "SPIRIT OF RESISTANCE"

Given these distortions of democratic ideals, it is no wonder that elite theory emerges as an appealing normative state of affairs. Much as democracy, in Winston Churchill's ironic quip, "is the worst form of government except [for] all those other forms," perhaps elite-driven democratic decision-making suffices because we can do no better. A full and fair consideration of whether we can do better is perhaps more suitably left to political philosophers. So let me close by submitting three key observations that bear on the proper consideration of democratic politics, elite theory, and public opinion. First, elite theories fit most coherently with a minimal democratic conception, to the exclusion of alternate conceptions. Second, a minimalist normative conception, coupled with an elite-driven empirical account of public opinion, makes the threat of elite manipulation and domination that much more menacing. Third, this linkage between empirical and normative accounts comes dangerously close to committing a "naturalistic fallacy"—wrongfully inferring how democratic politics *ought* to be from how democratic politics now *is*. I consider each of these points in turn.

If public opinion cannot be trusted and if ordinary individuals are at best minimally competent to render political judgments, a strong case can be made for a limited, procedural, elite-driven rendition of representative democracy. As Jack Walker commented during an earlier incarnation of academic debate about elite theory, "The elitist theory allows the citizen only a passive role as an object of political activity; he exerts influence on policy making only by rendering judgements after the fact in national elections . . . the elitist theorists have transformed democracy from a radical into a conservative political doctrine, stripping away its distinctive emphasis on popular political activity" (1966, 288). According to such a minimal conception, most commonly identified with Schumpeter (1962), what defines a democracy is the competitive, contested nature of elections.[13] The primary obligation facing ordinary citizens is to choose, periodically, the political agents who will do the work of democratic politics for us. We can expect no more from our fellow citizens because they are deplorably uninterested in and abysmally ignorant of political matters. Democracy survives despite this because elites effectively signal their policy positions and citizens make efficient use, through heuristics and other cognitive simplifications, of this information. Little trouble, then, that ordinary citizens are fed their information by elites, because this information is used to form and update their preferences concerning a nominal set of issues, and those preferences are expressed only episodically through formal instruments such as elections and opinion polls.

The first observation, recall, is that this is a conspicuously threadbare, procedural democratic conception that favors an elite account of public opinion. Certainly, it is more austere a notion than common colloquial evocations of the term "democracy." The basis for valuing a procedural conception, notably, is the suspicion that ordinary citizens are not fit for "thicker" notions of citizenship and democracy. Accepting, for the moment, that this suspicion is warranted, we should be cognizant of the trade-offs we are making. The risk of letting ill-equipped citizens exercise popular sovereignty is that democratic decision-making may be unstable and inefficient or result in collectively self-defeating outcomes.

Yet the risk of restricting the boundaries of citizenship and democratic decision-making too gives pause. Critically, a minimal conception of democracy is likely to be a self-fulfilling prophecy. A democracy that asks little of us is likely to get little from us. If opinion polls find us ill-informed and errantly motivated now, it will surely find us so in the future. As a result, the pay-off to such a minimalist, thin conception of citizenship is a democracy whose decision-making is impersonal and bureaucratic, whose outputs are largely predetermined by opinion polls, and whose daily practice is far removed from the pastoral New England town meeting ideal of popular sovereignty. On this point it is tempting to speculate that the historically high levels of citizen apathy, alienation, and inattention that we are currently witnessing in the United States may in no small measure stem from our normative expectations about civic life and the obligations of democratic citizenship.

The second observation is that if a minimal conception is indeed the most defensible form of democracy, then there is a great deal at stake in whether elections are sufficiently competitive and whether the democratic public is a sufficiently autonomous judge of their own interests and opinions. Adam Przeworski (1999) offers an elegant defense of minimalism on the grounds that it is a politically stable mechanism for resolving deep conflicts and for getting scoundrels out of office peacefully.[14] This is not an accomplishment to scoff at because we have reasonable grounds to expect that if decision-makers are chosen through a contested process, the political outcomes will be just, rational, egalitarian, representative, or reflective of some other cherished outcome. Yet the United States today, a veritably stable electoral system, is characterized by rampant economic, social, and political segregation and inequality. Stability and peaceful transitions of power in themselves will not guarantee the primary goods we seek from a political system. Achieving such primary goods will depend on whether there are significant, systemic barriers to political expression and electoral competition and whether citizens are able to reasonably, autonomously judge their own best interests and preferences.

Specifically, if opinion formation is a top-down process, it makes a critical difference whether elites exploit their influence and manipulate mass opinion. And it makes a critical difference whether non-elites are capable—when they rise above their ill-informed and errantly motivated state—of circumventing elite influence and voicing political demands that elites may not wish to hear. Interestingly, in the leading contemporary elite opinion accounts we have examined in this book by John Zaller and by Edward Carmines and James Stimson, the possibility of elite domination or manipulation of mass opinion is simply dismissed, by theoretical assumption and by an idealization of elite processes.

Carmines and Stimson, for example, tip their hand when they argue against party realignment theories *because* they "accord a fundamental role to mass electorates, treating institutional actors as responding to more central electoral forces" (1989, 179). This is misguided, according to Carmines and Stimson, because they render professional politicians less sophisticated than the "amateur electorate." In their account, the sole obligation of democratic citizens is "to respond to some issues and not to others" (179). Thus in describing mass preferences and realignment during the civil rights movement, they accord no role to ordinary individuals because, as the politically "unsophisticated," they were simply not cued in to the "subtle shifts in the objective political situation" (118). Furthermore, Carmines and Stimson belie throughout deep theoretical commitments to a structuralist, evolutionary view of political change in which only certain political elites (such as Barry Goldwater, who emerges as a clairvoyant) are endowed with strategic behavior, while the civil rights movement itself is reduced to an exogenous "external disruption" to the political system. Unsurprisingly, then, with neither rigorous arguments nor supporting evidence, they simply assert that "Although elites 'lead'—in the sense of acting first in time sequence—they neither control nor manipulate. . . . Issue evolution produces representation as a by-product . . . the by-product representation is inadvertent. It is systemic, not individual" (179–80).[15]

In Zaller's case, we are warned that ordinary citizens "pay too little attention to public affairs to be able to respond critically to the political communications they encounter; rather, they are blown about by whatever current of information manages to develop the greater intensity" (1992, 311). No surprise, then, that the onus is thus upon political elites to set straight the rudder of democracy. For Zaller, this elite basis is not viewed as a threat to democratic aims because existing elite-mass dynamics are not too far removed from the best political state of affairs we can expect. In this "parable of Purple Land," the predispositions of policy experts parallel those of the general public ("such that experts are motivated to examine issues from all viewpoints"). Such experts are presented with institutional incentives for problem-solving. The press does not favor particular expert viewpoints or neglect to represent those of others. Politicians and activists restrict themselves to the domain of expert opinion on a given issue. The only requirement of citizens, amid all this, is to be able to recognize elite disagreements when they happen and align themselves with the elites who share their beliefs and predispositions (313–14). Philosophically, such a starry-eyed ideal seems to assume away the basic "circumstances of justice" (that is, irreconcilably conflicting conceptions of the good) that are the starting points for much of Anglo-American liberal thought.[16] Empirically, the proposition that existing elite-mass dynamics come close to Purple Land is, of course, at best informed conjecture (testable) and certainly conjecture that would engender lively controversy.

The third observation is that there is sufficient reason to demur against such a pragmatic, perhaps cynical, ideal for democratic politics. Even within the empirical realm, recent survey research finds, for example, that individuals do indeed conform to some basic axioms of rational choice when faced with clear, intelligible choices; that the political reasoning of ordinary individuals does not look so different from that of elite actors when issues take the form of salient policy metaphors; and that the macro-foundations of mass preferences evoke a roseate "collective rationality." [17] Moreover, the ignorance, incoherence, and ideological innocence of mass publics is a contingent reality, not an immutable fact about democratic citizens.

In fact, elite theory comes perilously close to committing a "naturalistic fallacy" of inferring "ought" from "is." The linkage of the empirical fact that citizens appear to be minimally competent with the normative claim that elites ought to influence what, when, and how ordinary citizens think about politics is one that should be sustained by moral argument, not assumed by logical elision. Of course, the democratic ideals we defend and pursue should not make exorbitant demands on citizens, nor should they aspire to a romanticized, Elysian political realm that never was. How elites and non-elites reason and act in reality should have some bearing. But the imperfections of our current practices should not impose a binding constraint. On this point, neither should definitive judgments of democratic citizens be wrought out of theories and tools that belie our own prior judgments and aspirations. There are good reasons, in particular, to question the privileged status that knowledge and rationality hold as qualifications for active citizenship. Schattschneider articulates this suspicion very spiritedly:

> One implication of public opinion studies ought to be resisted by all friends of freedom and democracy; the implication that democracy is a failure because the people are too ignorant to answer intelligently all the questions asked by the pollsters. This is a professorial invention for imposing professional standards on the political system and deserves to be treated with extreme suspicion. . . . Who, after all, are these self-appointed censors who assume that they are in a position to flunk the whole human race? . . . Democracy was made for the people, not the people for democracy. Democracy is something for ordinary people, a political system designed to be sensitive to the needs of ordinary people regardless of whether or not the pedants approve of them. (1960, 132) [18]

Jack Walker raises a similar point even more incisively, arguing that political scientists who defend elite conceptions of democracy under these circumstances risk becoming "sophisticated apologists for the existing political order" (1966, 289).

In this book, I have been quite explicit and deliberate about considering the capabilities of the democratic public by choosing a particular episode of political conflict in which citizens were manifestly attentive, adequately informed, ideologically engaged, and properly incented to political action. I have also been quite explicit and deliberate about choosing multiple methods to undertake this consideration, including modes of public expression in which individuals enjoy free rein over what issues to address, what positions to take, what cross-cutting linkages to reveal, and how to frame their viewpoints. It is no surprise, perhaps, that under these conditions, there is ample evidence to support a more sanguine view of the capabilities of ordinary citizens than elite opinion theories would expect. These pages have shown quite vividly that ordinary citizens, under appropriately compelling circumstances, *will* take an active part in crafting politics rather than merely consuming the political outputs of elite actors.

We ought not, then, turn our scholarly gaze away from the contexts and conditions in which citizenship becomes more activated under the guise of science, objectivity, protocol, or habit. Discovering such contexts and conditions may require resorting to messier, noisier tools and theories. But in most cases, the messy and the noisy are what make it politics. Failing to grapple with the radically contingent circumstances of politics may push us down the narrow road of minimalist democracy and obscure and obviate the pathways to a vivid public life and a spirit of resistance against unjust conditions. If we simply accept the elite account of the civil rights era, then, we may well forget Frederick Douglass's still trenchant and apropos point that "[i]f there is no struggle, there is no progress . . . power concedes nothing without a demand" (1857). Even Michael Walzer, who takes a somewhat skeptical view of the merits of active citizenship in fractured and differentiated contemporary societies, argues that "the passive enjoyment of citizenship requires, at least intermittently, the activist politics of citizens" (1989, 217), if only because a ruling regime will not always secure the rights and freedoms of citizenship.

To invoke the epigraphs to this chapter, the story we remember about public opinion and the civil rights movement depends critically on whether we see mass opinion as moving to a single groove for everyone within a single "mass public" or to the separate grooves of white and black Americans, of those at the dominant mainstream of our political system and those at the oppositional margins. On this reading of "two nations, separate grooves," the pages of this book have spoken animatedly What I hope this coda on democratic theory has added is a sense of the normative import as well. As Hannah Arendt, an adoring advocate for active citizenship and a flourishing public life, frames it, the "question of representation actually implies no less than a decision on the very dignity of the political realm itself" (1965, 239). Viewed thus,

The age-old distinction between ruler and ruled . . . has asserted itself once again; once more, the people are not admitted to the public realm, once more the business of government has become the privilege of the few. . . . The result is that the people must either sink into "lethargy, the forerunner to death to the public liberty," or "preserve the spirit of resistance" to whatever government they have elected, since the only power they retain is "the reserve power of revolution." (240)

APPENDIX ONE

QUESTION WORDING, SCALES, AND CODING OF VARIABLES IN SURVEY ANALYSIS

Fair jobs and housing. "If Negroes are not getting fair treatment in jobs and housing, the government should see to it that they do." High = strongly supportive.

School integration. "The government in Washington should stay out of the question of whether white and colored children go to the same school." High = strongly supportive.

Perceived proximity to party position, given partisanship. Measured as the interaction term: party proximity x party identification. Party proximity is worded as "Would the Democrats or the Republicans be closer to what you want on this issue (of the government in Washington being concerned about white and colored children going to the same schools or of the government seeing to it that Negroes get fair treatment in jobs and housing) or wouldn't there be any difference?" Party identification is coded so that high = Strong Democrat for perceived proximity to Democratic Party position and conversely for perceived proximity to Republicans. Separate variables are examined for perceived proximity to the Democratic Party, perceived proximity to the Republican Party, and perceived proximity to the Democratic Party for southern whites on the two dependent variables of interest. A high score on the perceived proximity measure thus measures consonance between respondent's partisanship and the party that best approximates the respondent's ideal position on the two dependent variables. A low score measures dissonance.[1]

Perceived proximity to black movement groups, whites (1956, 1960). Measured as degree of trust in "Negro groups." High = strong trust of black groups.

Perceived proximity of black movement groups, African Americans (1956, 1960). Measured as an index of three items, the trust measure above and two measures of support for black movement organizations' political mobilization.[2] The latter items are worded as "How do you feel about Negro organizations trying to get Congress to pass laws that Negroes are interested in? Do you think it's all right for them to do that, or do you think they ought to stay out of that?" and "How do you feel about

Negro organizations trying to help certain candidates get elected? Do you think it's all right for them to do that or do you think they ought to stay out of that?" The questions were asked only of African American respondents. High = strong racial group identity. Cronbach's reliability scores: $\alpha_{1956} = .67$, $\alpha_{1960} = 0.58$.

Proximity to movement groups, whites (1964). This relative affect measure is calculated as the feeling thermometer differences between affect toward civil rights groups (the NAACP and CORE) and affect toward the Ku Klux Klan. High = very warm toward civil rights groups, relative to white supremacist groups.

Proximity to movement groups, blacks (1964). Measured as an instrumental variable reconstructed from the 1960 proximity to black organizations scale.

Activist government, social policy domains. Respondent support for or opposition to an active government role in the following three social policy domains: guaranteed jobs, school aid, and medical care. Cronbach's reliability scores: $\alpha_{1956} = .63$, $\alpha_{1960} = 0.69$, $\alpha_{1964} = 0.66$.

Party identification. High = strongly Democratic.

Age. Age of respondent in years. High = older.

Family income. Respondent's family income. High = greater income.

Education. Educational level of respondent. High = more educated.

Strong partisanship. Respondent identifies strongly with Democrat or Republican Party. Dummy variable, 1 = strong partisan.

APPENDIX TWO

BIBLIOGRAPHIC SOURCES
FOR RACIAL ATTITUDE ITEMS, 1937–1965

Brink, William, and Louis Harris. 1963. *The Negro Revolution in America*. New York: Simon and Schuster.

———. 1966. *Black and White: A Study of U.S. Racial Attitudes Today*. New York: Simon and Schuster.

Campbell, Angus, Gerald Gurin, and Warren Miller. 1971. *Survey Research Center 1952 Election Study (S400)*. Ann Arbor: Inter-University Consortium for Political Research.

Campbell, Angus, Philip Converse, Warren Miller, and Donald Stokes. 1975. *Survey Research Center 1958 American National Election Study*. SRC431-ICPR7215. Ann Arbor: Inter-University Consortium for Political Research.

———. 1974. *Survey Research Center 1960 American National Election Study*. SRC440-ICPR7216. Ann Arbor: Inter-University Consortium for Political Research.

Campbell, Angus, and Howard Schuman. 1973. *Racial Attitudes in Fifteen American Cities, January–March 1968: Black Data File Documentation*. Ann Arbor: Institute for Social Research.

Cantril, Hadley, and Mildred Strunk. 1951. *Public Opinion, 1935–1946*. Princeton, N.J.: Princeton University Press.

Converse, Philip, Jean D. Dotson, Wendy J. Hoag, and William H. McGee III. 1980. *American Social Attitudes Data Sourcebook, 1947–1978*. Cambridge: Harvard University Press.

Erskine, Hazel. 1962. The Polls: Race Relations. *Public Opinion Quarterly* 26 (1): 137–48.

———. 1967a. The Polls: Negro Housing. *POQ* 31 (3): 482–98.

———. 1967b. The Polls: Demonstrations and Riots. *POQ* 31 (4): 655–77.

———. 1968a. The Polls: Negro Employment. *POQ* 32 (1): 132–53.

———. 1968b. The Polls: World Opinion of U.S. Racial Problems. *POQ* 32 (2): 299–312.

————. 1968c. The Polls: Speed of Racial Integration. *POQ* 32 (3): 513–24.

————. 1968d. The Polls: Recent Opinion on Racial Problems. *POQ* 32 (4): 696–703.

————. 1969a. The Polls: Negro Philosophies of Life. *POQ* 33 (1): 147–58.

————. 1969b. The Polls: Negro Finances. *POQ* 33 (2): 272–82.

————. The Polls: *POQ*.

Gallup, George H. 1972. *The Gallup Poll: Public Opinion, 1935–1971.* 3 vols. New York: Random House.

Hastings, Philip K., and Jessie C. Southwick. 1975. *Survey Data for Trend Analysis.* The Roper Public Opinion Research Center.

Martin, Elizabeth, Diana McDuffee, and Stanley Presser. 1981. *Sourcebook of Harris National Surveys.* Chapel Hill, N.C.: Institute for Research in Social Science.

Marx, Gary T. 1967. *Protest and Prejudice: A Study of Belief in the Black Community.* New York: Harper Torchbooks.

Matthews, Donald R., and James W. Prothro. 1962. *Negroes and the New Southern Politics.* New York: Harcourt, Brace, and World.

Miller, Warren E., Arthur H. Miller, and Edward J. Schneider. 1980. *American National Elections Studies Data Sourcebook, 1952–1978.* Cambridge: Harvard University Press.

APPENDIX THREE

SAMPLING AND CODING OF CONSTITUENCY MAIL

The sampling was one out of every twenty letters for each month, with the following exceptions: (1) letters from the Truman Library, where one out of every ten letters was sampled in most months; (2) periods with an excess of public opinion mail, where anywhere from one out of every twenty (for 2/48 and 3/48) to one out of every forty (for 9/62 and 10/62) and one out of every eighty (for 2/65, 3/65, and 4/65) was sampled.

(1) *Truman Library.* Materials were not well ordered and were drawn from the following filing categories, all subheadings under White House Central Files: Official Files (#542–549), President's Personal Files (#500, 599, 309–14, 351, 482), Official Files (#265–267, under "Fair Employment Practices Commission"), Public Opinion Mail (#10, under "Civil Rights"), General Files (#1743, under "Paul Robeson"), and Official Files (#1235).

(2) *Eisenhower Library.* Materials were obtained from three filing categories: White House Central Files, Bulk Mail; White House Central Files, General File; and White House Office, Telegraph Office.

(3) *Kennedy Library.* Almost all materials were obtained from the Overflow Files in the following categories: "Pressure mail" on Tent City in Tennessee (#98–100), on Freedom Riders (#101), on Albany, Georgia (#101), on James Meredith (#102–165), on Birmingham, Alabama (#166–171), general mail on civil rights (#171–219), on the bombing of a Birmingham church (#220–223), and reaction to a national address on civil rights (#1224–1234). A few petitions were coded from the White House Central Files, under Human Rights.

(4) *Johnson Library.* Materials were primarily from the filing category "Public Opinion Mail," comprised largely of correspondence from 1965 regarding the march from Selma and Johnson's national address on March 15. Other filing categories in which letters were found were the White House Central Files, Human Rights (General). These letters include a sampling of letters from all

years. From 1966 to 1969, they included letters regarding the 1967 Detroit riot, Martin Luther King Jr.'s assassination, and the Poor People's Campaign. Only 50 percent of letters from the Poor People's Campaign were sampled (half of these letters did not concern civil rights directly).

In certain years, the number of letters that were identifiable by race was insufficient to extract percentages with any confidence to measure trends in constituent mail. As an arbitrary marker, I sought a minimum of twenty letters from correspondents who were identifiably black or white for each year. In years that fell short of this number of letters, an oversample was drawn. Oversamples were drawn for the following years: 1954–56, 1959, 1960, and 1964 for blacks; 1950, 1954, 1955, 1959, and 1964 for whites. Inter-coder reliability scores were drawn for coding race, issue position, and interpretive frames. a = 0.94 for race and for issue position, 0.85 for interpretive frames.

Race
Correspondents were coded as "black" or "white" if they explicitly identified themselves as such or if race could be strongly inferred from the content; with the exception of certain white ethnic surnames, race was not inferred from correspondents' names. An issue position in itself (e.g., southerner opposing school desegregation) was never used to infer race. Cues drawn from white ethnic surnames led to a possible overrepresentation of identified whites. Mail was also coded if from nonblack nonwhites and when racial attribution was ambiguous or indeterminate.

Region
1 =   South (Virginia, West Virginia, Kentucky, Tennessee, Missouri, North Carolina, South Carolina, Georgia, Florida, Alabama, Louisiana, Mississippi, Arkansas, Oklahoma, Texas);
2 =   North (Maine, New Hampshire, Vermont, Massachusetts, Connecticut, Rhode Island, New York, New Jersey, Pennsylvania, Maryland, Delaware, District of Columbia);
3 =   Midwest (Ohio, Michigan, Illinois, Indiana, Iowa, Wisconsin, Minnesota, Kansas, Nebraska);
4 =   West (Colorado, Utah, Wyoming, Montana, North Dakota, South Dakota, Idaho, New Mexico, Arizona, Nevada, Washington, Oregon, California, Hawaii, Alaska).

Region is drawn from the postmark of a letter. The exception to this practice is when correspondents identify themselves with a region different from their postmark (e.g., someone who grew up in the South, but moved west, or someone from the North serving in a military base in the South). I initially thought of constructing a category of "border states" to cover responses from places such as Maryland, Delaware, Virginia, the District of Columbia, Kansas, Missouri, Kentucky, and Tennessee, which often seemed qualitatively different from those of either the solid South or the Northeast.

Type

This category identifies whether the letter represents an individual's own point of view, that of an organization, that of a group of individuals, or that of a child. Telegrams were treated the same as regular mail, although in retrospect, the limited text contained in them probably warranted analysis of telegrams as a separate category. Letters from individuals or organizations that were elite voices (e.g., for African Americans, from elected officials, such as A.C. Powell, leaders of national organizations, such as Walter White, or people with special ties to the White House, such as Mary McCleod Bethune) were excluded from analysis.

Issue Position

Letters were coded for issue position on civil rights and racial equality. In some cases, the issue position of the correspondent is ambiguous; this is especially evident when correspondents offer to mediate differences of opinion or, toward the mid-1960s, when the civil rights movement itself becomes more fragmented and diversified and "pro" positions become less clear. That said, letters in which the issue position was indeterminate constituted less than 1 percent of all the letters sampled and, for the most part, were excluded from analysis as a result.

APPENDIX FOUR

TYPOLOGY OF INTERPRETIVE FRAMES

Cherished Political Principles. Describes support for and opposition to civil rights that are based on core principles, either in U.S. political discourse or in religious and moral discourse. General political principles thus range from equality (voiced more specifically as equality of opportunity, justice, and fairness) and liberty (also voiced as freedom, individualism, and opposed to coercion) to general references to democratic rule (majority rule, citizenship, and representation). Equal protection under the law is separated from general equality to denote the specific plea to protect civil rights activists against white-on-black violence and state-sanctioned brutality in the South. This category also incorporates a diversity of references to rights discourse: references to universal rights (equal rights, human rights, citizenship rights, basic rights) and three types of particularistic rights—rights to particular governing units (states' rights), rights to particular populations that belie a sense of perceived threat (whites' rights, taxpayer rights, property rights), and rights of particular disenfranchised populations used for rhetorical leverage (minority rights, blacks' rights). Finally, this category includes arguments based in religious or secular morality.

Group References. Describes support for and opposition to civil rights that are based on references to group interests, conflict, and domination. Group interests include references based on an understanding of a group from personal experience, group identity and consciousness (Third World consciousness, black identity, southern white identity), and group-based calls for militant action (southern white resistance, black retaliation for white-on-black violence). Viewpoints based on group conflict cover four broad categories of threat to whites: social or sexual threat, political threat, economic threat, and physical threat. Of these, the idea of social or sexual threat (of social integration and bi-racial marriages) and physical threat (anxieties about black crime, violence, and rape) are intertwined with racist defenses of segregation. Two other references that belie dimensions of group conflict and threat are relative well-being (comparing blacks with whites, South with North) and southern white violence and Jim Crowism. Finally, defenses of segregation based on group superiority distinguish religious essentialism (a natural order rooted in Christianity) from biological essentialism; this category also codes for references to southern paternalism (speaking on behalf of southern blacks' interests), dehumanizing racial stereotyping in general, and the welfare stereotype of African Americans as welfare cheats, lazy, lacking self-respect, and bearing illegitimate children.

Symbolic References. Describes support for and opposition to civil rights based in symbolic references to cherished principles and group conflict. Symbolic references to principles are divided into those referring to general political symbols of U.S. democracy (e.g., the Constitution, the Bill of Rights, the Declaration of Independence), those referring to the violations of democratic principles at home (e.g., police brutality, second-class citizenship, discrimination within the federal government), and those referring to the violations of democratic principles vis-à-vis world affairs, especially the Cold War (e.g., communism, Nazism, world opinion, and the specific charge that the civil rights movement was communist-inspired). Symbolic references also include the group dimensions of racial conflict. Symbols here are primarily historical, from the standpoint of southern white justifications of segregation (e.g., the slogan "the South shall rise again," carpetbaggers, Yankees, Jefferson Davis) and from the standpoint of the black rights struggle (e.g., Gettysburg, the Emancipation Proclamation, Crispus Attucks, Frederick Douglass). Symbolic principles also include religious symbols.

Issue Considerations. Describes support for and opposition to civil rights based on issue considerations. These include partisan-, president-, policy-, and movement-specific considerations. Partisan considerations encompass mentions of specific parties (including the Dixiecrats) and of changes in partisanship. "Presidential considerations" refers to specific actions and speeches, electoral considerations (from one's personal vote to accusations of pandering for black votes to promises of racial bloc voting), the influence of White House staff and advisors, and personal requests (from casework to monetary solicitations to requests for public statements). Policy-specific considerations range from references to Supreme Court rulings (*Brown v. Board, Aaron v. Cooper*) to specific civil rights initiatives (FEPC, civil rights, anti-lynching, public accommodations), economic and social policies not under legislative consideration (housing, health, jobs, labor, farming, community development), and minority political representation. Movement considerations encompass the events, leadership, and organizations of the movement and of its opponents (especially southern whites).

Affective Dimensions. Describes arguments that exemplify a strong affective component to the correspondent's position. The primary affective categories here are betrayal, disgrace, shame, gratitude, and pride.

NOTES

INTRODUCTION

1. In the South writ large and in Alabama, two of every five voting-age African Americans were registered in 1964. On African Americans and the Voting Rights Act, see Garrow 1978; Grofman, Davidson, and Niemi 1996; Lawson 1976, 1985; and F. Parker 1990.

2. Garrow 1978, 107. President Johnson compared Selma to Lexington, Concord, and Appomattox.

3. Representative samples can be found in Brody 1991; Carmines and Stimson 1989; Carmines and Kuklinski 1990; Gerber and Jackson 1993; Iyengar 1991; Lupia and McCubbins 1998; MacKuen, Erikson, and Stimson 2001; Neuman 1986; Page and Shapiro 1992; Stimson 1991; and Zaller 1992.

4. See also Lipset and Schneider 1987 and Hibbing and Theiss-Morse 1995.

5. See also Schudson 1995; Skocpol 1995; and Vallely 1995.

6. See Habermas 1984 and Cohen and Arato 1992. I do not mean to imply that these three dichotomies are equivalent. Most obviously, forms of private association are dissociable from civic life, and Habermas's systemic spheres of activity include both economic and political transactions (Young 1999).

7. Note that I do not mean by the term "counterelites" the same thing as the term "non-elites." That is, I view counterelites as that subset of individuals outside of mainstream, institutionalized spheres of political activity who exercise influence and leadership. There are, of course, less empowered and more alienated non-elites, to whom we might apply homogenizing terms such as "ordinary individuals" or "everyday people."

8. I do not mean to imply in this discussion that there were no African American elites within formal political institutions and channels prior to the civil rights movement. Clearly, elected officials such as Adam Clayton Powell, William Dawson, and Charles Diggs, and prominent activists such as W. E. B. Du Bois, A. Philip Randolph, Walter White, and Charles Houston befit the term "elites."

9. For an excellent discussion of the evolution of historiography on the civil

rights movement from top-down to more bottom-up perspectives, see Payne 1995.

10. Representatives of each position can be found in Branch 1988, Collier-Thomas and Franklin 1999, and McAdam 1982 for the *Brown v. Board of Education* decision; Hampton and Fayer 1990 for the killing of Emmett Till; Morris 1984 for the Baton Rouge boycott; Garrow 1986 and Raines 1977 for the Montgomery boycott; and Marable 1991 and Weisbrot 1990 for the Woolworth's lunch counter sit-ins.

11. In terms of opinion research, the period examined is also remarkable for encapsulating two relevant trends: (1) the emergence of polls as the primary source of opinion data; and (2) the demonstrable upsurge in presidents' interest in the measurement and manipulation of public opinion. See Eisinger 1996; Ginsberg 1986; Jacobs and Shapiro 1994, 1995; and Margolis and Mauser 1989.

12. also marked efforts to mobilize protest around the United Nations' Universal Declaration of Human Rights.

CHAPTER ONE

1. See, e.g., Converse 1964, 1970; Erikson et al. 1988; Delli Carpini and Keeter 1996.

2. See, e.g., Bartels 1996; Delli Carpini and Keeter 1996; Althaus 1998; and Converse 2000.

3. The important precondition to this aggregative defense is that individual measurement errors in survey response are independently random and that variations in individual response are also independent of each other.

4. See, e.g., Austen-Smith and Banks 1996 and Fedderson and Pesendorfer 1998.

5. See, e.g., Miller and Stokes 1963 and Page and Shapiro 1983, 1992.

6. Alan Monroe (1998) finds that whereas government policy outputs were largely consistent with the policy preferences of a majority of Americans from 1960 to 1979 (changes in policies matched changes in public opinion 63 percent of the time), this correspondence declined discernibly between 1980 to 1993 (to 55 percent), and markedly so in particular issue domains such as social welfare and economic policy. For an excellent analysis of how the relationship between mass preferences and elite policies changes over time, see Jacobs and Shapiro 2000.

7. As Arthur Lupia and Mathew McCubbins put it, "reasoned choice requires knowledge, knowledge requires information, and information requires attention. However, reasoned choice need not require either full information or unlimited attention" (1998, 25).

8. See, e.g., Brady and Sniderman 1985; McKelvey and Ordeshook 1986; Ferejohn and Kuklinski 1990; Popkin 1991; Sniderman, Brody, and Tetlock 1991; Lupia 1992; Mutz, Sniderman, and Brody 1996; Lupia and McCubbins 1998; and McCubbins, Popkin, and Lupia 2000. Several of these cases build on the work of Tversky and Kahneman on heuristics—"shortcuts that reduce complex problem solving to more simple judgmental operations" (1974, 247; see also 1973; Kahneman, Slovic, and Tversky 1982). Sniderman, Brody, and Tetlock 1991, for example, add to Tversky and Kahneman's "availability" heuristic the "likeability" and "desert" heuristics.

9. See, e.g., Calvert 1985; McKelvey and Ordeshook 1986; Lupia 1992, 1994; Lupia and McCubbins 1998; Jacobs and Shapiro 2000; and McCubbins, Popkin, and Lupia 2000.

10. All page references in this chapter are from *The Nature and Origins of Mass Opinion* unless otherwise specified. Although it has become standard, almost requisite, to cite Thomas Kuhn (1962) with any reference to research paradigms, it is debatable whether Kuhn himself viewed the social sciences (never mind more restricted domains within the social sciences such as political behavior or opinion research) as being in a "protoscientific" state or as engaging in "normal science." This controversy aside, Zaller's work is paradigmatic in that it is a particular, archetypal way of looking at our social and political world, where this particular way shares a conceptual approach and methodological tools.

11. To mention a few of RAS's undiscussed accomplishments, Zaller suggests a nonlinear relationship between awareness and opinion statements, offers insightful distinctions between mainstream and polarization effects and between persuasive and cueing messages, elaborates three types of resistance to political messages, and incorporates intensity of messages in his empirical analyses.

12. See Achen 1975; Erikson 1979; Jackson 1979.

13. This rendition of response instability is not solely due to Zaller but jointly developed with Stanley Feldman. See Feldman 1989, 1991, 1995; Zaller and Feldman 1992. A similar account is also developed in Chong 1996.

14. Zaller opts for Lippmann's term "stereotypes" rather than cognitive shortcuts or heuristics. The centrality of such stereotypes, however, is quite clear: "Stereotypes and frames . . . are important to the process by which the public keeps informed because they determine what the public thinks it is becoming informed about, which in turn often determines how people take sides on political issues" (8).

15. This shift in racially egalitarian beliefs is among the most established findings in public opinion research (see Taylor, Sheatsley, and Greeley 1978; Schuman, Steeh, and Bobo 1988; Page and Shapiro 1992; Bobo 1997).

16. Specifically, Zaller uses three questions from the biennial American National Election Studies (ANES) surveys: (1) the ability to correctly locate the issue positions of elite political actors (relative to one's own ideal point), (2) the ability to recognize political figures on "feeling thermometer" items, and (3) the subjective ranking that interviewers give on completion of recording the respondent's political knowledge. The third measure is also not neutral, strictly speaking, because interviewer evaluations can be systematically subjective. See, e.g., Schuman and Converse 1971, Sanders 1995, and Davis 1997 on race-of-interviewer effects.

17. Even in sections that test the hypotheses that Zaller deduces from RAS with survey data on racial attitudes, the elite or non-elite origins of the inputs (political messages) are not controlled for. Despite this honest self-appraisal, at times the search for evidence of an elite view seems to be at the heart of Zaller's project. Thus, for example, Zaller notes that "[t]he aim of this book is to show how variations in this elite discourse affect both the direction and organization of mass opinion" (14).

18. Zaller compares his knowledge and interviewer evaluation measures against education, participation, media exposure, and political interest (21) and discusses why issue-specific measures are inapt (336).

19. In my reading, this appears to be the only place in the text where this limi-

tation to "short-term situations" is noted. Elsewhere, Zaller seems to aim for a more general and broadly applicable account of the "nature and origins of mass opinion." At several points, Zaller also hints at RAS as a long-term model of opinion change as well. Thus he discusses attitude change as "a change in people's long-term response probabilities [that] results from change in the mix of ideas to which individuals are exposed. Changes in the flow of political communication cause attitude change not by producing a sudden conversion experience but by producing gradual changes in the balance of considerations that are present in people's minds and available for answering survey questions" (266).

20. U.S. Census Bureau 2000.

21. Put bluntly, it is the social, legal, historical, and ideological forces that define "race" in everyday life which give it the regulatory force it wields over our beliefs and sentiments. For range of examples, see Appiah 1996; Dawson 1995b; Du Bois 1992; Mills 1998; Omi and Winant 1986; Shklar 1991; Zack 1993; cf. Hacking 1999. See also Dawson 1994a; Dawson and Wilson 1991; Gilroy 1991; and Omi and Winant 1986 for arguments against the view that race is a peripheral influence on politics and in favor of the view that race is a central, defining ideology—and by corollary, that empirical studies ought to specify separate, race-specific models of political attitudes and behavior.

22. For white Americans, Donald Kinder and Lynn Sanders (1996) demonstrate that one's degree of "racial resentment" (also an enduring tendency for which ample statistical variation exists) powerfully defines one's racial attitudes and political preferences. See also Bobo and Hutchings (1996) for another variant on the centrality of in-group/out-group evaluations on racial attitudes and policy preferences.

23. Elsewhere, Zaller takes a much more plural view toward values and predispositions, noting that "*Values*, as I use the term, refers to any relatively stable, individual-level predisposition to accept or reject particular types of arguments. Values may be rooted in personality, philosophy, ideology, gender, experience, religion, ethnicity, occupation, or interest (among other things). Party attachments . . . also qualify as values under this definition" (1991, 1216).

24. See, e.g., Greenstone 1993; Horton 1995; Sanders 1994; Shklar 1991; and Smith 1996. More contemporary mono-tradition views are found in interpretations of mass preferences from the 1950s to the 1970s (Huntington 1981; McClosky and Zaller 1984; Verba and Orren 1985).

25. Smith argues that any mono-traditional, liberal account will fail to explain some of the defining features of American political development, such as the dogged persistence of racial and gender hierarchies.

26. See also McCartney 1991 and Robinson 1997. As Smith's and Dawson's discussions of racial ideologies suggest, our predispositions also intersect and interact in significant ways, a topic about which RAS is also silent. Political theorists such as Smith have long argued that race and liberalism are linked, jointly constituted belief systems. In opinion research, Donald Kinder, David Sears, and their colleagues argue that racially hostile sentiments are linked to and evoked by framing an issue in ideological terms. See, e.g., Kinder and Sears 1981, 1985 and Kinder and Sanders 1990, 1996. Against this view, Paul Sniderman and his colleagues (Sniderman and Piazza 1993; Sniderman and Carmines 1998) argue that opposition to controversial

policy issues such as affirmative action is possible on purely principled ideological grounds, without any symbolic or logical link to racially hostile sentiments.

27. Key defines latent opinion in essentially negative terms: "If public opinion has a quality of latency, discussion of such opinion would appear to present a singularly slippery problem. . . . So long as it remains latent, it cannot well be inspected. By the time it reaches a state of activation, it has ceased to be latent" (263).

28. The group-based determinants of racial attitudes are most often examined within the context of "realistic group conflict" theory (Bobo 1983, 1988), "racial group identity" theory (Allen, Dawson, and Brown 1989; Dawson 1994a), and "social dominance" theory (Sidanius and Pratto 1998). See also variants in Pinder-hughes 1987; Gurin, Hatchett, and Jackson 1989; Olzak 1993; Tate 1993; and Nelson and Kinder 1996. Racial group consciousness is also key to explaining black political participation (Gurin, Miller and Gurin 1980; Miller, Gurin, Gurin, and Malanchuk 1981; Shingles 1981). Racial group dynamics are also especially useful for understanding the role of group identity formation in mobilizing mass protest movements (from the formal side, see Uhlaner 1989; Chong 1991; Hardin 1996). For more general treatments of the primacy of social groups, see Blumer 1958; Conover 1988; Tajfel 1982; and Turner 1987.

29. Price (1992) offers a very helpful classification of the "public" into the general public, the voting public, the attentive public, and the active public. Within his framework, the activation of mass opinion during social movements can probably be described as the movement of individuals from the general public into the attentive and perhaps the active public.

30. This notion has been especially useful in recent work on African American mass opinion. For example, see the Black Public Sphere Collective 1996; Dawson 1994b; Herbst 1994; and Sanders 1994. Although I use the singular form of *a* black counterpublic, there is clearly a broad diversity of institutional and ideological forms—and a dominant center and excluded margins—even within the African American community. See, e.g., Cohen 1999; Cohen and Dawson 1993; and Dawson 2001.

31. This argument is due to Fraser (1992; see also Meehan 1995). The points made here, of course, vastly simplify both Habermas and Fraser. An important element of Fraser's discussion, for example, is an extended critique of the privilege Habermas confers on economic stratification in his focus on a *bourgeois* public sphere as *the* primary public sphere, to the neglect of other organizing principles, such as gender. Notably, Fraser writes, "We can no longer assume that the bourgeois conception of the public sphere was simply an unrealized utopian ideal; it was also a masculinist ideological notion that functioned to legitimate an emergent form of class rule" (1992, 116). Fraser's critique with respect to gender is paralleled with respect to race in Dawson 1994b.

32. The idea of counterpublics thus build on Gabriel Almond (1950) and V. O. Key's (1961) notion of "issue publics" and "attentive publics."

33. For one thing, identifying the African American protest movement as the primary oppositional counterpublic obviously obscures important interactions and intersections with other oppositional counterpublics at the time. The rise of a "countercultural" New Left after the McCarthy era clearly also played a role in the political

unfolding of the 1960s. See Gitlin 1980 and Miller 1994. Dawson (1994b) further sharpens this adjuvant public into a "white oppositional public" and notes the intersections between the constituent groups within the black counterpublic and white oppositional publics such as adherents to anti-war, feminist, and "white radical" movements.

34. To follow through with the equilibrium metaphor, the political system should return to equilibrium once the boundaries between elite and mass are redefined (e.g., through the co-optation of leadership of the counterpublic, repression of counterelite insurgency, incorporation of movement ideologies within conventional dimensions of political discourse) and sectors of the mass public realign themselves ideologically and institutionally in response to movement activism and elite response.

35. At risk of stating the obvious, the justification for disaggregating my analysis by race and region, at the most basic level, is because the era of black insurgency began in the 1950s as a demand to end *racial* segregation in the *South*. Empirically, Schuman, Steeh, and Bobo (1988) find marked differences between blacks and whites and among whites, as well as between southern and nonsouthern respondents across a range of questions about racial principles (e.g., school desegregation, employment discrimination, public accommodations, residential integration, miscegenation, and electing a black president) and racial policies (e.g., federal intervention in desegregation, aid to racial minorities, school busing, and appropriate response to urban revolts).

36. There are, of course, important exceptions, such as President Truman's efforts on civil rights and the subsequent salience of civil rights as an electoral issue in 1948.

37. That said, we should also see the emergent role of sympathetic white or biracial organizations such as the Congress of Racial Equality (CORE) and what Aldon Morris (1982) calls "movement halfway houses" such as the American Friends Service Committee and the Highlander Folk School.

38. I don't mean to suggest that a flourishing black counterpublic is omnipresent in any and all racial regimes. Certainly, in the absence of such a counterpublic, racial predispositions might be expressed in the kind of "everyday forms of resistance" that Scott (1985, 1990) discusses, or, if Marxian hegemony and false consciousness take root, such predispositions may never develop and the predispositions of a systematically marginalized group may perfectly mirror those of a dominant public.

39. One clear exception is the intensification of antiblack violence and repression by white supremacist organizations such as the Ku Klux Klan and White Citizens Councils following the NAACP's victory in *Brown v. Board of Education* in 1954.

40. Finally, although this will not be tested, to the extent that movement counterelites successfully reconfigure the link between predispositions and considerations on racial politics, these effects should persist after the decline of black insurgency in the 1970s. That is, these linkages should linger as influences on mass opinion on racial, political, economic, and social issues into the 1980s and 1990s (e.g., as an influence on contemporary debates on poverty, urban violence, and social policy).

41. On this point, we have thus far presumed a common understanding of what defines a social movement. Within political science, for example, boundaries be-

tween the study of "social movements," "interest groups," and "political participa-tion"—however crisply defined individual scholars might intend them to be—are ultimately somewhat arbitrary. For the present purposes, what matters is that the expression of a more activated public voice, influenced significantly by non-elite forces, should increase in likelihood as political engagement moves further away from conventional, equilibrium politics.

42. For example, on "technical" policy matters such as funding for NASA, ne-gotiating navigation treaties, or appointing mid-level bureaucrats, most ordinary citizens would neither care about, nor be knowledgeable about, nor have channels to express their views in a way that will have political influence.

43. On the fourth stage, see Foucault 1980; Gramsci 1971; and Lukes 1980. This continuum is also suggested in Touraine's (1977, 1988) categorization of forms of social conflict, although Touraine's view of social movements is contained in a broader theoretical and historical argument about sociology that is far beyond the scope of this book.

44. This typology of social movements and its relevance to the dynamics of mass opinion can be read as a call to return to the study of "issue domains." The important difference is that this return to issue domains comes with the assurance of, and in reference to, a generalized, integrated model like RAS. Thus, rather than falling prey to Zaller's characterization of a public opinion field that has "devolved into a collection of insular subliteratures that rarely communicate with one another" (1992, 2), the idea is to build an integrated account such as Zaller's into the study of particular issue domains.

45. See Zaller 1998. Clinton's "presidential approval" rating averaged about 60 percent just before the story of his affair broke; ten days later, his approval rating jumped to about 70 percent. Thus Zaller notes, "[h]owever poorly informed, psycho-logically driven, and 'mass mediated' public opinion may be, it is capable of recog-nizing and focusing on its own conception of what matters" (186).

46. See Cohen 1999 and Lee 1999. Political conspiracy theories broadly speak-ing also fit this kind of non-elite opinion. Another recent example, along these lines, would be the rise of white supremacist groups and white militia groups in the United States.

47. Bottom-up accounts are most often found among historians such as Rude (1964) and Hobsbawm (1965), or, more recently, Bourdieu (1977), Braudel (1969), and de Certeau (1984). In African American history, bottom-up accounts are promi-nent in Holt (1995), Kelley (1990, 1993), Lipsitz (1988), and Payne (1996). In polit-ical science and sociology, examples of bottom-up analysis can be found in Gaventa (1980), and Scott (1985, 1990).

CHAPTER TWO

1. See, e.g., Schuman, Steeh, and Bobo 1988; Page and Shapiro 1992; Mayer 1993; Bobo 1997; Taylor, Sheatsley, and Greeley 1978. Attempts to explain this gap between principles and policies have stimulated among the most vocal and en-gaging debates within opinion research today (for the most recent iterations, see Sniderman and Piazza 1993; Kinder and Sanders 1996).

2. See also Jean Converse (1987) and A. Wade Smith (1987) on the 1942 and 1944 NORC surveys. It is revealing that the prescience of the NORC/OWI surveys

appears to result not so much from the issue salience of racial politics in the 1940s but from the federal government's need for research on the potential impact of racial tensions on military service and the war effort.

3. There are several important milestones in the renaissance of academic interest in racial attitudes, perhaps most prominent among them being the first of the Brink and Harris studies of black public opinion in 1963 (see Brink and Harris 1964, 1966; see also Matthews and Prothro 1962).

4. In terms of credit for the shift in racial attitudes, Page and Shapiro note the importance of "broad historical development" and point to a motley assortment of events from the late 1950s to the early 1960s, with the influence of mass media coverage. Notably, they point to the 1956 Montgomery bus boycott, President Eisenhower's decision to send federal troops to Little Rock schools in 1957, lunch counter sit-ins in 1960, the freedom rides of 1961, James Meredith's enrollment in the University of Mississippi in 1962, and the 1963 March on Washington (see 76–77).

5. The vanguard of labor's opposition came from the American Federation of Labor. See Goings 1990; Hine 1977; and O'Reilly 1995, 105–7. O'Reilly notes that Herbert Hoover took special exception to the NAACP's opposition to Parker, resulting in Hamilton Fish's (D-N.Y.) Special Committee to Investigate Communist Activities' looking into the NAACP and J. Edgar Hoover's conducting background checks on Joel Spingarn, Walter White, and other NAACP leaders.

6. In 1900, African Americans comprised one of three southerners in the United States; by 1960, this figure decreased to one of five southerners.

7. As early as 1929, Oscar DePriest became the first African American since Reconstruction to serve in the U.S. Congress and the first northern black ever to do so. DePriest served as a Republican in the First Congressional District in Illinois from 1929 to 1935, eventually losing his seat to the first black Democrat elected to Congress, Arthur Mitchell. In short order, other African Americans from the North began occupying the U.S. Congress as well, such as William Dawson (D-Ill.), Adam Clayton Powell (D-N.Y.), and Charles Diggs (D-Mich.).

8. On prior efforts to mobilize the black community by Marcus Garvey, A. Philip Randolph, Hubert Harrison, Ida B. Wells, and the NAACP leaders, see, among others, Duster 1970; Gaines 1996; McCartney 1992; Marable 1985; and Naison 1983. More extensive accounts of the history of black insurgency can be found in Dawson forthcoming; Franklin and Moss 1994; and Robinson 1997.

9. On black insurgency in the South prior to the civil rights movement, see Kelley 1990; Morris 1984; Payne 1995; and Egerton 1994.

10. On the Harlem Renaissance, see Locke 1992 and Huggins 1971. As Kevin Gaines (1996) notes, there were considerable clashes at the time between Alain Locke and others, who wanted to define the "New Negro" in apolitical terms, and others such as Marcus Garvey and A. Philip Randolph, who insisted on explicit linkages between cultural redefinition and political empowerment.

11. Moreover, the onset of the twentieth century also saw the founding of numerous publications associated with specific movements and organizations, such as *Horizon,* the journal of the Niagara Movement (1907), *The Crisis,* the journal of the NAACP (1910), and *Opportunity,* the journal of the National Urban League (1923).

12. W. E. B. Du Bois coined the term "Talented Tenth" for this rising black elite

and described their mission to challenge these prevailing beliefs as nothing less than a quest for the truth, writing that "[t]he American Negro deserves study for the great end of advancing the cause of science in general. No such opportunity to watch and measure the history and development of a great race of men ever presented itself to the scholars of a modern nation. If they miss this opportunity—if they do the work in a slip-shod, unsystematic manner—if they dally with the truth to humor the whims of the day, they do far more than hurt the good name of the American people; they hurt the cause of scientific truth the world over" (1992, 60).

13. On the organization of a black elite, see Cruse 1967; Gaines 1996; and James 1997. On Myrdal, see Aphtheker 1977; Bunche 1973; Jackson 1990; and Southern 1987. From the standpoint of sociology of knowledge, Barkan (1992) suggests that the demise of biological theories of race should be attributed more generally to the emergence of previously excluded voices (e.g., those of women, Jews, and political leftists) in academic discourse (see also Harding 1993; Stepan 1986).

14. Although it may not be entirely fair to refer to Carmines and Stimson as micro-level theorists since they do intend to speak to aggregate shifts in partisanship and mass preferences, their method of doing so includes multivariate models in which the units of analysis are individuals.

15. Carmines and Stimson profess, in this regard, "We took up the research that led to this book without intending to study race per se. It was but one of many of the 'issues' scholars of electoral processes might examine in the early 1970s . . . for we were students of issue voting, and we shared in the procedural norm of that subdiscipline: issues, *in general,* were the proper focus of inquiry" (1989, xiv, emphasis in original).

16. See Downs 1957 and Enelow and Hinich 1981, 1984, 1989. Other works that adapt such voting models include Franklin and Jackson 1983, Erikson and Romero 1989, Gerber and Jackson 1993, and Rivers 1988.

17. As Gerber and Jackson describe it, "voters shift in direct response to the actions of the parties as they search for strategies to increase their likelihood of winning elections" (1964, 639).

18. In the probabilistic framework (Enelow and Hinich 1984, 1989) of spatial voting models, there will also be a zone of indifference, in which relative small differences between candidates will leave the individual indifferent.

19. See also Erikson and Romero 1989.

20. Details of question wording, coding, and scales used in this chapter are available upon request from the author.

21. One might also be tempted to note that the proportion of respondents who report being "undecided" on school desegregation increases from 1956 to 1964. This "eyeball" change does not fall within a conventional margin of statistical significance. Furthermore, as Keith Reeves (1997) and other have shown, the category of "undecided" is often chosen by individuals who do not wish to appear biased or inegalitarian in a public setting (e.g., a survey interview) but who endorse such hostile and inegalitarian positions in private settings.

22. As this example suggests, differences in the political elites who are giving the opinion cues and differences in the heterogeneity in ideal positions among political elites likely contribute to this interpersonal subjectivity in perceived ideological distance.

23. The degree to which perceived proximity matters should signify the issue salience of civil rights to the respondent. In this sense, it may be difficult to disentangle the force of elite influence from the public's engagement on a given issue. Note, however, that we are controlling for other factors as well. If the respondent were fully disengaged on an issue, these factors would also not be significant. The ideological distance measure, then, reflects the degree to which reliance on partisan cues affects one's opinion.

24. This specification of three separate measures removes us somewhat from formal (two-candidate) voting models. The model can also be specified without separating perceived proximity to elite actors by party. In this restricted form, the key result—namely, that movement-specific, non-elite cues were strong and significant influences on people's racial attitudes well before the mid-1960s and in the absence of elite influences—remains.

25. On the unique status of the Democratic Party in the South, see Key 1949; Sitkoff 1971; and Woodward 1966. Among the prominent examples of this is the umbrage that southern Democrats took in 1948 upon President Harry S. Truman's support of his presidential Committee on Civil Rights' recommendations for sweeping antidiscrimination measures (including establishing a Fair Employment Practices Commission, outlawing the poll tax, prohibiting segregated interstate public accommodations). Delegates from several states bolted the Democratic convention, and then South Carolina Governor Strom Thurmond ran (with considerable success in the South) as a third party candidate for the States' Rights Democrats.

26. These measures are asked only of African American respondents.

27. Franklin's method has been used in at least two existing studies of opinion change. Gerber and Jackson (1993) examine the role of political parties in the "endogenous" formation of policy preferences on civil rights from 1956 to 1964 and the Vietnam War from 1968 to 1972. Zaller (1992) looks at the role of "two-sided information flows" in shaping mass opinion on the Vietnam War from 1964 to 1970.

28. Franklin's estimator is carried out in two stages. First, regress the variable of interest onto a set of explanatory measures in an auxiliary data set. These auxiliary explanatory variables should be replicated in our primary data set. Second, use the parameter estimates from this first-stage regression with the same explanatory variables in our primary data set to generate our instrument. The critical assumption is that the primary and auxiliary data sets come from the same underlying population. If the primary and auxiliary data sets are fielded at different points in time, this implies that the relationships between the auxiliary measures and the measure of interest are time-invariant. In tables 2.1 and 2.2, the instrumental variable reconstructs an ideological proximity scale for African Americans using the 1960 CPS as our auxiliary dataset. An alternative dataset would be the 1972 ANES, which includes a black consciousness measure that better captures the role of racial group interest during the mid-1960s. The primary justification for using the 1960 CPS is the shorter lag between surveys. Details of the variables and data sets used with Franklin's method are available on request from the author.

29. In theory, one can use this method of calculating magnitude effects for any kind of respondent of interest (i.e., by holding the other variables in the model to other values of theoretical interest). Only predicted probabilities for strong support

are shown in figs. 2.3 and 2.4. Predicted probabilities for the remaining categories are available on request.

30. The course of this conflict within the Democratic Party during the civil rights era is well illustrated by comparing the nomination of a separate states' rights candidate for president in 1948 (when southern white Democrats could still view Democrats as closest ideologically to their preferred position on civil rights issues) to the successful candidacy of Republican Barry Goldwater in five southern states by 1964. This in a region where the Democrats had previously held a virtual hegemony on electoral matters (Key 1949).

31. Alternatively, the switch in signs might also be sensible if a sizeable number of racially egalitarian Democrats who experienced dissonance in 1956 between their personal partisanship and the party they felt closest to on civil rights issues felt more consonance by 1960.

32. King was initially arrested for picketing a department store in Atlanta, then re-arrested for a violation related to driving with an Alabama license while living in Georgia. The intervention from Kennedy, notably, extended beyond a phone call. Robert Kennedy engaged in some behind-the-scenes negotiations to get Dr. King out of jail. The positive impact of this incident on African Americans' support of candidate Kennedy is well established (Garrow 1986; Marable 1991; Stern 1992), although its impact on white voters is less clear (see, e.g., Brauer 1977).

33. The influence of perceived proximity to political parties for southern whites changed during the course of the Civil Rights Movement, while the influence of perceived proximity to movement groups was unchanged. To underscore an obvious but important point, the sensitivity of elite signals and steadfastness of movement signals indirectly illustrates the initial insight in this chapter: that social movements, when successful, upstage the political agenda of conventional elites.

34. To preserve degrees of freedom in our model, the three variations on perceived proximity to party position for fair jobs and housing and for school desegregation are combined into an additive scale. The Cronbach's reliability scores for these scales are: $\alpha_{1956} = .65$ and $\alpha_{1960} = 0.55$ for perceived proximity to Democrats, $\alpha_{1956} = .71$ and $\alpha_{1960} = 0.61$ for perceived proximity to Republicans, and $\alpha_{1956} = .48$ and $\alpha_{1960} = 0.21$ for perceived proximity to southern white Democrats. Because the reliability of perceived proximity for southern white Democrats in 1960 is rather abysmally low, alternate specifications that keep separate perceived proximity measures for each issue were also estimated, but the substantive results are essentially identical.

35. Alvarez and Brehm's discussion is adapted from Harvey's (1976) "multiplicative heteroskedasticity" model for estimating error variance. See also Greene 1997.

36. The authors' typology of unexplained response variance is a shifting target. In Alvarez and Brehm (1995), equivocation is held as the kind of sociability effects described in the text above. In Alvarez and Brehm (1996), this explanation is no longer proposed, and equivocation is now taken to describe cases in which the differences in underlying core values are not necessarily in conflict and under which additional information reduced the variance in responses. In Alvarez and Brehm (1995), two additional sources of variance are discussed: first, that in which respondents might vary in their responses because of ambiguity in question wording, or as

we more conventionally know it, measurement error (Achen 1975); and second, that in which respondents might vary in their responses as a manifestation of greater informedness (that is, better-informed individuals being better able to cite both sides of a debate).

37. Full results of the heteroskedastic probit estimates in this chapter are available from the author. The sign, significance, and magnitude of variables are largely unchanged from the specifications shown in tables 2.1 and 2.2.

38. Substantively, this difference in effects may reveal the greater uncertainty and ambivalence at work as black insurgency in support of desegregation occurs and as political parties begin to react to this mobilization.

39. This decrease in heteroskedasticity also lends indirect support to Carmines and Stimson's thesis that 1964 is a significant year in focusing national attention on the issue of racial equality. Of course, this result still falls short of their claim that 1964 is *sui generis* in punctuating an equilibrium shift in racial attitudes.

CHAPTER THREE

1. The terms "survey," "opinion survey," "opinion poll," and "poll" are often used as though synonymous. To most contemporary practitioners, these terms are interchangeable. Bradburn and Sudman, for example, state that "[t]here is no precise definition between the terms *poll* and *survey*" (1988, 2). That said, the two terms, of course, have different etymologies and conceptual histories. Bradburn and Sudman note that the use of the term "poll" has explicitly political origins (in fact, it shares an etymological root with the word "politics") in the Greek term for "citizen." "Polling" more recently described voting and taxation (e.g., the "poll tax") and only more recently came to denote opinion surveys. The use of the term "survey," on the other hand, had less explicitly political origins. The term originates from Latin (*sur* from *super*, *vey* from *videre*) and from Old French (*survoir*), and Jean Converse (1987, 18) notes at least three meanings: (1) to see over, or view from above; (2) to oversee, or scrutinize and supervise; and (3) to count, measure, take stock of.

2. See, e.g., Blumer 1948; Hobsbawm 1965; Tilly 1983; Farge 1994; Herbst 1993, 1994.

3. The deliberative poll refers to the National Issues Convention, held in January, 1996 in Austin, Texas, and televised over the Public Broadcasting Service (see Fishkin 1991, 1995). As Merkle (1996) notes, however, there have been other uses of the deliberative poll, e.g., by the Minnesota *Star Tribune* and KTCA-TV, and by the Corpus Christi, Texas, Central Power and Light Company.

4. Charles Tilly goes even further, claiming that "nowadays we can consider the opinion survey a complement to, or even an alternative to, voting, petitioning, or protesting" (1983, 462). The observation that the construct of public opinion was increasingly becoming conflated with one possible measure of that construct, opinion polls, can be found among early critics, most notably Herbert Blumer (1948), who cautions against the tautological construction in which "public opinion consists of what public opinion polls poll."

5. Brehm's compilation from 1986 suggests that the rise of research using survey data may well have peaked in the 1970s: 49.3 percent of articles from 1986 in the *American Sociological Review* and the *American Journal of Sociology* used survey data; 25.6 percent of articles from 1986 in the *American Political Science Review* used

survey data (1993, 15). The evidence for the salience of polls in economic and psychological research in both Presser and Converse is not as striking. In both disciplines, the rise of survey data peaks sooner and plateaus at a lower level than in sociology or political science.

6. Table 3.1 only includes *POQ* articles on race that present empirical results relating to public opinion—articles that discuss racial attitudes and politics in general terms (or book reviews in *POQ*, e.g., that for Myrdal's *An American Dilemma*) are excluded from this table. In addition, the conception of "race" coded for in these articles is limited to black-white relations in the United States. For the 1987–96 data, one item by Smith (1992) uses multiple data sources—organization names, media content, and survey data—but is coded under "poll data." This is because Smith's discussion of public opinion per se relies on the survey data. If this item is coded under "media" or "other," the percentage of articles for the period from 1987 to 1996 using poll data would be 87 percent.

7. Much interesting work on that evolution already exists (see, e.g., Ginsberg 1986; Gunn 1995a, 1995b; Herbst 1993; Jackman 1995; Peters 1995; and Price 1992).

8. See Gunn 1995b and Price 1992 on this same point.

9. See also Baker 1990. For more general treatments of this critical period in the origins of our contemporary conception of public opinion see Farge 1994; Gunn 1983, 1989, 1995a; Habermas 1989; Noelle-Neumann 1993; Peters 1995; and Price 1992. Ontological tensions in the concept of public opinion will be examined in more detail in chapter 7.

10. See also Manin (1997) on theories of representation. Manin's account of direct democracy and the "autonomy of public opinion" will be discussed in chapter 7.

11. See Gallup and Rae's influential *The Pulse of Democracy* (1940) for an extended normative justification of survey research and Gallup's intellectual debt to Bryce (see also Salmon and Glasser 1995 on this). Bryce views the optimal form of democracy as occurring "if the will of the majority of citizens were to become ascertainable at all times, and without the need of its passing through a body of representatives, possibly even without the need of voting machinery at all" (1895, 258).

12. As J. Converse (1987) and Salmon and Glasser (1995) note, Gallup and other early pioneers advocated opinion polls with the passion of social activism. Salmon and Glasser, in particular, note that by promoting opinion polls, Gallup was not studying "the democratic process as it actually existed, but as they would have preferred it to exist" (1995, 441). Herbert Blumer recognized this normative residue early on, arguing that "if one seeks to justify polling as a method of studying public opinion on the ground that the composition of public opinion *ought to be* different that what it is, he is not establishing the validity of the method for the study of the empirical world as it is. Instead, he is hanging on the coat-tails of a dubious proposal for social reform" (1948, 548, emphasis in original).

13. See Ross 1991, 1993; and Bulmer, Bales, and Shklar 1991. See also J. Converse 1987 on the ascendance of survey research within the social sciences and Dahl 1993 on the era of behavioralism. Scientism and behavioralism are not the only trajectories of academic inquiry that have influenced the rise of survey research, of course. Related others that have been noted are the paradigm of rationality (Edel-

man 1995; Noelle-Neumann 1995), methodological individualism, and the cognitive revolution in the human sciences (Beniger and Gusek 1995).

14. See, e.g., Gallup and Rae's acknowledgment of the media's role in promulgating polls as an authoritative mirror of the public's sentiments (1940). Gallup and Rae thank "the editors and publishers of American newspapers who have made this new venture in reporting public opinion possible. . . . The newspapers who have stood by the [American Institute of Public Opinion's] researchers since the earliest experimental days, and have played their part loyally in backing continuous and independent surveys of what people think. In publishing the results of surveys even when these results have violently disagreed with the opinions expressed in their editorial columns, these newspapers act as the twentieth-century weathercocks for a vast democracy" (viii).

15. This recognition of the dual influence of journalism and market research is due to J. Converse (1987). Accounts of this turning point in the history of opinion polls can also be found in Crossley 1937; Gallup and Rae 1940. Elmo Roper (with Paul Cherrington) conducted the first pre-election polls with *Fortune* magazine; Archibald Crossley's pre-election polls were published in Hearst newspapers; and George Gallup, through the AIPO (and with multiple newspapers), began conducting weekly national polls during the election. The AIPO polls not only correctly predicted the outcome of the election but also correctly predicted the degree of the *Literary Digest's* sampling error to within one percentage point (Gallup and Rae 1940, 47).

16. See, e.g., Beniger 1992; Peer 1992; and Sanders 1999.

17. For Habermas the term "public opinion" is reserved to describe an idealized conception that only occurs within a public sphere in which political discourse is characterized by rationality and deliberation. As such, "public" opinion is differentiated from "mass" opinion, which results from what he terms the "manufactured publicity" of ideas among a limited, elite group of political actors. For the masses, social psychological processes "liquidate" into an apparent consensus as "public opinion," which then legitimates the rule of the few.

18. For an excellent rebuttal to these critiques, especially Ginsberg's, see Converse 1996. As Converse notes, Ginsberg and others are never clear about the precise causal mechanism by which polls themselves would domesticate mass sentiments. Moreover, Converse points out that popular protest has not obviously declined since the advent of opinion polls and that ordinary citizens are not beyond giving their elites a "nasty surprise."

19. On the notion of controlling and shaping public sentiment, see also the collection of essays in Margolis and Mauser 1989.

20. Bourdieu's theoretical interest in the (non)existence of public opinion becomes more apparent in later works such as *Distinction* (1986), where much is made of a downward class bias in survey nonresponse. Thus, whether someone responds to a survey question depends, to Bourdieu, not just only whether the question asked has any import to the respondent but also on that respondent's "socially authorized and encouraged sense of being entitled to be concerned with politics, authorized to talk politics" (1986, 409). Bourdieu further argues that "forcing on everyone, uniformly, problems which only arise for a few . . . there is every likelihood of creating a pure artifact out of thin air. Opinions are made to exist which did not pre-exist the

questions, and which otherwise would not have been expressed" (413). As Bourdieu sees it, opinion polls thus legitimize and reproduce social hierarchies and muffle the unvoiced desires and needs of the politically dispossessed. See also Bourdieu 1990 and Herbst 1992.

21. Even for a non-positivist like the early Habermas, the question is as much about why researchers do not find a more precise term than "public opinion" as it is about the lack of such a notion itself. Moreover, authors such as Herbst, Tilly, and Bourdieu, I would argue, implicitly or explicitly accept that there is an underlying observable "public opinion" that merits study. Finally, some of this ambiguity can be clarified by differentiating what opinion polls and the discursive rendering of "public opinion" signify from whether or not there is an underlying construct that merits empirical study. Take Herbst (1993), who in the section "Defining Public Opinion" offers the categories "aggregation," "majoritarian," "discursive/consensual," and "reification" as definitions of the term. None of these categories actually describes what it is that survey researchers think they are measuring when they administer polls; rather, the categories describe particular meanings that interpreters of poll data or other political acts that might fall under "public opinion" attach to that act or praxis. Thus, Herbst's choice "to avoid discovering the true meaning of the phrase, and simply grant that the definition is fluid" (92), describes a different undertaking than that of survey practitioners.

22. See Brehm (1993) on nonresponse, Schuman and Converse (1971) and Sanders (1995) on race-of-interviewer effects, and Alvarez and Brehm (1995, 1996, 1997) and Rivers (1988) on response uncertainty and heterogeneity. A collection of influential treatments of these methodological refinements from *Public Opinion Quarterly* can be found in Singer and Presser 1989. See especially articles on nonresponse (Steeh), question wording (Smith), question order (Schuman and Presser; Sigelman), response scaling (Alwin and Krosnick), measurement error (Andrews), and race-of-interviewer effects (Schuman and Converse).

23. Zaller's sensitivity to what surveys actually measure is captured well in the subtitle of an article co-authored with Feldman (1992), "Answering Questions Versus Revealing Preferences." In this regard, the understanding of what surveys measure is remarkably similar to Habermas's and Bourdieu's understanding, albeit from radically different normative presuppositions.

24. For an excellent discussion of the prospects for democratic deliberation in the face of response instability, see Kinder and Herzog 1993. Among other things, Kinder and Herzog resuscitate Dewey against both Converse and Lippmann.

25. Although proponents of elite theories are wary of the potential for elite domination, they generally remain agnostic, or conclude that the elite influences and response instability do not pose a threat to democratic representation, or find inflections of collective rationality amid the apparent noise. Such defenses of survey research often reflect theoretical priors rather than well-grounded empirical analysis. These three positions on the possibility of elite domination are represented by Carmines and Stimson (1989), Zaller (1992), and Page and Shapiro (1992), respectively. And these priors are often grounded in the assumption that public opinion and survey data are equivalent. This is, of course, an oversimplification to which there are some noteworthy exceptions such as Margolis and Mauser 1989; Geer 1996; Lupia and McCubbins 1998; and Jacobs and Shapiro 2000.

26. This possibility is also shown in the way elite domination is characterized. To continue using Zaller, elite domination is defined as "a situation in which *elites induce citizens to hold opinions that they would not hold if aware of the best available information and analysis*" (1992, 313, emphasis in original). This definition is incomplete because it excludes some forms of elite domination. Zaller is primarily focused on the face of power describable in behavioral, pluralist terms, neglecting the kind of invisible agenda-control face of power that Bachrach and Baratz (1962) describe or the false consciousness that Lukes (1974) points out. Thus, the central point of elite domination for some—whether Gramscian hegemony or Habermasian manufactured publicity or Foucauldian power-knowledge—is not the completeness of information but authenticity of interests.

27. Examples of experimental or quasi-experimental design in surveys can be found in Iyengar and Kinder (1987), Kinder and Palfrey (1993), and Kinder and Sanders (1990). An example of fortuitous circumstances is the 1992 L.A. County Social Survey, which was in the field three months prior to the urban unrest in Los Angeles in the aftermath of the Rodney King verdict and remained in the field three months after the uprising (see Bobo 1994).

28. On the racism underlying biological and social scientific research in the nineteenth century, see, e.g., Gould 1981; Harding 1993; and Woodward 1966. On the history of research into racial politics within political science, see Dawson and Wilson 1991; McClain and Garcia 1990; Tucker 1994; and Walton et al. 1995.

29. Walton et al. also note the importance of the racial composition of political scientists in transforming not only the amount of research into race but the analytic focus and substantive implications of such research (see also Barkan 1992; Harding 1993).

30. See Gurin, Hatchett, and Jackson 1989 and Tate 1993 for a description of the 1984 and 1988 NBES; see Dawson 1995 for a description of the 1993–94 NBPS. Smith 1987 notes two other surveys on the viewpoints of African Americans: the National Survey of Black Americans and the Three Generation Family Study. Smith also notes the oversamples of African Americans in the 1982 and 1987 General Social Surveys, but the knowledge of black mass opinion accessible in these surveys is limited to questions that are relevant to the full sample (i.e., including, and compared to, white Americans).

31. Support for such legislation was quite high: in the October–November poll, 75 percent of New Englanders, 79 percent of respondents from the mid-Atlantic, and 57 percent of southerners favored such a bill. The breakdown of respondents by race and region from available sources is limited. In most cases, African Americans were not polled in these early surveys.

32. In both cases, it is interesting to note a disjuncture between generally encouraging levels of support for racially egalitarian principles and generally dismal levels of support for demonstrations in favor of legislation promoting such principles. Of the 63 percent of respondents who had heard of Freedom Riders, fully 64 percent disapproved of their activism; 57 percent of respondents from the same survey felt that the activism of blacks in the South was hurting their chances at integration; and of the 69 percent who had heard of plans for a march on Washington, 63 percent were unfavorable.

33. See appendix 2 for a description of the sources used. The following consti-

tute the set of surveys and survey organizations counted: American Institute of Public Opinion (later the Gallup Poll), American National Elections Studies, Harris National Surveys, National Opinion Research Center, *New York Herald Tribune*, Opinion Research Corporation, Public Opinion Survey (conducted by AIPO), Quality of American Life Study (conducted by the Center for Political Studies), the Roper Organization (commercial polls and for *Fortune* magazine), the Survey Research Center at the University of Michigan, Survey Research Service (conducted by NORC), and Surveys of Consumer Attitudes and Behavior (conducted by the Center for Political Studies).

34. See Converse 1987 and Smith 1987. An important exception to this is the NORC's two pioneering studies of racial attitudes in 1942 and 1944. Converse also notes that the interpretation and publication of NORC's survey met with resistance and that southern Democratic outrage at the OWI pamphlet praising the endeavors of the black soldier (titled *Negroes and the War*) led in part to a cut in OWI allocations from the $8.9 million requisition to $2.7 million.

35. Data for the number of movement-initiated civil rights events over time are taken from McAdam (1982, 121). See also Burstein 1979.

36. The results are available on request from the author. The term "autoregressive distributed lag" is from Harvey (1990). Autoregressive distributed lag models are a fairly general specification; they are very similar to ARMAX models, except that the disturbance term does not have its own dynamic structure (see Greene 1997). The model above actually estimates the first differences of each series. First differences were taken because Augmented Dickey-Fuller tests suggested that the series were most likely nonstationary. The particular lags were chosen on the basis of visual analysis and cross-correlograms. The time span chosen excluded years beyond 1962 because of the confounding periodicity in the survey questions series once the ANES begins to incorporate questions about race with regularity. A simple correlation between survey items and movement-initiated events, unsurprisingly, is quite strong (r=.78).

37. See, e.g., Dawson 1994b; Mink 1990; and Shklar 1991.

38. As Michael Dawson (1994a, 1995a) shows, for example, racial group identity and the sense of a collective fate strongly mark the political beliefs of African Americans.

CHAPTER FOUR

1. Letters to President Lincoln are quoted in Holzer (1998, 68–69).

2. Note that Einstein's letter to Roosevelt, contrary to popular mythology, was not simply the correspondence of a private citizen to the president of the United States. Rather, the letter was initiated by several prominent Hungarian physicist emigrés (especially Leo Szilard) that began as an effort to entreat the State Department to advise Belgium against selling uranium to Germany. By the time the letter had been redirected to Roosevelt, it bore the composition of Alexander Sachs as well, who pared down Einstein's celebrated correspondence to eight hundred words (Rhodes 1986).

3. The Office of Correspondence includes the mail room, Volunteer and Comment Office, Letters and Messages Office, the Agency Liaison Office, and the Gifts Unit (Patterson 1988).

4. Holzer (1998, xviii) reports estimates of constituency mail during the first Clinton administration at "routinely" between nine thousand and twelve thousand per day and as high as thirty thousand per day when an issue was explosive or when public debate was heated.

5. Holzer (1993) catalogues the following categories among letters to Abraham Lincoln: "advice and instruction," "requests and demands," "compliments and congratulations," "complaints and criticisms," "invention and innovation," "gifts and honors," "official business," "presidential invitations," "family matters," "threats and warnings."

6. There are, of course, exceptions. See, e.g., Buell 1975; Gustafson 1978; Hill 1981; Frantzich 1986; Thelen 1996; Sigelman and Walkosz 1991; and Hart 2000.

7. The study of constituency mail first appears in *Public Opinion Quarterly* in Anderson 1939; the special *POQ* issue on letter-writing includes articles by Bonilla 1956, Cohen 1956, Dexter 1956, and Sussman 1956. The Columbia studies can be found in Wyant 1941, Wyant and Herzog 1941, and Sussmann 1956, 1959–60, 1963.

8. Evidence on constituency mail from Lincoln's time is from Holzer (1993, 1998) and Sussmann (1963). The prominence of McKinley in existing studies of presidential mail is due to Ira Smith's account of his fifty-one years of service in the White House from McKinley to Franklin Roosevelt, most of it in the mail room (Smith 1949). Smith and Sussmann both note that McKinley distinguished between "pressure mail" and mail from ordinary individuals and kept count of the volume of mail.

9. For research on Roosevelt's use of polls, see Eisinger 1996. For more general historical treatments of the rise of presidential polling, see again Eisinger 1996 and also Jacobs and Shapiro 1994, 1995.

10. The discussion of the Roosevelt years draws on Smith 1949, Sussman 1956, and Gustafson 1978. The mention of Roosevelt's use of letters in press releases is from Howe 1934 and on his use of them as early signals is from Rosenman 1952. Roosevelt, of course, was also the first president to regularly make use of poll data (see Cantril 1967; Eisinger 1996). Truman, the first president in the period of interest in this book, apparently cared little for poll results, but Jacobs and Shapiro (1994, 1995) report that in the Kennedy, Johnson, and Nixon administrations, polling evolved into an institutionalized practice in the White House.

11. See Wyant 1941; Wyant and Herzog 1941; and Sussman 1956, 1959, 1963.

12. See, e.g., Rosenstone and Hansen 1993; Verba and Nie 1972; Verba, Schlozman, and Brady 1995; Nie, Junn, and Stehlik-Barry 1996.

13. This constancy of letter-writing over time is consistent with table 4.1's suggestion that the rate of letter-writing (to the president, in the case of table 4.1) has remained fairly constant since Franklin D. Roosevelt's presidency.

14. The figures for 1946 are from Sussmann 1959. The pooled 1973–90 figure is from Rosenstone and Hansen 1993. Note that the rate of letter-writing is quite sensitive to how the target of political contact is identified. In Verba, Schlozman, and Brady (1995), respondents are asked about a broader category of "contacting officials," which includes local officials and nonelected officials. Asked thus, 37 percent of white Americans and 24 percent of African Americans reported contact ac-

tivity. When contact is broken down to national elected officials (president, senator, congressperson), the figure falls back to a more familiar 13 percent.

15. See, e.g., Rosenstone and Hansen 1993; Verba, Schlozman, and Brady 1995; Nie, Junn, and Stehlik-Barry 1996.

16. Hart (2000) arrives at a contrarian conclusion about how letter writers compare to the general population. In this study, Hart conducted surveys after the 1992 and 1996 presidential elections that sampled individuals who wrote letters to newspaper editors in twelve small cities in the United States as well as residents of those cities. Hart concludes that letter writers are more likely to be Republican, older, and politically active but finds no differences in socioeconomic status. This conflicting result is possibly due to Hart's sampling frame (small cities in the United States).

17. This distinction is suggested by Rosenstone and Hansen's (1993) categorization of "personal" and "political" perspectives on political participation.

18. See Olson's (1965) classic statement of the "paradox of voting."

19. See Thelen's (1996) description of letter-writing in response to the Iran-Contra hearings.

20. This categorization of material, solidary, and purposive incentives is also from Rosenstone and Hansen (1993, 16).

21. With illegal acts, such as participation in insurrections or revolutions, a barrier to entry would also be the likelihood of getting caught and punished. There are, of course, other material and nonmaterial risks (e.g., losing one's job, social sanctions) to public expression, and the need for material and nonmaterial resources can deter public expression as well. This demonstrates the limitations of this category of barriers to expression: the formulation of such barriers could easily be disaggregated into material, solidary, and purposive disincentives.

22. One might argue that significant purposive benefits accrue from something like contributing to the quest for greater knowledge, or that there are significant solidary rewards to seeing "your" poll's results in the newspaper.

23. For an excellent discussion of the contrast between expressive and instrumental rationalities, see Schuessler 2000.

24. In addition, whereas surveys may yield collective solidary benefits vis-à-vis publicized poll results, letter-writing usually yields selective solidary benefits in the form of a response from the White House.

25. These dimensions certainly do not exhaust the possibilities. Another dimension of publicity we might consider is how well the public expression involved comports with a particular normative theory of politics. An example of a normatively defined conception of publicity is Habermas's public sphere; in Habermas's ideal conception of public opinion, of course, surveys are a poor indicator. Under an alternative normative conception such as pluralism or liberalism, the survey would fare better as a measure of public opinion.

26. These categories are described in Price (1992). Fenno (1978) similarly distinguishes between constituencies: "geographical constituency" (all the people in a representative's district), "reelection constituency" (those in her district who support her), "primary constituency" (those who support her most actively), and "personal constituency" (her personal, intimate acquaintances).

27. The term "issue public" itself can be traced before Converse at least as far

back as Almond 1950. The notion of a pivotal activated segment of the mass public is also noted by Key 1961, Lippmann 1925, and others.

28. See, e.g., Carmines and Stimson 1989; Mayer 1992; Page and Shapiro 1992; and Stimson 1991.

29. This proactive, freely formed characteristic is also what distinguishes letter-writing from other possible measures of public opinion like media content. The fact that the form and framing of letters is not screened or filtered is quite important, especially in a work that aims to challenge elite-driven theories of public opinion.

30. In some years, sampling every twenty letters yields either too small or too large a sample, and the systematic sampling is varied accordingly. For years with a low volume of mail, the sampling was one of every ten letters; for years with a deluge of mail, the sampling was one of every forty or even one of every eighty letters. See appendix 3 for details on sampling and coding of these letters.

31. The archivists from the presidential libraries were fairly certain that I had been given all the constituency mail on topics related to civil rights and racial politics during these administrations. My sample, however, is only as complete as the archives.

32. The estimated volume of mail on Selma drawn from my sample was 96 percent of the Johnson White House's tabulation, the differences likely due in part to alternate means of counting petitions. In all other periods, the estimated volume from my sample was only somewhere between 10 and 25 percent of all letters that the Johnson White House tabulated.

33. Since the Truman, Eisenhower, and Kennedy administrations do not appear to have kept summaries of constituency mail, there is no easy (i.e., short of prohibitive) means to determine the proportion of all constituency mail to the president consisting of letters on civil rights and racial equality. Such information would obviously be highly informative, if for no other reason than to compare the volume of mail on civil rights to the volume on other issues and to compare the responsiveness of letter-writing to the evolution of the civil rights movement with the other across-time measures of mass opinion.

34. Coding the region of the correspondent, unlike coding race and issue position, was almost always possible, since the letters are archived together with their postmarked envelopes. The assignment of states to regional categories is listed in appendix 3.

35. This category is also composed of jointly authored letters and letters from children. Again, what unifies all these letters is the need for some degree of collective action. In the case of letters from children, most come in the form of an entire class or school that was made to write a letter as a joint project. Mass mailings were seldom categorizable by race of correspondent; "race" was also not ascribed to organizations except in cases where the race of the membership was fairly explicit (e.g., white citizens councils, the Negro Council of Women).

36. Examples would be letters from Orval Faubus (governor of Arkansas during the Little Rock crisis), Adam Clayton Powell (Congressman from East Harlem), or Sam Yorty (at the time, the racially liberal mayor of Los Angeles). The limiting constraint in excluding such letters is my ability to recognize elite actors or the ability to infer elite status from the text of the letter itself.

37. The National Archives had not declassified letters from the first Nixon administration at the time the research was conducted. For obvious reasons, it would have been fascinating to compare the terms of racial discourse leading up to the mid-1960s with the terms of racial discourse following the explosion of urban uprisings from the mid-1960s on.

38. The greater representativeness of letters to the president results, of course, from the fact that the "sample" from which correspondents is drawn is the entire nation (cf. a county, congressional district, or state). And this "sampling frame" is constant over time.

39. Verba, Schlozman, and Brady (1995) suggest similar influences, although their findings apply to a generalized index of "overall participation."

40. These estimates are based on a maximum likelihood probit model. Results are available on request from the author.

41. I restrict my count to front-page items in order to filter out media coverage that even highly aware readers may ignore because they are buried in less prominent parts of the paper. Volume of mail is rescaled (divided by 100) to permit easy visual comparison.

42. Zaller (1992) discusses education, political knowledge, political interest, and media attention as alternative measures of political awareness.

43. Between 1948 and 1965 the correlation of the two series is 0.68. One explanation for the divergence of these trends in 1965 is that media coverage—especially on the front page—approaches a saturation point or upper bound. Put simply, the upper bound of letters is the population of literate persons in the United States (assuming each person writes the president only once), and the upper bound of media coverage is the number of possible articles on the front page of the *New York Times*, multiplied by 365.

44. Volume of constituency mail and issue salience in polls are rescaled (divided by 100 for volume of mail and multiplied by ten for issue salience). Marginals on the "most important problem" question are taken from Tom Smith (1980, 1985a, 1985b). The marginals and volume of constituency mail are rescaled for easy visual comparison. Ideally, it would be informative to know how both series track together if disaggregated by race (i.e., when civil rights becomes highly salient among whites and among African Americans), but the prohibitive costs of obtaining such analysis from the Roper Center prevent such a comparison.

45. Respondents to the ANES are also often asked what they like and dislike about the Democratic and Republican Parties, but this open-ended question is usually used simply to identify the *number* of likes and dislikes, not the actual substance of their replies.

46. Citizen activist who write to elected officials also appear to differ from those who write to newspaper editors. Results are available from the author upon request.

47. The volume of letters shown in figure 4.3 is divided by 100 to permit easy comparison with the number of movement-initiated events.

48. Bradley Patterson, on the president as "pen pal," writes that "[m]uch of the White House mail is exuberant—the folks want the president to know of their happiness as well as their problems. On the wall of the Correspondence Office are five bulletin boards, every square inch of them jammed with snapshots of weddings,

new babies, and anniversaries. The thousands of smiling little pictures are a daily reminder of the beleaguered correspondence staffers: the president is National Friend, sharer of joys as well as tribulations" (1988, 315).

49. For an overview of narrative as a methodological tool in the social sciences, see Patterson and Monroe 1998.

50. The starting point for research on race-of-interviewer effect is Schuman and Converse 1971. See also Finkel et al. 1991; Sanders 1995; and Davis 1997.

51. For example, unlike other possible political actors like state and local officials, presidents are unlikely to hear from ordinary citizens expecting material benefits. In fact, letters from other elite actors and personal acquaintances of the president's who might entertain such expectations are explicitly filtered out of my sample of constituency mail.

52. Other prominent addressees are James Hagerty (press secretary) and Sherman Adams (in the position currently known as White House chief of staff) in the Eisenhower administration and Lee C. White (special counsel), Harry McPherson Jr. (special counsel), Jack Valenti (special assistant), and Hobert Taylor Jr. (associate special counsel) in the Johnson administration.

53. The privileged voice of some correspondents—either political or social elites or personal acquaintances—will gain the president's ear; others will reach other influential staffers within the White House or other federal agencies; and letters from the common, anonymous citizen will likely remain within the White House mail room and receive the impersonal acknowledgment of an equally anonymous White House employee or volunteer. See Gustafson 1978; see also Bagdikian 1990, ch. 5.

54. There is a surge of interest, driven by profound advances in the cognitive sciences (e.g., Damasio 1994 and LeDoux 1996), in the role of emotion in political cognition (e.g., Marcus, Neuman, and MacKuen 2000).

55. This transformative element is a critical component of "new social movements" literature (see, e.g., Melucci 1989; Morris and Mueller 1992; Offe 1987; Touraine 1977). It is also one of the three central components of Doug McAdam's "political process" model of the civil rights movement; McAdam reserves the term "cognitive liberation" to describe such a shift from quiescence to activation (1982).

CHAPTER FIVE

1. See, e.g., Grossman 1990; Painter 1976; and Tolnay and Beck 1995.

2. See the introduction on the dating of black insurgency. On the importance of organizational capacity and resource mobilization to insurgent movements, see McAdam 1982; Oberschall 1973; and Zald and McCarthy 1979.

3. See, e.g., Branch 1988; Chong 1991; Edsall and Edsall 1991; and Graham 1990.

4. See Burk 1984; O'Reilly 1995.

5. The selection criteria is at least three hundred letters in response to an event.

6. The Little Rock case is typical of the movement-elite interaction that characterized many focal encounters during the civil rights movement. The issue came to fore when the school board of Little Rock, a relatively liberal southern city, decides to comply with the U.S. Supreme Court's *Brown* ruling (the Little Rock board was

the first in the South to issue a statement of compliance). Under the guidance of Daisy Bates (president of Arkansas' NAACP and publisher of the local black paper, *Arkansas State Press,* with her husband L. C. Bates) and superintendent Virgil Blossom, roughly seventy-five black students volunteered to enroll at Central High, of whom nine were chosen. Just as the Little Rock Nine were scheduled to be enrolled, Governor Faubus (by most accounts, as a result of cynical electoral considerations) responded to the presence of an angry white mob by ordering the Arkansas National Guard to prevent the students from entering the school. This set in motion a sequence of events that culminated in President Eisenhower's reluctant command for one thousand troops from the 101st Airborne Division to ensure the students safe entry to and exit from Central High. See Beals 1994.

7. One prominent exception one might infer from figure 5.3 is the relatively stable and high level of support for civil rights from 1959 to mid-1962. Note that this is, in figure 5.2, a period of relative latency in public views on race. Note also that the stability and supportiveness of letters is similar to that of the prior period of mass latency from the late 1940s to 1953. This parallel points to a tempting implication. Periods of relative calm in the mobilization of political action and relative stability in the substantive opinions of activated opinion appear to be related to periods of strong support. This is something we ought to expect, given our account of general publics and counterpublics. In the absence of active insurgency or elite action, correspondence is dominated by hard-core activists within oppositional counterpublics who are resolved to maintain a steady pressure for social change on elite actors.

8. The percentage of letters in which race of correspondent is neither identified nor inferred might appear high, even given the subjectivity in attributing race. This is of special concern if my coding of race of correspondent is systematically biased. Specifically, African Americans may be overcounted for two reasons: (1) blacks are likelier to identify themselves by race to the extent that their belief systems are strongly shaped by racial group interests and identity (see Allen, Dawson, and Brown 1989; Dawson 1994a); (2) whites are likelier to either be oblivious to racial group interests and identity or likely to equate "whiteness" with being "American." Having said that, there is also a systematic bias favoring white Americans: letters addressed by individuals with distinctly white ethnic surnames (eastern and southern European) were coded as white. The simple justification is, as James Baldwin put it, "it is a fact that every American Negro bears a name that originally belonged to the white man whose chattel he was" (1993 [o.p. 1963], 84), and that there were very few eastern and southern European immigrants to the United States before Emancipation. Thus the only obvious bias in my coding scheme is that letters from correspondents coded as "white" are probably disproportionately from whites of eastern and southern European (and perhaps Jewish) descent.

9. Historians point out that Truman may not have been entirely sincere in his advocacy of a civil rights plank. Facing a strong electoral challenge from Republican Thomas Dewey and former secretary of commerce Henry Wallace as a third-party candidate, Truman and his aides were apparently acutely aware of the importance of the black vote in 1948. See, e.g., Ruchames 1953; Berman 1970; and O'Reilly 1995.

10. See Burk 1984; O'Reilly 1995. President Eisenhower is infamous for his assertion that "You can't legislate morality" and for general dismay with the *Brown* decision. O'Reilly, for example, notes that Eisenhower promised James Byrnes, then governor of South Carolina, that school desegregation would not be enforced "with all deliberate speed" (as dictated by the Supreme Court).

11. White Americans were far more evenly distributed demographically across these regions in 1940 and in 1970, making up, respectively 31 and 27 percent in the North, 25 and 26 percent in the South, 33 and 29 percent in the Midwest, and 11 and 18 percent in the West.

12. Put simply, organizations whose memberships are predominantly white are coded as "white" and organizations whose memberships are predominantly black are coded as "black." Although racial ascriptions are possible in almost three of every four letters from individuals, such ascriptions are only possible in slightly more than half the cases of organizational mail and only about one of every eight instances of mass mailings.

13. In many of these organizations, especially specific labor union locals and progressive political parties, there may be a significant number of African Americans.

14. Roughly 26 percent of all mail was from organizational sources; 19 percent was from mass mailings. This breakdown may appear to contradict the visual impression from figure 5.8, but note that the baseline in figure 5.8 (total volume of letters) steadily increases with time and is far greater in the 1960s than in the late 1940s and early 1950s.

15. The idea for boycotts did not arise *de novo,* as scholars have noted. In fact, the Montgomery campaign was preceded by boycotts in Baton Rouge, Louisiana, and Tallahassee, Florida. Also, in 1956 African Americans began to organize bus boycotts in other southern cities—Tallahassee's led by Reverend C. K. Steele; Miami's led by Reverend Theodore Gibson; and Birmingham's led by Reverend Fred Shuttlesworth. See Morris 1984; Fairclough 1987; and Collier-Thomas and Franklin 1999.

16. The racial ascription of these cards is more subjective than in most cases. The uncertainty results from the name of the organization sending these cards, the "Florence Fair Employment Practices Committee." This names makes clear reference to the President's Committee on Fair Employment Practices, created in 1941 under Executive Order 8802 and subsequently named the Fair Employment Practices Commission. Although there is some record of regional offices of the FEPC, and some record of localized campaigns to create state-level committees, no evidence anywhere exists of FEPCs at the level of unincorporated metropolitan areas such as Florence. Given that the Florence FEPC is almost surely *not* related to federal or state FEPCs, it is categorized as a black organization for two reasons: (1) the Florence-Graham area is a neighborhood in South Central Los Angeles that was heavily African American in the 1950s; (2) there is a history of legal challenge and political mobilization by African Americans in Los Angeles to enforce existing FEPC law or to establish a California FEPC. See Garfinkel 1959; Patterson 1967; Reed 1992. One important point is that—whether this racial ascription is correct or not—1956 remains a clear, defining moment in the activation of mass opinion in the civil rights movement.

17. On repertoires of movement activism, see Tilly 1983.

18. The results are available from the author on request. The data on movement-initiated events come from Doug McAdam's (1982) work on the civil rights movement. McAdam's count is restricted to events that are attributable to movement activism and not elite-initiated events.

19. In fact, coverage during 1952, much of it campaign rhetoric about civil rights, exceeds that surrounding the *Brown* decision.

20. Interestingly, the spread of *New York Times* coverage also exhibits some political cycling. Front-page coverage of race and civil rights issues appears to increase in presidential election years. One notable divergence between these two time series is that letter-writing failed to manifest the kind of quadrennial upturns suggested by the *New York Times* coverage trend. In 1952 and 1956 there were relatively modest increases in letter writing relative to *New York Times* coverage; this difference was most striking in 1960.

21. This limitation results from the difficulty with making any discriminating inferences about time-dependent relationships when the data are (at best) quarterly: the kind of necessary lag between media reaction to counterelite activism or non-elite reaction to media coverage cannot be modeled.

CHAPTER SIX

1. On general treatments of the role that language plays in political change, see Pocock 1960; Shapiro 1984; and Tully 1988.

2. See Stoker 1998. On framing effects in survey experiments, see more generally Iyengar and Kinder 1987; Kinder and Sanders 1990; Iyengar 1991; Gilens 1996; Hurwitz and Peffley 1997; and Sniderman and Carmines 1998.

3. For more on Proposition 209, see Chavez 1998.

4. For a sampling of recent theoretical accounts of agency, see Swidler 1986; Alexander 1988; Archer 1988; Sewell 1992; and Emirbayer and Goodwin 1994, 1998.

5. Sewell's conception of social structure adapts Pierre Bourdieu's notion of habitus (1977, 1986) and Anthony Giddens's notion of "structuration" (1984), in which social structures and individual practices are defined by duality: structure shaping practices, practices constituting and reproducing structures. For Sewell, notably, the relation between schemas and resources is also captured by duality: not only will resources be the consequence of schemas, but schemas will also be the consequence of resources.

6. See, e.g., Festinger 1957; Petty and Wegener 1998.

7. My use of the term "cherished principles" is roughly analogous to the term "core values" among opinion researchers. I avoid the more conventional term since there is some debate about how "core" the core values really are (e.g., see Smith 1993). Moreover, satisfactory resolution of such debate notwithstanding, what really matters vis-à-vis public opinion is that these beliefs are dearly held. Cherished principles anchor the way we interpret the world, and thus there is a great psychic cost to surrendering them. This is precisely what makes the dissonance and contradiction between the lived racism of Southern blacks and principles such as equality,

citizenship, and justice so powerful. The term I use borrows from John Rawls's "cherished moral principles" (1971).

8. The variety of analytical uses of the term "frame" has burgeoned almost as rapidly as have articles that use the concept (e.g., see Gamson and Modigliani 1987; Iyengar and Kinder 1987; Snow et al. 1986; Tversky and Kahneman 1982). As a result it is often difficult to distinguish the use of "frame" from that of "schema" and, to a lesser extent, other close cousins, "heuristic," "signal," and "metaphor." One means to avoiding confusion between the different terms is to think of frames as interpretative mediators *external* to the individual and to schemas as their *internal* cognitive analogues—that is, as organizing structures, memory traces, or cognitive maps resulting from some mode of informational processing (see Fiske and Taylor 1991; Lau and Sears 1986).

9. In excerpts from letters, the names of the authors are omitted for copyright and confidentiality reasons, except for public documents such as pamphlets. In addition, the style and syntax of the author is kept intact despite occasionally awkward phraseology. Where spelling and grammar errors do not offend, they are left intact, but selective instances are amended.

10. See, e.g., Higham 1997; Klinkner and Smith 1999; and Parker 2001. Klinkner and Smith contend that racial progress succeeds when three factors converge: (1) the United States is embroiled in a large-scale war that requires the mobilization of large numbers of African Americans; (2) that war involves ideological demonization of America's adversaries vis-à-vis America's putative democratic tradition of inclusion and egalitarianism as a means of rallying public support; and (3) domestic protest movements can force the state to abide by those same democratic ideals at home. Klinkner and Smith find that all three factors were in evidence during the Revolutionary War, the Civil War, and World War II.

11. Burk (1984) suggests that this coordination around school desegregation was jointly the result of persistent litigation by the NAACP, the Supreme Court's decision to meet this litigation with a clear and steadfast voice, and the Eisenhower administration's decision to divert attention from some of the other demands of African American organizations to school desegregation. See also Marable 1991.

12. The Truman Committee report urged Congress to outlaw the poll tax and lynching, to pass an FEPC law, to desegregate interstate transportation, and to form a permanent civil rights commission. That same year Truman also issued executive orders to prohibit segregation in the military and racial discrimination in federal jobs.

13. Truman, of course, attempted to eliminate discrimination within the federal government and the military as early as 1948 with Executive Orders 9980 and 9981. In both cases, implementation was protracted and problematic.

14. At the same time, such diverse appeals never disappear completely, and their early presence suggests that demands for economic justice and community self-determination in the early and mid-1960s should rightly be seen as a part of a historical continuum rather than a novel issue that evolved from the demands for school desegregation in 1954.

15. This empowered (almost threatening) voice, importantly, exhibits the extent

to which engagement in mass movements can transform and reshape one's political and collective identity, described in the "new social movements" literature.

16. Morris (1984) identifies the Highlander Folk School as an example of a "movement halfway house" that offered critical training in activism to individuals who would be prominent in the civil rights movement such as Rosa Parks, Fred Shuttlesworth, E. D. Nixon, Septima Clark, and Marion Barry. See also Payne (1995) and Robnett (1997) on Highlander.

17. See Marable 1991, 232n.

18. The "warfare" mentioned in these cards referred to James Meredith's efforts to enrol at the University of Mississippi.

19. See also Cash 1941; Egerton 1994; Grantham 1994; Killian 1970; Odum 1936; and Williamson 1984.

20. Gillespie's pamphlet includes a section titled "The Principle of Segregation May Be Defended on Biblical Grounds and Is Not 'Unchristian.'" This section includes the following subheadings: "The First Separation (Gen. 4:11–26)," "Demoralization Resulting from Intermarriage (Gen. 6:1–7)," "New Divisions After the Flood Stemming from Sons of Noah (Gen. 9:18–29)," "Origin of Linguistic Differences (Gen. 11:19)," "Abraham Called to a Separated Life (Gen. 12–25)," "Prohibitions Against the Mingling of Diverse Things (Lev. 19:19)," "The Warnings of Moses Against Intermarriage with Other Peoples (Deut. 7:3)," "Ezra's Condemnation of Mixed Marriages (Ezra 9–10)," "The Attitude and Teachings of Our Lord—The Four Gospels," "The Attitude and Teachings of the Apostles—The Acts and the Epistles," and "Preview of the Church Triumphant" (Rev. 4–7).

21. In addition to explicit references (to social, sexual, political, economic, and physical threats and to relative group position), indirect manifestations of group threat and conflict are found in references to particularistic rights, to southern white identity and southern white militancy, to the communist bases of movement activism, to U.S. racial history, and to accusations of the president's wooing black voters.

22. The general argument that systems of racial domination are tangled in a web with sexual domination can be found in many theoretical treatments of race and gender (e.g., see Eisenstein 1996; hooks 1981; Stoler 1995).

23. More generally, table 6.3 suggests that the absolute number of identifiable interpretive frames in letters from northern whites increases over time. This quite clearly shows the increased issue salience of civil rights for northern whites as the struggle for civil rights began to take center stage in the national political arena.

24. This particular letter also illustrates a growing trend for such opposition to emerge from whites outside the South.

25. These references to cherished values by advocates of civil rights should highlight what Gamson (1992) refers to as the "injustice frame."

26. Manning Marable (1991), Doug McAdam (1982), and others identify these sit-ins as a decisive turning point in the evolution of movement activism.

27. Note that reference to these considerations is not the same thing as *responsiveness* to elite- or movement-specific considerations. That is, we cannot infer from the fact that correspondents frame their positions in terms of president-specific considerations that they are responding to elite cues. The direction of influence may be the exact opposite: in the absence of any elite cues, references to partisan consid-

erations may simply be a strategic reflection of the fact that correspondents are addressing a political elite. Of course, with some categories responsiveness is clearer than with others. Specifically, letters from southern whites that raise movement-specific considerations are likely doing so in response to cues and information about movement activists (since they aren't addressing a movement activist); letters that refer to partisan considerations are also somewhat likely to reflect some degree of responsiveness.

28. As Mustafa Emirbayer and Ann Mische note, "routine, purpose, and judgment all constitute important dimensions of agency [and] none by itself captures its full complexity" (1998, 963). Emirbayer and Mische propose an alternative, "chordal triad" notion of agency as "the temporally constructed engagement by actors of different structural environments—the temporal-relations contexts of action—which, through the interplay of habit, imagination, and judgment, both reproduces and transforms those structures in interactive response to the problems posed by changing historical situations" (1998, 970).

29. See also Gitlin 1980; Snow et al. 1986; Hanchard 1994; Melucci 1989; and Touraine 1977. Even within the "new social movements" tradition, discussion of the transformative elements of mass mobilization is usually reserved for movement activists themselves.

30. McAdam also specifies a fourth factor: the changing responsiveness of other organized groups, in particular opposition to black insurgency (1982, 231).

31. McAdam draws on Piven and Cloward (1979) and Edelman (1971) in developing the concept of cognitive liberation.

32. See McAdam 1982, 108–10. Later in the book, McAdam uses survey items on relative group position of blacks and whites, and perceived optimism on issues such as income, housing, voting rights, and whites' attitudes (161–63).

33. See Cohen and Dawson 1993; Hochschild 1995.

34. See Wilson 1961; Lipsky 1968.

35. See Chong 1991; McAdam 1986; Marwell and Oliver 1991; and Snow et al. 1986.

36. Research shows that aggregate shifts in public opinion, if sizeable and sustained, are reflected in corresponding shifts in public policy outputs. See Miller and Stokes 1963; Page and Shapiro 1983; Shapiro and Jacobs 1989; and Jacobs and Shapiro 2000.

CHAPTER SEVEN

1. See Johnson et al. 1992; Rutten 1992.

2. See also Baldassare 1994; Gooding-Williams 1993; Hunt 1997; Madhubuti 1993.

3. On genocidal, antiblack conspiratorial thinking, see Cohen 1999 and Lee 2001.

4. On the political socialization of Asians and Latinos, see Portes and Bach 1985; Cain, Kiewiet, and Uhlaner 1991; Portes and Rumbaut 1996; and Cho 1999. None of these studies, however, examine the political preferences and partisanship of Asians and Latinos in the context of elite opinion theory.

5. The discussion of this tension can be found in Palmer 1936 and Peters 1995. Plato deemed subjective opinions *(doxa)* as "darker than knowledge but clearer than ignorance" (1974, 273), and concluded, against the capacity of citizens, that "there will be no end to the troubles of states . . . till philosophers become kings in this world, or till those we now call kings and rulers really and truly become philosophers and political power and philosophy thus come into the same hands" (263). Aristotle, on the other hand, notes in *The Politics* (bk. 3, pt. 4) that "[p]ractical wisdom is the only excellence peculiar to the ruler: it would seem that all other excellences must equally belong to ruler and subject. The excellence of the subject is certainly not wisdom, but only true opinion; he may be compared to the maker of the flute, while his master is like the flute player or user of the flute" (1988, 57–58).

6. This modern conception is defined by Vincent Price as "[t]he combination of *public* and *opinion* into a single term, used to refer to collective judgments outside the sphere of government that affect political decision making" (1992, 8). There were, of course, numerous reconfigurations of public opinion between ancient Greece and eighteenth-century France, including Alcuin's *"vox populi, vox dei,"* Machiavelli's *publica voce,* Pascal's reference to the "Queen of the World," and Locke's "law of opinion." See Baker 1990; Bauer 1934; Gunn 1983, 1989, 1995a, 1995b; Herbst 1993; Noelle-Neumann 1993; Ozouf 1988; Palmer 1936; Peters 1995; and Speier 1950 on the origins of the modern conception of public opinion and the historical origins of the term.

7. Habermas understood the term "opinion" by itself to describe an amalgam of an individual's personal, subjective judgment (comparable to Plato's *doxa*) and, in social contexts, a collective understanding of reputation, mores, and interpersonal regard (which Locke terms the "law of fashion"). Hence opinion, "in the sense of a judgment that lacks certainty, whose truth would still have to be proven, is associated with 'opinion' in the sense of a basically suspicious repute among the multitude" (1989, 89).

8. See Baker 1990; Ozouf 1988. The idea of *publique* was counterposed with *particulier* (particular, individual) at the time; the juxtaposition with which we are more familiar, to *prive* (private), does not occur until 1835 (Ozouf 1988, S2). In addition, Ozouf notes the significance of the term retaining the singular form of opinion (cf. "public opinions") to embody that univocality. Thus she writes that *l'opinion publique* drew its "polemic efficacy from the adjective 'public' and, what is more, from the use of the term in the singular since Rousseau's public opinions in the plural were short-lived and returned immediately to the realm of personal prejudices" (S3).

9. From Ozouf 1988, S9n. See Condorcet (1785) for a rendition of his "jury theorem."

10. Thus Madison argued in *Federalist* 10 that representative government would "refine and enlarge the public views by passing them through the medium of a chosen body of citizens, whose wisdom may best discern the true interest of their country and whose patriotism and love of justice will be least likely to sacrifice it to temporary or partial considerations." Manin points out the double entendre in the phrase "chosen body."

11. This is evident in the very idea of public opinion itself. Bryce (1895) under-

stood public opinion to denote the rational deliberation of contentious political issues in a democracy. Thus Bryce argues that democratic theory demands that "every citizen has, or ought to have thought out for himself certain opinions, i.e., ought to have a definite view, defensible by arguments, of what the country needs, of what principles ought to be applied in governing it" (250).

12. Schumpeter, for instance, cautions that citizens "must respect the division of labor between themselves and the politicians they elect . . . they must understand that, once they have elected an individual, political action is his business and not theirs" (1942, 293).

13. Although the minimalist conception of democracy is mostly attributed to Schumpeter, the idea that citizens were otherwise too preoccupied to make a participatory conception of democracy workable dates back at least to Abbé Siéyès. Siéyès emphasized the need for representative democracy on the grounds that "commercial societies" required the primary arena of public activity to be economic production and exchange. On minimalist theories of democracy, see also Dahl 1956; Downs 1957; and Przeworski 1999.

14. Przeworski attributes this defense of minimalism to Karl Popper (1962). Democracy, the argument goes, achieves this stability *because* of the competitive and contested nature of elections.

15. In making this argument, Carmines and Stimson again reveal their strong structural theoretical bias, wherein even professional politicians are given no particularistic characteristics (i.e., their welfare functions, their decision-making rules, their incentives, and so on) other than the ability to be rational (although, even here, they suggest that issue evolution theory can do without it).

16. See, e.g., Rawls's discussion of such "circumstances of justice" (1971). For an excellent critique of Zaller's discussion of "Purple Land," see Shapiro 1998.

17. See Brady and Ansolabehere 1989 and Hansen 1998 on the microrationality of mass preferences; Page and Shapiro 1992 on the macro-rationality of mass preferences; Schlesinger and Lau 2000 on the constraining effect of metaphoric thinking.

18. Elite opinion theorists do not, of course, flunk the human race. One of the great strengths of Zaller's RAS model, as I noted in chapter 1, is precisely in the perfectly intelligible interpretation it gives to response instability without flunking the human race. Yet there is a strong imputation in Zaller's and in Carmines and Stimson's discussion of the possibility of elite domination that the top-down flow of influence is a good thing because mass preferences can be so seemingly incoherent, unstable, and inadequate to the task of "government by the people." And as a result, political representation is either a "by-product" that is "inadvertent" (Carmines and Stimson) or is achieved through preferences imputed to both elite and masses that are idealized beyond recognition (Zaller).

APPENDIX ONE

1. For ANES 1964, the model was also estimated with the interaction of party proximity to relative affect toward the Democratic and the Republican Parties. The relative affect measure is calculated as the feeling thermometer differences between affect toward the Democratic Party and affect for the Republican Parties. The results achieved using this alternate measure do not change substantively.

2. Another version of this perceived proximity measure was also tested wherein perceived proximity was measured attitudinally as racial group affinity and racial group interest. Racial group affinity: "Would you say that you pretty much feel close to Negroes in general or that you don't feel much closer to them than you do to other people?" Racial group interest: "How much interest would you say you have in how Negroes as a whole are getting along in this country? Do you have a good deal of interest in it, some interest, or not much interest at all?" The (alpha) reliability scores for the index were 0.95 for 1956 and 0.94 for 1960. The questions were also asked only of African American respondents. High = strong racial group identity. The results achieved using this alternate measure do not change substantively.

REFERENCES

Aberbach, Joel D., and Jack L. Walker. 1970. The meanings of black power: A comparison of white and black interpretations of a political slogan. *American Political Science Review* 64 (2): 367–88.

Abramson, Paul R., and William Claggett. 1991. Racial differences in self-reported and validated turnout in the 1988 presidential election. *Journal of Politics* 53 (February): 186–97.

Achen, Christopher. 1978. Measuring representation. *American Journal of Political Science* 22: 475–510.

———. 1977. Measuring representation: Perils of the correlation coefficient. *American Journal of Political Science* 21: 805–15.

———. 1975. Mass political attitudes and the survey response. *American Political Science Review* 69: 1218–31.

Adorno, Theodore, E. Frenkel-Brunswik, D. Levinson, and N. Sanford. 1950. *The authoritarian personality.* New York: Harper.

Alexander, Jeffrey C. 1988. *Action and its environments.* New York: Columbia University Press.

Allen, Richard L., Michael C. Dawson, and Ronald E. Brown. 1989. A schema-based approach to modeling an African-American racial belief system. *American Political Science Review* 83 (2): 421–41.

Allport, Floyd H. 1937. Toward a science of public opinion. *Public Opinion Quarterly* 1 (1): 7–23.

Almond, Gabriel. 1950. *The American people and Foreign Policy.* New York: Harcourt.

Alvarez, R. Michael, and John Brehm. 1997. Are Americans ambivalent towards racial policies? *American Journal of Political Science* 41: 345–75.

———. 1996. Uncertainty and ambivalence in the ecology of race. Paper presented at the annual meeting of the American Political Science Association, San Francisco.

———. 1995. American ambivalence towards abortion policy: Development of a heteroskedastic probit model of competing values. *American Journal of Political Science* 39: 1055–82.

Alwin, Duane F., and Jon A. Krosnick. 1985. The measurement of values in a surveys: A comparison of ratings and rankings. *Public Opinion Quarterly* 49 (4): 535–52.

Anderson, Dwight. 1939. Write your congressman immediately! *Public Opinion Quarterly* 3: 147–54.

Andrews, Frank M. 1984. Construct validity and error components of survey measures: A structural modeling approach. *Public Opinion Quarterly* 48 (2).

Aphtheker, Herbert. 1994. *A documentary history of the Negro people in the United States*. vol. 7: *From the Alabama protests to the death of Martin Luther King, Jr.* Secaucus, N.J.: Carol.

———. 1977. *The Negro people in America: A critique of Gunnar Myrdal's* An American Dilemma. New York: Kraus Reprint.

Appiah, Kwame Anthony. 1996. Race, culture, identity: Misunderstood connections. In *Color conscious*, edited by Kwame Anthony Appiah and Amy Guttmann. Princeton, N.J.: Princeton University Press.

Archer, Margaret. 1988. *Culture and agency: The place of culture in social theory*. Cambridge: Cambridge University Press.

Arendt, Hannah. 1965. *On revolution*. New York: Viking.

Aristotle. 1988. *The politics*. Edited by Stephen Everson. Cambridge: Cambridge University Press.

Asch, Solomon E. 1956. Studies of independence and conformity: A minority of one against a unanimous majority. *Psychological Monographs* 70 (9, Whole No. 416).

———. 1952. *Social psychology*. New York: Houghton Mifflin.

Bachrach, Peter, and Morton Baratz. 1962. The two faces of power. *American Political Science Review* 56: 947–52.

Bagdikian, Ben H. 1990. *The Media Monopoly*. 3d. ed. Boston: Beacon.

Baker, Keith Michael. 1990. Public opinion as political invention. In *Inventing the French Revolution: Essays on French political culture in the eighteenth century*. Cambridge: Cambridge University Press.

———. 1975. *Condorcet: From natural philosophy to social mathematics*. Chicago: University of Chicago Press.

Baldassare, Mark, ed. 1994. *The Los Angeles riots*. Boulder, Colo.: Westview.

Baldwin, James. 1993. *The fire next time*. New York: Vintage.

Banfield, Edward. 1970. *The unheavenly city*. Boston: Little, Brown.

Banks, William. 1996. *Black intellectuals: Race and responsibility in American life*. New York: Norton.

Barkan, Elazar. 1992. *The retreat of scientific racism*. Cambridge: Cambridge University Press.

Bartels, Larry M. 1993. Messages received: The political impact of media exposure. *American Political Science Review* 87 (2): 267–85.

———. 1990. *Presidential primaries and the dynamics of public choice*. Princeton: Princeton University Press.

Bauer, Wilhelm. 1934. Public opinion. In *Encyclopaedia of the social sciences*, edited by E. S. Seligman. New York: Macmillan.

Baughman, John R. 1995. Towards an interactionist model of survey response: The case of race and rated intelligence. Typescript.

Baum, Charlotte, Paula Hyman, and Sonya Michel. 1976. *The Jewish woman in America*. New York: Dial.

Beals, Melba Patillo. 1994. *Warriors don't cry: A searing memoir of the battle to integrate Little Rock's Central High*. New York: Washington Square.

Benhabib, Seyla, ed. 1996. *Democracy and difference: Contesting the boundaries of the political*. Princeton: Princeton University Press.

Beniger, James R. 1992. The impact of polling on public opinion: Reconciling Foucault, Habermas, and Bourdieu. *International Journal of Public Opinion Research* 4 (3): 204–19.

———. 1986. *The control revolution*. Cambridge: Harvard University Press.

———. 1983. The popular symbolic repertoire and mass communication. Comment on Charles Tilly. *Public Opinion Quarterly* 47: 479–84.

Beniger, James R., and Jodi A. Gusek. 1995. The cognitive revolution in public opinion and communication research. In *Public opinion and the communication of consent*, edited by Theodore L. Glasser and Charles T. Salmon. New York: Guilford.

Berelson, Bernard R. 1950. Democratic theory and public opinion. *Public Opinion Quarterly* 16: 313–30.

Berelson, Bernard R., Paul F. Lazarsfeld, and William N. McPhee. 1954. *Voting: A study of opinion formation in a presidential campaign*. Chicago: University of Chicago Press.

Berman, William C. 1970. *The politics of civil rights in the Truman administration*. Columbus: Ohio State University Press.

Black Public Sphere Collective, ed. 1996. *The black public sphere*. Chicago: University of Chicago Press.

Bloom, Jack M. 1987. *Class, race, and the civil rights movement*. Bloomington: Indiana University Press.

Blumer, Herbert. 1965. The future of the color line. In *The South in continuity and change*, edited by John C. McKinney and Edgar T. Thompson. Durham, N.C.: Duke University Press.

———. 1958. Race prejudice as a sense of group position. *Pacific Sociological Review* 1: 3–7.

———. 1948. Public opinion and public opinion polling. *American Sociological Review* 13: 542–54.

———. 1946. The mass, the public, and public opinion. In *New outline of the principles of sociology*, edited by Alfred McClung Lee. New York: Barnes and Noble.

Bobo, Lawrence. 1997. Racial attitudes and relations at the close of the 20th century: The color line, the dilemma, and the dream. In *Civil rights and social wrongs*, edited by J. Higham. University Park: Pennsylvania State University Press.

———. 1994. Public opinion before and after a spring of discontent. In *The Los Angeles riots*, edited by Mark Baldassare. Boulder, Colo.: Westview.

———. 1988. Group conflict, prejudice, and the paradox of contemporary racial attitudes. In *Eliminating racism: Profiles in controversy*, edited by Phyllis A. Katz and Dalmas A. Taylor. New York: Plenum.

———. 1983. Whites' opposition to busing: Symbolic racism or realistic group conflict? *Journal of Personality and Social Psychology* 45: 1196–1210.

Bobo, Lawrence, and Vincent Hutchings. 1996. Perceptions of racial group competition. *American Sociological Review* 61 (6): 951–71.

Bogart, Leo. 1972. *Silent politics: Polls and the awareness of public opinion.* New York: John Wiley.

Bonilla, Frank. 1956. When is petition "pressure"? *Public Opinion Quarterly* 20: 39–48.

Bourdieu, Pierre. 1990. *In other words: Essays toward a reflexive sociology.* Translated by M. Adamson. Stanford: Stanford University Press.

———. 1986. *Distinction: A social critique of the judgment of taste.* Translated by R. Nice. Cambridge: Harvard University Press.

———. 1979. Public opinion does not exist, translated by M. C. Axtmann. In *Communication and class struggle,* vol. 1: *Capitalism, imperialism,* edited by Armand Mattelart and Seth Siegelaub. New York: International General.

———. 1977. *Outline of a Theory of Practice.* Translated by R. Nice. Cambridge: Cambridge University Press.

Boyte, Harry C. 1995. Public opinion as public judgment. In *Public opinion and the communication of consent,* edited by Theodore L. Glasser and Charles T. Salmon. New York: Guilford.

Bradburn, Norman M., and Seymour Sudman. 1988. *Polls and surveys: Understanding what they tell us.* San Francisco: Jossey-Bass.

Brady, Henry, and Stephen Ansolabehere. 1989. The nature of utility functions in mass publics. *American Political Science Review* 83 (March): 143–64.

Branch, Taylor. 1988. *Parting the waters.* New York: Simon and Schuster.

Braudel, Fernand. 1969. *On history.* Chicago: University of Chicago Press.

Brauer, Carl M. 1977. *John F. Kennedy and the second reconstruction.* New York: Columbia University Press.

Brehm, John. 1993. *The phantom respondents: Opinion surveys and political representation.* Ann Arbor: University of Michigan Press.

Brink, William, and Louis Harris. 1966. *Black and white: A study of U.S. racial attitudes today.* New York: Simon and Schuster.

———. 1964. *The Negro revolution in America.* New York: Simon and Schuster.

Brody, Richard A. 1991. *Assessing the president: The media, elite opinion, and public support.* Stanford: Stanford University Press.

Bryce, James. 1895. *The American commonwealth,* vol. 3. London: Macmillan.

Buell, E. 1975. Eccentrics or gladiators? People who write about politics in letters-to-the-editor. *Social Science Quarterly* 56: 440–49.

Bullock, Charles S., III, and Harrell R. Rodgers Jr., eds. 1972. *Black political attitudes.* Chicago: Markham.

Bulmer, Martin, Keven Bales, and Kathryn Kish Sklar, eds. 1991. *The social survey in historical perspective, 1880–1940.* Cambridge: Cambridge University Press.

Bunche, Ralph J. 1973. *The political status of the Negro in the age of FDR.* Chicago: University of Chicago Press.

Burk, Robert Fredrick. 1984. *The Eisenhower administration and black civil rights.* Knoxville: University of Tennessee Press.

Burns, Stewart, ed. 1997. *Daybreak of freedom: The Montgomery bus boycott.* Chapel Hill: University of North Carolina Press.

Burstein, Paul. 1979. Public opinion, demonstrations, and the passage of anti-discrimination legislation. *Public Opinion Quarterly* 43: 157–72.

Cain, Bruce, Kiewiet, Roderick, and Uhlaner, Carole Jean. 1991. The acquisition of partisanship by Latinos and Asian Americans. *American Journal of Political Science* 35: 390–422.

Campbell, Angus. 1971. *White attitudes toward black people.* Ann Arbor: Institute for Social Research.

Campbell, Angus, Philip E. Converse, Warren E. Miller, and Donald E. Stokes. 1971. *The SRC American panel study: 1956, 1958, 1960.* Ann Arbor: Inter-University Consortium for Political Research.

———. 1960. *The American voter.* New York: John Wiley.

Campbell, Angus and Howard Schuman. 1968. Racial attitudes in fifteen American cities. In *Supplemental studies for the National Advisory Commission on Civil Disorders.* Washington, D.C.: United States Government Printing Office.

Cantril, Hadley. 1951. *Public opinion, 1935–1946.* Princeton: Princeton University Press.

Carmichael, Stokely, and Charles V. Hamilton. 1967. *Black power.* New York: Vintage.

Carmines, Edward G., and James H. Kuklinski. 1990. Incentives, opportunities, and the logic of public opinion in American political representation. In *Information and democratic processes,* edited by John A. Ferejohn and James H. Kuklinski. Urbana: University of Illinois Press.

Carmines, Edward G., and James A. Stimson. 1989. *Issue evolution: Race and the transformation of American politics.* Princeton: Princeton University Press.

Carmines, Edward G., and Richard A. Zeller. 1979. *Reliability and validity assessment.* Sage University Paper Series on Quantitative Applications in the Social Sciences. Newbury Park, Calif.: Sage.

Carson, Clayborne. 1991. *Malcolm X: The FBI files.* New York: Carroll and Graf.

———. 1981. *In struggle: SNCC and the black awakening of the 1960s.* Cambridge: Harvard University Press.

de Certeau, Michel. 1984. *The practice of everyday life.* Translated by Steven F. Rendall. Berkeley: University of California Press.

Chavez, Lydia. 1998. *The color bind: California's battle to end affirmative action.* Berkeley: University of California Press.

Childs, Harwood. 1965. *Public opinion: Nature, formation, and role.* Princeton: Van Nostrand.

———. 1939. By public opinion I mean . . . *Public Opinion Quarterly* 4: 53–69.

Cho, Wendy K. Tam. 1999. Naturalization, socialization, participation: Immigrants and (non-) voting. *Journal of Politics* 61 (4): 1140–55.

Chong, Dennis. 2000. *Rational lives: Norms and values in politics and society.* Chicago: University of Chicago Press.

———. 1991. *Collective action and the civil rights movement.* Chicago: University of Chicago Press.

Cohen, Bernard C. 1956. Political communication on the Japanese peace settlement. *Public Opinion Quarterly* 20: 27–39.

Cohen, Cathy. 1999. *Boundaries of blackness: AIDS and the breakdown of black politics.* Chicago: University of Chicago Press.

Cohen, Cathy, and Michael C. Dawson. 1993. Neighborhood poverty and African American politics. *American Political Science Review* 87: 286–302.

Cohen, Jean, and Andrew Arato. 1992. *Civil society and political theory.* Cambridge: MIT Press.

Cohen, Joshua, and Joel Rogers, eds. 1995. *Associations and democracy. The real utopias project,* vol. 1, edited by Erik Olin Wright. London: Verso.

Collier-Thomas, Bettye, and V. P. Franklin. 1999. *My soul is a witness: A chronology of the civil rights Era, 1954–1965.* New York: Henry Holt.

Condit, Celeste Michelle, and John Louis Lucaites. 1993. *Crafting equality: America's Anglo-African word.* Chicago: University of Chicago Press.

Condorcet, Marie-Jean-Antoine-Nicolas Caritat de. 1976. [1785.] Essai sur l'application de l'analyse a la probabilité des decisions rendues a la pluralité des voix. In *Condorcet: Selected writings,* edited by Keith Michael Baker. Indianapolis: Bobbs-Merrill.

Cone, James H. 1991. *Martin and Malcolm and America: A dream or a nightmare?* Maryknoll: Orbis.

Conover, Pamela. 1988. The role of social groups in political thinking. *British Journal of Political Science* 18: 51–76.

Converse, Jean. 1987. *Survey research in the United States: Roots and emergence, 1890– 1960.* Berkeley: University of California Press.

Converse, Philip. 2000. Assessing the capacity of mass electorates. *Annual Review of Political Science* 3: 331–53.

———. 1996. The advent of polling and political representation. *PS: Political Science and Politics* (December): 649–57.

———. 1990. Popular representation and the distribution of information. In *Information and democratic processes,* edited by John A. Ferejohn and James H. Kuklinski. Urbana: University of Illinois Press.

———. 1987. Changing conceptions of public opinion in the political process. *Public Opinion Quarterly* 51 (4, pt. 2): S13–S24.

———. 1970. Attitudes and non-attitudes: Continuation of a dialog. In *The quantitative analysis of social problems,* edited by Edward R. Tufte. Reading, Mass.: Addison-Wesley.

———. 1964. The nature of belief systems in mass publics. In *Ideology and discontent,* edited by David Apter. New York: Free.

———. 1962. Information flow and stability of partisan attitudes. *Public Opinion Quarterly* 26: 578–99.

Converse, Philip, Jean D. Dotson, Wendy J. Hoag, and William H. McGee. 1980. *American social attitudes data sourcebook, 1947–1978.* Cambridge: Harvard University Press.

Cornwell, Elmer E., Jr. 1965. *Presidential leadership of public opinion.* Bloomington: Indiana University Press.

Crawford, Vicki L., Jacqueline Anne Rouse, and Barbara Woods, eds. 1990. *Women* in the civil rights movement: Trailblazers and torchbearers, 1941–1965. Brooklyn, N.Y.: Carlson.

Crossley, Archibald M. 1937. Straw polls in 1936. *Public Opinion Quarterly* 1:24–35.

Cruse, Harold. 1967. *The crisis of the Negro intellectual.* New York: Morrow.

Dahl, Robert. 1961. *Who governs? Democracy and power in an American city.* New Haven, Conn.: Yale University Press.

———. 1956. *A preface to democratic theory.* Chicago: University of Chicago Press.

Damasio, Antonio R. 1994. *Descartes' error: Emotion, reason, and the human brain.* New York: Putnam.

Dates, Jannette L., and William Barlow. 1990. *Split image: African Americans in the mass media.* Washington, D.C.: Howard University Press.

Davidson, Chandler, and Grofman, Bernard, eds. 1994. *Quiet revolution in the South: The impact of the Voting Rights Act, 1965–1990.* Princeton, N.J.: Princeton University Press.

Davies, James C. 1960. The J-curve of rising and declining satisfactions as a cause of some great revolutions and a contained rebellion. In *The history of violence in America,* edited by Hugh Davis Graham and Ted Gurr. New York: Praeger.

Davis, Darren W. 1997. The direction of race of interviewer effects among African-Americans: Donning the black mask. *American Journal of Political Science* 41 (1): 309–22.

Davis, Mike. 1992. In L.A., burning all illusions. *The Nation* (June 1): 743–46.

Dawson, Michael C. 2000. *Black visions: The roots of contemporary African-American political ideologies.* Chicago: University of Chicago Press.

———. 1995a. Structure and ideology: The shaping of black public opinion. Typescript.

———. 1995b. Desperation and hope: Competing visions of race and American citizenship. Typescript.

——— 1994a. *Behind the mule: Race, class, and African-American politics.* Princeton, N.J.: Princeton University Press.

———. 1994b. A black counterpublic? Economic earthquakes, racial agenda(s), and black politics. *Public Culture* 7: 195–223.

Dawson, Michael C., and Ernest J. Wilson III. 1991. Paradigms and paradoxes: Political science and the study of African American politics. In *Political science: Looking to the future,* vol. 1, edited by William Crotty. Evanston, Ill.: Northwestern University Press.

Dearing, James W. 1989. Setting the polling agenda for the issue of AIDS. *Public Opinion Quarterly* (53): 309–29.

DeGroot, Morris H. 1986. *Probability and Statistics.* 2d ed. Reading, Mass.: Addison-Wesley.

Delli Carpini, Michael X., and Scott Keeter. 1996. *What Americans know about politics and why it matters.* New Haven, Conn.: Yale University Press.

De Sousa, Ronald. 1987. *The rationality of emotion.* Cambridge: MIT Press.

Dewey, John. 1927. *The public and its problems.* New York: Holt, Rinehart, and Winston.

Dexter, Lewis Anthony. 1956. What do Congressmen hear? The mail. *Public Opinion Quarterly* 20: 16–27.

Dionne, E. J., Jr. 1991. *Why Americans hate politics*. New York: Simon and Schuster.

Dittmer, John. 1995. *Local people*. Bloomington: Indiana University Press.

Dobkowski, Michael N. 1986. *Jewish American voluntary organizations*. Westport, Conn.: Greenwood.

Downs, Anthony. 1957. *An economic theory of democracy*. New York: Harper and Row.

Druckman, James N., and Arthur Lupia. 2000. Preference formation. *Annual Review of Political Science* 3: 1–24.

Du Bois, W. E. Burghardt. 1992 [1940]. *Dusk of dawn: An essay toward an autobiography of a race concept*. New Brunswick: Transaction.

———. 1989. *Souls of black folk*. New York: Penguin.

Duster, Alfreda, ed. 1970. *Crusader for justice: The autobiography of Ida B. Wells*. Chicago: University of Chicago Press.

Edelman, Murray. 1995. The influence of rationality claims on public opinion and policy. In *Public opinion and the communication of consent*, edited by Theodore L. Glasser and Charles T. Salmon. New York: Guilford.

———. 1988. *Constructing the political spectacle*. Chicago: University of Chicago Press.

———. 1971. *Politics as symbolic action: Mass arousal and quiescence*. Chicago: Markham.

———. 1964. *The symbolic uses of politics*. Urbana: University of Illinois Press.

Edsall, Thomas Byrne, and Mary D. Edsall. 1991. *Chain reaction*. New York: Norton.

Egerton, John. 1994. *Speak now against the day*. Chapel Hill, N.C.: University of North Carolina Press.

Eisenstein, Zillah. 1996. *Hatreds: Racialized and sexualized conflicts in the 21st century*. New York: Routledge.

Eliasoph, Nina. 1998. *Avoiding politics: How Americans produce apathy in everyday life*. Cambridge: Cambridge University Press.

Ellison, Ralph. 1952. *Invisible man*. New York: Random House.

Elster, Jon, ed. 1998. *Deliberative democracy*. Cambridge: Cambridge University Press.

———. 1993. *Political psychology*. Cambridge: Cambridge University Press.

Emirbayer, Mustafa, and Jeff Goodwin. 1994. Network analysis, culture, and the problem of agency. *American Journal of Sociology* 99: 1411–53.

Emirbayer, Mustafa, and Ann Mische. 1998. What is agency? *American Journal of Sociology* 103: 962–1023.

Enelow, James, and Melvin Hinich. 1989. A general probabilistic spatial theory of elections. *Public Choice* 61: 101–13.

———. 1984. *The spatial theory of voting*. Cambridge: Cambridge University Press.

———. 1981. A new approach to voter uncertainty in the Downsian spatial model. *American Journal of Political Science* 25: 483–93.

Erikson, Robert S. 1979. The SRC panel data and mass political attitudes. *British Journal of Political Science* 9: 89–114.

———. 1978a. Constituency opinion and congressional behavior: A reexamination of the Miller-Stokes representation data. *American Journal of Political Science* 22: 511–35.

———. 1978b. Analyzing one-variable three-wave panel data: A comparison of two models. *Political Methodology* 5: 151–167.

Erikson, Robert S., and David W. Romero. 1990. Candidate equilibrium and the behavioral model of the vote. *American Political Science Review* 84 (4): 1103–26.

Erskine, Hazel. 1969a. The polls: Negro finances. *Public Opinion Quarterly* 33 (2): 272–82.

———. 1969b. The polls: Negro philosophies of life. *Public Opinion Quarterly* 33 (1): 147–58.

———. 1968a. The polls: Recent opinion on racial problems. *Public Opinion Quarterly* 32 (4): 696–703.

———. 1968b. The polls: Speed of racial integration. *Public Opinion Quarterly* 32 (3): 513–24.

———. 1968c. The polls: World opinion of U.S. racial problems. *Public Opinion Quarterly* 32 (2): 299–312.

———. 1968d. The polls: Negro employment. *Public Opinion Quarterly* 32 (1): 132–53.

———. 1967a. The polls: Demonstrations and riots. *Public Opinion Quarterly* 31 (4): 655–77.

———. 1967b. The polls: Negro housing. *Public Opinion Quarterly* 31 (3): 482–98.

———. 1962. The polls: Race relations. *Public Opinion Quarterly* 26 (1): 137–48.

Euchner, Charles C. 1996. Public support and opinion. In *Guide to the presidency,* edited by Michael Nelson. 2d ed. Washington: CQ.

Evans, Sara. 1980. *Personal politics: The roots of women's liberation in the civil rights movement and the new left.* New York: Vintage.

Fairclough, Adam. 1987. *To redeem the soul of America.* Athens: University of Georgia Press.

Fan, David. 1988. *Predictions of public opinion from the mass media.* New York: Greenwood.

Farge, Arlette. 1994. *Subversive words: Public opinion in eighteenth-century France.* Translated by Rosemary Morris. University Park: Pennsylvania State University Press.

Farr, James. 1995. Remembering the revolution: Behavioralism in American political science. In *Political science in history,* edited by James Farr, John S. Dryzek, and Stephen T. Leonard. Cambridge: Cambridge University Press.

———. 1993. Framing democratic discussion. In *Reconsidering the democratic public,* edited by George E. Marcus and Russell L. Hanson. University Park: Pennsylvania State University Press.

———. 1989. Understanding conceptual change politically. In *Political innovation and conceptual change,* edited by Terrence Ball, James Farr, and Russell L. Hanson. Cambridge: Cambridge University Press.

Feagin, Joseph, and Harlan Hahn. 1973. *Ghetto revolts.* New York: Macmillan.

Feddersen, Timothy, and Wolfgang Pesendorfer. 1998. Convicting the innocent: The inferiority of unanimous jury verdicts under strategic voting. *American Political Science Review* 92 (1): 23–36.

Feldman, Stanley. 1995. Answering survey questions: The measurement and meaning of public opinion. In *Political judgment,* edited by Milton Lodge and Kathleen McGraw. Ann Arbor: University of Michigan Press.

———. 1991. What do survey questions really measure? *Political Methodologist* 4: 8–12.

———. 1989. Measuring issue preferences: The problem of response instability. In *Political analysis*, vol. 1, edited by James A. Stimson. Ann Arbor: University of Michigan Press.

———. 1988. Structure and consistency in public opinion: The role of core beliefs and values. *American Journal of Political Science* 32: 416–40.

Feldman, Stanley, and John Zaller. 1992. Political culture of ambivalence: Ideological responses to the welfare state. *American Journal of Political Science* 36: 268–307.

Fenno, Richard F., Jr. 1978. *Home style: House members in their districts*. New York: HarperCollins.

Ferejohn, John A., and James H. Kuklinski, eds. 1990. *Information and democratic processes*. Urbana: University of Illinois Press.

Festinger, Leon. 1957. *A theory of cognitive dissonance*. Evanston, Ill.: Row, Peterson.

Fields, Barbara J. 1982. Ideology and race in American history. In *Region, race, and reconstruction*, edited by J. Morgan Kousser and James M. McPherson. Oxford: Oxford University Press.

Finkel, Steven E., Thomas M. Guterbock, and Marian J. Borg. 1991. Race-of-interviewer effects in a pre-election poll: Virginia 1989. *Public Opinion Quarterly* 55: 313–30.

Fishkin, James. 1995. *The voice of the people: Public opinion and democracy*. New Haven, Conn.: Yale University Press.

———. 1991. *Democracy and deliberation: New directions for democratic reform*. New Haven, Conn.: Yale University Press.

Fiske, Susan T. 1986. Schema-based versus piecemeal politics: A patchwork quilt, but not a blanket of evidence. In *Political cognition*, edited by Richard R. Lau and David O. Sears. Hillsdale, N.J.: Lawrence Erlbaum.

Fiske, Susan T., and Shelley Taylor. 1991. *Social cognition*. 2d ed. New York: McGraw-Hill.

Foucault, Michel. 1980. *Power/knowledge*. New York: Pantheon.

Fox, John, and J. Scott Long, eds. 1990. *Modern methods of data analysis*. Newbury Park, Calif.: Sage.

Franklin, Charles H. 1989. Estimation across datasets: Two-stage auxiliary instrumental variables estimation. *Political Analysis* 1: 1–24.

Franklin, Charles H., and John E. Jackson. 1983. The dynamics of party identification. *American Political Science Review* 77: 957–73.

Franklin, John Hope, and Alfred A. Moss Jr. 1994. *From slavery to freedom: A history of African-Americans*. 7th ed. New York: McGraw-Hill.

Frantzich, Stephen E. 1986. *Write your Congressman: Constituent communications and representation*. New York: Praeger.

Fraser, Nancy. 1992. Rethinking the public sphere: A contribution to the critique of actually existing democracy. In *Habermas and the public sphere*, edited by Craig Calhoun. Cambridge: MIT Press.

Frazier, E. Franklin. 1963. *The Negro church in America*. New York: Schocken.

Fredrickson, George M. 1971. *The black image in the white mind: The debate on Afro-American character and destiny, 1817–1914*. New York: Harper and Row.

Fried, Amy. 1997. *Muffled echoes: Oliver North and the politics of public opinion*. New York: Columbia University Press.

Friedman, Debra, and Doug McAdam. 1992. Collective identity and activism: Networks, choices, and the life of a social movement. In *Frontiers in social movement theory*, edited by Aldon Morris and Carol McClurg Mueller. New Haven, Conn.: Yale University Press.

Furet, Francois, and Mona Ozouf, eds. 1989. *A critical dictionary of the French Revolution*. Translated by Arthur Goldhammer. Cambridge: Harvard University Press.

Gaines, Kevin K. 1996. *Uplifting the race: Black leadership, politics, and culture in the twentieth century*. Chapel Hill: University of North Carolina Press.

Gale Research. *Encyclopedia of associations*. 1956. Detroit: Gale Research.

Gallup, George H. 1972. *The Gallup poll: Public opinion, 1935–1971*. 3 vols. New York: Random House.

Gallup, George H., and S. F. Rae. 1940. *The pulse of democracy: The public-opinion poll and how it works*. New York: Simon and Schuster.

Gamson, William A. 1992. *Talking politics*. Cambridge: Cambridge University Press.

Gamson, William A., and Andre Modigliani. 1987. The changing culture of affirmative action. In *Research in political sociology*, vol. 6, edited by R. D. Braungart. Greenwich, Conn.: JAI.

Garfinkel, Herbert. 1959. *When Negroes march: The march on Washington movement in the organizational politics for FEPC*. Glencoe, Ill.: Free.

Garrow, David J. 1986a. *Bearing the cross*. New York: Vintage.

———. 1986b. Commentary. In *The civil rights movement in America*, edited by Charles Eagles. Oxford: University Press of Mississippi.

———. 1981. *The FBI and Martin Luther King, Jr.* New York: Penguin.

———. 1978. *Protest at Selma*. New Haven, Conn.: Yale University Press.

Gaventa, John. 1980. *Power and powerlessness: Quiescence and rebellion in an Appalachian valley*. Urbana: University of Illinois Press.

Geer, John. 1996. *From tea leaves to opinion polls: A theory of democratic leadership*. New York: Columbia University Press.

Gerber, Elisabeth R., and John E. Jackson. 1993. Endogenous preferences and the study of institutions. *American Political Science Review* 87 (3): 639–56.

Giddens, Anthony. 1984. *The constitution of society*. Berkeley: University of California Press.

Giddings, Paula. 1984. *When and where I enter: The impact of black women on race and sex in America*. New York: William Morrow.

Gilens, Martin. 1996. "Racial coding" and white opposition to welfare. *American Political Science Review* 90 (3): 593–604.

Gilroy, Paul. 1991. *"There Ain't No Black in the Union Jack": The cultural politics of race and nation*. Chicago: University of Chicago Press.

Ginsberg, Benjamin. 1986. *The captive public: How mass opinion promotes state power*. New York: Basic.

Gitlin, Todd. 1980. *The whole world is watching: Mass media in the making and unmaking of the new left*. Berkeley: University of California Press.

Goffman, Erving. 1974. *Frame analysis*. New York: Harper.

Going, Kenneth. 1990. *The NAACP comes of age: The defeat of Judge John J. Parker*. Bloomington: Indiana University Press.

Goldberg, David Theo. 1993. *Racist culture*. Oxford: Blackwell.

Gooding-Williams, Robert, ed. 1993. *Reading Rodney King, reading urban uprising*. New York: Routledge.

Gould, Stephen Jay. 1981. *The mismeasure of man*. New York: Norton.

Graham, Hugh Davis. 1990. *The civil rights era*. Oxford: Oxford University Press.

Gramsci, Antonio. 1971. *Selections from the prison notebooks*. Translated by Quintin Hoare and Geoffrey Nowell Smith. New York: International.

Grant, Joanne. 1998. *Ella Baker: Freedom bound*. New York: Wiley.

Grantham, Dewey W. 1994. *The South in modern America*. New York: HarperCollins.

Green, Donald P., and Ian Shapiro. 1994. *Pathologies of rational choice theory*. New Haven, Conn.: Yale University Press.

Greene, William H. 1997. *Econometric analysis*. 3d ed. New York: Prentice-Hall.

Greenstein, Fred I. 1978. Change and continuity in the modern presidency. In *The new American political system*, edited by Anthony King. Washington, D.C.: American Enterprise Institute.

Greenstone, J. David. 1993. *The Lincoln persuasion*. Princeton, N.J.: Princeton University Press.

Grofman, Bernard, Lisa Handley, and Richard Niemi. 1992. *Minority representation and the quest for voting equality*. Cambridge: Cambridge University Press.

Grossman, James. 1990. *Land of hope*. Chicago: University of Chicago Press.

Gunn, J. A. W. 1995a. *Queen of the world: Opinion in the public life of France from the Renaissance to the revolution*. Studies on Voltaire and the Eighteenth Century, vol. 328. Oxford: Voltaire Foundation.

——. 1995b. "Public opinion" in modern political science. In *Political science in history: Research programs and political traditions*, edited by James Farr, John S. Dryzek, and Stephen T. Leonard. Cambridge: Cambridge University Press.

——. 1989. Public opinion. In *Political innovation and conceptual change*, edited by Terrence Ball, James Farr, and Russell L. Hanson. Cambridge: Cambridge University Press.

——. 1983. *Beyond liberty and property: The process of self-recognition in eighteenth-century political thought*. Kingston and Montreal: McGill–Queen's University Press.

Gurin, Patricia, Shirley Hatchett, and James Jackson. 1989. *Hope and independence: Blacks' response to electoral and party politics*. New York: Sage.

Gurin, Patricia, Arthur H. Miller, and Gerald Gurin. 1980. Stratum identification and consciousness. *Social Psychology Quarterly* 43: 30–47.

Gurr, Ted Robert. 1970. *Why men rebel*. Princeton, N.J.: Princeton University Press.

——. 1968. A causal model of civil strife. *American Political Science Review* 62: 1104–24.

Guttmann, Amy, ed. 1998. *Freedom of association*. Princeton, N.J.: Princeton University Press.

Gutmann, Amy, and Dennis Thompson. 1996. *Democracy and disagreement*. Cambridge: Harvard University Press.

Habermas, Jürgen. 1989 [1962]. *The structural transformation of the public sphere*. Translated by T. Burger. Cambridge: MIT Press.

——. 1984. *Theory of communicative action*, vol. 2. Boston: Beacon.

——. 1981. New social movements. *Telos* 49: 33–37.

Hampton, Henry, and Steve Fayer, with Sarah Flynn. 1990. *Voices of freedom: An oral history of the civil rights movement from the 1950s through the 1980s.* New York: Bantam.

Hanchard, Michael. 1994. *Orpheus and power: The Movimento Negro of Rio de Janeiro and São Paulo, Brazil, 1945–1988.* Princeton, N.J.: Princeton University Press.

Hansen, John Mark. 1998. Individuals, institutions, and public preferences over public finance. *American Political Science Review* 3: 513–532.

Hardin, Russell. 1996. *One for all: The logic of group conflict.* Princeton, N.J.: Princeton University Press.

Harding, Sandra, ed. 1993. *The "racial" economy of science: Toward a democratic future.* Bloomington: University of Indiana Press.

Harley, Sharon. 1995. *The timetables of African-American history.* New York: Simon and Schuster.

Hartz, Louis. 1955. *The liberal tradition in America.* New York: Harcourt, Brace, Jovanovich.

Harvey, Andrew C. 1990. *The econometric analysis of time series.* 2d ed. Cambridge: MIT Press.

———. 1976. Estimating regression models with multiplicative heteroskedasticity. *Econometrica* 44: 461–65.

Hastings, Philip K., and Jessie C. Southwick. 1975. *Survey data for trend analysis.* Williamstown, Mass.: Roper Center.

Heith, Diane J. 1998. Staffing the White House public opinion apparatus. *Public Opinion Quarterly* 62: 165–89.

Herbst, Susan. 1998. *Reading public opinion: How political actors view the democratic process.* Chicago: University of Chicago Press.

———. 1995a. On the disappearance of groups: 19th- and early 20th-century conceptions of public opinion. In *Public opinion and the communication of consent,* edited by Theodore L. Glasser and Charles T. Salmon. New York: Guilford.

———. 1995b. Election polling in historical perspective. In *Presidential polls and the news media,* edited by Paul J. Lavrakas, Michael W. Traugott, and Peter V. Miller. Boulder, Colo.: Westview.

———. 1994. *Politics at the margin: Historical studies of public expression outside the mainstream.* Cambridge: Cambridge University Press.

———. 1993. *Numbered voices: How opinion polling has shaped American politics.* Chicago: University of Chicago Press.

———. 1992. Surveys in the public sphere: Applying Bourdieu's critique of opinion polls. *International Journal of Public Opinion Research* 4 (3): 220–29.

Hibbing, John R., and Elizabeth Theiss-Morse. 1995. *Congress and public enemy.* Cambridge: Cambridge University Press.

Higginbotham, A. Leon, Jr. 1996. *Shades of freedom: Racial politics and presumptions of the American legal process.* New York: Oxford University Press.

Higginbotham, Evelyn Brooks. 1993. *Righteous discontent: The women's movement in the black Baptist church, 1880–1920.* Cambridge: Harvard University Press.

Higham, John. 1997. Coda: Three reconstructions. In *Civil rights and social wrongs: Black-white relations since World War II,* edited by John Higham. University Park: Pennsylvania State University Press.

Hill, D. 1981. Letter opinion on ERA: A test of the newspaper bias hypothesis. *Public Opinion Quarterly* 45: 384–92.

Hine, Darlene Clark. 1977. The NAACP and the Supreme Court: Walter F. White and the defeat of Judge John J. Parker, 1930. *Negro History Bulletin* 40 (July–August): 753–57.

Hirschman, Albert O. 1994. Social conflicts as pillars of democratic market society. *Political Theory* 22 (2): 203–18.

Hobsbawm, Eric J. 1965. *Primitive rebels: Studies in archaic forms of social movement in the 19th and 20th centuries.* New York: Norton.

Hochschild, Jennifer. 1995. *Facing up to the American dream.* Cambridge: Harvard University Press.

———. 1981. *What's fair: American beliefs about distributive justice.* Cambridge: Harvard University Press.

Hogg, Michael A., and Dominic Abrams. 1988. *Social identification.* Oxford: Blackwell.

Holt, Thomas C. 1995. Marking: Race, race-making, and the writing of history. *American Historical Review* 100 (January): 1–20.

Holzer, Harold, ed. 1998. *The Lincoln mailbag: America writes to the president, 1861–1865.* Carbondale: Southern Illinois University Press.

———. 1993. *Dear Mr. Lincoln.* Reading, Mass.: Addison-Wesley.

Horton, Carol. 1995. Race, liberalism, and American political culture: Politics and ideology in the United States, 1865–1980. Ph.D. diss., University of Chicago.

Howe, Louis. 1934. The president's mailbag! *The American Magazine* (June).

Hsiao, Cheng. 1986. *Analysis of panel data.* Cambridge: Cambridge University Press.

Huckfeldt, Robert, and John Sprague. 1995. *Citizens, politics, and social communication.* Cambridge: Cambridge University Press.

Hunt, Darnell M. 1997. *Screening the Los Angeles "riots": Race, seeing, and resistance.* Cambridge: Cambridge University Press.

Hunter, Floyd. 1953. *Community power structure.* Chapel Hill: University of North Carolina Press.

Huntington, Samuel P. 1981. *American politics: The promise of disharmony.* Cambridge: Harvard University Press.

Hurtado, Aida. 1994. Does similarity breed respect? Interviewer evaluations of Mexican-descent respondents in a bilingual survey. *Public Opinion Quarterly* 58: 77–95.

Hurwitz, Jon, and Mark Peffley. 1997. Public perceptions of race and crime: The role of racial stereotypes. *American Journal of Political Science* 41: 375.

Iyengar, Shanto. 1991. *Is anyone responsible?* Chicago: University of Chicago Press.

Iyengar, Shanto, and Donald Kinder. 1987. *News that matters: Television and American opinion.* Chicago: University of Chicago Press.

Iyengar, Shanto, and William J. McGuire, eds. 1993. *Explorations in political psychology.* Durham, N.C.: Duke University Press.

Izard, Carroll E., Jerome Kagan, and Robert B. Zajonc, eds. 1984. *Emotions, cognition, and behavior.* Cambridge: Cambridge University Press.

Jackman, Simon. 1995. Liberalism, public opinion, and their critics: Some lessons for defending science. Paper presented at the conference "The Flight from Science and Reason," New York Academy of Sciences.

Jackson, John E. 1979. Statistical estimation of possible response bias in close-ended issue questions. *Political Methodology* 6: 393–424.

Jackson, Walter A. 1990. *Gunnar Myrdal and America's conscience: Social engineering and racial liberalism, 1938–1987.* Chapel Hill, N.C.: University of North Carolina Press.

Jacobs, Lawrence R., and Robert Y. Shapiro. 2000. *Politicians don't pander: Political manipulation and the loss of democratic responsiveness.* Chicago: University of Chicago Press.

———. 1994. Issues, candidate image, and priming: The use of private polls in Kennedy's 1960 presidential campaign. *American Political Science Review* 88 (3): 527–40.

Jacques-Garvey, Amy, ed. 1992. *Philosophy and opinions of Marcus Garvey.* New York: Atheneum.

James, C. L. R., et al. 1980. *Fighting racism in World War II.* New York: Pathfinder.

James, Joy. 1997. *Transcending the talented tenth: Black leaders and American intellectuals.* New York: Routledge.

Johnson, James H., et al. 1992. The Los Angeles rebellion: A retrospective view. *Economic Development Quarterly* 6 (November): 356–72.

Johnson, R. Benjamin, and Jacqueline R., eds. 1986. *The black resource guide.* Washington, D.C.: R. Benjamin and Jacqueline R. Johnson.

Katosh, John P., and Michael W. Traugott. 1981. The consequences of validated and self-reported voting measures. *Public Opinion Quarterly* 45: 519–35.

Katznelson, Ira. 1973. *Black men, white cities: Race, politics, and migration in the United States,1900–30, and Britain, 1948–68.* New York: Oxford University Press.

Kelley, Robin D. G. 1993. The black poor and the politics of opposition in a New South city, 1929–1970. In *The "underclass" debate: Views from history,* edited by Michael B. Katz. Princeton, N.J.: Princeton University Press.

———. 1990. *Hammer and hoe: Alabama Communists during the Great Depression.* Chapel Hill, N.C.: University of North Carolina Press.

Kelley, Robin D. G., and Earl Lewis, eds. 2000. *To make our world anew: A history of African Americans.* Oxford: Oxford University Press.

Key, V. O. 1966. *The responsible electorate: Rationality in presidential voting, 1936–1960.* Cambridge: Harvard University Press.

———. 1961. *Public opinion and American democracy.* New York: Knopf.

———. 1949. *Southern politics in state and nation.* New York: Knopf.

Killian, Lewis M. 1970. *White southerners.* New York: Random House.

Kilpatrick, James Jackson. 1962. *The southern case for school desegregation.* New York: Crowell-Collier.

Kinder, Donald R. 1998a. Opinion and action in the realm of politics. In *The handbook of social psychology,* 4th ed., vol. 1, edited by Daniel T. Gilbert, Susan T. Fiske, and Gardner Lindzey. Boston: McGraw-Hill.

———. 1998b. Communication and opinion. *Annual Review of Political Science* 1: 167–97.

———. Kinder, Donald R., and Don Herzog. 1993. Democratic discussion. In *Reconsidering the democratic public,* edited by George E. Marcus and Russell L. Hanson. University Park: Pennsylvania State University Press.

Kinder, Donald R., and Thomas Palfrey, eds. 1993. *Experimental foundations of political science.* Ann Arbor: University of Michigan Press.

Kinder, Donald R., and Lynn M. Sanders. 1996. *Divided by color.* Chicago: University of Chicago Press.

———. 1990. Mimicking political debate with survey questions: The case of white opinion on affirmative action for blacks. *Social Cognition* 8 (1): 73–103.

Kinder, Donald R., and David O. Sears. 1985. Public opinion and political action. In *Handbook of social psychology,* 3d ed., vol. 2, edited by Gardner Lindzey and Eliot Aronson. New York: Random House.

———. 1981. Prejudice and politics: Symbolic racism versus racial threats to the good life. *Journal of Personality and Social Psychology* 40: 414–31.

King, Martin Luther, Jr. 1998. *The autobiography of Martin Luther King, Jr.* Edited by Clayborne Carson. New York: Warner Books.

———. 1986. *A testament of hope.* Edited by James M. Washington. New York: HarperCollins.

———. 1967. *Where do we go from here: Chaos or community?* Boston: Beacon.

Klinkner, Philip A., with Rogers Smith. 1999. *The unsteady march: The rise and decline of racial equality in America.* Chicago: University of Chicago Press.

Kluger, Richard. 1976. *Simple justice: The history of* Brown v. Board of Education *and black America's struggle for equality.* New York: Knopf.

Krosnick, Jon A. 1990. Government policy and citizen passion: A study of issue publics in contemporary America. *Political Behavior* 12: 59–92.

Kuhn, Thomas. 1962. *The structure of scientific revolutions.* In *Encyclopedia of Unified Science,* vol. 2, no. 2. Chicago: University of Chicago Press.

LaBrie, Henry G., III. 1979. *A survey of black newspapers in America.* Kennebunkport, Me.: Mercer House.

Lane, Robert. 1962. *Political ideology.* New York: Free.

Lau, Richard, and David O. Sears, eds. 1986. *Political cognition.* Hillsdale, N.J.: Lawrence Erlbaum.

Lawson, Steven F. 1985. *In pursuit of power: Southern blacks and electoral politics, 1965–1982.* New York: Columbia University Press.

———. 1976. *Black ballots: Voting rights in the South, 1944–1969.* New York: Columbia University Press.

Lazarsfeld, Paul F. 1957. Public opinion and the classical tradition. *Public Opinion Quarterly* 21: 39–53.

Lazarsfeld, Paul F., Bernard Berelson, and Hazel Gaudet. 1944. *The people's choice: How the voter makes up his mind in a presidential campaign.* New York: Columbia University Press.

LeDoux, Joseph. 1996. *The emotional brain: The mysterious underpinnings of emotional life.* New York: Simon and Schuster.

Lee, Taeku. 2001. Government as enemy of the people: Conspiratorial beliefs in the African-American community. Typescript.

Lee, Taeku, and Mark J. Schlesinger. 2001. Signaling in context: Elite influence, partisan divides, and public support for health care reform, 1993–1994. Typescript.

Leonard, George B. 1965. Midnight plane to Alabama. *Nation* 200 (10 May): 502–5.

Lewis, David Levering. 1986. The origins and causes of the civil rights movement. In *The civil rights movement in America,* edited by Charles Eagles. Oxford: University Press of Mississippi.

————. 1978. *King: A biography*. 2d ed. Urbana: University of Illinois Press.

Lewis, Earl. 1991. *In their own interests: Race, class, and power in twentieth-century Norfolk, Virginia*. Berkeley: University of California Press.

Lien, Pei-te. 1994. Ethnicity and political participation: A comparison between Asians and Mexican Americans. *Political Behavior* 16: 237–64.

Lincoln, C. Eric. 1991. *The black Muslims in America*. 3d ed. Trenton, N.J.: Africa World.

Lincoln, C. Eric, and Lawrence H. Mamiya. 1990. *The black church in the African American experience*. Durham, N.C.: Duke University Press.

Lippmann, Walter. 1925. *The phantom public*. New York: Harcourt, Brace, Jovanovich.

————. 1922. *Public opinion*. New York: Free.

Lipset, Seymour Martin, and William Schneider. 1987. *The confidence gap*. Baltimore: Johns Hopkins University Press.

Lipsitz, George. 1988. *A life in the struggle: Ivory Perry and the culture of opposition*. Philadelphia: Temple University Press.

Lipsky, Michael. 1968. Protest as a political resource. *American Political Science Review* 62: 1144–58.

Locke, Alain, ed. 1992 [1925]. *The new Negro: Voices of the Harlem Renaissance*. New York: Atheneum.

Lodge, Milton, and Ruth Hamill. 1993. A partisan schema for political information processing. In *Experimental foundations of political science*, edited by Donald Kinder and Thomas Palfrey. Ann Arbor: University of Michigan Press.

Lohmann, Susanne. 1993. A signalling model of informative and manipulative political action. *American Political Science Review* 87 (2): 319–33.

Lowell, A. Lawrence. 1913. *Public opinion and popular government*. New York: Longmans, Green.

Lowi, Theodore J. 1985. *The personal president*. Ithaca: Cornell University Press.

Lukes, Steven. 1974. *Power: A radical view*. London: Macmillan.

Lupia, Arthur. 2000. Institutions as informational crutches: Experimental evidence from laboratory and field. Paper presented at the Annual Meeting of the American Political Science Association, Washington, D.C.

————. 1994. Shortcuts versus encyclopedias: Information and voting behavior in California insurance reform elections. *American Political Science Review* 88 (1): 63–76.

————. 1992. Busy voters, agenda control, and the power of information. *American Political Science Review* 86 (4): 390–404.

Lupia, Arthur, and Mathew D. McCubbins. 1998. *The democratic dilemma: Can citizens learn what they need to know?* Cambridge: Cambridge University Press.

Lupia, Arthur, Mathew D. McCubbins, and Samuel L. Popkins, eds. Forthcoming. *Elements of reason: Cognition, choice, and the bounds of rationality*. Cambridge: Cambridge University Press.

Macedo, Stephen, ed. 1999. *Deliberative politics*. New York: Oxford University Press.

MacKuen, Michael, Robert S. Erikson, and James A. Stimson. 2001. *The MacRo polity*. Cambridge: Cambridge University Press.

Madhubuti, Haki R., ed. 1993. *Why L.A. happened: Implications of the '92 Los Angeles rebellion*. Chicago: Third World.

Manin, Bernard. 1997. *The principles of representative government.* New York: Cambridge University Press.

Mansbridge, Jane. 2000. Everyday feminism. Typescript.

———. 1983. *Beyond Adversary Democracy.* New York: Basic.

Marable, Manning. 1991. *Race, reform, and rebellion: The second reconstruction in black America, 1945–1990.* Rev. ed. Jackson: University Press of Mississippi.

———. 1985. *Black American politics: From the Washington marches to Jesse Jackson.* London: Verso.

Marcus, George E., W. Russell Neuman, and Michael MacKuen. 2000. *Affective intelligence and political judgment.* Chicago: University of Chicago Press.

Margolis, Michael, and Gary A. Mauser, eds. 1989. *Manipulating public opinion: Essays on public opinion as a dependent variable.* Pacific Grove, Calif.: Brooks/Cole.

Markus, Gregory B. 1979. *Analyzing panel data.* Sage University Paper Series on Quantitative Applications in the Social Sciences, vol. 07–018. Newbury Park, Calif.: Sage.

Martin, Elizabeth, Diane McDuffee, and Stanley Presser. 1981. *Sourcebook of Harris national surveys: Related questions, 1963–1976.* Chapel Hill, N.C.: Institute for Research in Social Science.

Marwell, Gerald, and Pamela Oliver. 1991. *The critical mass in collective action.* Cambridge: Cambridge University Press.

Marx, Gary T. 1969. *Protest and prejudice: A study of belief in the black community.* Rev. ed. New York: Harper.

Matthews, Donald R. 1969. Political science research on race relations. In *Race and the social sciences,* edited by I. Katz and P. Gurin. New York: Basic.

Matthews, Donald R., and James W. Prothro. 1966. *Negroes and the new southern politics.* New York: Harcourt, Brace, and World.

Mayer, William G. 1992. *The changing American mind: How and why American public opinion changed between 1960 and 1988.* Ann Arbor: University of Michigan Press.

Mayhew, David. 1974. *Congress: The electoral connection.* New Haven, Conn.: Yale University Press.

McAdam, Doug. 1986. Recruitment to high-risk activism: The case of Freedom Summer. *American Journal of Sociology* 92: 64–90.

———. 1982. *Political process and the development of black insurgency, 1930–1970.* Chicago: University of Chicago Press.

McAdam, Doug, John McCarthy, and Mayer Zald, eds. 1996. *Comparative perspectives on social movements.* Cambridge: Cambridge University Press.

McCarthy, John, and Mayer Zald. 1977. Resource mobilization and social movements. *American Journal of Sociology* 82: 1212–41.

McCartney, John T. 1991. *Black power ideologies: An essay in African-American political thought.* Philadelphia: Temple University Press.

McClain, Paula D., and John A. Garcia. 1990. Expanding disciplinary boundaries: Black, Latino, and racial minority group politics in political science. In *Political science: The state of the discipline,* edited by Ada W. Finifter. Washington, D.C.: American Political Science Association.

McClosky, Herbert. 1964. Consensus and ideology in American politics. *American Political Science Review* 58: 361–82.

McClosky, Herbert, and John Zaller. 1984. *The American ethos.* Cambridge: Harvard University Press.

McCubbins, Mathew, and Arthur Lupia. 1998. *The democratic dilemma.* Cambridge: Cambridge University Press.

McGuire, William J. 1985. Attitudes and attitude change. In *Handbook of social psychology,* 3d ed., edited by Gardner Lindzey and Eliot Aronson. New York: Random House.

———. 1968. Personality and susceptibility to social influence. In *Handbook of personality theory and research.* edited by E. F. Borgatta and W. W. Lambert. New York: Rand-McNally.

———. 1966. Attitudes and opinions. *Annual Review of Psychology* 17: 475–514.

McKelvey, Richard D., and Peter C. Ordeshook. 1986. Information, electoral equilibria, and the democratic ideal. *Journal of Politics* 48: 909–37.

Mead, Margaret. 1937. Public opinion mechanisms among primitive peoples. *Public Opinion Quarterly* 1 (3): 5–16.

Meehan, Johanna, ed. 1995. *Feminists read Habermas.* New York: Routledge.

Meier, August, and Eliot Rudwick. 1973. *CORE: A study in the civil rights movement.* Urbana: University of Illinois Press.

Melucci, Alberto. 1989. *Nomads of the present.* Philadelphia: Temple University Press.

Merkle, Daniel M. 1996. The polls—Review: The national issues convention deliberative poll. *Public Opinion Quarterly* 60: 588–619.

Methvin, Eugene H. 1992. How to hold a riot. *National Review* (June 8): 32–35.

Milgram, Stanley. 1974. *Obedience to authority.* New York: Harper and Row.

Miller, Arthur H., Patricia Gurin, Gerald Gurin, and Oksana Malanchuk. 1981. Group consciousness and political participation. *American Journal of Political Science* 25: 494–511.

Miller, James. 1994. *Democracy is in the streets: From Port Huron to the siege of Chicago.* Cambridge: Harvard University Press.

Miller, Warren E., Arthur H. Miller, and Edward J. Schneider. 1980. *American National Elections Studies data sourcebook, 1952–1978.* Cambridge: Harvard University Press.

Miller, Warren E., and the National Election Studies. 1991. *American National Election Studies cumulative data file, 1952–1990.* 6th release. Ann Arbor: ICPSR [distributor].

Miller, Warren E., and Donald E. Stokes. 1963. Constituency influence in Congress. *American Political Science Review* 57: 45–56.

Mills, Charles. 1998. *Blackness visible.* Ithaca: Cornell University Press.

Mink, Gwendolyn. 1990. The lady and the tramp: Gender, race, and the origins of the American welfare state. In *Women, the state, and welfare,* edited by Linda Gordon. Madison: University of Wisconsin Press.

Morris, Aldon. 1984. *The origins of the civil rights movement.* New York: Free.

Morris, Aldon, Shirley J. Hatchett, and Ronald E. Brown. 1989. The civil rights movement and black political socialization. In *Political learning in adulthood,* edited by Roberta S. Sigel. Chicago: University of Chicago Press.

Morris, Aldon, and Carol McClurg Mueller, eds. 1992. *Frontiers in social movement theory.* New Haven: Yale University Press.

Morris, Lorenzo, Joseph McCormick, Maurice Carney, and Clarence Lusane. 1995. *Million man march: Preliminary report on the survey.* Typescript.

Morrow, E. Frederic. 1963. *Black man in the White House.* New York: Coward-McCann.

Moscovici, S. 1976. *Social influence and social change.* London: Academic.

Murray, Charles. 1992. Causes, root causes, and cures. *National Review* (June 8): 30–32.

Mutz, Diana, Paul Sniderman, and Richard Brody, eds. 1996. *Political persuasion and attitude change.* Ann Arbor: University of Michigan Press.

Myrdal, Gunnar. 1944. *An American dilemma.* New York: Harper and Row.

Naison, Mark. 1983. *Communists in Harlem during the Depression.* New York: Grove.

National Advisory Commission on Civil Disorders [Kerner Commission]. 1968. *Report of the National Advisory Commission on Civil Disorders.* Washington, D.C.: United States Government Printing Office.

Nelson, Thomas, and Donald Kinder. 1996. Issue frames and group-centrism in American public opinion. *Journal of Politics* 58: 1055–78.

Neuman, W. Russell. 1986. *The paradox of mass politics: Knowledge and opinion in the American electorate.* Cambridge: Harvard University Press.

Neuman, W. Russell, Marion K. Just, and Ann N. Crigler. 1992. *Common knowledge: News and the construction of political meaning.* Chicago: University of Chicago Press.

Nie, Norman H., Sidney Verba, and John R. Petrocik. 1979. *The changing American voter.* Cambridge: Harvard University Press.

Noelle-Neuman, Elisabeth. 1995. Public opinion and rationality. In *Public opinion and the communication of consent,* edited by Theodore L. Glasser and Charles T. Salmon. New York: Guilford.

———. 1993. *Spiral of silence.* 2d ed. Chicago: University of Chicago Press.

Nye, Joseph S., Jr., Philip D. Zelikow, and David C. King, eds. 1997. *Why people don't trust government.* Cambridge: Harvard University Press.

Oatley, Keith. 1992. *Best laid schemes: The psychology of emotions.* Cambridge: Cambridge University Press

Oberschall, Anthony. 1973. *Social conflict and social movements.* New York: Prentice-Hall.

Odum, Howard W. 1936. *Southern regions of the United States.* Chapel Hill, N.C.: University of North Carolina Press.

Offe, Claus. 1987. Challenging the boundaries of institutional politics: Social movements since the 1960s. In *Changing boundaries of the political,* edited by Charles Maier. Cambridge: Cambridge University Press.

Olson, Mancur. 1965. *The logic of collective action.* Cambridge: Harvard University Press.

Olzak, Susan. 1993. *The dynamics of ethnic competition and conflict.* Stanford, Calif.: Stanford University Press.

Omi, Michael, and Howard Winant. 1986. *Racial formation in the United States: From the 1960s to the 1980s.* New York: Routledge.

O'Reilly, Kenneth. 1995. *Nixon's piano: Presidents and racial politics from Washington to Clinton.* New York: Free.

————. 1989. *Racial matters: The FBI's secret files on black America, 1960–72.* New York: Free.

Ortony, Andrew, Gerald L. Clore, and Allan Collins. 1988. *The cognitive structure of emotions.* Cambridge: Cambridge University Press.

Ozouf, Mona. 1988. "Public opinion" at the end of the old regime. *Journal of Modern History* 60: S1–S21.

Page, Benjamin Y., and Robert Y. Shapiro. 1993. The rational public and democracy. In *Reconsidering the democratic public,* edited by George Marcus and Russell Hanson. University Park: Pennsylvania State University Press.

————. 1992. *The rational public: Fifty years of trends in Americans' policy preferences.* Chicago: University of Chicago Press.

————. 1983. Effects of public opinion on policy. *American Political Science Review* 77: 175–90.

Page, Benjamin Y., Robert Y. Shapiro, and Glenn R. Dempsey. 1987. What moves public opinion? *American Political Science Review* 81: 23–43.

Painter, Nell Irvin. 1976. *Exodusters: Black migration to Kansas after Reconstruction.* Lawrence: University of Kansas Press.

Palmer, Paul A. 1936. The concept of public opinion in political theory. In *Essays in history and political theory in honor of Charles Howard McIlwain.* New York: Russell and Russell.

Parker, Christopher Y. 2001. Military service and social change: The social and political context of war, 1945–1975. Ph.D. diss., University of Chicago.

Parker, Frank R. 1990. *Black votes count: Political empowerment in Mississippi after 1965.* Chapel Hill, N.C.: University of North Carolina Press.

Pateman, Carole. 1970. *Participation and democratic theory.* Cambridge: Cambridge University Press.

Patterson, Beeman Coolidge. 1967. The politics of recognition: Negro politics in Los Angeles, 1960–1963. Ph.D. diss., University of California at Los Angeles.

Patterson, Bradley H., Jr. 1988. *The ring of power: The White House staff and its expanding role in government.* New York: Basic.

Patterson, Molly, and Kristen Renwick Monroe. 1998. Narrative in political science. *Annual Review of Political Science* 1: 315–31.

Patterson, Thomas, and Robert McClure. 1976. *The unseeing eye: The myth of television power in national elections.* New York: Putnam.

Payne, Charles M. 1995. *I've got the light of freedom: The organizing tradition and the Mississippi freedom struggle.* Berkeley: University of California Press.

Peters, John Durham. 1995. Historical tensions in the concept of public opinion. In *Public opinion and the communication of consent,* edited by Theodore L. Glasser and Charles T. Salmon. New York: Guilford.

Petty, Richard E., and Duane T. Wegener. 1998. Attitude change: Multiple roles for persuasion variables. In *The handbook of social psychology,* 4th ed., vol. 1, edited by Daniel T. Gilbert, Susan T. Fiske, and Gardner Lindzeys. Boston: McGraw-Hill.

Pinderhughes, Dianne.1987. *Race and ethnicity in Chicago politics.* Urbana: University of Illinois Press.

Pitkin, Hanna Fenichel. 1989. Representation. In *Political innovation and conceptual change*, edited by Terrence Ball, James Farr, and Russell L. Hanson. Cambridge: Cambridge University Press.

————. 1967. *The concept of representation*. Berkeley: University of California Press.

Piven, Frances Fox, and Richard A. Cloward. 1977. *Poor people's movements*. New York: Vintage.

Pizzorno, Alessandro. 1978. Political exchange and collective identity in industrial conflict. In *The resurgence of class conflict in Western Europe since 1968*, vol. 2, edited by C. Crouch and A. Pizzorno. London: Macmillan.

Plato. 1974. *The Republic*. Translated by Desmond Lee. New York: Penguin.

Pocock, J. G. A. 1960. *Politics, language, and time*. Chicago: University of Chicago Press.

Popkin, Samuel L. 1991. *The reasoning voter: Communication and persuasion in presidential campaigns*. Chicago: University of Chicago Press.

Popper, Karl. 1962. *The open society and its enemies*. London: Routledge and Kegan Paul.

Porter, Theodore M. 1995. *Trust in numbers: The pursuit of objectivity in science and public life*. Princeton, N.J.: Princeton University Press.

———— 1986. *The rise of statistical thinking, 1820–1900*. Princeton, N.J.: Princeton University Press.

Portes, Alejandro, and Robert L. Bach. 1985. *Latin journey: Cuban and Mexican immigrants in the United States*. Berkeley: University of California Press.

Portes, Alejandro, and Ruben G. Rumbaut. 1996. *Immigrant America*. 2d ed. Berkeley: University of California Press.

Powledge, Fred. 1991. *Free at last?* New York: HarperCollins.

Presser, Stanley. 1984. The use of survey data in basic research in the social sciences. In *Surveying subjective phenomena*, edited by Charles F. Turner and Elizabeth Martin. New York: Russell Sage.

Price, Vincent. 1992. *Communication concepts 4: Public Opinion*. Newbury Park, Calif.: Sage.

Price, Vincent, and Hayg Oshagan. 1995. Social-psychological perspectives on public opinion. In *Public opinion and the communication of consent*, edited by Theodore L. Glasser and Charles T. Salmon. New York: Guilford.

Price, Vincent, and John Zaller. 1998. Who gets the news? Alternative measures of news reception and their implications for research. *Public Opinion Quarterly* 57: 133–64.

————. 1990. Measuring individual differences in likelihood of news reception. Paper given at the Annual Meeting of the American Political Science Association, San Francisco.

Przeworski, Adam. 1999. A minimalist conception of democracy. In *Democracy's value*, edited by Ian Shapiro and Casiano Hacker-Cordon. Cambridge: Cambridge University Press.

Przeworski, Adam, and John Sprague. 1986. *Paper stones: A history of electoral socialism*. Chicago: University of Chicago Press.

Putnam, Robert D. 1995a. Tuning in, tuning out: The strange disappearance of social capital in America. *PS: Political Science and Politics* 28: 664–83.

————. 1995b. Bowling alone: America's declining social capital. *Journal of Democracy* 6 (1): 65–78.

Raines, Howell. 1977. *My soul is rested: The story of the civil rights movement in the Deep South.* New York: G.P. Putnam.

Ralph, James R., Jr. 1993. *Northern protest: Martin Luther King, Jr., Chicago, and the civil rights movement.* Cambridge: Harvard University Press.

Rawls, John. 1971. *A theory of justice.* Cambridge: Harvard University Press.

Reed, Merl E. 1992. *Seedtime for the modern civil rights movement: The president's committee on fair employment practice, 1941–1946.* Baton Rouge: Louisiana State University Press.

Rhodes, Richard. 1986. *The making of the atomic bomb.* New York: Simon and Schuster.

Rivers, Douglas. 1988. Heterogeneity in models of electoral choice. *American Journal of Political Science* 32: 737–57.

Robertson, Stephen L. 1996. Executive office of the president: White House Office. In *Guide to the presidency*, 2d ed., edited by Michael Nelson. Washington, D.C.: CQ.

Robinson, Cedric J. 1997. *Black movements in America.* New York: Routledge.

Robnett, Belinda. 1997. *How long? how long? African-American women in the struggle for civil rights.* New York: Oxford University Press.

Rodgers, Daniel T. 1987. *Contested truths: Keywords in American politics since independence.* New York: Basic.

Roseman, Ira, Robert P. Abelson, and Michael F. Ewing. 1986. Emotion and political cognition: emotional appeals in political communication. In *Political cognition*, edited by Richard R. Lau and David O. Sears. Hillsdale, N.J.: Lawrence Erlbaum.

Rosenberg, Gerald N. 1991. *The hollow hope: Can courts bring about social change?* Chicago: University of Chicago Press.

Rosenman, Samuel I. 1952. *Working with Roosevelt.* New York: Harper.

Rosenstone, Steven J., and John Mark Hansen. 1993. *Mobilization, participation, and democracy in America.* New York: Macmillan.

Ross, Dorothy. 1993. The development of the social sciences. In *Discipline and history: Political science in the United States*, edited by James Farr and Raymond Seidelman. Ann Arbor: University of Michigan Press.

——— 1991. *The origins of American social science.* Cambridge: Cambridge University Press.

Ruchames, Louis. 1953. *Race, jobs, and politics: The story of FEPC.* New York: Columbia University Press.

Rude, George. 1964. *The crowd in history, 1730–1848.* New York: Wiley.

Ruffner, Frederick G., Jr., et al., eds. 1964. *Encyclopedia of associations.* 4th ed. Detroit: Gale Research.

Rutten, Tim. 1992. A new kind of riot? *New York Review of Books* 39 (June 11).

Saks, Michael J., and Thomas M. Ostrom. 1973. Anonymity in letters to the editor. *Public Opinion Quarterly* 37: 417–22.

Salmon, Charles T., and Theodore L. Glasser. 1995. The politics of polling and the limits of consent. In *Public opinion and the communication of consent*, edited by Theodore L. Glasser and Charles T. Salmon. New York: Guilford.

Sanders, Lynn. 1995. What is whiteness? Race of interviewer effects when all the interviewers are black. Typescript.

————. 1994. The racial legacy of American values. Ph.D. diss., University of Michigan at Ann Arbor.

Sanders, Lynn, and John R. Baughman. 1995. Seeing the "other" over the telephone: The politics of attributing ethnicity and race in a survey interview. Paper presented at the Annual Meeting of the International Society for Political Psychology, Washington, D.C.

Savage, Barbara Dianne. 1999. *Broadcasting freedom: Radio, war, and the politics of race, 1938–1948.* Chapel Hill, N.C.: University of North Carolina Press.

Schattschneider, Elmer Eric. 1975 [1960]. *The semi-sovereign people: A realist's view of democracy in America.* New York: Holt, Rinehart, and Winston.

Schlozman, Key Lehman, and John T. Tierney. 1986. *Organized interests and American democracy.* New York: Harper and Row.

Schmidt, Alvin J. 1980. *Fraternal organizations.* In *The Greenwood encyclopedia of American Institutions.* Westport, Conn.: Greenwood.

Schudson, Michael. 1996. What if civic life didn't die? *American Prospect* 7 (25) (March–April): 17–20.

Schuman, Howard, and Jean M. Converse. 1971. The effects of black and white interviewers on black responses. *Public Opinion Quarterly* 35 (1).

Schuman, Howard, and Shirley Hatchett. 1974. *Black racial attitudes: Trends and complexities.* Ann Arbor: Institute for Social Research.

Schuman, Howard, Graham Kalton, and Jacob Ludwig. 1983. Context and contiguity in survey questionnaires. *Public Opinion Quarterly* 47 (1): 112–15.

Schuman, Howard, and Stanley Presser. 1981. *Questions and answers in attitude surveys.* New York: Academic.

Schuman, Howard, and Jacqueline Scott. 1987. Problems in the use of survey questions to measure public opinion. *Science* 236 (4804): 957–59.

Schuman, Howard, Charlotte Steeh, and Lawrence Bobo. 1988. *Racial attitudes in America.* Rev. ed. Cambridge: Harvard University Press.

Schumpeter, Joseph A. 1962 [1942]. *Capitalism, socialism, and democracy.* New York: Harper and Row.

Schwartz, Mildred A. 1967. *Trends in white attitudes toward Negroes.* Report no. 119. Chicago: National Opinion Research Center.

Schwartzlose, Richard A. 1987. *Newspapers: A reference guide.* New York: Greenwood.

Scott, James C. 1990. *Domination and the arts of resistance: Hidden transcripts.* New Haven, Conn.: Yale University Press.

————— 1985. *Weapons of the weak: Everyday forms of peasant resistance.* New Haven, Conn.: Yale University Press.

Scott, Joan, and Howard Schuman. 1988. Attitude strength and social action in the abortion dispute. *American Sociological Review* 53: 785–93.

Sears, David O. 1988. Symbolic racism. In *Eliminating Racism: Profiles in Controversy,* edited by Phyllis A. Katz and Dalmas A. Taylor. New York: Plenum.

Sears, David O., and Jack Citrin. 1985. *Tax revolt.* Cambridge: Harvard University Press.

Sears, David O., and Carolyn L. Funk. 1990. Self-interest in Americans' political opinions. In *Beyond self-interest,* edited by Jane J. Mansbridge. Chicago: University of Chicago Press.

Sears, David O., Richard Lau, Tom Tyler, and H. M. Allen Jr. 1980. Self-interest versus symbolic politics in policy attitudes and presidential voting. *American Political Science Review* 74: 670–84.

Sears, David O., and John B. McConahay. 1973. *The politics of violence.* New York: Houghton Mifflin.

Sen, Amartya Kumar. 1993. Positional objectivity. *Philosophy and Public Affairs* 22 (2): 126–45.

Sewell, William H., Jr. 1992. A theory of structure: Duality, agency, and transformation. *American Journal of Sociology* 98 (1): 1–29.

Shapiro, Ian. 1999. *Democratic justice.* New Haven, Conn.: Yale University Press.

Shapiro, Michael J., ed. 1984. *Language and politics.* Oxford: Basil Blackwell.

Shapiro, Robert Y. 1998. Public opinion, elites, and democracy. *Critical Review* 12 (fall): 501–28.

Shapiro, Robert Y., and Lawrence R. Jacobs. 1989. The relationship between public opinion and public policy: A review. In *Political behavior annual,* edited by Samuel Long. Boulder, Colo.: Westview.

Sheatsley, Paul B. 1966. White attitudes toward the Negro. *Daedalus* 95: 217–38.

Sherif, Muzafer. 1935. A study of some social factors in perception. *Archives of Psychology* no. 187: 1–60.

Sherif, Muzafer, and Carolyn W. Sherif. 1964. *Reference groups.* New York: Harper and Row.

Shingles, Richard D. 1981. Black consciousness and political participation: The missing link. *American Political Science Review* 75: 76–91.

Shklar, Judith. 1991. *American citizenship: The quest for inclusion.* Cambridge: Harvard University Press.

Sidanius, James. 1993. Symbolic racism and social dominance theory. In *Explorations in political psychology,* edited by Shanto Iyengar and William J. McGuire. Durham, N.C.: Duke University Press.

Sigelman, L., and B. Walkosz. 1991. Letters to the editor as a public opinion thermometer: The Martin Luther King holiday vote in Arizona. *Social Science Quarterly* 73: 938–46.

Silver, Brian D., Barbara A. Anderson, and Paul R. Abramson. 1986. Who reports voting. *American Political Science Review* 80 (June): 613–24.

Simon, B., and R. Brown. 1987. Perceived intragroup homogeneity in minority-majority contexts. *Journal of Personality and Social Psychology* 53: 703–11.

Simon, Rita James. 1974. *Public opinion in America, 1936–1970.* Chicago: Rand McNally.

Singer, Eleanor. 1987. Editor's introduction. *Public Opinion Quarterly* 51 (4, pt. 2): S1–S3.

Singer, Eleanor, and Stanley Presser, eds. 1989. *Survey research methods.* Chicago: University of Chicago Press.

Sitkoff, Harvard. 1971. Harry Truman and the election of 1948: The coming of age of civil rights in American politics. *Journal of Southern History* 37: 597–616.

Skocpol, Theda. 1996. Unravelling from above. *American Prospect* 7 (25) (March–April): 20–25.

Skowronek, Stephen. 1993. *The politics presidents make: Leadership from John Adams to George Bush.* Cambridge: Harvard University Press.

Smith, A. Wade. 1987. Problems and progress in the measurement of black public opinion. *American Behavioral Scientist* 30: 441–55.

Smith, Darren L., ed. 1990. *Black Americans information directory.* Detroit: Gale Research.

Smith, Ira. 1949. *Dear Mr. President.* New York: Julian Messner.

Smith, Rogers. 1997. *Civic ideals.* New Haven, Conn.: Yale University Press.

———. 1993. Beyond Toqueville, Myrdal, and Hartz: The multiple traditions in America. *American Political Science Review* 87: 549–66.

Smith, Tom W. 1987. That which we call welfare by any other name would smell sweeter. *Public Opinion Quarterly* 51 (1): 75–83.

———. 1985. The polls: America's most important problems, Part I: National and international. *Public Opinion Quarterly* 49: 264–74.

———. 1985. The polls: America's most important problems, Part II: Regional, community, and personal. *Public Opinion Quarterly* 49: 403–10.

———. 1980. America's most important problem: A trend analysis, 1946–1976. *Public Opinion Quarterly* 44: 171.

Sniderman, Paul, and Edward G. Carmines. 1998. *Reaching beyond race.* Cambridge: Harvard University Press.

Sniderman, Paul, and Thomas Piazza. 1993. *The scar of race.* Cambridge: Harvard University Press.

Sniderman, Paul, and Philip Tetlock. 1986. Public opinion and political ideology. In *Handbook of political psychology,* edited by M. Hermann. San Francisco: Jossey-Bass.

Snow, David A., and Robert D. Benford. 1992. Master frames and cycles of protest. In *Frontiers in social movement theory,* edited by Aldon D. Morris and Carol McClurg Mueller. New Haven, Conn.: Yale University Press.

Snow, David A., E. Burke Rochford Jr., Steven K. Worden, and Robert D. Benford. 1986. Frame alignment processes, micromobilization and movement participation. *American Sociological Review* 51: 464–81.

Sonenshein, Raphael J. 1993. *Politics in black and white: Race and power in Los Angeles.* Princeton, N.J.: Princeton University Press.

Southern, David W. 1987. *Gunnar Myrdal and black-white relations: The use and abuse of An American Dilemma, 1944–1969.* Baton Rouge: Louisiana State University Press.

Speier, Hans. 1950. Historical development of public opinion. *American Journal of Sociology* 55: 376–88.

Spilerman, Seymour. 1971. The causes of racial disturbances: Tests of an explanation. *American Sociological Review* 36: 427–42.

———. 1970. The causes of racial disturbances: A comparison of alternative explanations. *American Sociological Review* 35: 627–49.

Steeh, Charlotte G. 1981. Trends in nonresponse rates, 1952–1979. *Public Opinion Quarterly* 45 (1): 40–57.

Stepan, Nancy Lays. 1986. Race and gender: The role of analogy in science. *Isis* 77: 261–77.

Stern, Mark. 1992. *Calculating visions: Kennedy, Johnson, and civil rights*. New Brunswick, N.J.: Rutgers University Press.

Stimson, James A. 1995. Opinion and representation. *American Political Science Review* 89 (1): 179–83.

———. 1991. *Public opinion in America: Moods, cycles, and swings*. Boulder, Colo.: Westview.

Stoker, Laura. 1998. Understanding whites' resistance to affirmative action: The role of principled commitments and racial prejudice. In *Perception and prejudice*, edited by Jon Hurwitz and Mark Peffley. New Haven, Conn.: Yale University Press.

Stoler, Ann Laura. 1995. *Race and the education of desire*. Durham: Duke University Press.

Stryker, Robin. 1994. Rules, resources, and legitimacy processes: Some implications for social conflict, order, and change. *American Journal of Sociology* 99: 847–910.

Sullivan, John L., James E. Piereson, and George E. Marcus. 1978. Ideological constraint in the mass public: A methodological critique and some new findings. *American Journal of Political Science* 22: 233–49.

Sussman, Barry. 1988. *What Americans really think*. New York: Pantheon.

Sussman, Leila A. 1963. *Dear FRD: A study of political letter-writing*. Totowa, N.J.: Bedminster.

———. 1959. Mass political letter writing in America: The growth of an institution. *Public Opinion Quarterly* 23: 203–12.

———. 1956. Communication to the policy-maker: Petition and pressure. *Public Opinion Quarterly* 20:5–16.

Swidler, Ann. 1986. Culture in action: Symbols and strategies. *American Sociological Review* 51: 273–86.

Tajfel, Henri. 1982. *Social identity and intergroup relations*. Cambridge: Cambridge University Press.

Tarrow, Sidney. 1994. *Power in movement*. Cambridge: Cambridge University Press.

Tate, Katherine. 1993. *From protest to politics*. Cambridge: Harvard University Press.

Taylor, D. Garth. 1986. *Public opinion and collective action*. Chicago: University of Chicago Press.

Taylor, D. Garth, Paul B. Sheatsley, and Andrew M. Greeley. 1978. Attitudes toward racial integration. *Scientific American* 238: 42–51.

Thelen, David. 1996. *Becoming citizens in the age of television*. Chicago: University of Chicago Press.

Thernstrom, Stephan, and Abigail Thernstrom. 1997. *America in black and white*. New York: Simon and Schuster.

Tilly, Charles. 1985. Models and realities of popular collective action. *Social Research* 52 (4): 717–47.

——— 1983. Speaking your mind without elections, surveys, or social movements. *Public Opinion Quarterly* 47: 461–78.

Tocqueville, Alexis de. 1969 [1835–40]. *Democracy in America*. Edited by J. P. Mayer, translated by George Lawrence. Garden City, N.Y.: Doubleday, Anchor.

Toennies, Ferdinand. 1922. *Kritik der Offentlichen Meining*. Berlin: Julius Springer.

Tolnay, Stewart E., and E. M. Beck. 1995. *A festival of violence: An analysis of southern lynchings, 1882–1930.* Urbana: University of Illinois Press.

Touraine, Alain. 1988. *Return of the actor.* Translated by Myrna Godzich. Minneapolis: University of Minnesota Press.

———. 1977. *The Self-Production of Society.* Translated by Derek Coltman. Chicago: University of Chicago Press.

Tucker, William H. 1994. *The science and politics of racial research.* Urbana: University of Illinois Press.

Tulis, Jeffrey K. 1987. *The rhetorical presidency.* Princeton, N.J.: Princeton University Press.

Tully, James, ed. 1988. *Meaning and context: Quentin Skinner and his critics.* Princeton, N.J.: Princeton University Press.

Turner, John C. 1987. *Rediscovering the social group.* Oxford: Blackwell.

Tversky, Amos, and Daniel Kahneman. 1982. The framing of decisions and the psychology of choice. In *Question framing and response consistency,* edited by Robin Hogarth. San Francisco: Jossey-Bass.

Uhlaner, Carole Jean. 1989. Rational turnout: The neglected role of groups. *American Journal of Political Science* 33: 390–422.

Uhlaner, Carole Jean, Bruce E. Cain, and D. Roderick Kiewiet. 1989. Political participation of ethnic minorities in the 1980s. *Political Behavior* 11: 195–221.

Valelly, Richard. 1996. Couch-potato democracy? *American Prospect* 7 (25) (March–April): 25–26.

Van DeBurg, William. L. M. 1992. *New day in Babylon: The black power movement and American culture, 1965–1975.* Chicago: University of Chicago Press.

Verba, Sidney. 1996. The citizen as respondent: Sample surveys and American democracy. *American Political Science Review* 90: 1–7.

Verba, Sidney, and Norman H. Nie. 1972. *Participation in America.* Chicago: University of Chicago Press.

Verba, Sidney, and Gary R. Orren. 1985. *Equality in America.* Cambridge: Harvard University Press.

Verba, Sidney, Kay Lehman Schlozman, and Henry E. Brady. 1995. *Voice and equality: Civic voluntarism in American politics.* Cambridge: Harvard University Press.

Vincent, Theodore. 1973. *Voices of a black nation: Political journalism in the Harlem Renaissance.* Trenton, N.J.: Africa World.

Walsh, Katherine Cramer. 2000. Making sense of who "we" are: Giving meaning to tools of political understanding through informal talk. Ph.D. diss., University of Michigan.

Walton, Hanes, Jr., Cheryl M. Miller, and Joseph P. McCormick II. 1995. Race and political science: The dual traditions of race relations politics and African-American politics. In *Political science in history: Research programs and political traditions,* edited by James Farr, John S. Dryzek, and Stephen T. Leonard. Cambridge: Cambridge University Press.

Walzer, Michael. 1989. Citizenship. In *Political innovation and conceptual change,* edited by Terrence Ball, James Farr, and Russell L. Hanson. Cambridge: Cambridge University Press.

Warren, Mark E. 2001. *Democracy and association.* Princeton, N.J.: Princeton University Press.

Washburn, Patrick Scott. 1986. *A question of sedition: The federal government's investigation of the black press during World War II.* Oxford: Oxford University Press.

Waskow, Arthur I. 1966. *From race riot to sit-in: 1919 and the 1960s.* New York: Doubleday.

Weisbrot, Robert. 1990. *Freedom bound: A history of the civil rights movement in America.* New York: Norton.

Weiss, Nancy J. 1983. *Farewell to the party of Lincoln: Black politics in the age of FDR.* Princeton, N.J.: Princeton University Press.

Wetherell, Margaret, and Jonathan Potter. 1992. *Mapping the language of racism: Discourse and the legitimation of exploitation.* New York: Columbia University Press.

Wexler, Sanford. 1993. *An eyewitness history of the civil rights movement.* New York: Checkmark.

Wiley, David E., and James A. Wiley. 1970. The estimation of error in panel data. *American Sociological Review* 45: 112–17.

Williamson, Joel. 1984. *The crucible of race: Black-white relations in the American South since Emancipation.* New York: Oxford University Press.

Wilson, James Q. 1961. The strategy of protest: Problems of Negro civic action. *Journal of Conflict Resolution* 3: 291–303.

Wilson, William Julius. 1978. *The declining significance of race.* Chicago: University of Chicago Press.

Winter, David G. 1992. Content analysis of archival materials, personal documents, and everyday verbal productions. In *Motivation and personality: Handbook of thematic content analysis,* edited by Charles Smith et al. Cambridge: Cambridge University Press.

Wolseley, Roland E. 1990. *The black press, U.S.A.* . 2d ed. Ames: Iowa State Press.

Woodward, C. Van. 1966. *The strange career of Jim Crow.* Oxford: Oxford University Press.

Wyant, Rowena. 1941. Voting the senate mailbag. *Public Opinion Quarterly* 5: 359–82.

Wyant, Rowena, and Herta Herzog. 1941. Voting the senate mailbag—Part II. *Public Opinion Quarterly* 5: 590–624.

X, Malcolm. 1965. *Malcolm X speaks.* Edited by George Breitman. New York: Grove Weidenfeld.

Young, Iris Marion. 1999. State, civil society, and social justice. In *Democracy's place,* edited by Ian Shapiro and Casiano Hacker-Cordòn. Cambridge: Cambridge University Press.

———. 1990. *Justice and the politics of difference.* Princeton, N.J.: Princeton University Press.

Zack, Naomi. 1993. *Race and mixed race.* Philadelphia: Temple University Press.

Zajonc, Robert. 1982. On the primacy of affect. *American Psychologist* 39: 117–23.

———. 1980. Feeling and thinking: Preferences need no inferences. *American Psychologist* 35: 151–75.

Zaller, John. 1998. Monica Lewinsky's contribution to political science. *PS: Political Science and Politics* 31 (2): 182–89.

———. 1994. Elite leadership of mass opinion: New evidence from the Gulf War. In *Taken by storm: The media, public opinion, and U.S. foreign policy in the Gulf*

War, edited by W. Lance Bennett and David L. Paletz. Chicago: University of Chicago Press.

————. 1992. *The nature and origins of mass opinion.* Cambridge: Cambridge University Press.

————. 1991. Information, values, and opinion. *American Political Science Review* 85 (4): 1215–37.

————. 1986. Analysis of information items in the 1985 pilot study. Report to the NES Board of Overseers, Center for Political Studies, University of Michigan.

Zaller, John, and Stanley Feldman. 1992. A simple theory of the survey response: Answering questions versus revealing preferences. *American Journal of Political Science* 36 (3): 579–616.

ACKNOWLEDGMENTS

This book is dedicated to the first and finest educators in my life, Dong Mock Lee and Jung Oak Choi. By word and deed, my parents have always tried to instill a deep respect for human dignity, a stubborn faith in human potential, and a fearless curiosity about the ways of the world, three aspirations without which this work would not exist. As a new parent, I am only now beginning to understand their infinite patience, love, and selflessness, and I will always be grateful to them for it.

I dare not stray too far from such intimate debts without also thanking three other Lees: brother, sister, and one and only partner. To Jinku and Jungku, thank you for your lifelong companionship, for your strength and guidance, and for softening the many bumps and bruises through the years. To Shirley, thanks for your brilliance, poise, wit, and friendship through all phases of this book. You (and our darling Ella) make the mornings brighter and the evenings more peaceful. I can only hope to nourish (and needle) your endeavors as enthusiastically and empathetically as you have this one.

In the years leading to this book, I have also incurred a great many intellectual and emotional arrears among friends and co-conspirators. I have not suffered as much as University of Chicago graduate students and Harvard University junior faculty are meant to suffer, and you are largely to blame. From this book's intellectual home base at Chicago and from numerous other "homes," my love and propers to John Baughman, Dan Carpenter, Ajay Chaudry, Michael Chwe, Pamela Cook, Nancy Crowe, Kevin Esterling, Andrew Grant-Thomas, Anna Greenberg, Sarita Gregory, Zoltan Hajnal, Karen Hoffman, Roger Larocca, Clara Lee, Namhee Lee, Sandra Lee, Frederick Nahm, Prexy Nesbitt, Chris Parker, Mark Sawyer, John Shon, Bobby Simmons, Jennifer Stewart, Dong Wook Suh, Arthur Vander, Julian Zahalak, and my University of Michigan gang.

In addition, numerous peers and "elders" in the academy have contributed invaluable insights and encouragements. Among them are Scott Althaus, Larry Bartels, Wendy Tam Cho, Dennis Chong, Cathy Cohen, Archon Fung, Vince Hutchings, Larry Jacobs, Michael Jones-Correa, Jane Junn, Rogan Kersch, Sanjeev Khagram,

Claire Kim, Dorinne Kondo, Karl Kronebusch, Ann Lin, Jenny Mansbridge, Ted Marmor, Harwood McClerking, Gary McKissick, Tali Mendelberg, Katharine Moon, Katherine Newman, Pippa Norris, J. Eric Oliver, Michael Omi, Tom Patterson, Adam Przeworski, Keith Reeves, Kira Sanbonmatsu, Robert Shapiro, Lester Spence, Katherine Cramer Walsh, Julie Wilson, Janelle Wong, and John Zaller. I also owe a special, enduring debt to Mark Schlesinger, who (during my earlier incarnation as medical student and itinerant rabble-rouser) introduced me to the radical, dazzling notion that political passions and moral convictions could achieve greater power and precision when disciplined by careful consideration and rigorous scholarship.

As for my mentors in the academy, I could not have dared for finer advisors than Michael Dawson, John Mark Hansen, and Lynn Sanders. To Michael—dissertation chair, guru, and friend—special thanks for training me in the ways of the insurgent scholar and for helping me see how all the dots are connected. To Lynn, thanks for your courage, confidence, clarity, and constant nudging to ask risky questions and pursue dangerous ideas. To Mark, thanks for asking the demanding but decisive question, "What if you are wrong?" It has been a cantus firmus throughout this project, and I will always cherish the integrity and spirit of intellectual inquiry it crystallizes. And to Susan Herbst and John Tryneski, thanks for your faith in this project, your superb editorial stewardship, and your general bonhomie in the making of this book. I hope the future brings many more opportunities to thank each of you.

Five distinguished institutions have also played a key role in the making of this book: the University of Chicago, the John D. and Catherine T. MacArthur Foundation, Pomona College, Harvard University, and Yale University. At these institutions, I have benefited from the administrative support and research assistance of Kathy Anderson, Victoria Bilski, Vanessa Bragg, Janet Gulotta, Albert Hahn, Charles Jung, Chinyelu Lee, Darlene Martin, Marian Rowan, and Lisa Sanbonmatsu. Thanks of an institutional nature are also due to participants in the American Politics Workshop at the University of Chicago, the Health Policy Seminar at Yale University, and the Faculty Research Seminar at Harvard University's Kennedy School of Government. Finally, from the ethereal to the material, I owe a large debt to some very generous institutions: the Searle Foundation, the Andrew Mellon Foundation, the Robert Wood Johnson Foundation, the presidential libraries for Truman, Kennedy, and Johnson, Pomona College, and, at the Kennedy School of Government, the Malcolm Wiener Center for Social Policy, the Dean's Fund, and the Shorenstein Center's Goldsmith Research Award. The idea that knowledge and understanding can better human affairs (and thus merit the financial backing of these various institutions) may yet be more a leap of faith than a reasoned, time-tested belief, but it is a heartwarming and wonderful faith.

INDEX

Page numbers in italics refer to figures and tables.

as an indication of public opinion, 188; individual's cost of responding to, 98, 239n. 22; information conveyed to elites by, 99–101, 239n. 25; judgmental competence of mass opinion, 222n. 3; lack of measurement of mobilized opinion, 81; lag behind political events, 197; methodological and theoretical refinements, 82–83, 235nn. 21, 22, 23; methodology and analysis, 211–12, 250–51nn. 1, 2; normative view of public manipulation, 79–80, 234nn. 17, 18; ontological view that public opinion doesn't exist, 80–81, 234–35n. 20; polls vs. surveys, 232n. 1; potential mismatch between survey responses and public's true opinion, 83–84, 236nn. 26, 27; research on race (*see* race research in surveys); rise to sovereignty (*see* survey data's rise to sovereignty); status as definitive measure, 72–73; "top of the head" considerations and, 25; treatment of racial attitudes changes, 45–46, 228nn. 3, 4
Sussman, Leila, 95–96

Talented Tenth, 228n. 12
Terrell, Mary Church, 47
Thernstrom, Abigail, 5
Thernstrom, Stephan, 5
Thurmond, Strom, 230n. 25
Till, Emmett, 141–42
Tilly, Charles, 232n. 4
TNOMO. See The Nature and Origins of Mass Opinion

Toennies, Ferdinand, 75
Truman, Harry S., 162, 243n. 9, 246nn. 12, 13

University of Mississippi, 132

Verba, Sidney, 75
Vivian, C. T., 2
Voting Rights Act (1965), 4

Walker, Jack, 207
Wallace, George, 2
Walton, Hanes, 85
Walzer, Michael, 208
Wells-Barnett, Ida B., 47
White, Walter, 47, 221n. 8
whites. *See* racially liberal whites; southern whites
Williams, Hosea, 3
Wilson, Ernest, 85
Wyant, Rowena, 96

Zaller, John: belief in elite bases of effective politics, 206; critical acclaim for *TNOMO*, 24, 223n. 10; elite definition, 9; goal of parsimony and generalization, 8; non-elite opinion dynamics, 41, 227nn. 45, 46; RAS model description, 18–19, 223n. 11, 250n. 18; on refinements to survey data, 83; on surveys, 73
Zelikow, Philip, 8